Stephen C. Ferruolo is Assistant Professor of History at Stanford University.

The Origins of the University

STEPHEN C. FERRUOLO

The Origins of the UNIVERSITY

THE SCHOOLS OF PARIS AND THEIR CRITICS, 1100-1215

Stanford University Press 1985
Stanford, California

Stanford University Press
Stanford, California

Printed in the United States of America

CIP data appear at the end of the book

To Beryl Smalley

Acknowledgments

I FIRST BEGAN thinking about this subject many years ago when, as a student at Oxford, I had the good fortune to be tutored in the Special Subject on the Schools of Paris and Chartres in the twelfth century by Sir Richard Southern, at St. John's College. Since then I have benefited from the challenges and criticisms of scholars at other universities. An earlier version of this work was submitted as a doctoral dissertation at Princeton under the supervision of Professors Joseph Strayer and Patrick Geary. Since then, my colleagues at Stanford, especially Professor Gavin Langmuir, have engaged me in fruitful discussions about education and the origins of the university. In addition to these medievalists, Professors Eugene Golob and Lawrence Stone, whose own scholarship is in other fields, taught me analytical skills applicable to medieval sources, and Father Leonard Boyle taught me the paleographical skills essential to using these sources.

Financial support for the research and writing of this book was generously provided by the Rhodes Scholarship Trust, the Danforth Foundation, the Dollard Fund of Bennington College, and the Pew Foundation Fund of Stanford University. I also wish to acknowledge my gratitude to the staffs of numerous libraries, especially those of the Bodleian and the Bibliothèque Nationale, for their courteous assistance.

No doubt those reading this book will recognize the influence of the many great scholars who have worked in the well-cultivated but still fertile field of thought and learning in the twelfth century. Among them none stands out more prominently than Beryl Smalley, whose vast scholarship touches upon each of the chapters here. As a modest token in recognition of the immense debt that the current generation of scholars working in this field owes to her, and also as a regrettably belated means of thanking her for the particular kindness and encouragement she offered during my stays in Oxford, I dedicate this book to the memory of Beryl Smalley—with the hope that whatever errors or omissions it may contain would not have led her to conclude that I have deliberately disregarded the advice she often gave young scholars, not to be in too much of a hurry to publish.

S.C.F.

Contents

The Origins of the University

Introduction

THE VALUE OF UNDERSTANDING the medieval origins of the modern university has been defended by scholars since they first began sifting through the accumulation of myth and legend that has obscured the institution's history. To Hastings Rashdall, author of the monumental three-volume *Universities of Europe in the Middle Ages* (1895), the university could only be understood as a distinctly medieval institution, as an enduring legacy of the same centuries that created the Gothic cathedral and parliament. Writing during an important period of educational reform in England, Rashdall believed that studying its medieval origins could shed light on the university's changing role in the modern world. Too great a historian, however, to look in the past for simple answers to contemporary questions, Rashdall ended his book with a wise caveat. "In education as in other matters," he wrote, "some knowledge of the past is a condition of practical wisdom in the present, but the lessons of history seldom admit of formal deduction or didactic exposition."[1]

Nevertheless, Rashdall still drew some helpful and practical lessons from his "purely critical and historical inquiry" into the origins of the university. That institution, he found, had shown a great deal of versatility and flexibility during its first centuries. Despite this "perpetual modification," or perhaps because of it, the university had managed to preserve and expand upon its essential form. This suggested to Rashdall that the educational reforms called for in his own time could be made without changing the basic institutional structure of the university. Moreover, he was convinced that the impetus for these reforms should come from within, rather than from outside, the university. To Rashdall, the university was more than a well-established institution made venerable by time and tradition. Far more important, it represented educational ideals worth preserving. From its earliest years, Rashdall concluded, the university had embodied three important educational values: a commitment to providing not only useful professional training but also the highest intellectual cultivation possible; a desire not only to conserve and transmit knowledge but also to advance it by research and writing; and, most essential of all, the idea of joining together teachers of diverse subjects into a single harmonious institution, the ideal of making the teaching body representative of the whole cycle of human knowledge.[2] It was, for Rashdall, within the "old university system," where professionalism and specialization still remained subordinate to a higher ideal of learning, that both teaching and research could best advance to serve the changing needs of modern society.

Nearly a century later, the university continues to be the primary locus of higher education and research, and the ideals praised by Rashdall endure despite the recurrent challenges of professionalism and of a degree of specialization that he probably could not even have imagined. Whereas Rashdall was committed to trying to defend an institution and educational ideal that then seemed to be seriously threatened, one must now try to explain the persistence of the university and how it has evolved. In recent decades, education has expanded more widely and knowledge changed more rapidly than at any time since the university was established. A look back at its origins in the twelfth century can help us to understand how and why the university has persisted into the twentieth century and may also tell us something about the seriousness of the new challenges it now confronts.

Rashdall was neither the first nor the last historian to write about the origins and early development of the university. All the institutions having a claim to be one of the first universities have been studied in detail. Bologna, Salerno, and Oxford, as well as Paris, all have well-established chronologies. Leaving their various claims to precedence unresolved, recent scholarly debate has focused increasingly on defining what constitutes a university rather than on interpreting new or contradictory evidence about where certain significant developments first took place. Much knowledge has been gained about the organization of teaching in the first universities, about the internal affairs of the guilds of masters and students, and about the relations between universities and external authorities. Yet there is one myth that still hinders our understanding of the university's origins and development: the idea that the university was born naturally, or even inevitably, out of the diversification of the utilitarian and professional demands made upon education in the later Middle Ages and that it was shaped by the struggle of scholars to gain freedom and autonomy from external, and especially from ecclesiastical, domination and control.

There is much that is appealing in this myth. As an account of the origins of the first universities, it has served the interests of modern educational reformers and defenders of academic freedom well. Like most myths, it also has some basis in fact. That most of those who attended the expanding schools of the twelfth century did so to receive practical training and to advance their professional careers cannot be doubted. Nor can it be denied that the university as a corporate entity originated in the joining together of scholars seeking to gain or to protect certain rights and privileges. These facts, however, tell only part of the story. From its very beginning, the university was established more as the embodiment of an educational ideal than as a workable means to organize learning and teaching. The sources and ramifications of this ideal are as much a part of the story of the origins of the university as are changing social and professional needs or the stages of the institution's legal and organizational development. The myth, moreover, is not only incomplete as an explanation for the origins of the university. It is also inconsistent with certain important but usually neglected aspects of the early history of universities and, in particular, of the university that came into being in Paris soon after 1200. This educational ideal better explains why scholars of diverse subjects and with diverse and often competitive professional goals continued to prefer to congregate in the same city and ultimately chose to join together to form a single corporation or guild.

This book is about that ideal or, stated another way, about the ideas and the values that gave shape to the university. I focus on developments in Paris during the century before the formation of its university, without trying to rewrite the institutional or the intellectual history of the city's schools. Rather than enter into the still unsettled debates about which specific school or schools survived to become part of the University of Paris, I have sought to answer the broader and more important question of why the university came into being at all.

By 1215 a "university of masters" had formed in Paris and had had its rights and privileges recognized by both the king and the pope. This "university of masters" was but one of the first prototypes of the university. By 1193 a "university of students" had formed at Bologna, whose scholars had earlier (in 1155 or 1158) been granted the first of the academic privileges that were to prove so important in the history of universities. And before the "university" was securely established in Paris, there were educational foundations modeled on those in Paris and Bologna at Oxford, Cambridge, Naples, and Toulouse, which were regarded by contemporaries as essentially the same type of institution and referred to by the common term *studium generale*. Whether spontaneous outgrowths of earlier schools or established by papal or imperial action, and regardless of the variations in subjects taught, they were all perceived as examples of a distinct and novel form of educational institution. By the later Middle Ages the term *universitas*, which originally meant any legally defined guild or corporation, was specifically and exclusively applied to this new institution.

Three basic characteristics were thought to distinguish this new educational institution from other types of schools. First, it was an enduring and autonomous corporate body. As a formal association with a significant degree of legal autonomy and the right of self-governance, the corporation exercised control over its membership and could make and enforce its own statutes. In this sense, the university was like any other medieval guild or *communia*. In its specific function, the university was a community engaged in study, a *studium*. It was an association of men of diverse social status drawn from a wide geographical area (the ability to attract scholars from beyond the local region is what first classified a school or *studium* as *generale*), studying a variety of subjects at different levels of expertise, and united only in that they were all involved in the pursuit of knowledge in the same place at the same time. Significantly, this pursuit was regarded not as a private vocation but as a public activity. The common endeavor of members of the guild was not so much independent study and research as teaching and learning. In the formation of the university, teaching took precedence over all else. The earliest university statutes were primarily concerned with establishing rules for what should be taught, when, how, and by whom, and with what should be the relationship between masters and their students. The second basic characteristic of the university was an emphasis on the sharing and the transmission of knowledge. The professional identity of the university consisted in teaching or being taught. Third, in contrast to other schools, the university was not narrowly specialized either in its constitution or in its goals. From early in its history, the university was intended to subsume the specialization of academic disciplines and division of faculties within a broader institutional structure defined by common educational goals and purposes. It was not necessary to offer instruction in all known subjects, but teaching was required in at least one of the higher faculties of theology, law (canon or civil), or medicine, as well as in the liberal arts. This is the essential concept of the university that has prevailed to the present.

Given how the university came to be defined, the decisive step in its development came when masters and scholars of various subjects and with diverse professional objectives first joined together to form a single guild or community. It was in Paris that the earliest such corporation was formed. Although in other respects the city's schools developed more slowly than those of Bologna, Paris can, in this definitive sense, be regarded as the location of the first university. It is my intention to show that the formation of the first "university of masters and scholars" in Paris resulted not so much from the pragmatic need of scholars to band together to secure their interests against an external adversary as from the prevailing influence within the schools of certain exalted educational principles and values. The scholars in Paris formed a single guild because, despite the diversity of the subjects they studied or taught, they considered themselves involved in a common endeavor, the pursuit of knowledge and truth. They thought of education as vital to the general improvement of society, not merely as training to fulfill specialized and utilitarian needs. The university they formed was a product not so much of narrow professional self-interest as of a higher educational ideal and a commitment to reform.

This is not to suggest that the increased demands for utilitarian learning and professional training were not important in the development of the university. Indeed, they were a precondition to it. Nor am I suggesting that the origins of the university can be explained as a steady progression or a decisive victory of this ideal of the unity of knowledge over the very real pressures to specialize. There was nothing certain, natural, or inevitable about the development of the schools into the university. The expansion of the schools to meet the needs of the increasingly wealthy and complex society of twelfth-century Europe was a sudden and, to contemporaries, surprising development. The streets of Paris were already filled with students and its classrooms were clamoring with the noise of disputations before there was any real awareness of, or serious concern about, the major educational changes that were occurring.

The first opposition to the schools came from a distance—the reaction of a few prominent churchmen alarmed about what they had heard or read was being taught. They were soon joined by other critics, who were often better informed about conditions in the schools. Yet even as the criticism of the schools spread, young men in search of instruction were converging on Paris in ever increasing numbers. Despite the opposition of a growing chorus of critics and intervention to challenge the teaching of several prominent masters, the schools continued to gain importance and influence. The specialization and professionalization of learning also advanced unabated. These developments could not be stopped, or even seriously impeded, for the social and intellectual demands that were transforming education were pressing, and those who opposed the schools could offer no other viable means of serving those practical needs. Many of the most vociferous critics failed to understand the educational changes they could witness only at a distance from the schools. However, others, who shared some of their same concerns, were better placed to observe the schools and to understand the changes, and these critics were eventually able to exercise a direct and positive influence on education. In this way, those who actively resisted educational developments came to play as important a role in the shaping of the university as those who uncritically accepted the learning the expanding schools offered.

The groups of critics studied here fall along a continuum of resistance to the schools. At one end are those leaders of the new monastic and religious orders who were the earliest and most vocal critics, as well as the only uncompromising opponents, of the schools. These monks viewed scholars as rivals whose growing influence posed a serious danger to the Church. Yet at the same time as monastic reformers were actively opposing the expanding urban schools, they were also closing their own schools to those who were not members of their orders. These policies were not as contradictory as they might appear, however. By closing their schools to outsiders, these reformers were wisely conceding that monasteries were no longer able to serve the educational needs of society. Instead, the cloister was to offer a retreat from the schools, a place where life was to be more tranquil and where learning was to serve a higher spiritual purpose. The frequent conversions of prominent masters suggest that this was an alternative not a few in the schools found appealing.

Perhaps the most important aspect of the uncompromising opposition of the religious reformers to the schools was the generally successful attempt they made, after about 1130, to prevent monks and canons regular from leaving the cloister to attend the schools. As I will argue, the withdrawal of members of religious orders from the schools was a significant factor in allowing for the increased corporate identity that was essential for scholars to form a single guild. In a sense, then, the opposition of the religious orders to the schools and the continued absence of their members from them can be said to have helped promote the development of the university. The frequent legislation specifically prohibiting monks and canons regular from studying law and medicine bears no less directly upon the history of the university as evidence of public concern about the moral value of academic specialization in what were known as the "lucrative arts." If monks and canons regular were prohibited by decree from learning these subjects, then there was certainly some question about whether specialization in them was acceptable at all.

At the other end of the continuum were those critics who were strongly supportive of the schools, but no less opposed to specialization and similarly concerned about the social effects of the growing numbers of students desiring the narrow professional training that would best further their personal ambitions. For these critics, who were themselves usually products of the schools, the potential benefits of the new learning far outweighed the more obvious risks. They were confident that the schools could provide the educated leadership capable of reforming all of society. But first the schools themselves would have to be reformed, the conditions of learning and teaching would have to be regulated, and above all the trends toward overspecialization and concentration in the lucrative arts would have to be checked.

In different ways and with varying degrees of effectiveness, these critics promoted a lofty ideal of what education could and should be and worked ardently to inspire those in the schools with a desire to pursue learning with a higher purpose than personal ambition. Satire was the one means some critics had to warn against what they saw as an ever-widening gap between true learning and the professional training that students wanted and society would support. Disappointment over their own careers was not a small part of what motivated many educated men to complain about the "decline of learning." But not all resorted to satire or bitter invective while somehow hoping for the return of an age ready to offer greater rewards for their learning. Some critics found more effective means of promoting their educational principles and values. As influential masters and as popular preachers, they actively gained support for educational reform both within and outside the schools. In their sermons, lectures, and treatises, they sought to translate an exalted idea of learning into a viable program of reform for the schools. The statutes promulgated by Robert of Courson for the University of Paris in 1215 owe a great deal to their efforts. More fundamental still, these critics are important as the most prominent proponents of the educational ideal that several years earlier inspired the formation of the first "university of masters and scholars."

In sum, I believe it can be argued that the university originated, not out of acquiescence to the demands for more specialized and practical learning, but out of resistance to these pressures. The university was a victory, if never a complete one, for a higher educational ideal. The examination of how this important victory was achieved might help to answer the questions of why the university has survived for so long and what are the most serious threats to its future.

PART ONE

THE SCHOOLS

ONE

Paris and the Expansion of Education

IN THE EARLY twelfth century, Paris established its preeminence as a city of learning both by surpassing the other cathedral cities of Northern France in the number and prominence of its schools and by becoming the undisputed educational center in all of Western Europe for the study of the liberal arts and theology. How Paris achieved this preeminence has never been satisfactorily explained. Before 1100 the city had no distinct advantage in attracting scholars. In fact, the schools of such nearby cathedral cities as Chartres, Laon, and Reims were far more distinguished than those of Paris. But in the early years of the twelfth century, when the numbers of young men seeking an education suddenly rose precipitously, it was the schools of Paris that increasingly attracted them. Why did Paris benefit disproportionately from the increased demand for learning? What drew young men from every part of Europe to a city that, at the time, lacked most of the amenities that would later account for its appeal? Simply to assume, as many historians have done, that the rise of Paris as an educational center was somehow inevitable given the increased demand for learning leaves unexplored an important aspect of the history of the origins of the university. As we shall see, the conditions that drew so many young men to Paris in the early decades of the twelfth century also fostered the development of the first university of masters and scholars in the final decades of the same century. Paris became the site of the first university for many of the same reasons that it had first become an important center of learning. But neither development was natural or inevitable. Both will have to be looked at more closely.

PARISIUS, PARADISUS

By the mid-twelfth century, Paris was often spoken of as a paradise, especially for those intent upon learning.[1] The rise of the city to educational preeminence did not escape the notice of contemporary observers. To an early-thirteenth-century observer, William the Breton, chaplain to King Philip Augustus (1180-1223), there was an obvious reason why Paris had become so great a center of education. In an entry in his chronicle under the year 1210, William praises the city's attractions and emphasizes the beneficent role of royal patronage. "In that time," he writes, "the study of letters flourished in Paris. Never before at any time or in any part of the world, neither in Athens nor Egypt, had there been so many scholars. The reason for this is not only the admirable beauty of the city and its affluence but also the freedom and special privileges that King Philip and his father before him conferred upon the scholars."[2]

As a former master and a member of the royal entourage, William the Breton had personal reasons to be grateful for royal patronage, and he no doubt overstates its importance. But at the same time, he is correct in recalling that support for scholars had long been an important precept of the Capetian policy for building the authority of the French monarchy. Patronage of the schools had cost the kings little of their precious material resources but had added greatly to their prestige.

From early in the reign of Louis VII (1137-80), scholars were outspoken in praise of the benevolence of the French monarchy. Walter Map, recalling his own period of study in Paris around 1160, is no less laudatory of Louis VII than William the Breton was later to be of Philip Augustus. "With such kind favor," Map writes of Louis VII in his scathing satire of courtiers and court life, *De nugis curialium*, "did he promote clerics that in his time they flocked to Paris from all quarters of Christendom and, nourished and protected under the shadow of his wings, have continued in the schools unto this day."[3] As a Welshman who spent much of his career in the service of the Angevin kings of England, Walter Map might be considered a more reliable source of evidence than a chronicler directly in the service of the French monarchy. But his praise of the Capetians was no less free of self-interest. Walter, like the group of humanists who will be discussed below, sought to hold up the French monarchy as an example to other kings, especially Henry II of England, of the advantages to be gained by supporting and advancing scholars. Ironically, the English monarchy was, as we now know, far ahead of the French in using scholars as administrators.[4] But this fact was probably not apparent to contemporary observers, and our sources often seem to reflect the frustrated expectations of ambitious men who, having left the schools confident in their future, years later looked back to Paris with nostalgia. We are wise, then, to read those like Walter Map, who were not in the employ of the Capetians, as cautiously as those who were.

At the same time, we must recognize that by the mid-twelfth century, the learned were already important as shapers of public opinion.[5] Patronage of scholars brought the praise of the literate, a useful asset in extending royal authority. Louis VII and Philip Augustus, anxious for any advantage they could gain over their materially and politically stronger rivals, learned this lesson early and well. Whether or not their patronage was as important to the schools as William the Breton and Walter Map assert, the kings of France certainly had a good practical reason for whatever support and encouragement they gave to the scholars who came to study or teach in the expanding capital of their realm.

But more than practical considerations seem to have influenced the Capetian policy toward the schools. Their patronage of the learned and the praise they received in turn from those who were, or who hoped to be, patronized were not simply an exercise of mutual admiration and assistance. An underlying ideology of kingship motivated both the monarchs and the scholars. According to a view prevalent at the time, the fates of learning and ruling were intricately linked. In a chronicle of world history completed in 1146, the Paris-trained writer Bishop Otto of Freising explains the course of history as the steady movement of political power and human learning from East to West. Both in this chronicle and in the more optimistic account of the deeds of Frederick Barbarossa, the *Gesta Friderici*, on which he was working at the time of his death in 1158, Otto aimed to demonstrate the historical process of how, as the power of a kingdom (or empire) grows, wisdom also flourishes and how, as one empire replaces another, a new center of learning is established.[6] William the Breton's comparison of Paris to Athens and Egypt is an implicit reference to the same idea of the *translatio studii*. Probably the best-known version of this idea is that found in the opening lines of Chrétien of Troyes's romance *Cligès*, written in the 1170's, which tells of the movement of both learning and chivalry to France: "Our books have informed us that the preeminence in chivalry and learning once belonged to Greece. Then chivalry passed to Rome together with that highest learning which now has come to France. God grant that it may be cherished here, and that it may be made so welcome here that the honour which has taken refuge may never depart from France."[7]

Given the connection made by Otto of Freising and other historians between the movement of learning and political power, between the *translatio studii* and the *translatio imperii*, the flourishing of the schools in Paris, which was also the capital of the Capetian kingdom, took on added significance. Not only had the great learning of the past been transmitted to Paris, so too had the great power. The preeminence of the schools of Paris was a sign that France was now heir to the *imperium* or, at the very least, to a partial share of the political inheritance of the Roman Empire and of the legacy of Charlemagne. This idea was an important asset in the Capetians' efforts to advance their exalted claims of royal authority. Much was to be made of the fact that Philip was, through his mother, a direct descendant of Charlemagne; he was also, after his great conquests, to be styled "Augustus" by his contemporaries. By their patronage of the schools, Philip and his father before him added to their imperial aura and bolstered their position relative to the other kings of Europe. There was much prestige to be gained in ruling a kingdom from Paris, the new Athens, the city of learning that made France the latest heir of the great world civilizations.[8]

The direct patronage of scholars was only one of the ways in which the Capetians contributed to the expansion of the schools. No less important were the policies that transformed the city of Paris into an important administrative and commercial center. The growth of the schools coincided closely with the development of Paris into the wealthy, beautiful, and well-defended capital of the expanding Capetian kingdom.

The rise of the city to commercial importance began, like the rise of the schools, no earlier than the first years of the twelfth century.[9] The city's political importance began decades earlier. From the first years of their dynasty, the Capetian kings had favored Paris above their other residences; as early as the reign of Henry I (1031-60), many more royal acts were dated from Paris than from anywhere else.[10] But the city's decisive period of growth occurred during the reign of Louis VII, who resided in Paris more frequently and for longer periods than his predecessors and who first established permanent locations in the city for several departments of the royal administration. Under Louis VII, Paris took on the definite functions of a capital.[11] It was left to his son, Philip Augustus, to make the capital into the greatest city in Northern Europe. During the same decades in which Bishop Maurice of Sully initiated the building of the great new Gothic cathedral of Notre Dame and in which the masters joined together to form their guild, Philip undertook a vast program of urban construction. The principal roads of the city were paved; a great covered market (Les Halles) was built on the Right Bank; the entire city, including both the Right and the Left Bank, was enclosed in a massive new wall; and a new castle (the Louvre) was erected to protect the capital from attack from the Vexin, then held by the English king.[12] The beauty and affluence of Paris resulted from the Capetians' deliberate efforts to establish a strong and suitable base for their royal ambitions. These same attributes made the city a secure and appealing place for scholars.

Thanks, then, to the policies of the Capetians, Paris offered scholars amenities that few other cities could rival. The thriving schools came to be regarded as one of the glories of the French kingdom. However, the conduct of the young men who flocked to the schools in ever-increasing numbers also created difficulties for royal administration and sometimes caused the king to wonder about the wisdom of having so many scholars resident in the capital. Nevertheless, when scholars threatened to leave Paris, in 1200, the king rallied to their support and granted privileges that gave scholars special legal status. The granting of these privileges, as William the Breton suggests, was a vital factor in establishing the educational preeminence of Paris and, as we shall see, was an important episode in the early history of the university.

As significant as these privileges and other aspects of royal patronage were to the schools, we should not be misled by William the Breton into overemphasizing the king's role in fostering the conditions in which learning could thrive. Historians now generally agree that the University of Paris had no single founder. But it did have many patrons and supporters. Among these, the papacy comes to mind first. Early-thirteenth-century decrees such as *Super speculam* (1219) and *Parens scientiarum* (1231) are often cited as the culmination of a long tradition of active papal support for the schools of Paris. Yet, as we shall see, before the pontificate of Innocent III (1198-1216) there was relatively little papal involvement in the schools or direct patronage of scholars. The much-lauded policies of Pope Alexander III (1159-81), who sought to increase educational opportunities by eliminating financial obstacles to teaching, benefited the schools of Paris disproportionately only because the city's schools had already surpassed those elsewhere in prestige and size. The policies were actually intended to improve education in all cathedral cities. More significant than any particular policies of the papacy to the rise of Paris to educational preeminence, especially in theology, may be the fact that scholars who had trained there were already established in prominent positions in Rome before the popes began to take a direct and active interest in what was happening in the schools.

The support of local ecclesiastical officials was considerably more important to the schools than that of the papacy. All the men who served as the bishops of Paris or as chancellors of Notre Dame in the second half of the twelfth century were former masters who maintained close ties to the schools. Although often outspoken in their criticism of the instruction offered by their former colleagues and of the immorality and misconduct of students, they used their influential positions to encourage the expansion and the reform of education in the city. The university owes much to their patronage.

There is much less evidence about the attitudes or actions of the bishops and chancellors of Paris in the first half of the century. Peter Abelard's difficulties trying to teach in Paris have left the impression that the local authorities were not entirely favorable to the new learning and exercised control over who taught in the schools. But Abelard did succeed in teaching in Paris, even at the cathedral school. Although once driven from the city by his former master William of Champeaux, the archdeacon of Paris and scholasticus at the cathedral school, Abelard was twice given the opportunity to teach at the cathedral school. In 1108 he lectured on dialectic in place of Master William's successor, until this unknown master was removed as scholasticus; and from about 1114 to 1118 he himself served as scholasticus and taught both dialectic and theology, presumably under the direct patronage of the chancellor of Notre Dame.[13] Moreover, when masters were prevented from teaching at the schools on the Ile de la Cité by the chancellor, they still had the option of crossing the Petit Pont to the Left Bank and settling in the area surrounding the abbey of Ste. Geneviève, which was exempt from episcopal jurisdiction.[14] That Abelard and other masters successfully established schools on Mont Ste. Geneviève suggests that the abbot was another of the patrons who welcomed and supported learning in Paris in the early decades of the twelfth century.

This divided jurisdiction contributed to another important advantage that Paris had over rival cities—its ability to attract scholars and to maintain a lively educational atmosphere. From the first decades of the twelfth century, academic life in Paris was relatively free from control and regulation. Scholars could choose among several prominent schools in close proximity. In addition to the cathedral school on the Ile, there were important monastic schools affiliated with two abbeys on the Left Bank, Ste. Geneviève and St. Victor, as well as independent or private schools such as those established by Abelard on Mont Ste. Geneviève and by the English master Adam of Balsham on the Petit Pont.[15] Although only the schools associated with Notre Dame seem to have remained in continuous operation, the monastic and independent schools played no less important a role in the rise of Paris to educational preeminence.

Throughout the twelfth century, there were always enough schools in the city to offer considerable freedom to masters and choice to students. Not subject to any one authority, masters were generally free to teach where, when, and what they chose. Only when those who lectured on the Bible strayed beyond, or sometimes only too near, the bounds of orthodox opinion did authorities intervene to restrict their teaching. A few masters, such as the scholasticus at Notre Dame, had set obligations for which they received the income from a prebend as a regular salary.[16] Where and for how long most other masters taught depended largely upon whether or not they could attract enough students to their lectures to support themselves until offered more secure positions in the Church or royal service. As for the students, they were free to remain in Paris without attaching themselves permanently to any school or master. Given the number of masters in the city, students with sufficient means could wander from school to school until they found the instruction that satisfied their needs or desires. The competition among teachers for these paying students stimulated the development of new teaching methods and new ideas and gave vitality to intellectual life in the city.

Such freedom did not exist elsewhere. Where teaching remained the monopoly of a single school, as in most cathedral cities, it was more restricted and learning more staid. In contrast, Paris, with its many schools and masters, could offer the growing number of young men seeking an education learning that was both exciting and demanding. It was of considerable importance to the development of the university that no effort was made to curtail this freedom and to regulate the schools until after the educational and intellectual preeminence of Paris had been securely established.

THE DIVERSITY OF SCHOOLS AND MASTERS

That Paris should have several prominent schools at one time was more fortuitous than inevitable. Up to 1100 the education available in the city seems to have offered no particular or unusual attraction. The cathedral school, which had probably been founded during the Carolingian educational reforms of the early ninth century, served its intended function as a seminary to train priests for the diocese and rarely drew students from outside the region.[17] The chief monasteries in the city and its suburbs—St. Germain des Prés, St. Maur des Fossés, St. Denis, and, especially, Ste. Geneviève[18]—had their own schools. Now and again, when a noted scholar was resident at one of them, learning flourished briefly and some students were attracted then from a distance. But students who traveled to France to study before 1100 were much more likely to have been destined for other nearby episcopal cities, such as Reims, Laon, and Chartres, whose schools were far more renowned than those of Paris.[19] Not until Peter Abelard arrived in Paris to study dialectic at the cathedral school under Master William of Champeaux does the educational history of the city's schools begin to emerge from obscurity.

Abelard's autobiographical letter, the *Historia calamitatum* (c. 1132), is a valuable and unique source for understanding the conditions that enabled Paris to rise so quickly to educational preeminence.[20] Abelard writes, first of all, as a representative of the young men who, around 1100, began to flock to the schools. Sometimes they were motivated by a sincere desire for learning, and perhaps more often by the increased opportunities for social advancement available to those who had received some education. Although Abelard boasts of the glory and wealth he acquired as a teacher, the love of learning had been his original reason for attending the schools. The eldest son of a literate Breton nobleman, Abelard had chosen to relinquish his right of inheritance and to "leave the court of Mars in order to be nourished at the bosom of Minerva."[21] Seeking instruction in dialectic, already the subject of first choice for the intellectually ambitious,[22] he spent several years traveling from school to school in northern France before arriving in Paris. Many of the first two generations of scholars who came to Paris in the twelfth century had undertaken similar wanderings in search of suitable places to study or teach.[23] Ambitious men like Abelard brought an enthusiasm and aggressiveness to the schools that, no less than the recovery of Aristotle's logical writings, stimulated the emergence of disputation as the new method of instruction.[24]

Although Abelard was in some ways no different from the many other young men who came to the schools, he was hardly typical of them. Considerably brighter and certainly more intellectually ambitious than any of his contemporaries, Abelard was a dominant figure, if not *the* dominant figure, in the schools during much of the next four decades. As the most renowned teacher of his time, he attracted scores of students to Paris while he taught there. And although many of these students followed him when he left to teach elsewhere, others remained to continue their studies with other masters or to teach to their own students what Abelard had taught them. The methods Abelard used with such skill in his lectures and disputations became the accepted means of instruction. His theological works, although twice condemned as heretical by Church councils and seldom used or cited directly, had a considerable influence on the subsequent development of scholastic theology.[25] But, perhaps above all, it was Abelard who brought a sense of excitement and controversy to the schools of Paris. As a teacher and scholar, no less than in his personal life, Abelard was provocative. Other masters found they had to take notice of what Abelard was saying and doing, and even if they did not always approve, they could not help but be influenced by him. More than anyone else, Peter Abelard made Paris the place to go for the best teaching and the newest learning.

Abelard's story of great success followed by terrible misfortune is well enough known not to require retelling here. But it is necessary to recall and to comment upon those episodes in his career that bear directly on the history of the Paris schools. Abelard, who had been drawn to Paris by what he had heard of the superior quality of the instruction available in dialectic, was soon disappointed in what he found there. The famous master, William of Champeaux, did not measure up to his reputation, and Abelard was quick to challenge him in class discussion. Once he had successfully debated the greatest dialectician of the day, Abelard was anxious to launch his own career as a teacher, preferably in Paris, where there would be a ready audience of students among those who had witnessed his arguments with Master William. As archdeacon of Paris, however, William of Champeaux was able to prevent Abelard from teaching anywhere in or near the city. Thus Abelard opened his first school in Melun, a royal town about fifty miles south and just outside the boundaries of the diocese of Paris. Although apparently able to attract students to Melun, Abelard wanted to be closer to his rival. As soon as possible, he moved his school to Corbeil, less than half the distance from Paris.[26] This phase of Abelard's teaching career ended when illness forced his return to Brittany.

Abelard did not realize his ambition to teach in Paris until several years later. In 1108, after a long convalescence, he returned to the city to find that William of Champeaux had retired from the cathedral school to establish a new community of canons regular at St. Victor, on the Left Bank. There William, despite his conversion to the religious life, continued to teach publicly and to draw a large number of students to his lectures.[27] Abelard again used the forum of William's own classroom to challenge the famous master before opening his own school in the city. Before long, William's successor as scholasticus ceased lecturing on dialectic and gave Abelard his first opportunity to teach at the cathedral school. After only a few days, however, William used his influence to remove this master and to drive Abelard again from Paris to Melun. But this time he did not stay away long. When William left Paris, Abelard returned and established a school on Mont Ste. Geneviève, an ideal location from which to lay siege to the man who had usurped his place at the cathedral school.[28] Although just across the Seine, the Mont was safely outside episcopal jurisdiction. The ambitious master now finally had a real opportunity to prove his teaching in Paris.

Abelard gives a highly self-flattering account of his success against William of Champeaux and other masters. In the early twelfth century a master's fame was measured by the number of his students. According to Abelard, he emptied the schools of his rivals. Whether or not Abelard dominated education in Paris to the extent that he boasts, the heated battle between his school on Mont Ste. Geneviève and those of William at St. Victor and of William's disciple on the Ile de la Cité was undoubtedly a great magnet for attracting young men from the schools of other cities. The rivalry among masters debating with the sharpened tools of dialectic must have made Paris the place where all the most ambitious scholars wanted to be.

When Abelard left Paris in 1112, the excitement may have diminished temporarily. But as Abelard's own brief experience trying to teach in Laon shows, the conditions that made Paris so appealing were not readily found elsewhere. As a theologian, Anselm of Laon proved as much of a disappointment to Abelard as William of Champeaux had been as a dialectician.[29] As scholasticus of the cathedral school, Anselm had effective control over education in Laon. When Abelard ceased attending his lectures and tried to establish a rival school, Anselm was able to drive his challenger out of the city for good. The situation in Laon, unlike that in Paris, would not allow for the establishment of a rival to the cathedral school.

It is from the time of Abelard's return from Laon that we can decisively begin to document the ability of Paris to draw young men to its schools from throughout Europe. With the removal of his influential rival, William of Champeaux—who became bishop of Châlons-sur-Marne in 1113—Abelard assumed the long-coveted position of scholasticus at the cathedral school. For several years he lectured there both on dialectic and theology, to what he proudly describes as a rapidly expanding audience of students.[30] One of these, Fulco of Deuil, provides corroborating evidence of Abelard's success in attracting students to Paris. "No distance of land, no heights of mountains, no depths of valleys, no thief or obstacle on the way," Fulco wrote Abelard in a letter of consolation after his castration and entrance into St. Denis, "held back anyone who hastened to you." Fulco tells how Abelard's lectures drew crowds from such distant lands as England, Brittany, Angers, Picardy, Gascony, Normandy, Flanders, Germany, and Swabia. "Nearly all the inhabitants of Paris and men both from nearby and from the remotest parts of France," Fulco continues, "were thirsty to learn from you, as if no instruction could be found except from you alone."[31] Given the other evidence we possess of Abelard's abilities and of his fame as a teacher, we would be mistaken to dismiss this as no more than the praise of a loyal disciple. Abelard, after all, then held unchallenged the position of master at the renowned cathedral school of Paris.

There is no need to recount the tragic events that brought a sudden end to this phase of Abelard's teaching in Paris and his entrance into the abbey of St. Denis in 1119. If he was the first in a long line of teachers whose academic careers have been hindered by an affair with a beautiful young student, neither the problems resulting from his liaison with Heloise nor the restraints of monastic life kept Abelard from teaching for very long. Save for the difficult years (c. 1126–34) as abbot of the remote Breton monastery of St. Gildas, Abelard continued to teach and to attract students to his lectures, wherever they were given, for the rest of his life. No doubt it was this very tenacity in the face of so many obstacles that gave rise to the many apocryphal legends about Abelard as a teacher. One of these, found in a sermon of Jacques of Vitry, tells how Abelard, when prohibited by the French king from teaching on the lands of his realm, began lecturing from a tall tree outside Paris to students congregated on the ground. Then, when the king forbade him to lecture either on land or in the air, he taught while floating on a boat in the Seine to students seated along the bank. He finally won over the king by his persistence, and the royal restrictions on his teaching in France were removed.[32]

Although this legend places Abelard in Paris, we know that he spent no more than a few of the last twenty years of his life teaching in or near the city. He taught briefly at the abbey of St. Denis, until conflicts with his brethren forced him to transfer his school to the distant priory of Maisoncelle-en-Brie, near Provins, in Champagne. He did not return to Paris until after resigning as abbot of St. Gildas. Between then and the convening of the Council of Sens in 1140, Abelard was back teaching at the school he had founded on Mont Ste. Geneviève. According to Otto of Freising, Abelard's lectures still attracted a great throng of students.[33] But as we know from the account John of Salisbury gives of his own education, Abelard was often away from Paris even during these years.[34]

Fortunately, given Abelard's long and frequent absences from the city, the educational draw of Paris did not depend upon him alone. Directly or indirectly, Abelard had provided the intellectual stimulus for three important schools in Paris, but by the beginning of the second quarter of the twelfth century, enough other distinguished masters had become associated with each of these schools to ensure the continuing educational vitality of the city. We know little of the actual masters who succeeded Abelard at the cathedral school, but we do know that they continued to attract so many students that, in 1127 the bishop, Stephen of Senlis, found it necessary, in order to restore peace and tranquility to the cathedral close, to transfer the school to a new site near the episcopal court.[35] On Mont Ste. Geneviève there continued to be a popular school of dialectic, run by masters who had been students of Abelard.[36] Not far away on the Left Bank, St. Victor, founded by William of Champeaux, became a major center of biblical studies. Hugh of St. Victor, head of that school, was probably – especially during Abelard's absence – the most renowned Paris master and the one whose lectures attracted the largest number of young scholars to the city.

There are three sources that attest to the continuing popularity and expansion of the schools in Paris in the decades after Peter Abelard. The first and best-known is the account given by John of Salisbury of his studies between 1136 and 1148.[37] During these twelve years, John was taught by a total of eleven masters. These include Peter Abelard, who ceased lecturing soon after John's arrival, and his two known successors at the school on Mont Ste. Geneviève, Master Alberic and Robert of Melun; six other renowned scholars, Gilbert of Poitiers, Thierry of Chartres, William of Conches, Robert Pullen, Peter Helias, and Adam of Petit Pont; and, finally, two more obscure men, Simon of Poissy and Richard the Bishop. Since John does not specify where he actually studied with several of these masters, there has been considerable debate whether he spent part of these twelve years in Chartres or remained in Paris throughout.[38]

The view that John never left Paris is supported by the evidence of the *Metamorphosis Goliae*. This allegorical poem, now generally agreed to date from 1142 or 1143, mentions fourteen contemporary masters by name, most of whom were known to have been teaching in Paris.[39] Among the masters present in the heavenly court are no fewer than six of the masters under whom John of Salisbury says he studied: Gilbert of Poitiers, Thierry of Chartres, Robert of Melun, Robert Pullen (here called Robert Amiclas),[40] Peter Helias, and Adam of Petit Pont. Two other masters present, the rhetorician Manerius and Peter Lombard, can be definitely placed in Paris. Named, but absent and seriously missed, is the recently deceased Peter Abelard. Like John of Salisbury, the author of the *Metamorphosis Goliae* provides testimony that though many other distinguished masters still taught in Paris, the loss of Abelard was keenly felt.

The third document is William of Tyre's long-lost account of his student years in Europe from 1145 to 1165.[41] Among the ten masters he names as having taught him the liberal arts and theology are many also mentioned in the other sources. Four appear in both the *Metalogicon* and the *Metamorphosis Goliae*: Peter Helias, Robert of Melun, Robert Pullen, and Adam of Petit Pont. A fifth, Master Alberic (here called "de Monte"), was also a teacher of John of Salisbury. Four more are named in the *Metamorphosis Goliae*: Manerius (called Mainerus by William), Peter Lombard, and Ivo of Chartres and Bernard Brito (who were identified only by their Christian names in the allegory, but both there and by William are associated with the school of Peter Helias). The final teacher named is none other than Maurice of Sully, the Paris master who succeeded Peter Lombard as bishop. Although William of Tyre never states explicitly where he studied with these masters, his account strongly suggests that they were all teaching in one place. This place could only be Paris.[42]

The combined evidence of these three independent sources supports the placement of no fewer than sixteen known masters in the schools of Paris in the three middle decades of the twelfth century. The majority of these men rank among the most distinguished scholars and teachers of the time. When one adds the masters teaching at the school of St. Victor, which the three sources exclude, the concentration of learned men in Paris becomes even more impressive. Although several of these scholars spent part or, in some cases, even most of their careers as teachers or as administrators elsewhere, no other city could claim to have had as many distinguished masters associated with its schools. By 1140, Paris was where scholars came to make their reputations. In Paris alone could they find so large and ready an audience of students. And Paris was the place where successful teaching was most likely to gain them the attention and support of a rich and powerful patron. The brightest and most ambitious young men in Europe were drawn to Paris by the unsurpassed opportunities its schools offered to advance and to prove their learning as students and then to gain their fame and fortune as masters.

By mid-century, Paris was unquestionably better endowed with masters and schools than any other city in France was or ever had been. More than anything else it was the presence of so many masters, some teaching at schools tied to existing communities but many more having established their own schools, that determined the educational future of Paris. The appeal of the other cathedral towns that had once been able to rival, or even to surpass, Paris as educational centers depended upon much more limited resources. At Laon, for example, the teaching of Master Anselm (d. 1117) and later of his brother Ralph (d. 1133) had drawn a steady stream of foreign students to the cathedral school for several decades. But once these distinguished masters were gone and the cathedral school, run by lesser scholars, had returned to its usual function as a diocesan seminary, this stream quickly dried—or, more likely, diverted to Paris. A similar history was repeated in other cities, including Reims and Chartres, where public instruction was offered only at the cathedral school, which could usually employ no more than one or two masters at a time.[43] When a famed master of one of these schools died, retired from teaching, or left to assume a position elsewhere, most of his students simply packed up their belongings and moved on. Students were still more likely to seek and to follow distinguished masters than they were to attach themselves to established institutions. One such student provides additional evidence of the advantages of Paris over other cities. Everard of Ypres followed Gilbert of Poitiers when, sometime before 1141, the great master left Chartres for Paris. Whereas, Everard records, there had been only three other students attending Gilbert's classes in Chartres, nearly three hundred filled the bishop's hall to hear him lecture in Paris.[44]

These figures are only suggestive of the size and importance of the schools of Paris relative to those of other cities. Given that Gilbert of Poitiers was only one of many distinguished masters teaching in Paris at the time, we can assume that at least several times this number of students were already attending the city's schools. So large and ready an audience of students attracted masters to Paris, no less than the large choice of masters attracted students to the city and kept them there. Paris would certainly have lost these students and suffered the same fate as other cities that had briefly flourished as educational centers, had it also had just one school whose draw depended upon the reputation of a single teacher—even if this master were of the stature of Peter Abelard, Hugh of St. Victor, or Gilbert of Poitiers. Paris was able to survive the loss of each of these renowned masters. There were even times when no single outstanding teacher appears to have been drawing students to the city. But there were always less famous masters who continued to offer students what was generally the best and most advanced instruction in both the liberal arts and theology available anywhere. Similarly, when public teaching ceased or was temporarily curtailed in one of the city's established schools, other schools opened or expanded to accommodate the ever-growing numbers of students.

The educational history of Paris in the twelfth century cannot be explained as the growth or evolution of any one or two schools into the university. Nor can the origins of the university in any way be traced to the continuing influence of the teaching of a single master, not even of Abelard. From soon after 1100, what distinguishes Paris is not the established reputation of a particular school or master but the expanding numbers of schools and masters in the city. This expansion both secured the educational preeminence of Paris and was the essential precondition for the eventual organization and development of a university. Only Paris could boast such a concentration of schools and so large a body of masters capable of offering instruction in the full range of academic disciplines to the rapidly growing numbers of young students.

If no single factor had made the existence of these conditions in Paris inevitable, several had helped to make them possible. Without the concurrent commercial growth of the city, the expanding population of masters and students could not have been sustained. Nor was it insignificant that Paris was already becoming the administrative capital of an increasingly wealthy and powerful kingdom. Both the king and the local officials welcomed scholars with support and protection while imposing only the most minimal restraints on their activities. Patronage and freedom combined as the ideal assets encouraging young men to come to Paris confident of finding an education that would be both materially rewarding and intellectually challenging. These were the very real advantages, not readily found elsewhere, that made the city a true educational paradise.

But not all agreed that Paris was a paradise. The schools had their critics as well as their admirers. In 1164, at the start of his exile, John of Salisbury returned to Paris and found the city almost heaven-like. To Thomas Becket, John wrote:

> There I saw such quantity of food; a people so happy; such respect for the clergy; the splendour and dignity of the whole church; the tasks so diverse of the students of philosophy—saw and marvelled at it, as Jacob marvelled at the ladder whose summit reached to Heaven, which was the path of the angels going up and down. The thrill of this happy pilgrimage compelled me to confess: "Truly the Lord is in this place, and I knew it not" [Genesis 28.16]. It came to my mind how the poet said: "A happy thing is exile in such a place as this" [Ovid, *Fasti*, i.540].[45]

Other alumni have been no less moved upon visiting their alma mater after a long absence. John's spirits must have been dampened somewhat when, shortly after his arrival in Paris, he received a letter from his friend, the Benedictine Peter of Celle. Peter described the city as a dangerous place "where vice reigns and where the soul is miserably enslaved and imperiled."[46] As a monk accustomed to the order and routine of the cloister, Peter of Celle could hardly have reacted favorably to what he heard of conditions in Paris—where masters, seldom attached to an organized community, lived and taught pretty much free from restriction, where disputation had replaced the traditional methods of instruction, and where the curriculum could be as fleeting as the desires of students, whose conduct was what one might expect of teenage boys left mostly unsupervised in a city already becoming known for its joie de vivre. But criticisms of Paris were voiced no less strongly from other quarters. And as we shall see, John of Salisbury himself looked askance at many of the new trends in the schools.

Throughout the twelfth century there was continuous controversy and discussion about what was happening in Paris. With the rapid expansion of the schools, education was changing in ways that no one could have anticipated and few were prepared to endorse wholeheartedly. Questions about what should be taught and who should teach were raised repeatedly, the basic problems of how masters could be supervised and students disciplined remained unresolved, and attitudes about the nature and purposes of learning often quite contradictory to those prevailing in Paris were proposed. Despite all this debate and criticism, however, the freedom that was essential to the expansion of the schools and to their continuing intellectual vitality was never seriously threatened. Fortunately, lack of a consensus about what should or could be done, as well as the absence of a single cognizant authority able to intervene, forestalled any serious limitations of the independence of the masters until they had begun to reform and regulate their own affairs and had secured their corporate autonomy. At the same time, the scholars of Paris were not unaware of or unaffected by the concerns expressed by their critics. As the next chapters will show, the continuing educational controversy and criticism were no less fundamental to the origins of the university than royal patronage and academic freedom were to the initial rise of the schools of Paris to preeminence.

TWO

The School of St. Victor

THE QUESTION of which of the schools of Paris actually evolved into the university has long been a topic of scholarly debate. The once prevalent view that Ste. Geneviève, on the Left Bank, was the cradle of the university or alternatively played midwife to its birth on the Ile de la Cité has generally given way to the opinion that the university is the direct successor of the cathedral school of Notre Dame.[1] Recently, however, at least one historian has returned the focus to the Left Bank—not to the schools on the Mont but instead to St. Victor, which he estimates to have been the most frequented school throughout the twelfth century.[2] Although the abbey certainly drew scholars to the Left Bank as long as its school remained open to outsiders, there are difficulties in proving a direct connection between St. Victor and the formation of the university. Well before the university formed, public instruction had ceased at the abbey. Moreover, there is no evidence that the Left Bank became the predominant educational quarter of Paris until years after the formation of the university, when the Dominicans established their house of study at St. Jacques.[3]

To focus on one school or location obscures the very conditions that made Paris so attractive for study and were the essential prerequisites to the university's formation—the large concentration of scholars and the freedom they enjoyed. Throughout the twelfth and early thirteenth centuries, masters and students settled in all parts of Paris, including the Right Bank as well as the Ile de la Cité and the Left Bank, and they remained quite free to move from one school or place to another—or even, if they chose, to leave the city entirely.[4] No one part of the city seems to have had a special hold on scholars yet, nor can any particular school be credited with giving birth to the university.

Why, then, single out the school of St. Victor for special treatment here? In explaining the origins of the university, it is important to distinguish the school *at* St. Victor from the school *of* St. Victor. St. Victor was most obviously a "school" in the sense that it was an educational institution, one of the places in Paris where learning and teaching went on and one that contributed to the fame of the city. As long as public instruction was allowed, scholars were drawn to the school there, though probably never in very large numbers. The exclusion of Victorine masters from the three contemporary accounts discussed in Chapter 1 suggests that the school, which was located outside the walls, remained somewhat isolated from other schools within the city. Moreover, since the Victorines were always somewhat ambivalent about keeping the school open, the enrollment of outsiders was probably limited intentionally. At the same time, the association of several outstanding theologians with its school did make St. Victor a powerful magnet to scholars intent upon studying theology, whether already in Paris or attracted from farther away. Yet although Peter Lombard comes to mind as a notable example of a young scholar who traveled to Paris specifically to study at St. Victor, it seems highly probable that the school drew most of its students because it was in Paris rather than the other way around. As an actual place of public teaching, the school *at* St. Victor was probably too small and too short-lived to have had a major impact on the development of the university.

The influence of the school *of* St. Victor, however, was more significant and enduring. In the twelfth century an important tradition of thought and learning was developed and maintained by the succession of capable biblical scholars associated with the abbey of St. Victor. This school *of* St. Victor embodied an intellectual tradition with a discernible set of common sources, methods, and doctrines, and it also represented an educational ideal with a distinctive program of learning and teaching. Even after the abbey ceased to be important as a place at which to study, the Victorine educational program endured as an ideal, as a set of intellectual methods and values against which the developments in the other schools of Paris were measured, and as a standard that ultimately played a vital role in the formation of the university by the masters and scholars of the city.

Focusing on St. Victor thus provides a doubly valuable perspective on educational developments in Paris. The history of the rise and decline of the school *at* St. Victor exemplifies the flux and controversy that surrounded the growth of the schools. And the enduring influence of the school *of* St. Victor as a tradition of thought and learning helps to explain how these diverse schools became a single university.

THE SCHOOL AT ST. VICTOR

In 1108 the renowned master William of Champeaux retired as archdeacon and scholasticus at the cathedral school of Notre Dame and, with several disciples, established a new community of canons regular in a building adjacent to a chapel dedicated to St. Victor, just outside the city walls on the Left Bank. William of Champeaux, as we are told by Peter Abelard, who briefly attended his lectures on rhetoric, did not give up teaching after his conversion. He established a school at St. Victor that was open to those outside the community. Abelard was not alone in charging William with duplicity.[5] Although—and, perhaps in some cases, because—William did not charge his students fees, his decision to continue teaching as a canon regular was controversial. At the time, reformers were insisting that canons, like monks, should be educating only their own novices within the cloister.[6] A letter from Hildebert of Lavardin, then bishop of Le Mans, urging him to continue teaching, suggests that William had encountered criticism strong enough to make him consider closing his school.[7] Despite both the controversy and his conflicts with Abelard, William kept the school at St. Victor open until he permanently left Paris to become the bishop of Châlons-sur-Marne.

William of Champeaux appears to have made arrangements to assure the future of both his community and his school before his departure in 1113. In the following year, St. Victor was officially consecrated as an abbey, was endowed by the king, and elected as its first abbot one of William's disciples, Gilduin. During Gilduin's long and distinguished tenure as abbot (1114–55), the new order thrived. St. Victor grew to have more than forty daughter houses.[8] Gilduin was no less successful in his recruitment for the abbey's school. "Under his reign," one near-contemporary source records, "many noble clerics, learned in secular and in divine letters, came to live in that place."[9] Nearly all of the great scholars in the Victorine tradition arrived during the four decades Gilduin was abbot. First came Hugh of Lotharingia, who entered the abbey before 1120; then the generation of scholars he taught, which included Richard, Andrew, and Achard (Gilduin's successor as abbot). Even Godfrey, with whom the teaching tradition of St. Victor comes to an end, probably arrived before 1155.

There is sparse but sufficient evidence to conclude that public instruction was offered continuously at St. Victor throughout this period. Hugh attracted students until his death in 1141, and under his pupils and successors, Andrew and Richard, St. Victor remained an important center of biblical scholarship.[10] Among the especially renowned scholars drawn to the school during these years were Peter Lombard, who arrived via Reims in 1134;[11] Robert of Melun, who studied and taught theology there before being made bishop of Hereford in 1160;[12] and Peter Comestor, who had probably spent part of his student years at St. Victor and who died as a member of the community, in 1179.[13] Beryl Smalley is certainly right in saying that "the experiment of reviving up-to-date teaching in the cloister was a brilliant success in the lifetime of Hugh and his pupils."[14]

However, the experiment did not last beyond the generation of Hugh's pupils. Even before the death in 1173 of Hugh's immediate successor as scholasticus, Richard of St. Victor, public teaching appears to have been curtailed and instruction offered only to members of the community. It is not clear when or why the school was closed to outsiders. The internal problems and conflicts experienced at St. Victor in the 1160's were a definite factor. A decade of misgovernment by the scandalous Abbot Ernisius (1162-72) must have disrupted the school no less than it did the community's life in general. As prior during these years, Richard probably had little time to attend to either his scholarship or his teaching. If any outsiders survived that period, they were certainly driven away when the intolerant and far less learned Walter succeeded Richard as prior and forced the head of the school, Godfrey, to leave St. Victor. Underlying these conflicts was the worsening of the tension between teaching and the religious life that went back to the foundation of the community by William of Champeaux. In describing both William and Hugh, Victorine sources emphasize their impressive combination of learning and piety.[15] After these great teachers and their pupils were gone, the two qualities appear to have become increasingly incompatible to members of the order. Some of those who read the *Didascalicon* might also have wondered if Hugh's criticism of monks teaching was meant to include canons regular.[16] The vehement hostility of the Cistercians to the schools had also made it much harder for the leaders of the community, even had they wished to do so, to resist the pressures William of Champeaux had endured in starting the school at St. Victor.

Unlike its opening, the closing of the school at St. Victor cannot be precisely dated. By the final quarter of the twelfth century, outsiders were apparently no longer welcomed into the cloister. The school at St. Victor became a place that provided training only for members of the order and grew increasingly isolated, educationally and intellectually, from the other schools of Paris.[17]

MASTER HUGH AND THE SCHOOL OF ST. VICTOR

Among the scholars and teachers who made Paris preeminent, few were as important as Hugh of Lotharingia—or, as he has come to be known, Hugh of St. Victor. It is incontestably true, as Roger Baron asserts, that "l'Ecole de Saint-Victor est vraiment l'Ecole de Hugues de St. Victor."[18] Not only did the abbey reach its apex as a place of study during his years as scholasticus, from about 1124 to 1141; it was Hugh who shaped the educational program followed at St. Victor and who articulated the enduring intellectual principles associated with the school.

We have only one contemporary account of Hugh's actual teaching, written by Lawrence, a monk of Westminster, who had attended Hugh's lectures on Scripture. According to Lawrence, Hugh was especially concerned that his students not misrepresent what he taught them. Only after their repeated requests did he allow them to take notes, with the stipulation that they turn in their wax tablets once a week for him to examine. He would read their notes carefully, erase what he found to be superfluous, add what had been omitted, revise what was unclear or badly stated, and support with more authority the doctrines he had propounded.[19] Lawrence's account provides valuable evidence both about Hugh's caution as a teacher and about the conditions at his school. The deliberate supervision of the *reportationes* of lectures was certainly a wise policy, since many contemporary masters, most notably Peter Abelard, suffered from having their ideas misrepresented by their students. But this practice could have been possible only at a school in which attendance at lectures was carefully controlled. It thus seems likely that, even during the time when Hugh was teaching, the school at St. Victor was limited in both its openness and its size.

In the early years of his teaching, Hugh of St. Victor compiled the *Didascalicon* as a concise guidebook for his students. As he explains in the preface, his purpose was to provide practical guidance to students on what they should read, in what order, and how.[20] Although it is uncertain whether Hugh actually followed the program of study he outlined, the *Didascalicon* has often and rightly been used as a source for knowledge about the texts and methods of teaching at St. Victor as well as for more general information about conditions in the schools of Paris. What has attracted less attention is the theoretical principles and educational ideals that underlie, but are sometimes obscured by, Hugh's efforts to offer practical pedagogical advice to his students.

In the interests of clarity, Hugh divides his treatise into two parts: the first three books are about secular texts for students of the arts and the last three about Scripture for students of the Bible. This division can be interpreted as a possible indication of the separation of students at St. Victor into two distinct groups, the younger concentrating on the liberal arts and the more advanced on biblical studies. It is especially important to understand, however, that the division was intended to be practical, not theoretical, and that it in no way corresponds to the distinction made by later thinkers between philosophy and theology. For Hugh of St. Victor, all knowledge was encompassed in philosophy. The entire structure of his thought rests solidly on the idea of the essential unity of all learning. The profound and enduring influence of the *Didascalicon* is due not to the practical advice it offers but to Hugh's success in developing this idea of the unity of knowledge into a systematic view of the nature and purpose of learning.[21]

Hugh beings with the Boethian definition of philosophy as "the love and pursuit of wisdom."[22] This pursuit, he explains, is a special prerogative given to human beings so that they can come to realize the dignity of their nature. Just as wisdom should guide humans in every aspect of their lives, so must philosophy provide instruction for all human activities. This point is made clear in Hugh's redefinition of philosophy as "the discipline which investigates comprehensively the ideas of all things, human and divine."[23] Philosophy is one in having the single purpose of providing the wisdom that enables humans to live and act according to their nature. However, in order to encompass all the varied needs and actions of humans, it is divided into distinct branches. There must therefore be as many divisions or separate disciplines of philosophy as there are varieties of human endeavor that require guidance. This is the essential principle of knowledge upon which Hugh builds his theory of education.

Consistent with this principle, the *Didascalicon* presents a comprehensive scheme of the unity of knowledge based on the division of philosophy into four main branches and twenty-one disciplines. According to Hugh, the fundamental division arose after the Fall, when humans were left with both the goodness of their created nature and the evil of their corrupted one. Confronted with the dual task of restoring the original integrity of their nature and of relieving the deficiencies that result from their sin and corruption, humans require two kinds of wisdom: understanding (*intelligentia*) and knowledge (*scientia*). In turn, because the restoration of human nature is a twofold process requiring the reorientation of both the reason and the will, understanding is divided into two branches. Hence the threefold division of philosophy into the theoretical arts, which guide reason in the search for truth; the practical arts, which guide the will in the practice of virtue; and the mechanical arts, which teach humans to procure the necessities of life. The fourth branch, eloquence or the logical arts, was discovered as the need later arose for rules to guide the discussion and teaching of the other arts.[24]

A simpler version of this scheme is found in one of Hugh of St. Victor's earlier works, the *Epitome Dindimi in philosophiam*, where he explains the divisions of philosophy as originating in the triple defects suffered by human nature as a consequence of the Fall: the ignorance of good, the desire for evil, and the weakness of mortality.[25] This account clarifies the practical implications of Hugh's unified scheme of knowledge. Each branch of philosophy, Hugh argues, has a distinct and essential role to play in remedying the defects of human life. The theoretical arts provide the wisdom necessary to overcome ignorance of the good. The practical arts instill the virtue to desire to do good. And the mechanical arts provide the skill to cope with the necessity of sustaining daily life. An education that aims to restore the full integrity of human nature must include study of each of these three branches of knowledge—and, no less essentially, of the fourth branch, the logical arts that facilitate learning in all the others.

Probably the best way to summarize Hugh of St. Victor's scheme of knowledge is the diagrammatic representation of it seen below. After discussing the four main divisions of philosophy, Hugh continues with a series of subdivisions among human needs and actions that result in a total of twenty-one distinct arts (italicized in the diagram). This account of the origins and purpose of these arts is conventional. Hugh's importance as a theorist lies not in what he says about any of the particular arts but in the orderly and systematic treatment he gives to them as a whole. In constructing a scheme that comprehended all human knowledge, Hugh of St. Victor gave coherent shape to the diffuse body of thought about the traditional disciplines. The practical purpose of the effort was to mold these disciplines into an educational program suitable for the schools. However, although the unified scheme of knowledge was an impressive and enduring achievement, it could not fulfill its intended purpose even in Hugh's own lifetime. Three inherent problems seriously limited its viability as a useful guide to study.

First, there is the place and definition of the discipline of theology. In Hugh's scheme, theology is not a distinct realm of knowledge but one of the twenty-one arts included within philosophy. Following Boethius, Hugh of St. Victor defined theology narrowly as the science of intellectible or incorporeal being, the highest of the three parts of theoretical knowledge. According to this definition, theology is limited to the study of God alone, to speculation about the nature of divinity and of the Trin-

- Philosophy
  - Theoretical Arts
    - *Theology*
    - Mathematics
      - *Arithmetic*
      - *Music*
      - *Geometry*
      - *Astronomy*
    - *Physics*
  - Practical Arts
    - *Solitary* (Ethics)
    - *Private* (Economics)
    - *Public* (Politics)
  - Mechanical Arts
    - *Fabric Making*
    - *Armament*
    - *Commerce*
    - *Agriculture*
    - *Hunting*
    - *Medicine*
    - *Theatrics*
  - Logical Arts
    - *Grammar*
    - Theory of Argument
      - *Necessary Argument*
      - Probable Argument
        - *Dialectic*
        - *Rhetoric*
      - *Sophistical Argument*

ity. Hugh viewed this art as quite distinct in both scope and method from the more general religious instruction given at St. Victor, which was based upon the study of the Bible and referred to as *lectio divina*, *sacra pagina*, or *studium sacrae scripturae*. But Hugh's narrow definition of theology was rapidly becoming outdated. In the schools, theology was being redefined and broadened in scope to include biblical exegesis and questions of doctrine, morality, and practice, as well as more speculative matters.[26] This new discipline no longer fit neatly into a unified scheme of knowledge. Theology was coming to be distinguished in status and purpose, as well as in sources and method, from philosophy. And, as we shall see, it was not only Hugh's scheme of knowledge that was challenged by these developments. This new theology was also incompatible with the Victorine program of biblical study itself.

The second problem with Hugh's scheme is the absence of any evident place for law. The reasons for the exclusion of law are unclear, but it is certainly not to be interpreted as an antecedent to the hostility toward law and lawyers expressed by Godfrey of St. Victor. At the time he was writing the *Didascalicon*, Hugh was probably still unaware of the important advances in the study of law then occurring in Italy. Moreover, no tradition of thought gave law an explicit role in the restoration of human nature or in the correction of human defects. Nevertheless, law's exclusion is a serious flaw. As civil and canon law developed as distinct branches of study and became popular subjects of specialization in the schools, the absence of law from Hugh's scheme significantly reduced its value as an accurate guide to learning.

The third problem is the inclusion of the mechanical and the logical arts as integral parts of philosophy. By including the mechanical arts, Hugh was explicitly acknowledging his departure from the prevailing tradition, which divided philosophy into physics, ethics, and logic.[27] At the same time, he made clear his difference from those of his contemporaries who, like him, preferred the Aristotelian division of philosophy into the theoretical and practical sciences but excluded the mechanical arts and, in addition, viewed the logical arts as useful tools or instruments that are mere appendages rather than an integral part of philosophy.[28] According to this division, the theoretical and practical sciences as true wisdom or philosophy proper (*de philosophia*) are a higher form of knowledge than both the logical arts, which exist to serve philosophy (*ad philosophiam*), and the mechanical arts, which do little more than proceed according to philosophy (*secundum philosophiam*). Hugh accepted the distinction between higher and lower forms of knowledge but strongly criticized those who then proceeded to define philosophy, too narrowly, as the search for truth and thereby, as he describes their error elsewhere, "eliminate certain arts [i.e., the logical and mechanical] from philosophy by an excessively rigid test."[29] For Hugh, more than just the integrity of his scheme of knowledge was at stake here. The danger of the narrow definition of philosophy was that it could be used to justify the elimination of these arts from the curriculum of the schools.

The danger was real. Efforts to include the mechanical arts in the curriculum did not survive long even among Hugh's students at St. Victor. However, as Hugh seems to have been aware, the real battle was being fought over the logical arts of the trivium. He was therefore especially emphatic in limiting the subject matter of the trivium to what he believed could be taught and learned in a reasonable time. Moreover, in defining these arts Hugh deliberately avoided the common distinction that the logical arts studied words (*verba*) and the theoretical and practical arts studied things (*res*). It was on this distinction that his contemporaries, such as William of Conches, based their assertion that the logical arts were only preparatory, not integral, to philosophy.[30] The distinction was also later used as an excuse by those who, anxious to specialize, sought to defend their avoidance or hasty study of the trivium. Despite the skill and care Hugh demonstrated in fitting the logical arts into his scheme, it proved impossible to save the trivium from the growing pressures toward specialization in the schools.

What about the seven liberal arts as a whole? As the diagram indicates, Hugh did not distinguish the trivium and quadrivium in any particular or obvious way from the other arts. However, although the liberal arts do not have a distinctive place in his theoretical scheme of knowledge, they stand out prominently in the actual educational program Hugh proposes. All twenty-one arts are defined as integral parts of human knowledge, but only the seven liberal arts are prescribed as necessary disciplines of formal instruction. According to Hugh, because training in the trivium and quadrivium can provide the tools for all the rest of philosophy, once someone has been adequately taught these seven arts, he has the ability to learn all the others on his own.[31] Few educational principles have been more influential or enduring than this one. Hugh's argument enabled him to retain the particular importance of studying the seven traditional liberal arts while advancing the broader concept of the essential unity of knowledge. His purpose was to secure the place of these arts in the schools by making them not only introductory to the study of the Bible but fundamentally necessary to the pursuit of all knowledge.

No less strong is the case Hugh makes for the liberal arts as a coherent program of study. In order to advance in knowledge, a scholar must study each and every one of the seven liberal arts. "These," he insists, "so hang together and so depend on one another in their ideas that if only one of the arts is lacking, all the rest cannot make a man into a philosopher. Therefore, those persons seem to me to be in error who, not appreciating the coherence among the arts, select certain of them for study, and leaving the rest untouched, think they can be perfect in these alone."[32] The defensive tone noticeable here and elsewhere in the *Didascalicon* suggests that Hugh perceived the threat already being posed to the liberal arts by academic specialization. While seeking to affirm the virtue and viability of the educational program at St. Victor, he wrote with a critical eye on what was happening in the other schools of Paris.

Specialization was only one of the educational trends undermining the study of the liberal arts. No less serious a problem was the hasty attention given to them by students anxious to complete their education and to advance their careers. Hugh contrasts the students of his own day to the pupils of Pythagoras, who spent seven years diligently studying the seven liberal arts.[33] This example was hardly likely to appeal to the young men who came to the schools with limited funds and unlimited ambitions. More helpful to them was Hugh's advice on how the arts could be studied in reasonable time. Hugh maintains that the schools too often failed to distinguish between the material or rules proper to the arts, which can be learned by studying the standard texts prescribed for them, and literary works, which are no more than appendages of the arts.[34] To study the liberal arts it is not necessary, and can even be harmful, to peruse poems, plays, fables, and histories. This literature, although entertaining to read and sometimes helpful in refining knowledge of the arts, too often distracts students from completing their other studies. Unlike the humanists, Hugh believed that the purpose of the liberal arts curriculum was to provide the knowledge and training needed for more advanced learning, not to cultivate a broad literary culture.

Students were failing to acquire a solid foundation in the liberal arts not only because they themselves did not want it but also because their masters did not provide it to them. Too many masters, Hugh complains, "do not know how to give each art what belongs to it but, while treating one, lecture on them all."[35] No doubt, from the orderly milieu of St. Victor, conditions in the other Paris schools seemed chaotic. Hugh accuses some masters of confusing and distracting their students by filling their introductory lectures with superfluous details designed to show off their knowledge. With other teachers the problem was not so much vanity as actual ignorance of how to teach the arts.[36] If masters used the traditional textbooks—such as Priscian and Donatus for grammar—and kept their instruction as brief and simple as possible, students would be able and, presumably, more willing to learn all seven of the liberal arts. Hugh's argument is clearly directed against those scholars who justified specialization on the grounds that it was simply no longer feasible to learn or to teach all the arts.[37] For Hugh, mastery of both the trivium and quadrivium was not only necessary; it was also still possible.

There is more than a hint of competitiveness in Hugh's criticisms of the teaching of other masters. As head of a school, Hugh was not professionally disinterested in or unaffected by what happened in the other schools of Paris, and we should not overlook the ways in which his arguments served to promote St. Victor. When advancing the traditional idea that learning requires a combination of innate ability, practice, and art or discipline,[38] for example, Hugh defines discipline not as academic training but as moral excellence. This definition seems intended to suggest the clear advantage of studying at St. Victor, where the rules of learning were inseparable from the rules of the canonical life.

No less notable is Hugh's treatment of the well-known lines of verse that John of Salisbury later attributed to Bernard of Chartres:

> A humble mind, eagerness to inquire, a quiet life,
> Silent scrutiny, poverty, a foreign soil.
> These, for many, unlock the hidden places of learning.[39]

Discussing the first of these keys to knowledge, Hugh offers the kind of sound and timeless advice that has won him so much admiration. The properly humble student should hold no learning in contempt, be willing to learn from anyone, and not be condescending to those less learned. Often overlooked, however, is the fact that Hugh combines his advocacy of these educational principles with some very harsh invective against other scholars and rival masters, including what appears to be an ad hominem attack on Peter Abelard. He lashes out first against proud and overly ambitious scholars who, having studied (often for only a short time) under great masters, publicly advance opinions on the most profound matters.[40] Even more vehement is Hugh's criticism of those whom he calls "triflers" (*nugigeruli*), scholars with inflated egos who condemn great masters as simple-minded, deny the value of their teaching, and claim to be able to interpret the mysteries of Scripture by personal ingenuity alone – all of which sounds very much like Peter Abelard's own account of his treatment of Anselm of Laon.[41] Perhaps to remove any doubt that he was alluding to Abelard, whose poems made him as renowned a lover as he was a teacher, Hugh goes on to urge scholars to free themselves from vain cares and sensual indulgences.[42]

Hugh's discussion of the other keys to wisdom is similarly directed against the attitudes and conditions prevailing in other schools. His criticism is most explicit when he comes to the merits of poverty. "What can be said of the scholars of our time," he asks sarcastically, "who not only are contemptuous of frugality in their studies but actually work to become richer? Each boasts not about what he will learn, but about what he will earn."[43] As a canon regular vowed to poverty, Hugh was in a stronger position to protest against venality than were many subsequent critics of the schools, but this does not mean that he was disinterested. To Hugh, moreover, the principle that "all the world is an exile to those who philosophize" suggests not only the advantages of leaving home to study but also the necessity of exile as the first step in preparing to be indifferent to worldly fame and fortune.[44] Few of those flocking to the schools were likely to have found much appealing in Hugh's advocacy of poverty—indeed, this was the condition of which so many scholars complained. Nor could many among them have honestly denied that they had chosen to exile themselves in Paris for no other reason than to seek the fame and fortune to which Hugh of St. Victor thought they should be indifferent.

There is no need to discuss or summarize the specific advice Hugh offers to the student of Scripture in the last three books of the *Didascalicon*. As taught by Hugh and his disciples, the prescribed curriculum was the foundation of the vigorous biblical scholarship that was St. Victor's particular contribution to the development of scholastic theology. The important point is that even in Hugh's own lifetime, the actual program of studies was outdated and impractical.[45] At a time of growing specialization, it required scholars to be generalists. At a time when scholars elsewhere in Paris were developing the new discipline of theology by applying the sharpened tools of analysis to increasingly difficult questions of doctrine and morality, the Victorines were defending the older conception of *lectio divina* and broadening the scope of biblical exegesis. When theologians like Peter Lombard went to St. Victor, they learned methods and doctrines valuable to their future studies, but they did not attempt to follow the program as a whole. Only parts of the Victorine program were transferable from the cloister, where biblical study was expected to be fulfilled in meditation and contemplation, to the other schools, where theology was being oriented to the more practical needs of teaching, of preaching, and of fighting heresy.

Some of the more general recommendations and criticisms first voiced by Hugh in the *Didascalicon* were echoed repeatedly by critics of the schools throughout the twelfth century. One was Hugh's timeless and often quoted educational principle, "Learn everything; you will later see that nothing is superfluous"[46]—which, characteristically, he balanced by emphasizing that learning should be pursued in an orderly, deliberate, and disciplined way.[47] Hugh was also, apparently, the first to complain that many scholars choose to study the insignificant subtleties of the philosophers only because they fail to understand the complexities of Scripture.[48] Finally, Hugh anticipated other critics in suggesting that the motives and worldly ambitions prevalent among scholars were the root cause of many trends harmful to true learning: "There are not a few," he writes, "who seek knowledge of Holy Scripture in order to gain riches, obtain honors, or acquire fame. . . . And there are others who desire to hear the words of God and learn of his works not because these bring salvation, but because they are marvels. They wish to search obscure matters and know new things, to learn much and do nothing."[49] In the face of growing specialization and professionalism, Hugh of St. Victor saw education as having no less exalted a purpose than the restoration of human dignity. While neither the integrity of his scheme of knowledge nor the viability of his program of study could long withstand the impact of the rapid new intellectual developments, the educational values and principles that Hugh had so eloquently defended continued to appeal to those who were looking for alternatives to the prevailing trends in the schools.

THE SCHOOL OF ST. VICTOR AFTER HUGH

Under Hugh's successors, the intellectual vitality of the school of St. Victor was threatened by its increasing isolation from the developments at the other schools. The antischolastic current swelled within St. Victor, as within other religious orders, making it ever more difficult for new sources and methods to flow from the schools into the cloister. Meanwhile, the rapid expansion of knowledge and the pressure of specialization were distancing the Victorine program of study ever further from the realities of practical education. Still, until the climate within the abbey became inhospitable to their efforts, a series of Victorines diligently worked to carry on the scholarly tradition of Master Hugh.

The divergence of this tradition from the intellectual life elsewhere in Paris is clearly reflected in the teaching and scholarship of Richard of St. Victor, Hugh's immediate successor as head of the school. The vast difference of method and purpose can best be seen by comparing Richard's intended compendium of knowledge, the *Liber exceptionum* (which he planned and for which he began to compile material during his active period as a teacher between 1153 and 1162) and the systematic summae, such as Peter Lombard's *Sententiarum libri IV*, being produced in other schools at the same time. The surviving fragments of Richard's encyclopedic work include a synopsis of the *Didascalicon*, notes on geography and world history, biblical commentaries exemplifying all three types of exegesis, and a collection of sermons.[50] In nearly every respect, Richard's massive endeavor recalls the synthetic florilegia of the cloister more than the systematic collections of sentences then being produced in the schools. Richard intended the *Liber exceptionum* to trim the Victorine educational program down to manageable size. That the work was never finished perhaps indicates that even Richard of St. Victor had recognized that task as impossible.

By the time Godfrey of St. Victor had succeeded his teacher Richard as head of the school, the challenge of defending and preserving the Victorine program had become even more difficult. In at least one respect, however, Godfrey was better prepared for the task than Richard had been.

Prior to entering St. Victor in about 1155, Godfrey had studied both the liberal arts and theology elsewhere in Paris. His direct personal experience of the learning offered in other schools allowed him to speak with greater authority about the relative advantages of St. Victor.

Soon after 1176, Godfrey dedicated and sent to Stephen of Tournai, then abbot of Ste. Geneviève, a number of his writings. Among them was the *Fons philosophiae*, an autobiographical poem that allegorically recounted his education in the schools and his entrance into St. Victor.[51] The poem uses the familiar biblical figure of wisdom as a complex of streams all flowing from one fountain, or source, to represent Hugh of St. Victor's scheme of knowledge. Godfrey writes of himself as a traveler journeying from stream to stream and drinking from each. Emphasizing the need for order, he begins at the tributaries of the trivium, drinking in sequence the waters of grammar, dialectic, and rhetoric; then he moves on to the quadrivium and the streams of arithmetic, music, geometry, and astronomy; next he comes to the river of physics and to the three waters of the practical arts (ethics, economics, and politics); and finally his journey ends at the great river of theology, of whose waters he can never drink too much.

The *Didascalicon* is Godfrey's Baedeker for this journey. But like most travelers, he does not always follow the suggested itinerary. As he sets off, Godfrey first comes upon the seven streams of the mechanical arts. Although these flow from the fountain, he does not choose to join the undiscriminating mob in drinking from these muddy and polluted waters.[52] Likewise, he complains along the way that much of the scenery has changed, usually for the worse. The rivers of the trivium are especially disappointing to him. On the riverbanks once settled by prominent scholars whose eloquence was greatly valued and richly rewarded by society, he finds only ruins and a few unemployed inhabitants reduced to begging. (In contrast, in the new suburbs nearby, rich physicians and lawyers can be found in abundance.) Moreover, instead of the order described by Hugh of St. Victor, Godfrey finds terrible disorder. Like confused travelers rushing from place to place, students of the trivium drink randomly from the three rivers without heeding the proper order of study or the prescribed texts. Then, having drunk far too shallowly of the waters of the logical arts, which are so essential a preparation to the rest, they rush on to more distant rivers. Godfrey thinks it no wonder this happens, given the poor guidance available to students in the corrupt and disorganized schools along these riverbanks.[53]

Worst of all are the conditions Godfrey finds at the river of dialectic. Since the time of William of Champeaux, this subject had been the glory of the Paris schools. None of the other liberal arts had attracted more students—or more criticism. How this powerful but potentially dangerous discipline was being taught and how it should be used had long been issues of serious concern. "Stultum dialectica facit insanire," Godfrey warns in his turn. Dialectic is a sharp sword that should be handled only by wise men, not carelessly entrusted to the hands of fools.[54] But dialecticians, preoccupied with their ceaseless bickering over universals, are failing to provide students with the orderly training in the texts of Porphyry and Aristotle necessary if they are to know and use the art well. Rather than nourishing their students from the deep waters of the river, these masters are leaving them parched and stranded on treacherous rocks. Specifically criticized for their bad teaching are the disciples of Gilbert of Poitiers, the Porretani, as well as Abelard's two known successors at the school of dialectic on Mont Ste. Geneviève, Alberic and Robert of Melun.[55] On the other hand, Godfrey tells of finding one solid bridge of learning and teaching spanning the turbulent river of dialectic—an obvious reference to the much-praised school of Master Adam of Balsham on the Petit Pont.[56]

There is no need to follow Godfrey's travels along the rivers of the quadrivium, the practical arts, and physics. These were not, nor had they ever been, especially vital subjects of scholarship or teaching in the Paris schools. Godfrey himself reveals more than a passing interest in only two of the arts of the quadrivium, music and astronomy. After merely pausing at the rivers of the other arts, Godfrey arrives at the ultimate destination of his travels, the river of theology. Significantly, his journey culminates not in the troubled and tumultuous waters of scholastic disputation but at the calm and peaceful oasis of *lectio divina*. In advancing to theology, Godfrey has also moved from the secular schools to the cloister of St. Victor.

The second half of the *Fons philosophiae* gives a lengthy description of the sources, methods, and doctrines of Victorine biblical studies. Continuing his allegory, Godfrey provides an eloquent testament to the continued intellectual vitality of the school of St. Victor. But no less significant is what he tells about his decision to leave the schools and become a canon regular. For Godfrey, converting and entering St. Victor represented a rejection both of conditions in the schools and of the methods of scholastic theology. He had become dissatisfied with the unnourishing disputations over the profound mysteries of the divinity that preoccupied theologians in the schools and had chosen to retire to the tranquility of the cloister to reflect on subjects more accessible to human understanding, such as Creation, the Fall, and Redemption.[57] The decision was the deliberate choice both of a different life and of a different theology. Godfrey's account clearly indicates that, by the last quarter of the twelfth century, St. Victor was no longer seen as being like the other schools of Paris but had come to represent an educational alternative to them.

How different this was from the time when William of Champeaux had moved his school to St. Victor or when students had traveled back and forth from the lectures of Master Hugh to those of other Paris scholars. When Godfrey left the schools, he was probably not fully aware of how isolated St. Victor was becoming. He certainly could not have foreseen that the ever-present tension in the abbey between learning and the religious life would worsen into an open and bitter conflict that would harm him personally. Soon after he completed the *Fons philosophiae*, Godfrey was forced to leave St. Victor. Perhaps other internal conflicts, unrelated to the school, played a role in his departure. But there can be little doubt that his position as head of the school had become increasingly untenable since 1173, when Richard had been succeeded as prior by Walter of St. Victor, an uncompromising and outspoken opponent of the schools.

Perhaps not coincidentally, Walter's polemical treatise, the *Contra quatuor labyrinthos Franciae*, appeared just about the time Godfrey was expelled from St. Victor. In the *Fons philosophiae* Godfrey had expressed some definite reservations about the soundness of theological disputation, but his criticisms of the way in which theology was being taught in the schools were both informed and moderate. In contrast, Walter's treatise was nothing less than a virulent and impassioned attack on the teaching of four of the greatest theologians of the schools—Peter Abelard, Gilbert of Poitiers, Peter Lombard, and Peter of Poitiers, all of whom he accuses of being heretics.[58] Unhindered by his own lack of understanding, Walter completely rejected the validity of the sources, methods, and doctrines of scholastic theology. At the same time—as Godfrey no doubt found—Walter was no less intolerant of what had long been taught at St. Victor. In his treatise, Walter not only opposes the use of dialectic by theologians in the schools but also questions the application of any of the liberal arts to the interpretation of Christian doctrine. He describes the arts not as the handmaidens but as the enemies of theology, not as useful preparations for the study of the Bible but as unworthy of study at all.[59]

The attitudes expressed by Walter of St. Victor in the *Contra quatuor labyrinthos Franciae* represented a clear repudiation of the Victorine program of study. After trying unsuccessfully to counter such attitudes with his thoughtful and eloquent *Fons philosophiae*, Godfrey must have had little choice but to leave St. Victor and pursue his scholarship elsewhere.[60]

Although Godfrey was eventually able to return, it was not as head of the school. In Godfrey's absence Walter seems to have used his position as prior to disband permanently whatever remained of the school at St. Victor.

The unfortunate exile of Godfrey also put an end to the intellectually distinct and rich tradition of the school of St. Victor. Some have recently tried to argue that the school continued, citing as evidence the classical learning found in the sermons of Absalon, who served as abbot of St. Victor for several years, and the rich imagery in the mystical writings of Thomas Gallus, who spent his early years at the abbey. But these arguments are unconvincing.[61] As we have seen, the presence of one or two learned men in a place does not necessarily make it a center of scholarship and teaching. Moreover, there is no evidence that either Absalon or Thomas Gallus either taught or found intellectual disciples at St. Victor. After Godfrey, it was as preachers and confessors, not as scholars or teachers, that the Victorines continued to make their presence felt in Paris. The promotion of the educational ideals and values associated with the school of St. Victor was left to others.

PART TWO

THE CRITICS

THREE

Monastic Opposition to the Schools

SOMETIME SOON after Easter in 1139, Bernard of Clairvaux visited Paris and preached to the scholars of the city. The theme of his sermon was conversion, not doctrine. On this occasion he was concerned with the motives and morals of scholars, not with the new methods and sources of the schools. Curiosity, ambition, worldliness, and lust—these were what he then saw as the serious dangers emanating from the schools, not dialectic or disputation. With his characteristic eloquence and exaggeration, Bernard railed against the vices of scholars, exhorting them to flee the evil city for the safe refuge of the cloister. "I beg you brothers," he urged,

> to spare your souls, spare the blood that was spilt for you. Beware of the horrible peril. Avoid the fire that was prepared. . . . Don't you realize that your chastity is imperiled by delights, your humility by riches, your piety by mundane affairs, your truth by excessive chatter, your charity by your worldly life? Flee from the middle of Babylon! Flee and save your souls! Flee together to the cities of refuge where you can do penance for your past and obtain grace.[1]

Bernard's preaching was a great success. According to Cistercian sources, more than twenty scholars were converted. Among those to leave Paris and accompany him back to Clairvaux were such notables as Geoffrey of Auxerre, later to be Bernard's official biographer, and Goswin of Anchino, a disciple of Peter Abelard.[2]

This was the opening salvo in the long conflict between monks and scholars, the symbolic start of a bitter struggle between the Cistercians and the masters of Paris that continued for the rest of the century. Historians of the schools have often overlooked the significance of this conflict. Monastic opposition to the schools was more than a marginal nuisance or a minor obstacle that could be ignored until it went away. The recurrent attacks of monks repeatedly forced scholars to defend their learning, as well as their lives, and increased the pressure on scholars to organize both to secure their independence and to regulate their own affairs. Likewise, the nature of the conflict has often been misunderstood. The monks were concerned not just with the methods of the schools and the morals of scholars but, above all, with the growing influence of education.

The fact that monks and scholars were competing for many of the same positions in the Church partly explains the monastic opposition to the schools. But great monastic thinkers like Bernard of Clairvaux certainly knew that there was a greater issue at stake. The expansion of the schools and the advances of scholars posed a considerable challenge to the religious and intellectual order that the monasteries and monks had dominated for so long. Thus, with all the means at their disposal, these monastic leaders sought to reverse or, at least, to check the growing influence of the schools. In retrospect, it may appear that the monks were fighting a losing battle against the inevitable advance of learning. But to the scholars of the time the situation must have looked more dangerous, especially when Bernard himself was watching over their activities. As long as monks remained hostile to the schools, a serious obstacle stood in the way of scholars seeking to advance both learning and their careers.

Because of his later attacks on Peter Abelard and Gilbert of Poitiers, Bernard's visit to Paris soon took on a significance in the dispute between the cloister and the schools that bore little resemblance to its original purpose. Bernard seems to have regarded the visit as an opportunity to see the schools for himself and, perhaps too, to gain some prominent recruits for Cîteaux. Having only recently returned to Clairvaux from Rome after years of hard politicking to secure the papacy for Innocent II, he apparently had no intention of becoming embroiled in another conflict.[3] At that time Bernard seems to have known and to have cared little about what was going on in the schools. Cîteaux and Rome had been his spheres of action, not Paris. William of St. Thierry had recently written warning of the dangers of Peter Abelard, but Bernard had not been alarmed.[4] Although Abelard regarded Bernard's visit as part of a concerted attack against him, there is no reference to the controversial master or his doctrines in Bernard's sermon or in accounts of his visit.[5] The renowned abbot went to the great city of Paris in 1139 to preach the monastic life, not to challenge the methods and doctrines of the schools.

In one of his sermons to scholars, Jacques of Vitry tells the story of

Bernard's shock upon hearing his first scholastic disputation in Paris.[6] Even if such an encounter did occur during this visit, Bernard was apparently not yet alarmed about Abelard or the schools. Having won some prominent recruits for Cîteaux, he left Paris with good reason to be pleased. What then happened to increase his alarm is a matter of speculation. Goswin and other converted scholars may have told him worrisome things about conditions in the schools.[7] But it was not until after his initial efforts against Abelard failed that Bernard truly became aroused against the schools. Only then did he realize the true extent of their influence and begin to see scholars as dangerous rivals to monks.

For the remainder of his life Bernard of Clairvaux waged a two-part battle against the growing influence of the schools, attacking the doctrines and methods of prominent masters and defending the superiority of the monastic life and learning. His notable victories, if never decisive enough actually to endanger the schools, were harmful to individual masters and disruptive of learning. And Bernard did not hesitate to use deceptive tactics that ultimately tarnished his own reputation. But in his view the stakes were high enough to require the use of all his skill and power. It was a battle between Cîteaux and Paris, the new Babylon, for influence in Rome and for the direction of the Church.

Once Bernard of Clairvaux had established the terms of the opposition between Cîteaux and Paris, between the cloister and the schools, there could and would be no accommodation between them. Each side was forced not only to defend its position but also to challenge the other on its own ground. Finding that they were rapidly losing influence, the monks tried to promote the cloister as a viable educational alternative to the schools and as the only place where true philosophy could be learned. At the same time, the monks, especially the Cistercians, had no intention of offering the learning of the cloister to scholars unless they were also willing to convert to the monastic life. Monastic schools had been closed and were not to be reopened. Before turning to what Bernard of Clairvaux and other monks were opposing in the schools and offering as an alternative in the cloister, we must first briefly reexamine the history of monastic schools.

THE DECLINE OF MONASTIC SCHOOLS

Most historical accounts give the impression that there was a sudden decline of monastic schools and a major change of attitude toward learning among monks after 1100. The schools within the cloister, it is suggested, rapidly disappeared as monasteries, after centuries of providing the best education available, lapsed into intellectual quiescence because they were either unable or unwilling to meet the challenges posed by the expanding urban schools. It is certainly true that the monasteries did irrevocably lose their dominance over education and scholarship to the cathedral schools. Bec, the last of the renowned monastic schools, was quickly superseded by Laon and Paris once St. Anselm departed for Canterbury. But despite the lessened importance of their schools, the essential function and purpose of learning within monasteries remained the same. The cloister had always been intended as a place of devotion, not education—of prayer, not teaching.[8] As their schools closed, the monks did not lose a responsibility they had actually sought. Rather, they ceased to provide a service no longer essential to, and increasingly viewed as incompatible with, the purpose of their lives. What concerned monastic reformers was not that the cathedral schools had taken over education but that society was coming to value the intellectual training provided by the schools more and to reward it better than the spiritual training of the cloister. The monks were competing with the expanding urban schools not over students but over influence and authority.

Even during the greatest age of Benedictine monasticism, in the tenth and eleventh centuries, monastic schools had remained generally small in size and limited in purpose. It is too often assumed that an active monastic scriptorium and a large library are sufficient evidence of thriving scholarship and teaching. They are not.[9] Nor is the presence of an important scholar, if, as often happened in monasteries, he lacked both suitable students to teach and disciples interested in continuing his work. Although it is certainly true that in the absence of other schools, monasteries alone had kept learning and intellectual life going, no single monastery seems to have had a continuous history of educational distinction. For a generation or two—or at most three—scholarship and teaching might thrive at a certain monastery and bring its school some renown. Then the activity would decline. The main limitation of monastic schools came from the nature of the students taught. In addition to the novices being trained in Latin for the monastic office, a few sons of local noble families might be admitted to attract donations or secure patronage, and a limited number of young clerics might be in training for the priesthood. This was the normal enrollment in monastic schools. If a scholar of great repute happened to be in residence, other students would often come to study with him, sometimes drawn from a considerable distance. In most cases, these older and more advanced students would be taught separately from the others. Their instruction fell outside the usual teaching done within the cloister and was not an integral part of the monastery's function. The presence of such "external" students at a monastery, wholly dependent upon the personal reputation of the teacher as well as the toleration of his monastic brethren, was never considered more than a temporary arrangement.

A notable example of such an arrangement is provided by Bec while Lanfranc was teaching there. Already a renowned teacher when he joined the recently founded Norman house in 1042, Lanfranc was given the likely duty of running the monastic school. Only after several years of exclusively teaching the oblates and novices, however, was Lanfranc permitted to open his school to external students. Bec's founder and first abbot, Herluin, approved this innovation for the specific reason of providing an additional source of revenue for his new monastery. In a short time this school acquired an international reputation. Lanfranc's teaching of both the liberal arts and the Bible attracted students to the monastery not just from northern France but also from Germany and Italy. Although some of these students, such as Anselm of Aosta, became monks and joined the community, many did not, instead moving on to study or to teach elsewhere after a few years of study under Lanfranc. The school was closed in 1063, when Lanfranc left Bec, and it stayed closed even when Lanfranc's great disciple, Anselm, began to teach. Whether by personal choice or community consensus, Anselm, even as his reputation as a scholar grew, continued to have as pupils only members of Bec itself and a few monks from elsewhere. This restriction deprived Anselm of the disciples who could have continued his work and taught his methods to others. When Anselm went to Canterbury, the great scholarly tradition of Bec ended. What to us seems like the unfortunate decline of an important school, the monks of Bec probably regarded as a return to a more normal and acceptable state of affairs.[10]

What happened to the school opened at Bec by Lanfranc was not exceptional. Efforts to restrict or curtail the educational services provided by monasteries date as far back as the ninth century. At the Council of Aix, in 817, legislation was promulgated requiring that monasteries separate their teaching into "cloister" schools, reserved for oblates, novices, and monks, and "external" schools, for those who were not members of the community.[11] Thus, if outsiders were to be taught in the monastery, the school should be outside the cloister. The arrangement at Bec apparently complied with this long-standing regulation. At the time that Lanfranc was opening his school, reforming monasteries were already beginning to close their external schools entirely or to arrange for secular clerics to take them over. Monte Cassino, if the testimony of Peter Damian is correct, achieved its greatest influence as a center of both humanistic learning and religious reform under Abbot Desiderius (1059-87), after the monastery had closed its school to outsiders.[12] In the twelfth century examples of this trend multiply. Among the first set of codified statutes promulgated by the General Chapter of the Cistercian Order (1134) is a regulation prohibiting the instruction of any pupils, other than novices, either within the cloister or in any buildings belonging to a monastery.[13] A well-documented example of the change occurred at the Benedictine monastery of Lobbes, in Lorraine. In addition to a school within the cloister for young monks, the monastery had, since the ninth century, maintained a school for external students, staffed by a monk, at nearby St. Ursmer. As part of a program of reform, Abbot Leonius (1131-37) conferred the duties of scholasticus of St. Ursmer on a secular cleric, rather than a monk.[14] To reformers from the mid-eleventh century on, it was preferable that monks not teach others either within the cloister or in external schools.

At the same time, other reforms were affecting the cloister, or internal, schools. New restrictions limiting the number of child oblates or, in certain cases, prohibiting them completely lessened the need for monasteries to provide instruction in Latin and the elementary arts. Cistercian novices had to be at least fifteen, by which time most would already have been taught enough grammar to understand the Rule and to learn the monastic office. At Cluny the customs established by Abbot Hugh (1049-1109) reduced to six the number of boys who could be accepted as oblates and trained as novices at any one time. This reform changed the purpose of the school as well as its size. With older and usually literate novices to train, instruction at Cluny took on the new emphasis of inspiring devotion and a better understanding of the Rule and customs of the order. This trend was accentuated after 1132, when Cluny promulgated an even stricter regulation requiring all novices to be at least twenty.[15] At Lobbes, Abbot Leonius, after turning the school of St. Ursmer over to a cleric, later also tried unsuccessfully to close the cloister school on the grounds that the education of boys conflicted with the religious life.[16]

Such reforms were seldom fully effective. As Leonius found at Lobbes, some novices, young or old, were still likely to be illiterate and to need instruction in Latin. And where instruction in grammar and other elementary arts was offered within the cloister, an occasional external student appears to have been tolerated, even in houses of the reformed orders. Some external schools also managed to escape being closed. Often staffed, as at Lobbes, by secular clerics rather than monks, they remained small and local institutions, providing elementary instruction for no more than a few clerics and noble children in the more rural or remote parts of Europe. They could not and did not try to compete with the instruction being offered at the cathedral schools in the expanding towns. It was still not rare for those who attended cathedral schools to have first learned their Latin grammar at a monastery near their homes.[17] But scholars seldom traveled to monasteries anymore to be taught by a renowned master. By the early twelfth century it was no longer socially acceptable to do what Lanfranc had done when he opened his school at Bec to outsiders. Peter Abelard's difficulties after his conversion were in no small measure due to the opposition he confronted, the antagonism he provoked, and the suspicion he aroused when he tried to teach publicly as a monk.

There is another aspect of monastic learning that is no less relevant to the conflict between the cloister and the school. Despite the diminished importance of monasteries as centers of education, learned monks continued to play an important part in the intellectual life of the twelfth century, if not often in the mainstream of theological or philosophical advances, still in vital areas of religious thought and literature.[18] Monasteries flourished intellectually as centers of biblical exegesis, historical writing, devotional literature, and preaching. The learning and scholarship of such monks as Bernard of Clairvaux and William of St. Thierry rivaled the achievements of even the most prominent masters in the schools. These learned monks could write sophisticated Latin, construct complex arguments, and cite a broad spectrum of classical and patristic authorities. Although they usually limited their actual teaching to the training of the novices in their own monasteries, they regarded themselves as the guardians of doctrine. When they challenged the renowned schoolmasters of the time, they did so fully confident in their ability to prove them wrong.

Bernard of Clairvaux and William of St. Thierry stand out, in part, because of the major controversies in which they got themselves involved. Many other intellectually distinguished monastic scholars worked and wrote more quietly within the cloister. Their scholarship was aided by the many manuscripts, both of ancient and contemporary authors, to which they had access. The libraries of the rich Benedictine monasteries had been built up over centuries, and the houses of the newer orders like Cîteaux had active scriptoria that provided the monks with their needs. Those who entered monasteries from the schools brought their personal libraries with them and thereby updated the community's holdings. The arrival of these new recruits also kept those within the cloister informed of what was happening intellectually in the schools. As the experience of Isaac of Stella shows, some monks were eager to be taught the newest doctrines and methods from the schools. When renowned masters like Odo of Soissons, Serlo of Wilton, and Alan of Lille relinquished their positions in the schools for the monastic life, they left neither their learning nor their scholarship behind. They renounced teaching and often expressed serious doubts or regrets about what they had once learned and taught, but they continued to write and to influence those around them with the accumulated knowledge of their years in the schools. The claims of monastic scholars to intellectual superiority were not idle boasts or simple pretense. Twelfth-century monasticism lacked neither the scholarly resources nor the personnel to defend the benefits of monastic life and learning against the advances of the schools.

BERNARD OF CLAIRVAUX'S ATTITUDE TOWARD THE SCHOOLS

As the young son of a Burgundian nobleman, Bernard had, like many others of his class, confronted a difficult decision: whether to attend the schools, as his elder brothers were urging him to do, or to enter the cloister, as his devout mother had requested before her death. According to his biographer, Geoffrey of Auxerre, Bernard agonized greatly over the choice and even set out for the schools before finally deciding to enter Cîteaux in 1112.[19] Cîteaux was then still a small, austere community of monks who had recently left far larger and wealthier Benedictine houses, seeking to withdraw from the world and to pursue a simple life in complete obedience to the Benedictine Rule. It was simplicity and solitude that apparently attracted Bernard and his companions to Cîteaux, the same ideals that had inspired the new monastery's founders.[20] But there was an important difference in what they had left behind. The founders of Cîteaux had rejected the established routine and social obligations of such great abbeys as Molesmes. Others were to follow in their footsteps, leaving Benedictine houses for the stricter observances of the Cistercians. Bernard, in contrast, had come straight from the world; and in doing so, he added another important ideal to those that had inspired the order's original founders. He viewed Cîteaux as an alternative not so much to other monasteries but to the schools. In entering the new order, Bernard had rejected not another form of monastic life but the learning and the careers open to those who attended the schools.

Bernard's conversion thus followed the never-forgotten precedent of Benedict of Nursia, whose decision to become a monk, according to Gregory the Great, had involved the explicit rejection of the schools and of learning.[21] The steady stream of students and masters who left the schools and gave up their careers to enter Cîteaux in the twelfth century gave this precedent an important role in defining the identity of the order. The stability and tranquility of the cloister were increasingly seen as an alternative to the turbulence and competitiveness of the schools. Cîteaux stood in opposition to Paris.

Bernard of Clairvaux was not the first monk to use the language of education to describe the monastic life. Again, Benedict provided a precedent. In the *Rule*, the cloister is called "a school for the service of God."[22] But it was probably Bernard more than anyone else who created the vocabulary that set the cloister and the schools up as mirror images. Two passages from his letters will suffice as examples of his use of this language. The first is from a letter written to Master Henry Murdach, urging him to follow the example of two of his former students who had joined the Cistercian order. Bernard echoes the *Rule of St. Benedict* in speaking of the cloister as a "school of piety." But it is greater knowledge that Bernard promises the master if he will leave the schools for the cloister. "Believe an expert," he writes without modesty. "You will find something much greater in the woods than in books. The woods and stones will teach you what you cannot learn from other masters."[23] The second is from a letter addressed to a young student who had reneged on an earlier vow to enter Cîteaux because he had been attracted to the schools. Warning the young man that he is mistaken to think he can learn more in the schools, Bernard writes that it is Christ himself who will be his master in the cloister. "You should forward no excuse," he insists. "If study is the reason and you still wish to be taught and to be under a master, a master approaches and calls you, a master in whom all the treasures of wisdom are concealed. It is the very master who teaches man knowledge and makes the tongues of children eloquent."[24] The cloister's superiority as a place to learn as well as to live could not have been made clearer.

The use of such language seems to have come naturally to Bernard. But it was also a tactic that he deliberately used in recruiting for his order. To Bernard, it was obvious that many young men who might have entered a monastery had been attracted to the schools instead and were reluctant to give up the wordly fame and fortune that learning promised them for the less tangible benefits of the monastic life. He seems to have harbored few doubts that such men would be converted once they were shown the clear superiority of the cloister. Some notable scholars, as we have seen, were converted, and such successes gave Bernard good reason to be confident. It was not until the difficulties he encountered in trying to silence Peter Abelard made him aware of the extent of the influence wielded by the scholars and graduates of the schools that what had been an intense but essentially cordial rivalry between Cîteaux and Paris turned into a serious conflict.

Bernard's actions and writings against Abelard grew progressively more antagonistic and alarmed. At first he had been reluctant to get involved. Responding to the letter William of St. Thierry wrote him during or just before Lent in 1139, Bernard had expressed confidence that the doctrines of Abelard that concerned William could be easily refuted in good time and had postponed any action until after Easter.[25] Whatever personal animosity their previous encounters and disagreements might have occasioned does not seem to have made Bernard at all anxious to take Abelard on as an adversary.[26] After Easter, Bernard met with William of St. Thierry and was probably then convinced of the seriousness of Abelard's doctrinal errors. He also appears to have met with Abelard himself at least twice but to have been unable to convince him to admit or retract his errors.[27] That these meetings were amicable, as some sources suggest, adds to the difficulty of explaining why Bernard subsequently became so worked up against Abelard.[28] It seems likely that Abelard, anxious to avoid another Soissons, was cordial to Bernard, willing to give ground on some minor points but firm in defending the essentials of his doctrine. Perhaps Bernard had been partially placated by these discussions but later grew increasingly worried by reports of what Abelard's students were saying and finally decided that the popular master should be prevented from teaching.

In his initial efforts to silence Abelard, Bernard approached the archbishop of Sens and the bishop of Paris, neither of whom was willing to intervene in the matter. He then decided to appeal directly to Rome and sent a long letter to the papal curia detailing Abelard's errors.[29] It is impossible to know how far his efforts had progressed when Bernard visited Paris and preached at the schools. There is no evidence that he went to Paris to attack Abelard or became alarmed by anything he learned during this visit. It was probably not Bernard but Abelard who first forced the issue into the open, when he learned of the accusations Bernard had made to the pope. In a letter sent to his supporters just before Sens, Abelard writes that Bernard, who had been friendly in their private meetings, had betrayed him and publicly attacked him in Paris. Under the circumstances, Abelard felt he had no other choice than to seek an opportunity to answer the accusations Bernard had been making against him.[30] The meeting, scheduled to be held during the Council of Sens on June 3, 1140, was instigated by Abelard and his supporters, who wanted to engage the abbot in a public debate over the disputed doctrines.

During the year between his visit to Paris and the convening of the Council of Sens, Bernard launched a full-fledged attack against Abelard with a flood of letters addressed to Rome. His charges and tactics escalated as he became aware of the considerable support that Abelard enjoyed among members of the papal curia. When pointing out the obvious errors of Abelard's teaching was not enough to get his opponent silenced, Bernard resorted to more serious allegations against Abelard's conduct, integrity, and influence. He increasingly saw Abelard as dangerous as well as erroneous. "The faith of the simple is being scorned," Bernard wrote, "the secrets of God are being eviscerated, questions about the most sacred matters are being heedlessly discussed; the fathers are reviled for thinking that such matters are better allowed to rest than to be solved. . . . So human ingenuity usurps everything for itself, leaving nothing to faith."[31] No longer was the conflict just a disagreement over certain points of doctrine. It had become a battle between two different and fundamentally irreconcilable approaches to the knowledge of faith, one of which Bernard viewed as a serious danger to the Church.

The strong ad hominem attacks in the letters are a clear indication of Bernard's growing personal antagonism toward Abelard as well as of a deeply embedded suspicion of his behavior as a teacher and a monk. "Abelard argues with boys and consorts with women," Bernard charges in a letter to one cardinal.[32] To another cardinal, he calls Abelard, who had resigned as abbot of St. Gildas, "a monk without a rule, a prelate without responsibility."[33] As Bernard had shown during the papal schism, he would resort to ruthless tactics when he was defending an endangered Church against an unworthy adversary—and temperamentally he tended to see all his battles in these terms. This explains the explicit comparison he makes in several of his letters to Rome between his two adversaries. Abelard, "Peter the Dragon," is likened to the recently deceased antipope Anacletus II, "Peter the Lion." "We have escaped the roaring of Peter the Lion," Bernard proclaimed. "We now encounter the hissing of Peter the Dragon. . . . The former did damage only as long as he lived; and death was the end both of him and of his evil. But this man [Abelard] has arranged to pass his virus on to posterity, to harm every generation in the future. He has written down his leprous inventions with pen and in ink."[34] Despite a steady barrage of such letters to Rome, Bernard did not succeed in having Abelard quickly silenced by papal action. There was apparently more sympathy and support for Abelard among the cardinals than Bernard realized. Perhaps owing to their influence, no action was taken by Rome until after the meeting already scheduled for Sens had taken place.

Unfortunately for Abelard, his strategy of seeking a decisive confrontation with his opponent failed. Although he had been unable to secure Abelard's condemnation prior to Sens, Bernard proved to have enough influence and skill to manipulate the council to serve his purpose. He had tried at first to prevent the meeting. While still hoping for preemptive action from Rome, he refused the invitation of Archbishop Henry of Sens to attend the council. He was reluctant to confront Abelard in public debate. "I refused," Bernard later explained in a letter to the pope, "since I am but a child [in disputation], and he has been a warrior since his youth."[35] Bernard's previous encounters with Abelard made him concerned that the skilled dialectician could better him in debate. But when he realized that his choice was either to appear at the widely publicized meeting at Sens or to risk leaving Abelard unopposed to win the support of those present, Bernard decided he had to attend. To ensure that Abelard's supporters did not dominate the meeting, Bernard summoned the French bishops attending the council to come to his aid.[36] He outmaneuvered Abelard by changing what was to have been a public debate before an assembly of scholars and churchmen (which even Louis VII had decided to attend) into a tribunal before which Abelard would have to answer to specific charges of heretical teaching. At a closed meeting arranged by Bernard the day before the scheduled public debate, the bishops were presented with a list of nineteen propositions from Abelard's writings and pronounced them to be heretical.[37]

Under the circumstances, Abelard's fate before the council was predetermined. He had wanted a discussion; he was facing a trial. Realizing that he had been outmaneuvered, Abelard refused to appear before the council or to answer to the charges against him. Instead, he would take his case directly to Rome, where he hoped his supporters could assure him a fair and open hearing. As Abelard expected, the Council of Sens voted to condemn him of heresy. But the conflict was not yet over. The venue had merely been switched, by Abelard's action, back to Rome.

The letters that Bernard wrote to Rome after the Council of Sens giving his version of the dispute provide the clearest evidence of the reasons for his growing concern about Abelard. Like the first set of letters written before Sens, they reveal how much Bernard disliked Abelard personally and distrusted him as a monk who had left his monastery and, even worse, as an abbot who had given up his prelacy to return to teaching in the schools, as well as how strongly convinced he was that many of Abelard's opinions and doctrines were erroneous, heretical, and dangerous. In his view, the danger came not just from the specific errors of doctrine, which Bernard remained confident could be proven wrong, but from Abelard's intellectual method, from his basic approach to questions of faith, from the way in which he taught and discussed doctrine. This danger was made all the worse by Abelard's popularity as a teacher and his great influence in the schools. Abelard's former students and intellectual disciples were everywhere – even in the papal curia, as Bernard had found to his dismay – and they were prepared to defend their master and his errors. Bernard's realization of the extent of Abelard's influence and support convinced him that the pope should move quickly and decisively to silence him.

There had been a discernible increase in Bernard's alarm since the time that William of St. Thierry had first warned him about Abelard. William had insisted that it was Bernard's responsibility to intervene because the deaths of Anselm of Laon and William of Champeaux had left the schools without soundly learned masters able to challenge Abelard and defend the faith.[38] Initially unworried, Bernard had proceeded deliberately. Then, apparently after his meetings with Abelard, Bernard had begun to understand the nature of the intellectual changes that had been occurring in the schools under the influence of Abelard and other dialecticians. By the time he wrote his first letter to the pope, Bernard no longer saw the problem as simply a matter of refuting a few obvious errors of doctrine. It had become clear to Bernard that Abelard's basic methods were at fault.

In his letter to Innocent II, Bernard makes four major criticisms of Abelard's method. He charges (1) that Abelard erroneously applied dialectical reasoning to the most profound mysteries of the faith, (2) that he foolishly believed these mysteries could be made intelligible, (3) that he equated faith with opinion rather than certainty, and (4) that he depended more on his own understanding than upon the authority of the Fathers.[39] These charges reveal the extent of Bernard's opposition to the new theology of the schools. For him, faith and authority were sufficient means of knowing. Bernard's letter makes it apparent that although he understood something of their methods, he saw no purpose or justification in what dialecticians like Abelard were doing. Questions of faith were better resolved by reading and reflecting upon Scripture within the cloister than by speculating and disputing in the schools. Bernard was defending the monastic tradition of *lectio divina* against the challenge of the new scholastic discipline of *theologia*.[40] His mocking references to Abelard as "another Aristotle" and "the new theologian,"[41] which would have been regarded as epithets of praise in the schools, are clearly indicative of the irreconcilable differences that had developed between the methods of monastic and scholastic learning.

For Bernard, what made the new scholastic methods especially dangerous was the fact that they were being used publicly. The profound mysteries of faith had become matters of public discussion. Writing to Innocent II in the name of the French bishops, after Sens, Bernard warned that it was dangerous to allow Abelard to go on teaching when issues of faith, including the very nature of the Trinity, were already being disputed everywhere and by everyone, "in cities, villages, and castles; by scholars, not only in the schools but also in public places; and not only by those learned and advanced enough but also by boys and the uneducated, and even by fools."[42] Abelard's methods, dangerous enough when used by learned men, would really cause havoc as they spread outside the schools. Public disputation of doctrinal questions had to be stopped before faith became a matter of personal opinion rather than of revealed and accepted truth. "Our theologian," Bernard wrote to Cardinal Aimeric, the papal chancellor, "impugns the law with the words of the law. He throws what is holy before dogs and casts pearls before swine; he corrupts the faith of the simple and defiles the purity of the Church."[43] In several letters Bernard compared Abelard to Pelagius, Arius, and Nestorius.[44] This comparison was not merely polemical, nor was it really doctrinal, although Bernard did see some parallels in their errors. Bernard had actually come to view Abelard as a new heresiarch, who was using the schools and his students to spread his heretical doctrines and dangerous methods throughout the Church.

To heresy was, in Bernard's mind, added the danger of schism. In the light of his failure to get Abelard condemned by the pope before the meeting at Sens, Bernard feared that Abelard had a great deal of influence and support in Rome. To Bernard, Abelard's decision to appeal to Rome rather than answer the charges advanced against him at Sens gave his supporters in the curia another chance to delay action. Abelard was boasting, Bernard reported in several post-Sens letters, that there were cardinals and clerics in the curia who would protect him and his writings.[45] Bernard was clearly worried about what might happen were Abelard to get to Rome. If Abelard's supporters managed to keep him from being silenced, there was a danger that the wounds of the recently healed schism would reopen. "I can no more bear," Bernard wrote to Innocent II, "to see the Church suffer than I could have ignored the injuries done to my lord, the pope."[46] Bernard enforced his warning to the pope by repeatedly linking "Peter the Dragon" and "Peter the Lion."[47] The scars of faction within the curia remained evident. Bernard was seriously concerned that the controversy over Abelard, if not quickly settled, could resplit the Church. For this reason above all, he thought it was imperative that Abelard be condemned and silenced as soon as possible, preferably before he had a chance to rally his support in Rome.

Abelard never did reach Rome. Within only a few weeks of Sens, Innocent II confirmed the decision of the council by declaring the nineteen disputed propositions to be heretical. Abelard was to be confined within a monastery and forbidden from further writing or teaching, his theological works were burned, and his defenders were excommunicated.[48] Bernard got exactly what he had wanted, the complete condemnation and silencing of his opponent. Abelard had no choice but to submit to the judgment of the pope. Confined to Cluny, where he had found refuge on his way to Rome, Abelard was never able to teach again. Numerous copies of Abelard's works were destroyed and scholars were discouraged from referring to him by name or from quoting his works directly. But those who had heard Abelard's lectures still carried on his work and thought.[49] Bernard had won an important battle over the schools, but he was going to lose the war. He had managed to silence the greatest teacher of the time, seriously damaging Abelard's reputation and preventing him from becoming an authority who could be quoted by name. Meanwhile, the influence of the schools and of scholastic theology continued to grow. As a scholar and teacher, "Peter the Dragon" had indeed made provision for "passing his virus on to posterity."

After silencing Abelard, Bernard kept a watchful eye over the schools for new signs of this virus. Eight years after Sens he became involved in a conflict with another scholastic theologian, Gilbert, then bishop of Poitiers but formerly a master in Paris.[50] Geoffrey of Auxerre tells the story that Abelard, as he departed from Sens, had warned Gilbert that he would be next.[51] There are clear similarities between the two disputes. Bernard again took the lead, challenging the teaching of a prominent master, and he again tried to manipulate a Church council to defeat his rival. This time, however, he was not as successful. Two contemporary sources, both reliable though neither completely neutral, question Bernard's motives in trying to have Gilbert's doctrines condemned in a private caucus before the public discussion scheduled at the Council of Reims, as he had done to Abelard at Sens. Significantly, both suggest that Bernard's failure this time may have been as much a political as a doctrinal defeat.

The first of these sources is the *Historia pontificalis* of the humanist John of Salisbury, who was an actual eyewitness of Gilbert's trial at Reims in 1148.[52] According to John, there was from the beginning more to the attack on Gilbert of Poitiers than a mere dispute over statements of questionable orthodoxy in the bishop's commentary on the *De Trinitate* of Boethius. John suggests, cautiously but clearly, that Gilbert's original assailants, who included Masters Peter Lombard and Robert of Melun and Abbot Suger of St. Denis, might have had personal or political reasons for challenging Gilbert. "I cannot say," he writes, "whether they acted out of zeal for the faith, or jealousy of his fame and merit, or a desire to propitiate the abbot [Bernard], whose influence was then at its height and whose counsel was most weighty in the affairs of church and state alike."[53] In even more diplomatic language, John raises doubts about Bernard's motives. Others may disagree, he writes, but he cannot believe that a man of such sanctity was not acting out of his love for God.[54]

John arouses further suspicions by his description of the reactions to the private meeting Bernard called at which he pressed unsuccessfully for the condemnation of the disputed questions. Bernard had invited French and English prelates and scholars to this meeting, urging them to take action then because it was their duty to remove scandals from the Church.[55] Excluded from the meeting had been the large group of cardinals present in Reims for the council, which had been called during a papal visit to France. According to John, the cardinals were infuriated when they heard of the meeting. To them this was, like Sens, a deliberate attempt by Bernard to undermine the authority of the curia to decide such cases. John's comments deserve quotation in full:

> When the news came to the hearing of the cardinals, they were indignant against the abbot and against those who had assembled at his request. They therefore decided to support the case of the bishop of Poitiers, saying that the abbot had attacked Peter Abelard using the very same tactics. . . . The cardinals suspected, or pretended to suspect, that the abbot wished to draw the French and English prelates to his side, because he thought that the Roman curia would be able to do nothing against their judgment, especially then and there in Reims, nor be able to absolve Master Gilbert, if he had already been condemned by them, without risking sedition. As I recall, there was not a single cardinal other than Alberic, of holy memory, bishop of Ostia, who was not completely opposed to the abbot in spirit and deed. They said, I believe falsely, that Bernard had called together the abbot of St. Denis, then regent of France, and the most powerful men in the Church in order to pressure the papacy to agree with him under threat of schism.[56]

However the dispute began and whatever Bernard's actual motives were, his questionable tactics, combined with the memory of what had happened to Abelard at Sens, turned the decision of Gilbert's case at Reims into a power struggle. But this time Bernard lost.

John's interpretation of the events at Reims is corroborated by the similar account found in the *Gesta Friderici* of Otto of Freising.[57] Although he places the private meeting later in the proceedings of the council, Otto reports virtually the same indignation on the part of the cardinals against Bernard and the French prelates. United in their anger, the cardinals, according to Otto, sent a long letter of protest to Eugenius III, the Cistercian pope who was a disciple of Bernard. Complaining that Bernard had usurped their prerogatives, they wrote: "What has your abbot done and the French Church with him? With what effrontery, with what audacity has he raised his head against the primacy and supremacy of the Roman see? . . . It alone has the right to conduct investigations of the Catholic faith."[58] The two sides of the conflict are again clearly drawn in Otto's account. He reports that the entire group of cardinals (as opposed to all but one, in John of Salisbury's version) were allied against Bernard and the French prelacy. Gilbert of Poitiers was caught in the middle and so, in a way, was the pope. The doctrinal questions were clouded by the more energetic struggle over the extent of Bernard's power and influence.

Under the circumstances, both accounts agree, the doctrinal questions could be resolved only by compromise. With the strong support of the cardinals, Gilbert was given the chance to answer the charges against him. He denied those doctrines that were not his, defended or agreed to correct those that were, made a profession of faith, and returned to his diocese acquitted of heresy and with his reputation intact. Although some of Gilbert's doctrines had been found to be erroneous, it was Bernard's reputation that suffered most from the confrontation. The abbot, both John of Salisbury and Otto of Freising concur, should never have been involved in the affair. Each of the chroniclers raises the possibility that Gilbert escaped condemnation by clever use of his subtle intellectual and dialectical skills, but both conclude that it was more likely that Bernard was just not equal to the task of debating so great a master.[59] Both accounts emphasize that the doctrinal issues in dispute were very complex—in fact too complex, John and Otto both seem to think, to be understood by anyone, including Bernard, who had not himself been trained in the schools. "His speech was difficult," Otto of Freising writes of Gilbert, "and what he meant was never clear to child-like minds, scarcely even to men of education and learning."[60]

Otto, himself both a Cistercian monk and a former Paris student, raises a further objection. In his view, it had been a mistake for Bernard to try to silence Gilbert of Poitiers as he had Peter Abelard eight years earlier, because there was "neither the same reason nor like material. For Gilbert," he goes on to explain, "from his youth subjected himself to the instruction of great men and put more confidence in the weight of their authority than in his own intellect. . . . His moral sense and the seriousness of his living were not at variance with his intellectual attainments."[61] Gilbert's spotless career and his status as a bishop made him a more formidable adversary than the controversial Abelard. Both accounts also suggest that the political situation had changed, reducing Bernard's influence and allowing for a more effective resistance to his interference in the schools.

But it would be a mistake to look to personal and political factors alone in accounting for the different outcomes of the two trials. Gilbert and Abelard, however great the differences in their personal reputations, were not really very different in their methods or doctrines. Both were skilled dialecticians who had made their reputations as speculative theologians teaching in Paris. What happened at Reims may be an indication that in the few short years since Sens, the Church's attitude toward scholastic theology had become generally more favorable.[62] There was—and would continue to be—controversy over specific points of doctrine and concern that the new methods, if improperly used, could result in heretical opinions. But the value and the usefulness of scholastic theology in defining, clarifying, and systematizing Christian doctrine was being increasingly recognized. After what happened at Reims, Bernard himself may have been forced to accept the fact that the influence of the schools had reached the point where their independence was assured.

It is difficult to sympathize with Bernard of Clairvaux if one looks only at his conflicts with Peter Abelard and Gilbert of Poitiers. These disputes reveal only one side of his character—Bernard the reactionary opponent of the schools, desperately struggling to check the growing influence of what he saw to be dangerous new methods and doctrines. The polemics of his letters and antischolastic treatises make a far different impression than the profound insights and beautiful language of his treatises on the monastic life, his sermons, and his biblical commentaries. As a contemplative theologian Bernard had no equal, and his influence on later medieval thought was immense.[63] Bernard opposed certain masters and intellectual trends, not learning per se. This having been said, we must look beyond his words and actions against Peter Abelard and Gilbert of Poitiers to evaluate Bernard's view of the schools and his expectations of them.

Despite his obvious dislike for and distrust of the schools, Bernard recognized their necessity and, at times, intervened in their affairs in a positive as well as a negative way. An analysis of his impact on the schools must take into account the close ties he maintained with William of Champeaux and Hugh of St. Victor, and the support he provided to such scholars as Peter Lombard, Alberic of Reims, and Robert Pullen, as well as his attacks on Abelard and Gilbert.[64] The case of Robert Pullen provides what is probably the most telling example of the positive side of Bernard's concern and involvement in the schools.

A short time after succeeding Gilbert of Poitiers as theology master at the cathedral school in Paris, Robert Pullen was ordered by the new bishop of Rochester, Ascelin, either to return to England or to resign the archdeaconry of Rochester, which he had held in absentia since 1134. Many masters depended upon nonresident prebends to supplement the fees they got for teaching, and Pullen, even though he had the secure income of a chair at the cathedral school, resisted giving up the revenues of his archdeaconry. When Ascelin confiscated the archdeacon's property, Bernard intervened on Pullen's behalf. In a forceful letter to Bishop Ascelin, Bernard wrote that Pullen, a master known for his sound doctrine, must be allowed to continue teaching in Paris.[65] Bernard's estimation of Robert Pullen presumably derived more from the master's virtuous reputation than from a familiarity with his theological writings, which reveal the strong influence of Peter Abelard. This issue aside, the greater question is why Bernard, given his strong views on the superiority of life and learning within the cloister, bothered to intervene on behalf of any master in the schools. The answer, quite simply, is that Bernard was practical enough to realize that not all men could be educated as monks, that a secular clergy was needed, and that these men would have to be trained in the schools. His responsibility was to make certain that they were taught by masters reputed for their sound doctrine and virtuous lives – by men like Robert Pullen, not like Peter Abelard.[66]

"Who will grant that I might see learned and holy men presiding in the Church, if not everywhere or in most places, at least in some?"[67] This plea, found in a letter to a Carthusian prior, suggests the personal responsibility that Bernard felt for the state of the clergy and prelacy and the reasons that he kept so watchful an eye on the schools and learning. But his complaints in this letter about being preoccupied with worldly affairs also suggest something of his ambivalence. Bernard confesses that he feels it monstrous for him, as a monk, to be involved in such affairs.[68] Perhaps it was because of this ambivalence that Bernard never explained his educational attitudes or tried to justify his actions toward the schools. At times Bernard seems to have felt he had no other choice than to use all the means at his disposal to oppose dangerous masters, methods, and doctrines, and at those times he urgently intervened in the schools. Then, as soon as possible, he returned to his own rich life of contemplative learning within the cloister.

It is through one of his contemplative works, the beautiful commentary on the Song of Songs, that we can gain some deeper insight into the educational ideals and values that shaped Bernard's reaction to the schools. In Sermon 36 on the verse, "If you do not know yourself, go forth" (Cant. 1.7), Bernard preaches about knowledge and how it is to be acquired. After an introduction that, he recognizes, might be construed as an attack upon learning, he emphasizes, somewhat defensively, that he regards education as vital to the Church. "Perhaps I seem to go too far in my scorn of knowledge," he says, "as if to censure the learned and to prohibit the study of letters. Not at all! I am not ignorant of how much her learned members have benefited and still do benefit the Church, whether by refuting her opponents or by instructing the ignorant."[69]

This sermon predates Bernard's conflict with the schools and was delivered within the cloister, but his next comments seem to be addressed as much to scholars as to monks. There are, he explains, two kinds of knowledge. One is useful and necessary to salvation; the other serves merely to puff men up with useless pride. The distinction being made is not between the learning of the cloister and that of the schools. Bernard is preaching not about where but about how and, above all, about why knowledge is sought. Order, application, and a sense of purpose are, he emphasizes, the essential keys to fruitful knowledge. Most important is the third of these, the intent or purpose of learning. Many men, argues Bernard, study only for the sake of knowledge itself, or out of the desire for fame, or to sell what they know for money and honors. These base motives—curiosity, vanity, and ambition—abuse and corrupt learning. Only those who study either to serve others or to improve themselves become truly learned. Charity and prudence alone make knowledge useful.[70]

This distinction between good and bad motives seems to have been the primary standard that Bernard applied to judging the scholars and the schools of his time. When he preached in Paris in 1139, he warned scholars that curiosity and ambition were corrupting both their lives and their learning.[71] Conversion was the answer for some. But what was to be done about those left behind in the schools, where there were too few masters motivated by charity and prudence to provide the right kind of education? The excessive questioning, public disputations, dangerous new methods, and erroneous doctrines fostered by masters like Peter Abelard could all be traced back to their base motives. These were, Bernard believed, the inevitable consequences of leaving education to masters who had become scholars to satisfy their curiosity and who taught to acquire worldly fame and fortune. The overweening ambitions of scholars for both their methods and their careers were at the very root of the problem Bernard perceived in the schools.

Bernard of Clairvaux never did propose a practical solution to the problem. Later critics who shared his concerns about the motivations of scholars concluded that curricular reforms and the regulation of students and masters would improve conditions in the schools. Bernard seems to have doubted that there could ever be any real improvement in the schools. For him there remained the alternative of the cloister, which offered a more virtuous life and superior learning. Although Bernard obviously cared that masters of sound doctrine should be left teaching in the schools, it was a higher priority for him to recruit such masters and their students for the cloister. This was the dilemma of Cistercian opposition to the schools, one that neither Bernard nor his successors managed to resolve.

THE CLOISTER VS. THE SCHOOL: THE CISTERCIAN EVANGELISTS

The opposition of the cloister and the school is a recurring theme in the Cistercian literature of the twelfth century. Not surprisingly, given the importance of the idea in the life and writings of Bernard of Clairvaux, it was taken up by four of the other great evangelists of Cistercian spirituality: William of St. Thierry, Guerric of Igny, Isaac of Stella, and Adam of Perseigne.[72] Their treatments of the theme provide important evidence of the grounds upon which monks continued to renounce the schools and to reject the validity of scholastic learning. Although none of the Cistercian evangelists was as influential or as powerful as Bernard, each helped shape attitudes to the schools within – and, to a lesser extent, outside – the cloister. The theme also appears frequently in the writings of less prominent Cistercians, in letters of vocation, in stories of conversion, and in the legends of the order. Before the four great evangelists are discussed, a few examples from these sources will first serve to demonstrate just how important and pervasive opposition to the schools was in shaping the mentality of the Cistercians.

Probably the best-known and most repeated story about renouncing the schools for the cloister is the legend of the conversion of Master Serlo of Wilton that, having become a popular *exemplum* in sermons to scholars, will be discussed below.[73] A similar story is found in a late-twelfth-century manuscript from the Cistercian abbey of Aulne, near Liège. A scholar dies after having promised a close friend that if he met Virgil in hell, he would ask the poet the meaning of two obscure lines of verse and return to report the answer. The dead scholar does reappear, to pass on Virgil's warning that if the friend does not renounce poetry and the liberal arts while he is still alive, he will be damned to hell like them. The friend takes the advice to heart and enters a monastery – presumably, though it is not stated explicitly, a Cistercian one.[74] Another variation on the same story is found among the several examples of scholars' conversions in the *Dialogus miraculorum* of the German Cistercian, Caesarius of Heisterbach. In this case it is not the appearance of a dead friend that brings about the conversion but the actual death of the scholar himself. According to Caesarius, a certain abbot of Morimond had, as a young man, done homage to the devil in exchange for greater intelligence and a stronger memory. As a result, he had become the greatest scholar in Paris. Only God's mercy in giving him another chance after his death enabled the scholar to escape the pains of hell, renounce the schools, and convert to the Cistercian order.[75]

These stories make especially vivid the dangers the Cistercians saw in the schools and in secular learning. They were warnings to those who chose to remain in the schools no less than confirmations for those who had already chosen the cloister. Yet in their reliance on spiritual intervention, they may also hint at some underlying concern among the monks about the cloister's ability to compete on equal terms with the worldly attractions of the schools.

Seeking new recruits, the Cistercians often wrote their friends telling them of the advantages of the monastic life. As the letters of vocation that have been collected and edited by Dom Jean Leclercq demonstrate so clearly, the Cistercians saw the schools as the primary obstacle to their efforts to attract others into the cloister.[76] More than any other theme, these letters emphasize the superiority of the knowledge to be gained within the cloister. It is hardly surprising, given the social backgrounds of the Cistercians and the fact that many of them had themselves spent some time in the schools, that a large number of the letters are addressed to friends who were scholars and that they so often describe conversion as a matter of overcoming the seductiveness of academic life and the dangerous illusions of scholastic learning. The pervasiveness of this competitive attitude toward the schools does become remarkable, however, in letters written from the remoter Cistercian houses, which one might have expected to feel the rivalry less strongly.

An example not discussed by Leclercq is a letter to a certain Adam, a student of the liberal arts, written by Gilbert of Hoyland (d. 1172), abbot of the Cistercian house of Swineshead in Lincolnshire, far from any direct contact with the expanding urban schools. In urging Adam to convert, Gilbert actually echoes the argument often used within the schools to convince students of the arts to move on to the higher discipline of theology:

> It is not that I disparage instruction in the arts and a sound understanding of the liberal disciplines, on which the integrity of all knowledge rests. For knowing the arts is good, but only if one uses them properly, that is, only up to a certain level or point. They should not be fixed upon or adhered to but used to prepare for a certain superior, holier, and more intimate secret of wisdom, to enter secret and pleasant places, and to see that inaccessible light that God inhabits.[77]

It is not to the theology of the schools that Gilbert is urging Adam to advance, however, but to the monastic life. It is fine to study the liberal arts in the schools, but once they are learned, it is time to move to the cloister. Only there, Gilbert insists, can true wisdom be found. Only the cloister provides such an abundance of sources and such a wide scope for the intellect that even the most zealous and capable scholar will never exhaust his abilities. In his final appeal, Gilbert warns Adam not to be deceived by what might appear to be the more demanding and profound learning of the schools:

I have emphasized these things so that you will not excuse yourself on the grounds that you are busy studying letters and, deprived of light, continue to follow the shadow, and also so that you will not use your distorted Aristotelian arguments to attack our silence and simplicity. . . . Do you not realize that the leisure and peaceful silence of our lives is that very art, taught and learned as if in a direct line from God, that transforms and changes one into a new man, a new Adam, and that reaches all the way to the perception of Christ, in whom all the treasures of wisdom are concealed?[78]

This is a confident letter. Gilbert himself seems to have little doubt that the silence, peace, and simplicity of the contemplative life are far surer means to wisdom than the methods and arguments of the schools. But both the language and tone of his letter prove just how deeply embedded the Cistercian rivalry with the schools had become.

What happened to the scholars who followed the advice of these letters and renounced the schools for the cloister? To judge from the case of Isaac of Stella, the change of life did not always mean an immediate change of learning. English in origin, Isaac joined the Cistercian order apparently after teaching for several years at the schools. The details of his scholarly career are uncertain, but it is likely that he had studied in Paris and perhaps had been a student of Peter Abelard. He must have converted at least several years before 1147, when he was elected abbot of the Cistercian house of Stella, or L'Etoile, near Poitiers. One of the great Cistercian preachers of the twelfth century, Isaac is known primarily from a collection of fifty-four sermons dating from his years as abbot (1147-69). An impressive synthesis of monastic and early scholastic theology, these sermons represent Isaac's efforts to make the doctrines and methods he had learned in the schools suitable for instructing monks within the cloister.[79]

After a time Isaac abandoned these efforts and changed his techniques of teaching, apparently much to the dismay of the monks in his abbey, who became less attentive to his sermons and openly critical of his learning. In one of his sermons he describes their reactions and explains apologetically why he had decided to reform his way of teaching. As he begins one senses Isaac's concern that he had lost his effectiveness as a teacher:

For some time, my dearest brothers, I have detected that you have become more languid and slothful in listening to me. Whence I have become tedious and feeble in speaking. For it is the attention of his students that elicits the diligence of the teacher: the more devoted the listeners, the more zealous the speaker. But I recognize that you do not know why I have changed my style of speaking and why I, who used to be subtle and speak of new things, now talk only of the commonplace and repeat the trivial. Many of you comment, "How depressed that man is! How obscure his intelligence has become! How changed his great eloquence! He used to say wonderful things wonderfully, was particularly original in his thinking, made obscure things easily understandable, dissolved obscurities, and plainly demonstrated articles of disputation with examples. How is it now that he confuses and muddles everything, he touches upon everything but resolves nothing?"[80]

These words recall Abelard's reaction to the lectures of Anselm of Laon.

What must be remembered, however, is that Isaac was talking about the reaction of Cistercian monks. In fact, as Isaac goes on to say, it was their too-favorable response to his former teaching techniques that motivated him to renounce them. "I changed my mode of speaking since your curiosity was getting out of hand," he tells them.[81] They had demanded more and more novelties and he had struggled to provide them. It had reached the point where they would reject anything that was familiar to them from the Scriptures. This description of the monks' craving for novelty corresponds to a criticism often made of the schools. It is an important reminder that the young men who entered Cîteaux were not all that different from those who went off to Paris.

Whereas Abelard and other masters would often seek to blame the pressures their students put on them for the excesses or errors that appeared in their lectures and writings, Isaac accepts full responsibility for having recreated in the cloister the situation he had intended to leave behind in the schools. It was, he confesses, his curiosity and vanity that were at fault:

I am to blame. I am the cause for this insolence in you. . . . Why was I, first of all, led into such things by my curiosity, and why have I now suddenly relinquished these familiar things? The reason for both is readily apparent. For some time, certain men of spectacular ingenuity and remarkable creativity (whom I care not to name) have, if not actually perverted the sense of the Scriptures like heretics, neatly accommodated them to their own ideas, only minimally holding to the legitimate sense. . . . I followed them because the world followed them; the whole world sought after them and everyone thought that no one had ever spoken as they did. Anyone who did not speak their way was derided, condemned, and avoided. Thus, lest I be reproached for envy or be thought of as lacking intelligence for not speaking in their way, I followed them. And, as you know, I was not inferior to anyone in these ways of speaking.[82]

Isaac appraised the masters of his time less critically than Bernard did. He describes them—and Abelard and Gilbert of Poitiers must certainly be among those whom he will not name—as intending not to use their novelties against the faith or truth but to provide useful learning and to live honest lives.

Yet despite his insistence that the masters—including himself—were basically well intentioned, he shares Bernard's concerns about the dangers of their teaching. He was aware from the beginning, he confesses, that he and other masters might be establishing a dangerous precedent, that a time would come when not so well intentioned men would advance false and subversive new ideas. They would even cite the teaching of their predecessors as license for abandoning authority, responding to their criticism by asking "If you did it, why can't we?"[83] Isaac admits that he had decided to prove himself as a teacher of scholastic theology, despite his awareness of these dangers, because he had not wanted to be thought envious or unlearned. Willingly and knowingly, he had succumbed to the pressures of public opinion while in the schools. And once in the cloister, he had used the same methods and novelties because he had also wanted to be esteemed as a teacher there.

Thus Isaac explains why he had desired to study and to teach scholastic theology. Less clear is his explanation of why he suddenly renounced the methods of the schools and changed the way he taught. Perhaps it was, as he says, his concern that the curiosity of the monks whom he was teaching was getting out of hand. Coming sometime soon after his election as abbot, the change may have been motivated by his conviction that it was now his pastoral duty to give up theological speculation and disputation for clearer and simpler moral instruction. Isaac's renunciation of scholastic theology might also have been related to developments outside his monastery. The events surrounding the Council of Reims might have seemed like those dangerous times whose coming he had feared.[84] Whatever the immediate cause, or causes, of the sudden decision, it marked the completion of his conversion. Like other Cistercians, Isaac had ultimately come to define the monastic vocation in opposition to both the life and the learning of the schools.

Isaac's delay in renouncing scholastic learning and his account of his experience tell us something about both the schools and the cloister. Within the schools, we see scholars feeling pressured to advance new ideas in order to prove their intelligence. Within the cloister, we find a receptive audience for the doctrines and the methods of the schools. Isaac's monks were not—and some clearly did not want to become—cut off from scholastic learning. He chose to renounce that learning not because he was ignorant or intolerant but because he had seen its effects both in the schools and in the cloister. In explaining the reasons behind his decision, Isaac was hoping to change the attitudes of the monks who still found scholastic learning attractive.

For the Cistercians, as we have seen, the choice between the cloister and the school was a choice not just between two different ways of life but between two different ways of learning and knowing. It remains to be shown that their assertions of the superiority of monastic learning did not rest only on their praise of the peace, silence, and simplicity of life within the cloister. Bernard might write in his letters of vocation about learning from woods and stones and being taught directly by Christ, but he certainly did not depend upon such methods in refuting the complex doctrines of Abelard and Gilbert. Cistercians who had actually been trained in the schools were even more aware of the need to debate the scholars in their own terms. To do so, they recognized that they had to be able to articulate the methodological differences between monastic and scholastic learning. To confront the challenge of scholastic theology, they had to define a monastic theology.[85]

None was more successful in this cause than William of St. Thierry, the monk who had first warned Bernard of the dangers of Peter Abelard. While he depended upon Bernard to lead the battle for Abelard's condemnation, William provided the weapons by pointing out the doctrinal and methodological errors in Abelard's writings. But this was not the end of his efforts. Realizing that the problem was not limited to Abelard alone, William set out to articulate a monastic theology that would serve as an alternative to the theology of the schools and that could be used to refute the erroneous opinions that the scholars, using dialectic, were advancing as doctrine. The two treatises William wrote for this purpose, the *Speculum fidei* and the *Aenigma fidei*, explicate the intellectual differences between the monastic and scholastic approaches to learning with a clarity and force that leave little doubt that he was equal to the task.

William had studied in the schools, perhaps at Laon at the same time Abelard was there.[86] Most of his adult life was spent as a Benedictine, first at St. Nicaise in Reims, which he entered in 1113, then as abbot of St. Thierry, from 1119. Having long desired to become a Cistercian but dissuaded by Bernard from giving up his prelacy, William finally joined the order in 1135, when he entered the community at Signy. There he lived until his death in 1148. William wrote prolifically throughout his life as a monk, but his early treatises, though learned and original, lack the clear sense of method and purpose of those inspired by his opposition to the doctrines of Peter Abelard and William of Conches. From the time he first read Abelard's *Theologia*, William seems to have regarded it as his duty, in the absence of responsible masters in the schools, to defend the doctrine of the Church.[87] His disputations against Abelard and William of Conches, as well as his two treatises on faith, mark his temporary intellectual—not physical—return to the schools. His previous experience there helped him both to refute the two masters on specific points of doctrine and to articulate an alternative theology. Whereas Bernard of Clairvaux tended to see the conflict in personal terms, William of St. Thierry was aware that the problem was essentially one of method. No less critical of his opponents than Bernard, William did not impugn their motives but focused on contesting the dangerous results of their new and misguided methods.

In the opinion of William of St. Thierry, Peter Abelard and William of Conches had both made the same methodological mistake. Each had tried to speculate or to "philosophize" about the most profound matters of doctrine by making human reason independent of authority and the test of faith. Their fundamental error was that they did not understand what faith is. In his *Disputatio adversus Petrum Abaelardum*, William places Abelard's definition of faith as "the estimation of things not seen" (*estimatio rerum non apparentium*) at the very top of his list of thirteen errors.[88] According to William, "estimation" is no different from opinion. By making faith into a matter of opinion rather than an absolute certainty, Abelard was thereby opening every question of doctrine to determination not by the sound authority of the Scriptures but by disputation in the schools. "Truly that man," William wrote of Abelard, "loves to question everything, wants to dispute everything, divine as well as secular."[89] Whereas Abelard and other scholastic theologians claimed that authority needed to be interpreted and faith explained, William worried that they were weakening, not strengthening, authority and faith by their excessively rational approach. The "new theology," by subjecting the simple truths of faith to the complexities of dialectical reasoning, was, in William's view, only obscuring what learning should make clearer.[90]

More serious than obscurity were the dangers of scandal and heresy, which, according to William, were already present in Abelard's works, but which would grow worse as less capable and more daring scholars attempted to advance upon his arguments.[91] How was doctrinal error to be prevented when faith was reduced to a matter of opinion and the authority of Scripture was undermined? This is what worried William more than specific doctrinal errors. He mockingly describes Abelard's approach: "'It appears to me,' he says. Would it not be better if he asserted something to which all the doctors after the apostles consented and agreed? Is something revealed to him or invented by him better than what they taught us who were taught by the Lord? Is their wisdom not more profound, their understanding more acute, their lives holier, and their authority weightier?"[92] Abelard, unintentionally in William's view, was making the authority of his reason greater than that of the Scriptures and the Fathers. The danger of such intellectual presumption was that one person's opinion on a question of doctrine became as valid as another's. This was the situation in the schools that William believed had to be combatted.

Alarmed first by the "new theology" of Peter Abelard, William of St. Thierry only needed the "new philosophy" of William of Conches to convince him that the problem lay not in the doctrinal errors of one or two masters but in the basic flaws of the new scholastic methods. In the *Summa philosophiae* of William of Conches he saw the same presumption, the same disregard for authority, the same daring to assert opinions as doctrine as in Abelard's *Theologia,* along with a host of new errors that needed to be refuted.[93] Writing against these errors, William of St. Thierry articulated for the first time the precepts of an alternative theology. Though the scholastic theologians claimed they were using dialectic to interpret and clarify the meaning of authority, not to challenge it, he argues that limits must be placed on the application of reason to matters of faith:

> When we speak of God we should hold not only to the form of sound faith but also to the form of sound words in faith. Just as our philosopher here [William of Conches] loves to speak from the authority of the philosophers, thus we should take whatever we say from the Fathers, our teachers and leaders, making use of the understanding of their words, following in their footsteps, presuming nothing of our own. Indeed, it is exceedingly dangerous to venture into such things except where trustworthy authority supports us or the certain reason of faith leads us. The reason of faith, however, is to put all human reason after faith or to reduce reason to captivity in obedience to faith, and not to ignore the limits of that faith our Fathers established, nor to disregard them in any way.[94]

The interpretation and understanding of doctrine, no less than the establishment of what was to be believed, must, in his view, rest upon patristic authority. There is no place for opinion or invention in William of St. Thierry's theology. But, when kept within the limits of understanding established by authority and subordinate to the certainty of faith, there is a role for reason.

In his two treatises on faith, William explains just what he believes the role of reason should be, how reason can be used to advance knowledge without undermining faith. The first of these treatises, the *Speculum fidei,* is a refutation of Abelard's definition of faith as an estimation of what is unknown. William seeks to establish his alternative epistemology by showing the superiority of the knowledge of faith, which is certainty, over the knowledge of reason, which, if unsupported and not kept subordinate to faith, can only produce uncertainty and doubt.[95] It is in the second treatise, the *Aenigma fidei*, that William actually seeks to demonstrate how reason can be used by discussing the subject of the Trinity, at the time probably the most disputed topic in the schools. William thus takes on the speculative theologians directly, by offering a "contemplative" theology that boldly fuses aspects of the rational methodology of the schools with the contemplative approach of the cloister.[96]

William bases his theology on the idea of a three-stage process of understanding, which can be briefly summarized. At first, he argues, we know only the single truth that God exists. The desire to know more is hindered by the weakness of our natural reason. Without the aid of divine grace, our understanding can advance no further. The gift of grace, which is faith, is the only certain means of knowing God. Because the Trinity is inaccessible to our senses and beyond anything that our reason can conceptualize, it must be approached first through faith—faith being defined as belief in the certainty of something that cannot be seen or rationally understood. True understanding must begin with an assent to the certainty of faith. This "act of faith," the first stage of knowledge, involves knowing and accepting the truths revealed in the Scriptures and explained in the writings of the Fathers. Only after this stage can we move on to the second one, that of applying the tools of reason to understanding the accepted truths of faith. The final and highest stage of mystical knowledge is reached through contemplation.

William describes this process succinctly as follows:

> The first step, grounded upon authority, is of faith, having the form of faith [and] based upon the proven testimonies of established authority. The second is of reason—not of human reason but of that reason that belongs to faith, consisting in sound concepts of what is believed in full agreement with divine authority. To know belongs to this stage, not only how to think and speak about God rationally according to the reason of faith, but also how faith comes to be where it is not, how it is nourished and aided where it is, and how it is defended against its enemies. The third step is that of illuminating or sanctifying faith in love and advancing from faith to vision.[97]

Of these three stages, the first two are equivalent to what the schools meant by theology: establishing the truths of the faith, conceptualizing and expressing them so that they can be understood, and explaining and defending them. The third and highest stage is not theological, in the scholastic sense, but contemplative—an understanding accessible not through authority and reason but through a special state of grace that, as we shall see, William thought was attainable only within the cloister.

William's explanation of the second stage of understanding and the "reason of faith" makes it clear that he disagreed not with the legitimacy or importance of what the theologians of the schools were trying to do but with the way they were going about it. There is, he insists, nothing wrong with the desire to know more about God; it is natural to human piety and curiosity to want to understand the divinity. What is wrong is a search for knowledge that becomes vain and presumptuous when reason is applied to mysteries beyond the capacity of human understanding. To keep from falling into doctrinal error, one must carefully follow the guidance of authority and always keep reason subordinate to faith.

According to William, there are two major flaws in the methods used by speculative theologians such as Abelard. First, they presume that rational concepts are applicable to God. Instead of relying on the "sound words" provided by the authority of the Scriptures, they attempt to explain divine nature by drawing analogies from the created world or by applying the laws of logic. Authority must be strictly followed, he insists, not just in establishing the truths of the faith but also in developing a language to conceptualize and explain them.[98] The second and more serious error is that these masters do not recognize the limits of human reason, applying it vainly to things that are beyond its scope. They fail to distinguish between human reason and the "reason of faith." "In human things," William writes of this distinction, which was fundamental to his thought, "human reason prepares faith for itself; in divine things, faith precedes reason, then faith *sui generis* forms reason to itself."[99] Human reason is limited to the realm of experience, where knowledge comes before belief; the "reason of faith" is applicable to profound truths that must first be believed, then understood. Human reason cannot establish new truths—and this is what William of St. Thierry accused both Peter Abelard and William of Conches of trying to do. But if reason serves faith, then it is possible to advance to a better understanding and a deeper penetration of those truths that have already been established by authority. This is the limit of the second stage of knowledge.

Although highly critical of the errors and excesses of the schools, William of St. Thierry nevertheless recognized the difficulties and the practical importance of the work of analysis and interpretation being done by the theologians. He knew from experience that certain questions could not be solved simply by citing a truth already established by authority, that authority could be obscure and equivocal on vital issues, and that some passages in Scripture posed problems of interpretation resolvable only by the use of the analytical tools of reason. In an early treatise, *De sacramentis altaris*, William had argued that when authorities are obscure or contradictory, one must exercise critical judgment, weigh the relative merits of the authorities in dispute, and evaluate the historical context in which the sources were written.[100] This analytical approach to interpreting authority is strikingly similar to that outlined by Peter Abelard in the prologue to *Sic et non.*[101] The difference between the two is not in their method but in their emphasis. William relied more on the authorities themselves to explain the variations and reconcile the apparent contradictions, allowing little scope for the independent exercise of reason. For William, reason was not to be used for speculation but for interpretation. There was a surer means than reason to higher truths.

This brings us, at last, to the significance of the idea of a third stage of knowledge. William conceives of this stage not so much as the inevitable completion of the other two but as an alternative means of reaching the highest level of understanding. Here lies his real challenge to the schools. For in William's opinion, even if scholastic theologians corrected the flaws in their method and followed the reason of faith, they would not advance beyond the second level of knowledge. They still could not arrive at a full understanding of the mysteries of faith. For that, study and intellectual effort are not sufficient; one must reach the special state of grace attainable only through a life of contemplation. Whereas the theologian advances his understanding through reason alone, the contemplative combines reason with love, the intellective with the affective, in an alternative and far more certain ascent to wisdom. "There are two eyes of contemplation: reason and love," William writes in his commentary on the Song of Songs. "Often the two of these eyes become one eye when they faithfully cooperate with each other, since in the contemplation of God, in which love is more effective, reason changes into love and is transformed into a kind of spiritual or divine understanding that surpasses and absorbs all reason."[102]

For William, the advantages of learning within the cloister were clear. It was only within the cloister, "the school of love," where solitude, stability, peace, and poverty prevailed and where one could concentrate on contemplation, that the third level of knowledge could be reached. In the schools, where vanity, curiosity, contention, and ambition prevailed, there were far too many distractions.[103] The contemplative in the cloister, using both eyes, had the means to advance from faith to a full vision of the divine. The theologian in the schools, where understanding depended upon reason alone, remained blinded in one eye.

William of St. Thierry thought of the cloister as a "school of love." His contemporary Guerric, abbot of Igny, the mother house of William's monastery at Signy, took the idea a step further, referring to the cloister as "the school of Christian philosophy."[104] There is nothing new or original in this use of the term *philosophia* to describe the monastic life.[105] Nor was its usage in the twelfth century limited to Cistercian monks. The Benedictine Peter of Celle, in one of the several letters he wrote to John of Salisbury about the monastic life, describes the cloister as "the school of heavenly philosophy."[106] Peter the Venerable, abbot of Cluny, calls the discipline of his monastery "the true philosophy" in one of his letters.[107] And in his well-known letter to Heloise reporting the death of Abelard, the Cluniac writes that Abelard "had converted to the true philosophy of Christ."[108] In each of these examples, "philosophy" was used to compare the contemplative life of the cloister with the speculative thought of the schools and to suggest the superiority of the former. The force of the comparison becomes more apparent when one realizes that the schools were using the term "philosophy" increasingly to mean, not all knowledge and every aspect of human life, as Hugh of St. Victor had used it in his *Didascalicon*, but only intellective knowledge, learning acquired through the use of reason. To the monks, "philosophy" encompassed both the life and the learning that were equally necessary to attain wisdom.

The examples cited above are all taken from letters or writings directed to those in the schools or referring to the conversion of a scholar. In each case, "philosophy" is used consciously and tactically as a challenge to the schools. But these examples do not tell the full story of how the monks used educational language to talk about life in the cloister. Cistercian literature often refers to the cloister as "the school of philosophy" when the intention is not to criticize the schools, either explicitly or implicitly, but to describe the monastic life to those already converted. The frequent use of an educational vocabulary in Cistercian sermons, treatises for novices, and devotional writings suggests that opposition to the schools had a profound effect on the way in which the monks conceptualized their experience. Indeed there was a major change in the spiritual identity of the order. The first Cistercians had spoken of the monastery as a desert and described the advantages of the monastic life in terms of solitude, silence, and simplicity. It was a vocabulary that emphasized withdrawal from the world and that was implicitly hostile to learning. In contrast, describing the monastery as a school and the monastic life in terms of learning and teaching, philosophy and wisdom, seems designed to portray the cloister as a more attractive alternative than the schools to those reluctant to renounce either learning or involvement in worldly affairs.

Guerric of Igny refers to the monastery as "the school of Christian philosophy" only once, but the idea lies at the very center of his thought about the monastic life. Guerric had studied at the cathedral school of Tournai under the renowned Master Odo of Orléans and had taught there himself as scholasticus before entering Clairvaux, under the influence of Saint Bernard, in 1122.[109] When he became abbot of Igny, Guerric again assumed the role of teacher. The sermons he delivered during his years as abbot (1138–57) reveal him preaching to his community about many of the same theological topics being discussed in the schools.[110] But although the topics were the same, the methods were different. Preaching about the mysteries of the Incarnation, his favorite subject, Guerric explained them not in the logical order that would be followed by a master lecturing in the schools but in the order in which they appeared in the cycle of the liturgical year. Guerric's teaching was thus less systematic than that of the scholastic theologians, but it was no less intellectually rigorous. Guerric's purpose as abbot and teacher was to integrate such learning into the devotional life of his community.

For Guerric of Igny, there were clear advantages to learning and teaching where study was fostered by the structured routine and stability of life in the cloister. In the monastic school, silent meditation and prayer completed the education begun by reading and preaching. The profound mysteries of faith, which were inaccessible to the intellect and beyond the reach of study alone, could be understood only through contemplation. In the monastery are found none of the "fallacious theories" and "useless philosophies" that impede learning in the schools. The routine of the cloister makes the monk into a truly "teachable student" able to learn directly from the inspiration of the Holy Spirit and from the examples of the true teachers, the saints, especially Benedict.[111]

For the many Cistercians who had chosen to leave the schools, there was a strong appeal to the idea of the monastery as the "school of Christian philosophy." But, as Guerric of Igny articulated it, this idea had obvious limitations as an alternative to the schools. The "philosophy" learned in the cloister was personal, not practical; it was intended for contemplation and for individual edification, not for action or for teaching others. Guerric offered monks an attractive alternative to the schools but gave no indication of how his monastic school could serve the educational needs of society.

The Cistercians never did manage to resolve this dilemma. As it became more urgent later in the century to advance reform and combat heresy, however, some of the leaders of the order did begin to recognize the need to defend the social value of monastic life and learning. No one was more effective at this task than Adam of Perseigne (1145–1221), the last of the great Cistercian evangelists. His writings, both those directed outside the cloister and those intended for internal instruction, emphasized that monastic education could satisfy the practical needs of society as well as the spiritual needs of monks. In building his defense of the monastic life, Adam gave new meaning to the theme of the opposition between the cloister and the school, and added considerably to the idea of the monastery as the "school of Christian philosophy."

Adam, born a serf on an estate of the count of Champagne, is one of those rare examples of a man who advanced through intelligence and learning rather than noble birth and good social connections. After being educated probably at one of the cathedral schools in the Champagne region (Troyes, Reims, or, perhaps, Sens), Adam spent several years as a secular cleric at the court of the count before leaving to join, first a community of canons regular, then a traditional Benedictine monastery, and finally the Cistercian order.[112] It has been suggested that he is the Adam written to by Gilbert of Hoyland, but the evidence is inconclusive.[113] Sometime before 1188, Adam was elected abbot of the monastery at Perseigne, in Normandy. As abbot he undertook several important missions for the papacy as well as for the kings of England in their struggles with Philip Augustus over Normandy. According to Jacques of Vitry, Adam of Perseigne was one of the preachers recruited by the popular evangelist Fulk of Neuilly.[114]

Like Bernard of Clairvaux, Adam spent a great deal of time outside his abbey, and his writings also show him to have been frequently preoccupied with political and social affairs. Most of the more than sixty letters that survive from his years as abbot are addressed to recipients outside the cloister: to bishops and chapter officials, priests, canons, students or masters, a knight, and married women or virgins.[115] His career, sermons, and correspondence are evidence of the important role a Cistercian abbot could still play in ecclesiastical and secular affairs at the end of the twelfth and in the early thirteenth century. But it is probably more significant to understanding Adam's defense of the monastic life that he was the one nonmaster among the seven preachers recruited by Fulk, as well as the only one not educated in the schools of Paris.[116]

Adam of Perseigne had all the arrogance and confidence of a self-made man. His letters exhibit an annoying tendency to criticize and exhort others, especially nonmonks, by comparing their lives and learning to his own. Probably the best example of this is the forceful letter Adam wrote to Master Philip of Balon, a Paris-educated doctor of law and a canon of Le Mans (1197-1213) who was apparently worried that Adam did not think well of him.[117] In response to Philip's expression of concern, Adam commends his personal qualities but attacks his profession. The letter sternly warns Philip that as a lawyer, he risks earning the enmity of God in exchange for the friendship of the world. To improve his life, he should do as Adam himself has done and aspire above all else to know God and to follow divine law. Holding himself up as a model, Adam contrasts their two professions. "The abode of Cîteaux taught me knowledge of the law. Here Christ, the teacher and giver of justice, teaches his followers knowledge of heavenly law. . . . You, on the other hand, because you are of the world, have different tastes, and your search for the wisdom of this world attests that you have no taste for this great wisdom."[118] By now this language should be familiar enough to require no comment. Here it is applied to the practice of law rather than to the study of the arts or theology, but its purpose is still to urge conversion.

Adam embarks next on a long attack against lawyers that repeats the criticisms usually made of the profession at the time. There are plenty of lawyers for those who can pay but none for the poor; too many positions and too much of the wealth of the Church are going to them; lawyers use their learning and verbal skill to subvert justice, justify impiety, and convict the innocent. The motives of lawyers are primarily to blame. Law should be studied to ensure justice for others, not for personal gain. But this calls for a legal education different from that offered in the schools. In Adam's view, the desire for worldly honors and wealth will inevitably corrupt the study of law in the schools and the careers of those trained there. "Oh would, dearest friend," Adam exhorts, "that you studied to seek the virtue of the soul, which engenders the contempt of the world."[119] Adam seems to be suggesting not only that Philip switch professions but that the cloister, where one learns the heavenly law of divine justice, would ideally be a better law school for those who will have jurisdiction over the legal affairs of the Church.

It was not just lawyers that Adam addressed in these terms. His letters to bishops contain the same combination of criticism and exhortation, as well as similar comparisons of their lives to his own as a monk. In a strongly worded letter to Odo of Sully, bishop of Paris (1196–1208), Adam complains of the actions the bishop had taken during his first year in office to relieve the debts of his diocese. Admonishing Odo to be aware of both the burdens and responsibilities of his office, Adam draws an uncomplimentary contrast between their lives. "I, happier and more secure as a resident of the cloister, chose to remain in the cottage of Cistercian philosophy rather than to follow my friend and visit from city to city him whom I bemoan having nearly lost as a bishop."[120] Adam apparently had known the much younger and better-born bishop since his childhood and acted as a mentor to him. An earlier letter, dating from before Odo was elected bishop, suggests that Adam once hoped Odo might follow him in giving up worldly honors for the philosophy of Cîteaux.[121] Since Odo chose otherwise, however, Adam's only consolation is that he might overcome his initial failings, correct his errors, and henceforth exemplify mercy and truth in the exercise of his episcopal duties. "You are a pillar of salt," he admonishes. "Conduct yourself in a way that nourishes and improves all the animals."[122] Adam's imagery is not appealing, but his warning is forceful. The letter has the same admonitory tone as Bernard's *De consideratione*, the treatise he wrote for the Cistercian pope, Eugenius III. Like Bernard, Adam paradoxically decries the dangers of assuming a prelacy while insisting on the necessity of fulfilling its duties.

In a letter to another recently elected prelate, William of Perche, who became bishop of Châlons in 1215, Adam charges that "most of the bishops of our time, since they wretchedly indulge in the love of the wisdom of the world, usurp to themselves and rape the patrimony of the Crucifixion."[123] Adam, like many of the reformers of his time, attributes the bad state of the Church to the fact that the clergy and prelacy do not set a good example for the laity. "Live and teach," he admonishes William, "so that your conduct does not contradict your words."[124] A bishop must be able to teach both by word and example, which he can learn to do only by acquiring and practicing seven disciplines. "The teacher of that wisdom that comes from above," Adam exhorts, "must in every way follow chastity, be a master of peacemaking, and conserve modesty; he ought to be persuasive and affable, have a good conscience, be full of good works, and always do justice that is free from hypocrisy."[125] This "wisdom from above" is the antidote that can purify the Church, which has been corrupted by the "wisdom of the world."

How and where a bishop is to learn such wisdom, Adam does not specify. Although he does explicitly refer to the "school of Christ,"[126] he does not refer explicitly in this letter to the cloister or the contemplative life. But it is certainly significant that he defines the wisdom in terms of the ability to learn and to teach seven disciplines, implying that there is an alternative set of disciplines more important for a bishop to know than the seven liberal arts taught in the schools.

This idea of seven spiritual disciplines is developed more fully in a letter Adam sent to Robert Poulain, archbishop of Rouen (1208–21).[127] After responding only perfunctorily to a request the archbishop had apparently made for a treatise on the vices and virtues, Adam turns to the subject of the contemplative life and the "school of Christian philosophy":

He who philosophizes in the school of this wisdom ought not to ignore the liberal disciplines through which this philosophy is understood and taught. The letter of St. James (3.17) enumerated them: "The wisdom that is from above is first pure, then peaceable, modest, persuasive, of good conscience, full of good works, and judges without hypocrisy." Behold they are seven, and they are disciplines, and they are called liberal.

They are seven since the spirit of wisdom is septiform. They are disciplines because they make the followers of this philosophy full of learning, mature, and patient in their endurance of pressures. In fact, the word *discipline* is used for learning, sometimes meaning a well-ordered seriousness and more often the endurance of tribulation. . . . They are called liberal since he who is taught and retains them is free and exempt from sins and vices and elevated to heavenly love.[128]

To the best of my knowledge, this interpretation of the septiform wisdom as seven distinct disciplines, in the academic sense of branches of learning, and the comparison of them to the liberal arts are original to Adam. In pointing out to the two bishops the contrast between the seven spiritual disciplines and the seven liberal arts, Adam was apparently suggesting that the responsibilities of the episcopacy would be better served by men prepared by the contemplative life of the cloister than by years of studying and teaching in the schools. It is not masters who make the best bishops, but monks.

The sermons Adam preached to those within the cloister often describe the advantages of the contemplative life in similar ways. These sermons represent, in a way, the culmination of the Cistercian tradition of defining the monastic life in opposition to the schools. As a preacher, Adam gave eloquent expression to the rich vocabulary of this tradition, elaborating on the ideas and themes found in his letters to make a compelling case for the social value of life and learning within the cloister.[129]

Especially notable among these sermons is one for the important monastic feast day of St. Benedict.[130] Adam again lists seven spiritual disciplines, as in his letters to the two bishops, but this time the set of arts is significantly different. From the opening words, the language of the sermon is explicitly educational. Adam describes Benedict as "the principal teacher of monastic philosophy," a master who taught heavenly wisdom both by the example of his life and by the words of his rule.[131] Benedict's "true philosophy," according to Adam, differed from the "worldly philosophy" of the schools both in its methods and its motives:

How true and how praiseworthy is this philosophy, which does not argue needlessly in the Platonic way about the stars or the natural world but, with the reason of faith and the instruction of our father [Benedict], deliberates humbly and usefully about the correction of morals, the restoration of virtue, and the observation of the commandments, not seeking to delight in the applause of men but to join in the delights of the saints.[132]

The choice of Plato, rather than Aristotle, to exemplify the learning of the schools is at first sight surprising, but it probably suited a monastic audience more likely to know the *Timaeus* than Aristotle's *libri naturales*, which were just finding their way into the schools.

Adam continues to speak of Plato when he introduces the idea of an alternative set of liberal arts – "not those that worldly philosophy noisily teaches in the classroom, but those that the true Plato teaches from the lectern of the cross."[133] Christ, as the "true Plato," taught the rules of these arts, which Benedict then made the instruments of his Rule. These are rightly called the liberal arts, Adam explains, because they free the mind from the "slavery of philosophy" and the soul from the burdens of the world. "Just as that worldly and secular philosophy is taught in seven disciplines that are called liberal," Adam explains, "thus in the classroom of monastic philosophy where Benedict presides as master there are seven rules of the divine art, by which the just are taught and exercised in the true life."[134] The *Rule of St. Benedict* is the only textbook needed in the classroom of the cloister for a monk to learn all seven of these arts.

Like their secular equivalents, the spiritual liberal arts are divided into a trivium and a quadrivium. First to be learned is the trivium, the three ways to a wise life, which are the arts of knowledge (*scientia*), goodness, and discipline. In describing each of these, Adam emphasizes its difference from the equivalent art of the secular trivium. Knowledge, like grammar, provides the basis for learning all the other arts. But it does not make the monk proud and arrogant, as grammar does the scholar; rather, it teaches the monk about human nature and shows him the way to live a good life. Goodness, the second art of this trivium, is like dialectic in that it teaches how to separate truth from falsity. The difference is that this art is applied not to arguments, as dialectic is in the schools, but to life. It teaches the monk to distinguish between good and bad conduct and to exercise knowledge in the practice of the virtues of prudence, fortitude, temperance, and justice. Finally, discipline, like rhetoric, provides the skills the monk needs to be able to teach and to persuade others: timidity of expression, modesty of posture, seriousness of approach, humility of deportment, and sanctity of action.

Summarizing the relationship of the arts of the spiritual trivium to their secular counterparts and to each other, Adam concludes, "For in the same way that rhetoric adorns the discourse that grammar constructs from words, and that dialectic sharpens it by distinguishing truth from falsity, thus discipline embellishes the life that knowledge teaches and that the love of goodness ignites within us."[135] If the analogy is a little strained, Adam's distinction between the scholastic trivium, concerned only with learning eloquence, and the monastic trivium, concerned with learning how to live, comes through clearly. To the logical arts of the schools, which teach only about words, Adam contrasts the arts of the cloister, which teach virtue, how both to live well and to set a good example for others.

Next comes the quadrivium, whereby, according to Adam, the virtue taught by the trivium is practiced within the cloister. This spiritual quadrivium consists of the four standard exercises of the contemplative life: "the study of Scripture [*divina lectio*], holy meditation, devoted prayer, and indispensable manual labor."[136] Adam does not bother, as he does in his discussion of the trivium, to draw explicit comparisons between these four exercises and the arts of the scholastic quadrivium. There is no need for him to do so: his purpose is to compare not what is learned but how and why learning is undertaken. In preaching about this quadrivium, Adam is first of all emphasizing that in the cloister the study of Scripture is part of a complete spiritual program that gives the monk the advantage of being able to achieve a higher level of understanding than the theologian studying in the schools.

Adam is more concerned, however, with motives than with methods and, above all, with the practical implications of learning. Study in the cloister also has the advantage that it is undertaken not for the sake of learning per se or to appear learned, but in order to learn how to live. Adam considers the spiritual quadrivium superior not so much because it leads to a knowledge that is intellectually higher as because it is more conducive to the living of a better and more exemplary life. Instruction in the seven arts of monastic philosophy is, Adam emphasizes, preparatory both to contemplation and to action:

> Study, meditation, and prayer pertain to contemplation, manual labor to the active life, to which one should aspire no less than to the contemplative. . . . Study teaches what we should seek, prayer procures what study teaches, meditation unfolds what was procured, and contemplation gives what was promised. If, therefore, you join these four to the three preceding arts—that is, knowledge, goodness, and discipline—you will have a trivium and a quadrivium, seven ways to the treasure of celestial philosophy and seven guides to immortal wisdom.[137]

Preaching to monks, Adam makes the same point that he made in his letters to bishops. He defines the seven spiritual arts here to refer more explicitly to the contemplative life of the cloister, but they still embody the same idea that spiritual learning is superior to the education one acquires by studying the liberal arts in the schools. In this sermon it is clearer that Adam believes this learning to be inseparable from the monastic routine. Adam sees the education of the cloister as an alternative to the schools not just for those who intend to spend their lives as contemplatives but also for those preparing to assume the active leadership of the Church.

If other Cistercians spoke more eloquently about the "school of true philosophy," none was more emphatic than Adam in trying to convince his contemporaries that the cloister did offer a practical and socially useful educational alternative to the schools. He perceived a clear distinction between the "worldly philosophy" and seven secular arts of the schools, where learning was corrupted by vanity and ambition, and the "true philosophy" and spiritual arts of the cloister, where the monastic routine enabled one to attain the wisdom necessary to live a good life. From Adam's perspective, the problem was both that too many were making the mistake of choosing the former and that too few with the right kind of training were being advanced to positions of influence in the Church. His solution, like that of his Cistercian predecessors, was not to try to reform the schools but to reject them completely and to make the strongest case possible for the alternative education offered within the cloister.

OTHER VIEWS OF THE SCHOOLS: PETER OF CELLE AND PHILIP OF HARVENGT

Comparing the educational attitudes of the various religious orders, Dom Jean Leclercq concluded that "tendencies were basically the same everywhere and differences in color were only varieties in shading."[138] Although the Cistercians had by far the predominant voice among monastic critics of the schools, members of other orders expressed similar concerns about the growing popularity and prestige of the schools and were active in publicizing the educational alternative offered by the cloister. Other monks and religious shared the Cistercians' suspicion of learning not pursued within the peace and quiet of the cloister as well as their doubts about the new methods and intellectual trends of the schools. However, although they often followed the lead of the Cistercians in criticizing the schools and used many of the same themes in expressing their opposition, other monks did not necessarily agree about what could or should be done.

The Cistercians opposed the schools as institutions and, usually no less strongly, also the introduction of the methods and doctrines of scholastic learning into the cloister. To them, the appeal of the cloister was not that it provided an alternative place to study the same things being taught in the schools but that it offered an alternative way of living and learning—one that was more affective than intellective, more dependent upon experience than upon formal instruction. The essential purpose of the Cistercian "school of philosophy" was not to offer a practical education but to provide a more certain means to knowing and loving God. In contrast, members of other religious orders did not necessarily reject the schools or scholastic learning completely. When they opposed the cloister to the schools, it was often to show that the monastery could be a superior place for learning, and particularly for training in the pastoral theology important to the clergy and the prelacy. Their criticisms of the schools were sometimes intended less to convince secular clerics to convert to the monastic life, as the Cistercians so obviously wanted them to do, than to demonstrate the advantages they could gain by combining learning with the disciplined life of the cloister.

Among those who worked to promote education within the cloister as a viable alternative to the schools, two critics stand out: Peter of Celle and Philip of Harvengt. One a Benedictine monk and the other a Premonstratensian canon, they provide examples of the educational attitudes at both ends of the spectrum of the religious orders that were competing with the Cistercians for spiritual authority and political influence.

Peter of Celle's well-known letter warning John of Salisbury of the perils of remaining in Paris has already been mentioned.[139] As an alternative to the noise and clamor of the schools of Paris, the abbot offered John the sanctuary of the cloister, where he might end his exile and find a home, "not in words and speech but in actions and truth." This contrast between the schools and the cloister is made in terms no different from those used so frequently by the Cistercians. There is no suggestion in Peter's letter, however, that he was attempting to convert his friend permanently to the monastic life. Rather, he was offering the displaced cleric a temporary refuge, a place where he could peacefully reflect and write about his experience as a courtier. Knowing how much John of Salisbury valued learning and would be tempted to remain in Paris, Peter emphasized the contrast between the cloister and the schools:

> There [in the cloister] you will discern not rudiments and allusions but that which is divinity and truth face to face, without the hard work of study, without any aversion from seeing, without any fallacies or errors in understanding, without any apprehension about retaining, and without any fear of forgetting. O what a blessed school, where Christ teaches our hearts with the word of his power, where without study and reading we learn how we should live happily eternally! No book is bought there, a writing master is not hired, there are no circumvented disputations, nor intricate sophisms, but the simple determination of all questions

and the simple understanding of all reasons and arguments. There life teaches more than study, simplicity advances more than sophistry.[140]

Whether because he found this description of the peace and tranquility of the cloister appealing or because he found Paris too expensive, John of Salisbury did accept the invitation to spend his exile at Peter's monastery in Reims. But it is the language Peter of Celle used in his invitation, not the reasons John of Salisbury accepted it, that concerns us here. Like the Cistercians, Peter here describes the simplicity, order, and clarity of life in the cloister as an alternative to the difficulty, disorder, and confusion of the schools. His implicit criticism of the motives and methods of scholars also recalls theirs. However, what Peter says elsewhere about the schools and education reveals an important difference in his perspective and purpose.

Although he could criticize the scholars no less vehemently than the Cistercians, Peter of Celle was more specific about what he saw as the failings of the scholastic curriculum. The fundamental problem, in his view, was that the liberal arts were being studied too much and the Scriptures not enough. "Why do you exhaust yourselves," he asks scholars in one of his sermons, "in vanities and inane falsehoods, seeking the vain lucre of the world, admiring philosophical ingenuity, reading poetical deceits, neglecting the gospel of God and transgressing the law?"[141] Education, Peter emphasizes repeatedly in his synodial sermons, is failing to prepare the clergy to serve the Church and society. It is theology, not the liberal arts, that must be given precedence. No less important, he insists, theology must be studied in a way that is consistent with its purpose. The cleric must approach this study with devotion and adoration, not irreverently question the secrets of God by making them the subject of disputation and argumentation.[142]

Peter, as one would guess from his letter to John of Salisbury, was especially unsympathetic to the dialecticians. "Surely," he argues in one of his commentaries, "the things of God must be explained by divine words and the wood of Aristotle must not be planted near the altar lest we encumber the sacraments of the faith with innumerable and superfluous questions."[143] Nonetheless, in his treatise on the monastic life, *De disciplina claustrali*, Peter commends the study of the liberal arts. If learned in combination with the discipline of the cloister, they are valuable preparation for reading and understanding Scripture as well as useful tools in defending the faith and refuting heretics. This is the education that he deemed necessary for the clergy. Significantly, it is in the cloister—"within the confines of angelic purity and free from worldly impurity"[144]—and not in the schools that Peter believed this education should take place. Although never stated explicitly, the realization of Peter's educational ideal would have involved reviving the teaching of both the liberal arts and pastoral theology within the cloister in order to train the clergy.

In a letter he wrote as abbot of the Premonstratensian house of Bonne Esperance (1157–82) to another learned John, this one apparently a canon regular who had studied theology with Anselm of Laon before his conversion, Philip of Harvengt echoes Peter of Celle's advice to John of Salisbury about the superiority of learning within the cloister:

> In the cloister, where vanity is easily resisted and sanctity especially sought, there night and day the just man, in submission to divine will, devotes himself to hymns, prayers, silence, tears, and study. There, I say, the sincere desire for purified life cleanses the intellect, making it possible to attain perfection more easily and efficaciously. For you, however, no knowledge is commendable unless it has been forged in the tumult of the secular schools, as if among those who have studied for a long time in the schools there is the certainty that no error or heresy can be found. You are indignant because I said you had learned sacred letters in the cloister, as if I had insulted you, and you consider it more commendable that you studied at Laon and sat in the classroom of the celebrated Master Anselm. But blessed is not the man who heard Master Anselm, nor he who has pursued knowledge in Laon or Paris, but "Blessed," it is written, "is the man whom you instruct, Lord, and whom you teach your law" (Ps. 93.12).[145]

To defend the education of the cloister to John, who had clearly been offended that his study of theology in the schools had not been mentioned, Philip speaks regretfully of the time he himself spent in the schools:

> Would that I had been taught sacred letters in the cloister from my childhood, so that all my life I would have been interested in sacred studies and, raised as a boy in the house of god, like Samuel, I would have burned with desire to know, like Daniel. Since it seemed to me commendable to be nourished in the school of religion from childhood, I certainly did not think I was doing anything offensive when, in commending your knowledge, I made mention of the cloister and not the secular schools.[146]

Here we get a hint of the rivalry among learned clerics in the twelfth century. Where one had been educated clearly mattered both in establishing one's authority in discussing theological questions, which is the issue of contention between Philip and John, and in advancing one's career in the Church. While John flaunted his scholastic credentials, Philip, who had himself been educated in the cathedral school of Cambrai and in Paris, firmly defended the quality of learning available within the cloister.

According to Philip of Harvengt, the cloister's advantages as a place of learning are twofold. First, he believes, the discipline of the monastic routine prevents one from pursuing the vain and useless subjects that distract students in the schools. Within the cloister, where one is sheltered from the noise and competition of the schools, error and heresy are far less likely. Second, free from the burdens of worldly cares and ambitions, one can direct all one's efforts toward understanding Scripture. In the cloister, as it should also be in the schools, theology truly reigns supreme.

Although confident of the cloister's educational superiority, Philip of Harvengt was not opposed to the schools. In other letters he expresses great enthusiasm for the schools, particularly for Paris, which he commends as the "city of letters."[147] Nevertheless he was concerned that too many scholars were limiting their studies to the liberal arts and never advancing to theology.[148] By not providing training suitable to the pastoral duties of the clergy, the schools were failing to serve the needs of society. To Philip, the essential purpose of education was to teach clerics enough about both the arts and theology to be able to preach and to minister to the laity. Whether this education occurred in the schools or in the cloister did not so much matter to him. While Philip clearly thought that it would be more likely to occur in the cloister, where learning was combined with the discipline of monastic life, he accepted the fact that most destined for the clergy would continue to be educated in the schools.

For Philip of Harvengt, the primary obstacle to improving the learning of the clergy was, in fact, not the state of the schools but the attitudes prevalent in the Church and, especially, among members of religious orders. In his treatise on clerical education, *De institutione clericorum*, he harshly accuses both monks and canons regular of ignorance and duplicity. They cannot, he argues, continue to deny the value of education and yet still seek to assume responsibilities and positions in the Church that require learning. It was, Philip suggests, their own vain ambition for ecclesiastical advancement and office that too often motivated the attacks made by monks and canons on their rivals in the schools.[149] The unbiased Philip questioned the motives of the monks and canons who rejected learning no less than the ambitions of the scholars and masters who pursued it. In his view, both were equally responsible for the generally poor state of education among the clergy. The situation would only improve when there was less competition between monks and scholars over office and influence and more cooperation in advancing the cause of reform. Philip was among the first of the religious reformers to conclude that the pressing need for a clergy who possessed the knowledge and practical skills to instruct the laity and to combat the spread of heresy required the reconciliation of the cloister and the schools.

The problem was that the means did not yet exist, nor was public opinion conducive, to achieving this reconciliation. The dominant voice among the religious orders continued to be that of the Cistercians, who remained adamant in their opposition to the schools and to scholastic learning. Peter of Celle and Philip of Harvengt are representative of a more moderate body of opinion, one that was more attentive to the growing importance of education. Their criticisms of the schools were more tempered – more directly aimed at correcting what they saw as the failure of masters to provide their students with a sound and practical education – and less the expression of any inherent opposition to the schools as institutions or to scholastic learning per se. When they contrasted the cloister to the schools, they were less concerned to entice secular clerics to leave the schools for the contemplative life of the monastery than to suggest that in the cloister both the arts and theology could be learned in ways more suitable to the needs of those preparing for the active life of the ministry. Philip of Harvengt and, to a lesser extent, Peter of Celle spoke for the many men committed to living in the cloister who also desired to have knowledge of the new methods and doctrines of the schools, to be involved in the instruction of the clergy and laity, and to assume a role in the leadership and reform of the Church.

One means for them to do so – and both Peter of Celle and Philip of Harvengt seemed to have preferred this option – was to revive the educational role of the cloister, to open or in some cases reopen the schools in their houses for the instruction of the clergy. Such action, however, would have required the monks and canons to assume a public role as teachers, which was now both contrary to the reformed practices and statutes of most orders and also incompatible with canon law.[150] Moreover, even had monastic schools been revived, it is unlikely that they could have successfully competed with urban schools in attracting students or that they could have kept pace with the rapid advance of scholastic thought. The other possible option would have been to allow some monks or canons to leave the cloister to study or to teach temporarily at the schools. To judge from Philip of Harvengt, this course would probably have been more acceptable to canons than to monks. As one historian has written, "If Philip had had the whole order behind him – which he did not – the Premonstratensians would have been among the first to take root in the developing University of Paris."[151] It was not just the less enthusiastic attitudes of other Premonstratensians, however, that kept them out of the schools. There was also to be legislation prohibiting members of religious orders, both monks and canons, from leaving the cloister to study in the schools.[152]

Under these circumstances, the reconciliation of the cloister and the schools was delayed until 1218, when the Dominicans solved the dilemma by establishing their own house of studies in Paris, making it possible both to study and to teach others without leaving the cloister. As we shall see, this delay was probably fortunate for the history of education. That the religious orders continued to oppose and to be excluded from the schools may ultimately have helped more than hindered the corporate development of the university in Paris.

FOUR

The Satirists

MONASTIC OPPOSITION probably did keep a sizeable number of men away from the schools, including some who might have made significant contributions to the quality of learning and teaching. After 1218, members of religious orders rapidly swelled the population of scholars and added to the ranks of distinguished masters teaching in Paris. But even before then, despite the exclusion of members of religious orders, there was never a shortage of young men ready to fill the expanding schools.

What attracted these young men in increasing numbers to the schools throughout the twelfth century? A few among them could, like Peter Abelard, claim to be motivated by the love of learning, but most had more practical reasons for pursuing their studies. Learning had become a good means—perhaps the best means for those not born into a noble family or, more often, for the younger sons of such families—to advance their careers. The twelfth century was the zenith of what has been called "the golden age of careerism via the schools."[1] This is not the place to examine in detail the sources and nature of the growing demand for learning. But something does need to be said about this demand to explain the impact of the new careerism on attitudes toward the schools.

Beginning in the second half of the eleventh century, as European society became more peaceful, ordered, and wealthy, a new premium was put upon education. The reform movement in the Church and the efforts of secular rulers to improve the administration of their territories served both to increase the immediate demand for educated men and to provide expanding opportunities for them to demonstrate the practical usefulness of their learning. The significant number of witnesses with the title "magister" found in early twelfth-century charters is only one indication of how quickly educated men established their places in the courts of princes and prelates. What these masters offered their employers was not the specialized training in administration or law that would later become desired credentials but basic literacy, the ability to read and to write Latin, which was still a rare and precious commodity. For some time, this learning continued to be considered valuable enough to ensure those who possessed it employment. The basic and elementary arts of the trivium provided these men with the requisite tools—grammar for drafting letters and other documents, rhetoric for polemic and persuasion, and dialectic for argumentation and debate. The first of these was essential for the daily business of any government; the others could be called into service in times of disputed claims and rights, of which the upheavals of the Gregorian Revolution provided an abundance. Few periods have looked so bright for those with an education in the liberal arts.

Attracted by such excellent prospects, more and more young men flocked to the schools after 1100. That they chose to study the arts of the trivium does not mean that they were not primarily, or even exclusively, motivated by the desire to advance their careers. As of yet there was little awareness that more specialized learning would be required. Study of the liberal arts was assumed to ensure the success of one's career. The general expectation was that such an education would pay off quickly and well in both prestige and material rewards.

The problem with these prospects was that golden ages are always in the past. The monk Guibert of Nogent, writing in 1115, certainly had good evidence for praising the thriving educational situation of the time and comparing it to his youth, when there had been an actual scarcity of masters.[2] But his was the perspective of an outsider. The situation looked quite different to those within the schools, who were already feeling the adverse effects of the expansion. The increase in numbers meant increased competition—competition among masters to attract students; among students to impress, and perhaps eventually to succeed, their masters; and among both masters and students to gain the attention and the support of those with wealth, power, and, above all, jobs to offer. From the time of Peter Abelard on, scholars were continuously complaining of the dire effects this competition had on teaching and on the education of those who were, as John of Salisbury charges, "trying to seem rather than to become wise."[3] The anticipation of reward pressured scholars to distinguish themselves quickly, to challenge their masters and gain recognition for their intelligence, and to find the means of getting a head start on their classmates in advancing their careers. Avarice and ambition, always the most invidious corrupters of learning, had entered the schools as the companions of careerism.

So too had arrogance. Aware of the already considerable advances they had made intellectually and socially, the learned had come to regard themselves as an elite in possession of a nobility of learning more worthy, as well as more useful, than a nobility of blood. They had an increasingly exalted view of themselves and of the social value of the knowledge they had acquired. In their opinion, the faults of the Church and of society would be eliminated—or, at least, lessened—if they, the educated, held more positions of influence and responsibility. To an extent, of course, they were correct. The practical skills taken by the masters promoted from the schools to the courts had already contributed significantly to improving justice and refining the tools of government. Indeed, it was because this contribution was recognized that the demand for men with such training was increasing. However, for the expanding number of educated men, the opportunities would never increase fast enough.

In the absence of precise evidence of the actual numbers of students in the schools, we have no means of estimating even approximately the relationship between the supply of learned men and the demand for them. One must depend on indirect evidence, on what was said about the situation by the learned themselves, as self-serving or biased as such comments might be. Recently, Alexander Murray has argued that "the golden age of careerism via the schools" continued through the twelfth and the thirteenth centuries. It was not until after about 1300, he contends, that the supply of educated men actually did begin to exceed the demand and that university graduates, anxious about their diminishing career prospects, became outspoken critics of the unlearned and of the adverse social effects of illiteracy and ignorance. According to Murray, ignorance and lack of education were not especially prominent among the abuses for which the clergy was attacked or satirized in the twelfth century. The criticism voiced then primarily concerned how men were advanced, not who, suggesting that the educated continued to see their career prospects as good.[4]

Murray's argument draws too stark a contrast between the two periods. It may be true that the charges of clerical ignorance were made less frequently and more timidly in the twelfth than in the fourteenth century, but those who made them were no less serious or concerned, nor were their criticisms any less motivated by self-interest. Although the supply of learned men probably did not exceed the actual demand, there is good evidence that it exceeded expectations. The expanding bureaucracies of secular and ecclesiastical courts probably offered more than enough positions for those trained in the schools. The problem was rather that the careers of the educated did not advance as quickly as they had hoped. However valuable and useful education had become, good birth and wealth still counted for more. The masters had to compete not only among themselves but also with the well-born and well-connected for prominent positions in secular courts and in the Church. Moreover, as Abelard suggested when he questioned William of Champeaux's motives in becoming a canon regular, the religious life was still considered a more likely path to the prelacy than was the position of a secular master. Those who had flocked to the schools with great hopes for their futures as masters often found themselves struggling to survive as teachers until the right job came along or, alternatively, spending long years working in the lower echelons of a court bureaucracy. Both the arrogant claims these men made about their learning and their bitter criticisms of the unlearned have the distinct ring of frustrated expectations.

Whatever the actual employment situation in the twelfth century was, many of the learned, especially those who had exclusively or primarily studied the liberal arts, believed that the prospects of men like themselves had been much better in the past. It is a social fact, which each generation of ambitious young men must realize for itself, that the opportunities for advancement seldom match their expectations. The few renowned successes of the previous generation make it appear that the situation had once been different. We must keep this fact in mind when we read and try to interpret the frequent complaints made in the twelfth century about the decline in learning. It helps to explain why, even though the opportunities for the learned were almost certainly increasing, those in—or recently out of—the schools often complained they were decreasing. By any objective measure, learning was on the rise, but the unrealistic ambitions and expectations of many young men led them to think otherwise.

This chapter and the next are concerned with two groups of critics who came to feel disappointed in and embittered by their education—or, perhaps more accurately, by how society regarded their education. The members of both groups have much in common. They had all gone to the schools and had primarily studied the arts of the trivium. Then, some having first taught for several years, they spent their lives struggling to support and advance themselves largely by means of their learning. What distinguishes the two groups of critics is not the object or motive of their criticisms but the form they used to express them. Some of these critics wrote satires, in which they overstated, caricatured, and parodied what they found objectionable in the schools and in society. Others wrote more sober treatises and letters that defended the "humane" value of their learning against educational and social trends detrimental to it. These two groups, the satirists and the humanists, agreed in their overall estimation of the state of learning, criticized the same educational trends, and had similar views of what needed to be done to improve the situation. The two groups are treated in separate chapters because the interpretation of their writings requires two distinct methods of analysis.

"It is difficult not to write satire."[5] This line from Juvenal's *Satires* often occurred to learned men when they thought about what had happened in the schools and to education since the days when they had studied their grammar. The poetry of the classical Roman satirists had been part of their grammatical training. They had been required to memorize poems and had practiced writing Latin verse, using the models of Juvenal, Persius, and Horace. It was natural that men so trained in their youth found themselves later in their careers turning again to these models to express their criticisms of society.

The twelfth century, it has long been recognized, was a great age of Latin satirical writing. Although much has been written of the literary quality of this satire, however, less attention has been given to its social significance. To be sure, it is often difficult, in interpreting satire, to distinguish between literary imitation and conventional themes, on the one hand, and the expression of serious concerns and personal opinions about conditions actually observed or experienced, on the other. Satirical verse was usually first written as a school exercise, in which students diligently imitated themes set by their grammar teachers. Some of the extant satires appear to have originated as such exercises. But this fact does not lessen the significance of the ideas, attitudes, or values expressed in many satires. After getting their start in the schools, some men turned satire into a powerful tool for voicing their very real concerns and criticisms of the developments of their times. Their grammatical training provided the means. We have to look elsewhere to understand their motives.

Satire usually thrives in the context of rapid social change. Recent studies have shown that the writing of satire was revived amidst the disputes and debates of the Gregorian Revolution, which in the last quarter of the eleventh century severely disrupted the existing order and challenged long-established practices and widely accepted social values.[6] The earliest satire was aimed directly at the revolutionary ambitions of Rome and the papacy. However, once the power of the weapon was rediscovered, no part of the prelacy or clergy remained unscathed. Conservative resistance to reform and the inevitable discrepancies between the new ideals and the ability to realize them provided a plethora of targets for the sharpened pens of the satirists. Clerical incontinence and ignorance and the simony and nepotism of prelates soon joined the avarice and corruption of the Roman curia as the familiar themes of satire. A second front opened with the advent of new forms of religious life. The vehement rivalries among the new monastic and religious orders quickly fostered another war of words, in which satire again proved to be an especially powerful weapon.

With the rapid expansion of the schools, educational conditions became the third arena in which the satirists could prove their skills. Here, especially, there were excellent classical precedents and themes to be imitated. The great Roman satirists, especially Juvenal, had written many verses criticizing the education of their time. Juvenal had been primarily concerned with the lack of rewards for learning and with the corrupting influence of urban schools upon the morals of the young. The satirists of the twelfth century found a more general theme that encompassed these as well as newer concerns. That theme was the decline of learning.

WALTER OF CHATILLON

No one wrote of the decline of learning with greater force or authority than Walter of Châtillon (c. 1135-1203). Most of Walter's satires, written during the long schism caused by the conflict between Frederick Barbarossa and Alexander III, attack Church prelates and secular princes equally for the scandalous state of society. Walter probably passed his early career in the service of Henry II until forced to leave because of his support for Thomas Becket. From that time on, he seems to have had trouble gaining secure patronage. His skillful satires gained him recognition and prominence, but prospective patrons apparently feared that Walter would one day use his sharp pen to attack them as he had already done to others.[7] Walter suffered for his learning, not because it was unrewarded but because it had made him too critical to accept the rewards offered. He failed to learn that there is less freedom of criticism outside the schools than within. When Walter of Châtillon complained of the decline of learning, it was with all the bitterness of a disappointed courtier.

This does not diminish the importance of his criticism. Although he blamed most of the decline of learning on prelates and princes who did not sufficiently reward learned men, Walter was also critical of what was happening within the schools. No less than the worsening prospects for the learned to advance in society, his poems criticize the lessened regard for the trivium among scholars. Indeed, he saw a close connection between the two developments. One of his poems tells how a learned but poor scholar approaches a bishop to request a living, only to be driven away as soon as it is discovered that he cannot pay. Advancement is given not to the learned but to those who have money or good social connections. There is no one to sponsor the poor scholar. This is why so few are willing to undergo the expenses and hardships of study, especially in the liberal arts. "Now," Walter laments, "the chorus of poets begs miserably. None come to drink at the font of letters."[8] Like so many other scholars of his time, Walter believed things had once been different. In another poem he vividly contrasts a former era, when learning had flourished, to modern times, when "it is more useful to farm than to study in the schools of Paris."[9] Walter portrays himself as a defender of educational values no longer esteemed either in the schools or in society. As we shall see, these values were shared more widely than Walter, perhaps blinded by his own desperation, realized.

The contrast of a once golden age of learning to the present state of decline was already a literary commonplace at the time Walter was composing his satires. But few writers could express the theme with the force and directness found in the poem *Felix erat studium*. Walter begins by describing how the philosophers of antiquity regarded learning as its own reward. Seeking only to understand the Creator by studying the world and created things, these scholars voluntarily chose a life of poverty. As an example of the scholar uninterested in material rewards, Walter cites the learned Diogenes, who was willing to speak bluntly even to the great Alexander. In contrast, modern scholars are interested only in being rewarded for their learning. "Scholars," Walter complains, "have become idle and unfruitful; they learn only in order to say, 'I have disputed.'" Books are read only superficially and many abuse the title of master. Walter blames this situation on the corrupting influence of Rome, where one gains a place or position through simony alone. Given the bad example of Rome, is it any wonder that scholars pursue learning for material rewards alone and that the title of master has become no more than a valuable credential to be sold to an employer?[10] For Walter of Châtillon, as for so many others critical of the state of the schools, all the roads of Paris led directly to Rome.

In the poem *Tanto viro locuturi*, Walter again makes a connection between the decline of learning and the corruption of Rome, this time with all the ironic wit of which he was master. Supposedly a poor cleric's request to the pope for a prebend, the poem compellingly reveals how simony and corruption in the Church had affected the prospects of the educated. Walter here speaks in the voice of a learned but unrewarded lover of virtue struggling to survive in a world that has become a moral desert, where prelates love money and ravage their flocks to fill their pockets, and only those able to pay or willing to flatter are offered positions. At the end of a long description of ecclesiastical corruption, the cleric asks bitterly, "What do the arts give other than toil and sorrow?"[11]

Walter again compares this situation to a golden age of learning, this time in the not-too-distant past, when education was still valued and rewarded. It is now law and lawyers that Walter explicitly blames for the decline of learning. "The arts flourished for a long time," he writes, "but since the law has reigned, the arts are useless."[12] He savagely attacks the hypocrisy, avarice, and simony of the lawyers. The poor scholar complains that lawyers achieve their ambitions of becoming deacons, abbots, or bishops because they can and will pay, while he, without money, must demonstrate the value of his education in the arts and in theology. This clear expression of the frustration many young scholars seem to have felt in trying to procure a living is given additional force by the supplicant's threat to leave the clergy if the pope will not aid him: "You will be dishonored, good pastor, if I give up the study of theology and become a layman."[13] Although the poem ends with a humble petition for some means of support, this does not lessen the seriousness of the point Walter was making in having the scholar threaten to quit his studies.

In *Missus sum in vineam*, another satire on the lack of rewards for learning, the complaining scholar—this time a poet rather than a theologian—does actually choose to give up study rather than suffer the hardships of poverty. Lamenting his own inability to find patronage, the poet advises others of the uselessness of learning. Why honor books or spend time studying in Paris when even Homer, if he went to a court empty-handed, would be thrown out? No more of this learning, he exclaims. Why should he endure poverty and the miserable life of a scholar? It is far better to sleep in a soft bed with a woman than to endure long nights of study in a cold room alone. For him, life without wealth is no better than death, and besides, money is needed to support love. So why not quit? Learning only makes men proud and causes young men to boast. The poem ends with a call to others, too, to give up their studies and spend their time eating and drinking.[14]

Walter's obvious contempt for such attitudes among the learned is only thinly veiled. He considers the materialism within the schools no less responsible for the decline of learning than the corruption prevalent outside. In his view, education had become a source of pride; instead of inculcating virtue, as it should, learning was making good conduct impossible. Walter of Châtillon clearly believed that reversing the decline of learning was as much a matter of reforming the values of scholars as of changing the attitudes of the rest of society.

In other satires, Walter also makes scholars share the blame with prelates and princes for the decline of learning. In *Felix erat studium*, superficial learning and the abuse of the title "master" are shown to be the unfortunate effects of the struggle for rewards.[15] In *Stulti cum prudentibus*, Walter is especially critical of the corrupting effect the city of Paris has on the morals of young students.[16] Masters, he complains, are leaving the schools unlearned and immoral. Is it any wonder that they are not proving their worth and gaining advancement? Such criticisms should not be interpreted as rebellious invective. They had a serious moral purpose. Walter had spent much of his life as a student in the schools of Paris, Reims, and Bologna and as a master at Laon and Châtillon. He knew well what he was criticizing. Like many of his learned contemporaries, he had also suffered the frustration of not attaining the worldly success that he had expected his education would bring him. Unlike the poet he portrays in *Missus sum in vineam,* however, Walter was no less committed to the value of his learning because of these experiences.

As Walter saw it, the fundamental problem was that society had become too corrupted by wealth to value learning for itself, and this materialism had adversely affected conditions in the schools. That Walter's satires at times appear bitter, self-serving, and irreverent should not lead us to misjudge his attitude and intent. He was genuinely concerned about the decline in learning and was motivated by conviction as much as by frustration to rail against it. Like most satirists, Walter of Châtillon was fundamentally a conservative. "We moderns," he laments in one of his poems, "no longer follow in the footsteps of the ancients, . . . but we stride forward ardently on the road to hell."[17] Walter looked back to that golden age in the past when true learning had flourished and learned men had received their just rewards.

In addition to satires, Walter's surviving works include a sermon, *In domino confido*, preached to the masters of the schools in Bologna. A mixed composition of prose and verse, this work shows the serious, positive side of his educational thought better than his satires do. The sermon begins, in the conventional way, with a prose peroration on the liturgical text of the day, the fourth Sunday in Lent ("In domino confido. . . ," Ps. 10.1).[18] Walter cleverly uses the peroration to excuse himself from speaking exclusively about canon and civil law, the chief subjects of study at Bologna, on the grounds that his legal education is too limited. To allow himself to discuss all branches of learning, he chooses for the body of the sermon the text of Proverbs 9.1 ("Sapientia aedificavit sibi domum"), a theme often used by preachers when addressing groups of scholars. "The house of which I speak is the house of knowledge that the Lord gave to men that they might harvest the fruit of prudence," he begins.[19] Structurally, the sermon has three parts, corresponding to a threefold grouping of the masters in the schools: masters of arts, lawyers and physicians, and theologians.

The first group, the faculty of arts, comes out less well than one might expect. Although Walter praises the sincerity of their academic endeavors, he criticizes those who teach the trivium or quadrivium for spending too much time on learning that should be only preparatory. Too many of these masters, he complains, never seek to apply their learning to improving their lives or to furthering their understanding of God. They prefer to concentrate on the secular arts, either because they enjoy them or because they want to boast about their knowledge of the natural world. Walter warns these masters that their knowledge of the liberal arts, although often pursued diligently and without concern for material rewards, will remain fruitless unless they turn their attention to higher goals.[20]

As critical as Walter had been of the faculty of arts, masters in the lucrative professions come out still worse. Although Walter addresses physicians, canon lawyers, and civil lawyers collectively, he is most critical of the civil lawyers—the faculty that likely dominated his audience at Bologna. Mocking their learning as useless and vain, he begins with what is probably a reference to his own youthful exuberance for civil law. "O how happy our study would be," he says, "how happy our labors if we could live eternally learning the law! But when you see the body of the king [Justinian], who worked to resolve the mysteries of the law, rot in the ground, why do you spend long nights laboring to learn law? If I may be allowed to conclude this matter briefly: it is vain for these scholars to rise before dawn."[21]

Walter's criticisms of the lawyers at first echo those made of the arts faculty. Salvation cannot be achieved through Roman law, nor can life thereby be improved. Knowing the law, even the entire Codex, does not assure good conduct. If the law God gave to Moses did not make men perfect, what can be expected of laws merely promulgated by Roman princes? Walter poses a similar challenge to the faculty of medicine. What, he asks, is medicine's value if a physician can heal a person's body but leave the soul sickened by sin? But law and medicine—unlike the arts—are attracting scholars in increasing numbers because these subjects are a sure means to wealth. "Grammar sows but is always in need," he comments. "Law and medicine harvest bundles."[22] Money is not the only difference. The increased number of men pursuing the lucrative professions, especially law, also has serious social consequences. The study of law is not only a distraction from the search for true wisdom; it can actually be dangerous to society. The disputes raging among masters of the arts over such issues as universals are intellectually fruitless and unfortunate, but they are socially innocuous. The masters of arts are harming only themselves and the schools. In contrast, the conflicts that occur among lawyers can cause terrible injuries and injustices to be done to others. Thus Walter of Châtillon boldly and sternly warns the law masters in Bologna of the social responsibility incumbent in their knowledge, a warning that we shall find echoed repeatedly by those who preached in Paris.

According to Walter, the prudent scholar understands that the true measures of all learning are its usefulness in improving human life and conduct and its necessity to the attainment of salvation. Evaluated by this twofold standard, only theology comes out favorably. The third part of Walter's sermon is full of praise for theologians. He repeats none of the criticisms made by others about either their methods or their motives. Rather than telling of their faults, which he doubtless knew existed, Walter chooses to make the theologians the exemplars of an educational ideal. It is they alone, among all the faculties, who recognize the higher purpose of all learning and who, by concentrating their studies on the understanding of Scripture, are able to attain the wisdom needed to improve their lives and be saved. For all other masters, the theologians provide the model of those true workers whose intellectual labors do harvest the "fruit of prudence" and who make education truly beneficial both to themselves and to the rest of society.[23]

There is little unique or original in all this. Walter's sermon at Bologna, like those preached by his contemporaries in Paris, is a plea to scholars to reconsider their motives, to recognize the limitations of the secular arts, and to redirect their learning to higher objectives. His criticisms differ from theirs in form rather than substance. Like many of the learned men of his time, Walter of Châtillon strongly believed in the importance of education in improving the Church and society. He was convinced that the advancement of properly educated men would decrease corruption and immorality. At the same time, he was more pessimistic than most about the prospects for reform, partly because of his own experiences and partly, too, because he realized better than most that there was a major new obstacle to be reckoned with—the growth of a professional establishment in the Church and secular courts that was dominated by lawyers. Satire had become an effective means of protest against growing specialization and professionalism both in the schools and in society. The pen may have been the only weapon literary men like Walter of Châtillon had to wield against their powerful rivals, but they could wield it with considerable force and skill.

OTHER SATIRISTS ON THE DECLINE OF LEARNING

Walter of Châtillon portrayed himself as a lone voice, struggling to defend educational and social values that were no longer fashionable. From his perspective, the decline of learning was a relatively recent event, something that had happened since his own days in the schools, when the opportunities had seemed so bright for men soundly educated in the liberal arts. He wrote with all the force and conviction of someone who believed that he alone stood against the currents of change and was willing to suffer personally to point the dangers out to others. There is some validity to this view. Walter did live at the time of the most rapid advance of the new professions. And, although exceptionally learned and a prominent writer, he died poor and miserable, apparently as a leper. Still, though he certainly stands out both for the strength of his protest and the skill of his verse, neither his experiences nor his complaints were unique. Other poets both before and after Walter wrote satires likewise complaining of the decline of learning.

Several of the themes found in Walter's poems can be traced back to the verse of an obscure canon of St. Omer, Peter the Painter, who wrote during the first third of the twelfth century.[24] Among his satires is found the earliest of the many laments of poor scholars skilled in the arts but unable to find employment. "Cur ultra studeam?" Peter asks, when it is money and not learning or worthiness that gains one social advancement.[25] The poem *Temporibus nostris mutari* likewise laments the lack of rewards for learning. Peter blames the ignorance and corruption of worldly clerics and prelates for the situation, not lawyers. But, like Walter of Châtillon, Peter the Painter writes as a witness to the decline of learning and refers back to a golden age:

> Temporibus nostris mutari secula cerno;
> Omne vetus studium perit accedente moderno.
> Artes scire bonas fuit olim gloria cleri. . . .
> Nunc inhonesta sequi, nunc sectari levitatem
> Gens hodierna studet, morumque fuit probitatem.
> Artes scire bonas nunc pro nichilo reputatur,
> Nummos scire bonos, hoc prevalet, hocque probatur.
> Hoc hodie studium deducitur absque labore:
> Quod quicumque tenet, cito sublimatur honore.
> Hoc studio baculus donatur pontificalis,
> Venditur hoc studio gradus omnis symonialis.
> Hoc erismeticam studium dixere priores,
> Hoc etenim multi sunt affecti potiores. . . .

Est gravius studium bene scribere, versificari,
Discere grammaticam, prudenter versificari,
Quam nummos nummis, libras libris cumulare
Aut ex usuris usuras multiplicare.[26]

[I discern the world changing in our times; ancient learning perishes completely with the advance of modern times. It was once the glory of the clergy to know the arts. . . . Now men strive daily to gain disgraceful things and to attend to vanity, and they flee good conduct. Now to know the arts counts for nothing; counting money is what prevails and is valued. This learning does not require work; whoever has money is quickly honored. The bishop's staff is given for money; every position is sold as simony. Indeed many of those who formerly devoted themselves to learning this art of making money have done well. . . . It is more difficult work to learn to write well, to learn grammar, and to write skillful verse than to add pennies to pennies and pounds to pounds or to increase one's gain through usury.]

Peter demonstrates the decline by contrasting a poor, scholarly cleric to a rich, ignorant one. His descriptions of each become satirical conventions. The worldly cleric, named *Domnus vobiscum* (a pun on the blessing of the Mass, "Dominus vobiscum"), is wealthy, well dressed, and well fed, rides an excellent horse, has scant regard for learning, and charges for saying Mass. The one vice he lacks is that of keeping a concubine. In contrast, the poor scholar, a grammarian named Aristotle, is a diligent student and a good poet, but he must beg for his food and travel everywhere on foot. The contrast is especially pointed in the descriptions of the contents of the two clerics' purses. Whereas that of *Domnus vobiscum* is overflowing with money, Aristotle's holds nothing but the supplies needed for learning – writing tablets, pencils, and grammar books. These, Peter writes ironically, may be valued by philosophers but are a poor defense against poverty. Without money, Aristotle will go begging in the kingdom of priests. He should give up grammar, follow the example of *Domnus vobiscum*, and learn the more useful art of moneymaking.

Temporibus nostris mutari is apparently the first in the long line of satires that contrast the rich, beneficed cleric to the poor scholar, a tradition best known in Chaucer's clerk of Oxenford. This Aristotle is one of the more sympathetic of the many poor scholars portrayed in twelfth-century satire. Peter the Painter's description seems to ring with the truth of bitter experience, rather than merely to repeat a literary convention or represent an educational ideal.

Another poet who wrote from personal experience of the miserable rewards for learning was Hugh of Orléans (1093 to c. 1160), whose repute won him the epithet "the Primate." His frequently autobiographical satire tells of the struggles of a famed poet and erstwhile master at Orléans and Paris. Although sometimes loved and supported, he never gained secure employment but remained, even at the apex of his career, subject to the whims of wealthy patrons. Finally, in old age, he suffered the worst abuse and impoverishment. How much of this depiction of the poet's life – with his endless boasts of drinking, gambling, and womanizing – is actually true is open to question. Like the artists of modern times, the poets of the Middle Ages liked to portray themselves as scornful of conventional morality. The satirical verse of Hugh of Orléans is distinguished by its highly personal quality. Rather than attack the leaders of the Church and society in general for the decline of learning, he directed his invective against specific people who had wronged him – a prelate who offered him no more than an unlined cloak during the cold of winter or a rich lord who kicked him down the stairs just for begging.[27]

Amidst all these personal complaints about the lack of rewards for the learned, one of Hugh's poems, *Ambianis, urbs predives*, does give more concrete information about the changing conditions in the schools. The poem is not, as one would guess from its opening words, primarily about Amiens, which Hugh does initially thank for the gracious hospitality he received there after being robbed on the highway, but about the city of Reims and its schools. Hugh is effusive in his praise of the flourishing schools and especially of Master Alberic, the disciple of Anselm of Laon who opposed Peter Abelard at Soissons and who was then serving as scholasticus (1132–36).

Remis enim per etatem	Reims owes to an old tradition
Primam tenet dignitatem:	Her most dignified position.
Sed, quod habet ab antiquo	What was famous as of old
Nunc augetur sub Albrico.	Now is glorious to behold.
Per hunc Remis urbs suprema,	Alberic raised her supreme,
Per hunc portat diadema;	Graced her with a diadem,
Per hunc fulget in corona.	Set in the resplendent crown
Quam commendant multa bona:	Of an old and great renown.
Sed pre cunctis hanc divine	Above all that makes her shine,
Fons illustrat discipline,	Reims is fount of lore divine,
Fons preclarus atque iugis,	Fount of promise and salvation,
Fons doctrine non de nugis,	Not of petty altercation.
Non de falsis argumentis,	Banned are all false arguments;
Sed de Christi sacramentis.	She upholds Christ's sacraments.
Non hic artes Marciani	Martian's arts are nearly blighted,
Neque partes Prisciani,	Even Priscian's grammar slighted.
Non hic vana poetarum:	No one lectures here on poets,
Sed archana prophetarum,	But what God revealed to prophets,
Non leguntur hic poete:	Not on poets' vanities

Sed Iohannes et prophete;	But on Christian verities.
Non est scola vanitatis:	Not the school of vanity,
Sed doctrina veritatis;	But teaching of verity,
Ibi nomen non Socratis:	Socrates is here rejected,
Sed eterne trinitatis;	Holy Trinity respected.
Non hic Plato vel Thimeus;	None hears Plato or Timaeus
Hic auditur unus deus.[28]	Schools at Reims teach *unus deus*.

The criticism of the secular arts is surprising coming from "the Primate," the most disreputable of the satirists. Walter of Châtillon was evidently not alone in proclaiming the superiority of theology over the liberal arts. But there is an important difference in the situation the two satirists describe. Whereas to Walter the threat to sacred learning was the increased interest in law and medicine, when Hugh of Orléans was writing in the 1130's, the battle was still over the applicability of the art of dialectic to Scripture. To Alberic's sound and tranquil teaching of Scripture at Reims, Hugh contrasts the conditions in "the schools of disputation" – can there be any doubt he means Paris? – where competition, disagreement, and conflict make it impossible to learn the truth and where the false opinion of one master is soon replaced by that of another.[29] Although Hugh confidently asserts that Master Alberic can withstand any challenge ("doctor totum contradicit"), he worries that the concord and tranquility of Reims are being threatened by the attacks made on Alberic's teaching by a disreputable monk living in a nearby abbey. Is Hugh's object of vilification none other than Peter Abelard? Although Abelard's previous encounter with Alberic makes him a likely candidate, several of the details of Hugh's description do not exactly fit what we know of the controversial master's career.[30] Hugh's contemporaries probably had a better idea of whom he was vilifying on Alberic's behalf.

Ambianis, urbs predives provides an excellent example of the power of satire as a weapon in the bitter educational conflicts and interscholastic rivalries of the first half of the twelfth century. The satirist, unlike a master engaged in disputation, did not have to refute his opponent's teaching point by point. Rather, as Hugh of Orléans does in attacking the unnamed enemy of Alberic of Reims, he could build his offensive on parody and on ad hominem attacks.

The anonymous author of the *Metamorphosis Goliae* employs the powerful weapon of satire to defend Peter Abelard and to attack monastic interference in the schools. Abelard, an assembly of great masters explains to his mournful bride, is not among their company at the celestial court because he has been silenced by "the hooded abbot of the hooded people who dress in three tunics like an onion" – a mocking description of Bernard of Clairvaux. The poem includes a harsh attack on monks:

Grex est hic nequicie, grex perdicionis,
Impius et pessimus heres Pharaonis,
Speciem exterius dans religionis,
Set subest scintillula supersticionis.

Gentis gens quisquilia, gens hec infrunita,
Cuius est cupiditas mentis infinita:
Istos ergo fugias et istos devita
Et hiis ne respondeas: "non est *sic* vel *ita*."[31]

[Here is a flock of worthless men, the flock of destruction, the impious and most evil heirs of the Pharoah, giving the external appearance of religion but beneath glittering with superstition. They are the rubbish of mankind, senseless men, whose cupidity is infinite. You should flee them, avoid their company, and not bother arguing, "It is not *thus* but *so*."]

The poem ends with the gods issuing a decree expelling all monks from their court and excluding them from the schools of the philosophers. Unfit to learn the secrets of philosophy, they will be forced thenceforth to stick to the filth of the mechanical arts.

The poet's vicious attack on monks probably reflects the bitterness and helplessness felt by Abelard's disciples after what happened to their master at Sens. Few who heard the satire could have failed to understand that Bernard of Clairvaux was the primary object of ridicule. The satirist's strategy was to make an ad hominem attack on Bernard's character and motives rather than to attempt a judicious defense of Abelard. Boldly, he goes even further and launches an offensive against the monastic critics of the schools, accusing them of being superstitious, stupid, and cupidinous. It is monks who are not worthy and who should be silenced, not scholars. It is the ignorance of monks that is truly dangerous, not the learning of the schools.

In the *Apocalypsis Goliae*, another dream poem often attributed to the same author, satire is used in a different way to defend the schools. Golias here tells of three distinct visions. In the first he is guided by Pythagoras into a land inhabited by classical poets and philosophers. Next an angel directs his gaze to heaven, to watch the opening of the book with seven seals described in the Apocalypse. In this second vision the opening of each seal reveals a different aspect of the corruption of the clergy, with the last seal and the most savage satire reserved for the monastic orders. The final vision is that of the third heaven where, according to Paul (2 Cor. 12.2–4), the unspeakable mysteries of the faith were to be revealed.[32]

The complex allegory of the *Apocalypsis Goliae* obscures the relationship that the poet sought to make between the three visions. The first, in particular, seems only vaguely related to the others. But when we realize that the poet was writing about education, it becomes clear that the first vision is meant to be preparatory to the next two. The classical scholars Pythagoras shows to Golias are a selection of the primary *auctores* read in the arts curriculum in the schools; they represent secular learning. How this first vision leads to the third should be obvious. The poet is expressing, albeit somewhat obscurely, the familiar idea of the secular arts as propaedeutic to theology. More difficult to discern is the relationship between the first vision and the second. What does the poet's bitter satire of the immorality and corruption of the clergy and religious orders have to do with his beautiful vision of the classical authors peacefully going about their proper tasks? The contrast of the first two visions seems to be intended to suggest that the true obstacle to the wisdom of the third vision is not the curriculum of the schools but, rather, the corruption of the Church. Yet this is only part of the lesson. The structure of the poem also implies that it is only the knowledge that Golias has gained from the first vision that enables him to avoid the vices revealed to him in the second vision and to advance to the third vision of wisdom. Thus, not only is the poet defending the study of the secular arts as useful both in teaching morality and in preparing for theology, he is also asserting that those educated in the schools would be better suited than worldly clerics or ignorant monks to lead the Church and to reform society. There seems to be some hope in his optimistic vision that this might yet happen.

The satirists of the second half of the twelfth century were often less confident than Golias about the prospects for the learned. At the same time, their complaints were usually more personal than social, and their pessimistic expectations focused more on their own careers than on the general state of learning. One finds, especially in anonymous verse, increasingly bitter and hostile protests against the relative paucity of the rewards available to students of the arts. "What does careful study of the arts confer?" asks one unknown poet, and he answers, "Destruction of the body and weariness of the mind." The arts may be called liberal, but they imprison rather than free. Those who labor in the arts are forced to beg and to suffer the mockery of the vulgar and the derision of the rich. It is the study of canon law that is rewarded.[33]

The author of *Meum est propositum* echoes Walter of Châtillon in contrasting the riches of lawyers and physicians to the poverty of those who study the arts.[34] Other needy men should learn from his mistake: "It is good for poor men to stick to the law: I chose to waste too much sweat on the arts."[35] He warns bitterly that no material benefits can be gained from studying the logical arts; those who do so will be despised in old age by younger men who think they are senile. Why waste your time on dialectic if you have no money from other sources? Leave such study to the rich. A rich logician is rarer than a black swan. If you want to study something profitable, turn your attention to Galen and Justinian. Another unknown satirist mockingly suggests that although the liberal and the mechanical arts are equally unlikely means of gaining advancement or making money, the art of flattery is a certain path to riches.[36]

How seriously we should take some of these satires as evidence of the actual state of learning or of attitudes particular to the twelfth century is open to question. Scholars always seem to make the same complaints about how hard they work and how little they are rewarded. In some cases, especially when the verse is anonymous, it is impossible to tell to what extent the themes are dictated merely by literary convention. Many of the extant anonymous satires do read like school exercises for which the master set the theme. Also, to judge from the successful careers of some of those poets we can identify, a good deal of the satirical verse was written by young men anxious about their future prospects or bitter over some early setbacks who later, when they achieved success equal to their ambitions, must have been embarrassed by their words.

A notable, if exceptional, example of such a satirist is Philip of Grève, chancellor of Paris from 1216 to 1237. It is hardly surprising that there is a marked difference in tone and attitude between the satires he wrote as a young scholar seeking to establish his reputation and the sermons he delivered as chancellor exhorting other scholars to improve their conduct. The poems written in his youth are filled with bitter protests against the limited opportunities for the learned. "Math, logic, and poetry count for nothing," he laments in one poem, "gold counts for more than learning."[37] In another he complains that money has destroyed all incentive to become educated, since only those who are wealthy can gain advancement. "He who has more [money] is judged more learned and is more loved. Those without are derided. And a poor man, however noble in character, is reviled."[38] A third poem, Philip's famous song, *Veritas, aequitas*, singles out nepotism as the most serious obstacle for the learned:

Dum cognati praebendati
Surgunt ad honores,
Pulsant dati paupertati
Ostia doctores.

Literati spe fraudati
　　Egent post labores,
Probitati ac aetati
　　Desunt provisores.[39]

[While the relatives of those who have good livings advance in honors, learned men suffering in poverty are left knocking at the door. Men of letters, who had falsely hoped for advancement, beg after years of hard work. Worthy and aged, they remain without patrons.]

But Philip, even in this youthful verse, does more than complain about the lack of rewards for learning. He voices equally strong criticisms of the decline of learning within the schools. One of his most forceful satires, *De Artium conditione*, tells how the dignity of the arts is being tarnished by what he describes as the corruption of modern teaching. Masters of arts are harshly satirized for being too wrapped up in words and circuitous logic to be able to teach the truth. No less than those outside the schools, they are attacked for being content to "babble like infants" and for neglecting or defaming what they do not know and cannot understand. Most serious of all, Philip accuses scholars of being interested only in learning that can be readily used for material benefit.[40] These were the three standard criticisms at the time Philip was writing, and they offer no new insights into the state of learning. But they show that even as a young man chiefly concerned about his own prospects, Philip of Grève did not overlook the problems within the schools that he would later work to rectify as chancellor.

Whereas Philip of Grève's concerns about the decline of learning are undoubtedly sincere, the complaints of other satirists are often less convincing. This is especially true of their frequent tales of poverty and suffering. Some quite successful poets exaggerated the meanness of their lives in order to embarrass their patrons into augmenting their stipends. The renowned and rebellious "Archpoet" is an excellent example of this ploy. Known to have been patronized by Rainald of Dassel, the wealthy archbishop of Mainz and chancellor to Frederick Barbarossa, the Archpoet seems to make a mockery of the poor scholar's plight. A typical example of his many complaints of poverty is found in these stanzas from *Sepe de miseria*:

Poeta pauperior omnibus poetis
Nichil prorsus habeo nisi quod videtis,
Unde sepe lugeo, quando vos ridetis;
Nec me meo vitio pauperem putetis.

Fodere non debeo, quia sum scolaris
Ortus ex militibus preliandi gnaris;

Sed quia me terruit labor militaris,
Malui Virgilium sequi quam te, Paris.

Mendicare pudor est, mendicare nolo;
Fures multa possident, sed non absque dolo.
Quid ergo iam faciam, qui nec agros colo
Nec mendicus fieri nec fur esse volo?[41]

[I am the poorest of all poets; I have absolutely nothing save for what you see. Whence I often mourn when you laugh. Do not think I am poor because I want to be. I ought not to dig because I am a scholar and the son of a knight. But since I am afraid of fighting, I preferred to follow Virgil rather than Paris. I will not beg, since begging is disgraceful. Thieves are wealthy but not without grief. What, therefore, am I to do, since I care not for farming, nor to become a beggar, nor do I wish to be a thief?]

Given his relative good fortune, it seems unlikely that the Archpoet's cries of poverty won him much sympathy, either in court or in the schools.

Other complaints of poverty give every indication of being little more than the school exercises done by students when learning rhyme and meter in their grammar classes. Like the letters appealing to parents for money written by later generations of students learning the *ars dictaminis*,[42] these poems are all identical in theme and similar in form. Among the several examples found in the *Carmina Burana* is *Exul ego clericus*, a typically moving appeal for support written by a scholar to a patron—for whose name a blank space is conveniently left. Listing all the conventional attributes of a needy scholar—exile, poverty, a thin cloak to shelter him from the cold—the poet warns that unless he gets support soon, he will have no choice but to quit his studies: "Litterarum studiis vellem insudare, / nisi quod inopia cogit me cessare."[43] One can only wonder how often patrons heard nearly the same lines of verse from young poets, each claiming originality and each lamenting the hardships of scholarly life.

On the other hand, as we know from the testimony of John of Salisbury and others, it was expensive to live in Paris. Many scholars must have found it difficult to pay for lecture fees, books, food, and lodging out of the modest stipends they brought with them. No doubt, given the situation, some did try to use their literary skills to acquire additional support to continue their studies. One notable example of this is the parody *Evvangelium secundum marcam auri et argenti*.[44] Although similar to and perhaps begun as a classroom exercise, this clever satire was apparently used to make a serious request for support. Composed by a certain John, a scholar of the arts in Paris, the parody survives in a desperate letter written to his brother, an archpresbyter, after his three previous requests for money had not been answered.

John humorously and artfully describes the dire situation in which he finds himself, seriously in debt and unable to hold off his creditors. His plea for support parodies Luke's account of Martha's plea to Jesus (Luke 10.40-41). "At that time," he writes, "there was John studying the arts in Paris without any money. Thus he was bothered and busy over many things and, raising his eyes to heaven, he said to Jesus, 'Lord, does it not concern you that my brother has left me in Paris with no money? Tell him, therefore, that he should help me.' And Jesus responded: 'Indeed, money is needed for those studying in Paris.'"[45] Next, John describes the visit of two friends to whom he owes money, this time parodying the story of the two apostles' approach to Christ's tomb on Easter morning. When his friends arrive at his room, John, mimicking the Gospel (Matt. 25.12), denies that he knows them: "Amen, amen, I say to you who come for my money; I know you not."[46] Then, when they finally come into his room, he convinces them to wait for their payment with a speech that echoes the Beatitudes and the lamentations of Job:

And sitting down he taught them, saying: "Blessed be the merciful, for they shall obtain mercy; and blessed be those who do not irritate nor molest their debtors, for they shall soon be reimbursed for what is owed. Have mercy on me, my friends, since I suffer from an empty purse. Behold, I have no clothes other than my tunic and my underwear, which is ripped to shreds. Let not your heart be troubled or afraid because of this. I go away and I am coming back to you. And whatever I owe you, I acknowledge, as my debt is always against me [cf. Ps. 50.5]. I know that my redeemer lives and in a short time he shall return, and what is yours will be restored. Go therefore and tell your brethren what you have seen and heard."[47]

When a "redeemer" does give John some money, his creditors hear of it and congregate at his room demanding to be paid. The humorous scene imitates the story of Christ feeding the thousands in John, chapter 6, and Matthew's account of Christ's Passion. As the creditors argue among themselves over who should be paid first, John leaves the room and prays, just as Christ prayed in the garden of Gethsemane on the night of his arrest (Matt. 26.36-44):

John said to them, "Sit down here while I go yonder to pray." And taking three of his friends with him he said to them, "My soul is sad at the emptying of my purse." And bending his knees he prayed: "Father, if it is possible, let these creditors pass from me." Returning to his room he found the creditors still quarreling, for they were troubled by want. And again he went away and prayed the same words: "Father, if it is possible, let these creditors pass from me. The finger is indeed willing to count, but the purse is weak."[48]

When, at last, John is forced to relinquish his purse, the contention among the creditors increases. They, like Christ's guards, cast lots for the last remnants of the poor scholar's clothing. In sum, we are told, although "twelve bushels" were collected (as after Christ fed the thousands), many debts remain to be settled. "Have patience with me," John pleads, "and I shall return. Truly many coins are owed, but few are handed over."[49] Thus ends the humorous parody as well as a poor Paris scholar's desperate plea for financial help. As far as we know, the author, like the John in his parody and many other students since then, never received the support he needed from his family and left the schools hopelessly in debt.

THE SCHOLAR IN SATIRE

The scholar complaining of his poverty was a common figure in the satires of the twelfth century. His poverty, whether a genuine concern or a literary convention, gave him authority as a critic of society. The learned but poor cleric became a foil for the wealthy and worldly priest, as well as an obvious example of the decline of learning. But this is only one side of the picture. Some satirists hailed the poor scholar as an ideal, and poverty as not just a likely consequence of studying the arts but as a prerequisite of learning. Walter of Châtillon contrasted the scholars of his own time, who were overly concerned with material rewards, to the ancient philosophers, like Diogenes, who voluntarily chose a life of poverty in order to continue unobstructed in their pursuit of the truth. For him, as for Bernard of Chartres, poverty was one of the necessary conditions for study.[50] The same ideal inspired Peter the Painter's description of the poor grammarian Aristotle, whose only possessions are his books and writing materials. In spite of the cynical conclusion of *Temporibus nostris mutari*, there can be no doubt that Peter truly admired the poor Aristotle, contemptuous of riches, not the worldly priest.

When the anonymous author of the late-twelfth-century satire *In sublimi solio* took up the theme of the poor scholar and the rich cleric, he made it even clearer where his sympathies lay. This time, representatives of each class actually debate the matter before the wise King Solomon, who pronounces the poor scholar to be in the right. Although there is little new or surprising in this satirist's treatment of the theme, his poem reveals how completely such critics felt the values and ideals of the learned to be at odds with the rest of society.

The worldly priest begins the debate: "The scholar's life brings hunger and thirst. I choose to accumulate a lot of money so I can relieve the misery of poverty. I could never be satisfied with learning, however much I had." To which the scholar replies: "Everyone ought to learn in their youth and, through their studies, select the path of virtue. Certain men, however, wish to live like animals and struggle to preserve their hides above all else." The difference in values is clear, and the debate continues as the two adversaries grow increasingly hostile:

> *The priest:* If good morals are given to the learned, the simple are far better off without them. The afflictions of miserable scholars are obvious. Great honors are given to rich priests.
>
> *The scholar:* Why do you neglect scholars, however needy they are? Why do you love the avaricious, however fat they become? You are a disgrace to your age, for you should have given up the sweet drink of infants.
>
> *The priest:* Knowledge requires hard work. Strong wine is a pleasant delight. I greatly love the juicy honey of honeycombs, which has made me enviably fat.
>
> *The scholar:* Good sense is more valuable than wealth. The wealthy man gathers gold with enormous pain and guards it with fear. Knowledge reigns and endures in honor; it reveals what is unknown and glows in the love of virtue.
>
> *The priest:* Rich clerics dress ornately and eat fish and nourishing foods. They live just like prelates. They travel on horses with large retinues. But scholars travel on foot unattended.
>
> *The scholar:* A scholar is humble, simple, just, chaste, pallid, and thin. Immense work oppresses him. The wealthy man is horrible, full of great arrogance, abounding in luxury, drunk and fat.
>
> *The priest:* Why should you study except so that you will acquire wealth? You sharpen your mind in order to flatter. You need support from your friends to study. Abundance provides support for me.
>
> *The scholar:* You do not know what you should preach in church. You fill the pews but do not know how to speak. We scholars know what you ought to do. But you, full of avarice, do not even know how to say Mass.
>
> *The priest:* I, a wealthy man, do not envy the miserable scholar, since I know that no honor is given to him. But I have prebends and preside at the altar. I have power and prestige.[51]

The debate is clearly getting nowhere, and Solomon mercifully brings it to an end once all the conventional contrasts between the poor scholar and the rich priest have been made. Neither side is likely to give in. The priest is too content with the material benefits of his position, the scholar no less firmly committed to the less tangible rewards of the pursuit of learning. The scholar may sound too self-righteous in his criticisms, but there is nothing admirable about the priest. He represents the stereotypical avaricious and ambitious cleric, the corruption of the Church so evident to those in the schools. His are the worldly attitudes of the ignorant churchmen unconcerned with their spiritual duties whom scholars saw as the principal enemies of learning and reform. His adversary, the poor scholar, represents more than simply the ideal of learning for its own sake. As his challenges to the priest suggest, many social improvements would follow if men like him, rather than his worldly adversary, were rewarded prebends and presided in churches. The poor scholar, in this debate, has become a standard for moral reform.

In *Hora nona sabbati*, another late-twelfth-century debate, many of the same conventions appear, but both contestants are criticized equally.[52] This time the encounter is between a simple priest, doing his duty of preaching to his congregation on Sunday, and a scholar traveling home from the schools, his head filled with logical tricks. Every detail of the physical description of the logician is ironic. As per convention, he is walking barefoot—but in this instance it is suggested that because it is a hot day, he has chosen to carry his shoes. Richly dressed and accompanied by a servant weighed down with a bundle of books by Aristotle, Socrates, and Plato—significantly, no Christian authors are mentioned—the logician hardly fits the ideal of a poor scholar.

The debate begins when the scholar interrupts the priest and criticizes his sermon. While it is true that the priest is expounding Scripture poorly, what bothers the logician is the priest's imperfect grammar and logic, not his inability to teach the lesson of the text. "You are murdering Priscian," he charges.[53] Humiliated before his congregation, the priest first defends the simplicity of his preaching, then attacks the learning of the logician for being hateful to God and useless to understanding Scripture. To which the logician replies boastingly, "We teach many things that you don't even know."[54] The charges and countercharges continue after Mass, invoking nearly all the abuses and vices that concerned contemporary reformers. When the priest says that he is guilty of simony for selling his learning, the scholar accuses the priest of the same sin for selling burial plots and pardons. Then, partly contradicting his previous charge, the priest mocks the scholar for traveling on foot and not wearing shoes. The logician's response, praising the merits of poverty as a "happy misfortune," is certainly intended as ironic. When the priest boasts of his great wealth and honor, the logician tells him he is a selfish glutton who keeps a concubine and is unworthy to administer the sacraments—a wiser strategy than attempting to prove his own poverty and humility. In his own defense, the priest then raises a question that was a sensitive point for reformers: "If you prohibited all unworthy priests from serving at the altar, the sacraments would cease. If that happened, how would we be saved?"[55]

At this point the debate degenerates into lewdness, as the two opponents exchange charges of various types of sexual immorality and personal misconduct. Only the ringing of the bell for Vespers ends the debate and saves the priest from having to respond to some particularly embarrassing charges. It also gives him the opportunity to plan his revenge. The priest gets the scholar to agree that they should continue the debate in public, and that whoever admits defeat is to be thrashed by the congregation. While the confident logician plans his arguments, the priest makes sure that no other cleric will be present to recite the responses during Vespers. When the unsuspecting logician loudly sings a verse that implies an admission of defeat, the priest exclaims, "You are defeated!"[56] As previously agreed, the congregation attacks the beguiled logician, who barely escapes with his life. Let this be a warning, the poet concludes, to both scholars and priests to improve their lives!

This satire represents a major variation on the theme of the poor scholar and the rich cleric. It is the pretentious scholar who gets the thrashing—both physically, from the congregation, and verbally, from the satirist. The worldly priest, although he fits all the conventions of the rich cleric, is shown to be performing his duties adequately. The scholar, straight from the schools, is really anxious not to reform the priest but only to engage him in a dispute in order to demonstrate his own logical tricks. Both the scholar's criticisms of the priest's preaching—significantly, for poor grammar rather than any errors of substance—and the priest's attacks on the scholar's learning raise serious questions about the value of studying the arts. The satirist seems to be impugning the abilities and the aspirations of those educated in the schools. Not only is the logician's learning of little practical use, he is also as guilty of simony as the priest, since he is seeking to profit from his knowledge. Nor are his morals any better. Indeed, the logician possesses none of the attributes of the ideal scholar, as articulated by the author of *In sublimi solio*. He has neither humility, simplicity, justice, nor chastity. His poverty is nothing but a pretense. As a parody of the poor scholar, the logician serves to show the risk posed by those who leave the schools, trained only in the arts and filled with pride and ambition, yet who pretentiously claim that they deserve advancement because of their learning and their superior morality. In this satirist's view, the scholars needed to reform their behavior no less than other clerics.

The logician in *Hora nona sabbati* is not the only scholar who gets bested in a confrontation. A similar story is told by Vital of Blois in the *Geta*, the earliest (c. 1150) and one of the most popular Latin comedies of the Middle Ages, about two scholars—or, perhaps, more accurately, of a scholar and his pretentious servant—who return home from the schools skilled in logical reasoning but completely lacking in common sense.[57] This hilarious satire is based on a classical Roman comedy, the *Amphitruo* of Plautus, in which Jupiter seduces Alcmena, the beautiful wife of the general Amphitryon, who is away at war, by disguising himself as Amphitryon and Mercury as the general's servant Geta. Vital uses essentially the same plot but changes both the identities of some of the characters and the ending in order to turn the story into a satire of the schools. In the

Geta, Amphitryon becomes a scholar away studying logic in Athens (i.e., Paris). And, whereas the general in Plautus's comedy eventually realizes what has happened in his absence, Vital's Amphitryon is completely deceived by both Jupiter and his adulterous wife. At the conclusion of the comedy, Alcmena, disrobed and disheveled, convinces Amphitryon that she had not slept with anyone else, but had been in bed dreaming of him. By having Amphitryon accept his wife's story, Vital of Blois makes the husband into a fool as well as a cuckold.

A still greater fool, however, is the servant Geta who, in Vital's comedy, replaces Amphitryon as the central character. Geta thinks of himself as a scholar and has ambitions to gain fame as a great logician. His thoughts as he walks along carrying his master's books are clearly intended to mock the complaints and the claims of the typical poor scholar:

> Woe, woe is me! It will take a long time to tell of what I endured in Athens. I was cold, always hungry and thirsty; I slept little and ate horrible food. My master managed to survive on second-quality bread and what I ate was barely even fourth-quality. But as a reward for my troubles, I carry home wonderful sophisms and can even prove that a man is an ass! While the other servants hand me plates, dishes, and utensils in the kitchen, I will prove that some men are asses and other are oxen. I am a logician. I can make them any animal whatsoever! [58]

Geta dreams that his learning will bring him fame and prestige in the kitchen. "Dicor Geta magister," he boasts.[59]

Not unexpectedly, Geta's learning thoroughly fails him when he arrives home to find Mercury disguised to look like him. He first tries to use logic to explain how there could be two Getas. When his foolish syllogizing gets him nowhere, Geta asks Mercury to describe himself and his character. The intimate and lewd description the disguised Mercury gives convinces the dumb servant that Mercury must, in fact, be he. "You are I, and I am nothing," Geta exclaims as he wanders off defeated, but still hoping that his education will help him resolve the dilemma of his identity. His ruminations parody the arguments of dialecticians:

> Woe, woe is me! Woe is me, who I was; now somehow I have become nothing! Geta, who can you be? You are a man. No, by Hercules, for what man is Geta unless he is Geta? I am Plato. Perhaps the arts have made me Plato. I am not Geta and cannot be called Geta; if I am not Geta, I ought not to be called Geta. I was called Geta? What will be my name? There will be no name, since I am nothing. Alas, I am nothing.[60]

Only after becoming completely confused and discouraged does Geta stop his syllogizing and confess that dialectic has made him insane. Finally, when he meets up with Amphitryon, Geta recovers his identity.

"By Hercules," he says when his master calls him by name, "I am Geta, since he has called me Geta."[61] Common sense again proves far more valuable and trustworthy than logical reasoning.

Geta, the foolish servant, is a clever mockery of the familiar figure of the scholar returning from the schools with loud complaints about the hard life of scholarship, exalted claims for his learning, and obvious contempt for those less learned. It is through the character of another servant, the rude and unlearned Birria, however, that Vital of Blois expresses the major lesson of his satire. Seeing the foolish predicaments into which logic has got his master and Geta, Birria is thankful that he has stayed in the kitchen and not gone to the schools. "Greece received these men sane and sent them away crazy," he says. "Dialectic does make men insane. Birria, remember to have nothing to do with that art, which lacks any good and, through its reasoning, makes men either asses or nothing at all. Let anyone be a logician. You, Birria, always be a man. Study may please them; a good meal is all you want."[62]

That the simple, uneducated Birria speaks for common sense and sound reason adds force to Vital's attack on dialectic and on the schools where it was being taught. Not just trying to amuse, Vital of Blois was writing as a representative of the masters of the schools of the Loire Valley who were still teaching the traditional arts curriculum, strong in grammar and classical literature, and who viewed the Parisian craze for dialectic with alarm and contempt.[63] Geta's logical tangles are a mocking imitation of the same arguments that John of Salisbury criticizes. But Vital of Blois is uncompromising in his opposition to logic. The complete deception of Amphitryon and the utter confusion of Geta ridicule the idea that the dialectic taught in Paris could be of any practical value whatsoever. As an ardent defender of the traditional literary studies of Blois and Orléans, Vital reveals his educational convictions clearly by making the ignorance of Birria so obviously preferable to the insanity of Geta.

SATIRISTS OF THE SCHOOLS OF PARIS: JOHN OF HAUTEVILLE AND NIGEL WIREKER

Enough examples have been cited to demonstrate that the satirists criticized the schools as forcefully as the rest of their society. Scholars certainly got their share of the blame for the decline of learning. In this rich tradition of satire about the schools, two major works remain to be discussed, the *Architrenius* of John of Hauteville and the *Speculum stultorum* of Nigel Wireker. Each of these works includes a visit to Paris in its survey of the institutions of contemporary society. Neither the visit of John's young man nor of Nigel's old ass provides a very complimentary view of the state of the schools. Paris, as described in these satires, suffers from many of the same corruptions and vices that plague the rest of society. The unfortunate experiences of both the Archmourner and Brunellus in the city's schools vividly exemplify the disappointment felt by many critics over the failure of education to serve either personal or social needs.

Little is known about John of Hauteville, the author of the *Architrenius*, or *Archmourner*, but his satire can be precisely dated. The long and often obscure work was sent to Walter of Coutances on the occasion of his transfer from the bishopric of Lincoln to the archbishopric of Rouen, in 1184.[64] After a lengthy introduction moralizing about the vice of sloth, John tells the story of a young man weeping over his misspent youth and setting out to find the path of virtue. Sure that Lady Nature will remedy his grief, if he can but find his way to her, the Archmourner travels through a landscape filled with various temptations and obstacles. Before reaching Paris, he successfully avoids being diverted by the Palace of Venus and the House of Gluttony. But he does delay his journey to stay in Paris, hoping that the city's great learning will help him on his way and give him respite from his grief. Instead, he finds nothing but misery.

Book 3 of the *Architrenius* gives a lengthy description of the miserable lives of Paris scholars.[65] The Archmourner finds conditions in the schools to be wretched. Scholars are poor, ill fed, and meanly clothed, live in awful rooms, and have the vilest servants. Most work all day and night diligently studying the arts with little prospect of reward. Haunted by their studies, they are unable to sleep at night and, although still exhausted, rise well before dawn to return to their books. A few "soldiers of Venus" do miss sleep for other reasons. But for the most part, the Archmourner finds Paris to be populated by "followers and soldiers of Phoebus" who, despite their unrelenting diligence, are treated rudely by their masters and gain no advantage from their education. "The rewards Davus received," John laments, "Homer merited."[66]

John blames this sad state of affairs on both internal and external factors. While he attacks masters especially harshly for their excessive pride and vanity, John also complains that if these masters exemplified the ideal qualities of the philosopher—modesty, serenity, and humility—they would be even less likely to gain the favor of the rich and powerful. His bitter words against "superficial philosophers" who "grasp only the name and shadow of Minerva and, only tasting wisdom, think they are filled"[67] echo John of Salisbury's complaints against the Cornificians. Like so many other critics, John of Hauteville tells how the poor learning, bad morals, and arrogance of a few masters make matters worse for all the others. Rich patrons do not escape the blame for filling their courts with minstrels and entertainers instead of the learned. But his description of conditions in Paris suggest that he holds unqualified and immoral masters far more responsible for the decline of learning.

Disappointed by his experience in Paris, the Archmourner moves on along the path followed by many upon leaving the schools. He comes first to the Mount of Ambition, symbolizing the life of the courtier. Court life is superficially attractive, but he finds the vices and manners of the courtiers competing for favor so shocking that he quickly leaves. The next stop is the Hill of Presumption, the tallest peak on the landscape and a place densely populated by men from every social order. Prominent among them are ambitious young scholars boasting the title of master.[68] Ever more grieved by the corruption he finds on his journey, the Archmourner is finally overwhelmed when he meets the monster Cupidity, who is accompanied by a vast army of avaricious prelates, and gets caught in the middle of a raging battle between prodigals and misers. Miraculously rescued from that horrible conflict, he is transported to the distant and peaceful land of Thule where, like Golias in the first vision of the *Apocalypsis*, he finds the ancient philosophers declaiming against the many vices of mankind. Their words add to his sorrow but also give him the wisdom he needs to find his way to Lady Nature. Before allowing him to relate his grief, Lady Nature lectures the Archmourner on natural philosophy. Then she provides him with a remedy for his grief and a protection against every vice by giving him the virgin Moderation to be his bride. Once the marriage is solemnized, the Archmourner is finally ready for the virtuous life.

There is little either very new or original about John of Hauteville's description of the state of society. The Archmourner's visit to Paris merely adds some colorful detail to the familiar accounts of the poor, hard life of the scholar. However, although there are precedents for much of what he says about the decline of learning, John is the only satirist who makes so explicit a connection between the pretensions of the learned and the lack of rewards offered to them. His obscure verse and allegories make it difficult to discern his solution to the problem. That the Archmourner hears the ancient philosophers and receives a lecture on natural philosophy before being married to Moderation is apparently meant to suggest the value of a sound education in the liberal arts as preparation for the virtuous life.[69]

The *Speculum stultorum*, or *Mirror for Fools*, of Nigel Wireker is less obscure and better known than the *Architrenius*. Written about the same time, the *Speculum stultorum* tells the adventures of Brunellus, an aging ass with monstrous ears, who journeys in search of a longer tail.[70] At the start of his travels, Brunellus experiences a series of unfortunate mishaps. First he is deceived by a physician called Galen who, after unsuccessfully warning him of the foolishness of his quest, writes a prescription that is guaranteed to lengthen his tail and sends the happy Brunellus to Salerno to get it filled. Next he is cheated by an English merchant who sells him ten jars of waste that supposedly contain the drug prescribed by Galen. Then a worldly Cistercian monk sets a pack of dogs on Brunellus for trespassing on monastic lands. As a result, all his bottles are broken and half of his tail is bitten off. Instead of learning from his misfortunes and returning home, Brunellus decides that an education will suit his ambitions quite as well as a longer tail, and he sets off for Paris.

The foolishness of this decision is made clear from the start. Brunellus himself recognizes that it is his nature, as an ass, to remain stupid and also that some might consider him far too old to begin his studies. Still, he insists he is not yet one hundred, and attending school at such an age can have its advantages. He will be better able than the young to bear long nights of study and to withstand the blows of his masters, as well as less likely to be distracted from his studies by love.[71] All this foolish rationalizing serves to remind the reader of the common view that it is impossible to learn when old. "Just as an old horse or ass cannot be taught to trot," Jacques of Vitry advises in one of his sermons, "so you cannot be taught in old age what you did not learn in your youth."[72] But Brunellus is intent upon a full course of study: ten years learning the arts in Paris, followed by training in both canon and civil law at Bologna, and finally some instruction in theology. And the foolish ass dreams of returning home after these years of study with the proud title of master, to revel in the fame and honor that learning can bring in the farmyard.[73] Brunellus is meant to be a complete parody of the ambitious scholar. It is hardly surprising, then, that his experience in Paris turns out to be much less successful than Brunellus had hoped.

When he reaches Paris, Brunellus chooses to associate with the English students because he likes their good manners, charming speech and appearance, keen minds, and good judgment. But most appealing of all are their generosity, good food, and unrestrained drinking. The English, he finds, are completely praiseworthy save for the three vices of "washeyl," "drinkheyl," and whoring. And these, he decides, are not necessarily bad, because "the first two are banishers of grief and make way for happiness [and] the third prevents the passion that France is said to be full of from doing harm."[74] Enjoying the good company of the English, Brunellus spends seven years studying grammar. Despite all his efforts and the threats and brutality of his masters, he learns nothing nore than the words *hee haw*. Finally, he realizes that all the time and money he has expended on his education have been of no use whatsoever. "What madness drove me to Paris and its schools?" he laments. "I have learned little and forgotten everything I knew before."[75] Still, he remains hopeful that even a little knowledge will bring him fame and fortune. Confident that he will be able to remember at least one or two French (not Latin) words when he gets home, Brunellus bids farewell to his friends and leaves Paris now dreaming of the day when he will be made a bishop.

Only after he leaves Paris for Italy does Brunellus realize how much he has forgotten. When he stops on a hill just outside Paris—is it Mont Ste. Geneviève?—he turns around and cannot even remember the name of the city he has just left. He thinks for a while that it must be Rome. But soon, realizing he has not traveled that far, he despairs over his ignorance. How will he be able to boast of his learning if he cannot remember where he has been? The ruminations of Brunellus mock the boasts of scholars:

> If I go home now, and my parents ask
>   Where I have studied, how shall I explain?
> Perhaps they'll say I'm worthless and have failed
>   To learn a thing, but wasted all their means.
> So I'll go back and learn the name I've lost,
>   Lest I'll be called a fool when I get home.
> It will be something just to name the towns
>   And to pretend I've studied in their schools.
> But if I cannot even give the names,
>   Not one thing which I say will they believe.[76]

Brunellus is luckily saved from having to return to Paris when he meets a peasant, who asks the foolish old ass sarcastically whether he is going to Paris to learn or to teach. Reminded of the name of the city, Brunellus then vows not to speak another word for the fifteen days it will take him to complete his journey home. He will keep *Paris* alone on his lips. All goes well until the thirteenth day, when he meets a pilgrim making his way to Rome. The pilgrim's recital of the *Pater noster* drives the word *Paris* from Brunellus's mind; he can remember only the first syllable, *Pa*. After much despair, Brunellus decides that knowing just one syllable is quite enough learning and comes up with excellent excuses for his ignorance:

> If from the seven arts one syllable
>   Is left, I deem it not a small thing.
> And as instruction often makes men err,
>   It also causes them to be puffed up.

Lest knowledge of a letter bring me ruin,
 One syllable's enough for me, no more.
Sometimes superior training breeds disgust,
 And learning makes men's characters austere.
More often nature serves you better in
 A few things, and more strongly shows her power.
Those satisfied with just a letter gain
 Thereby, while constant care disturbs the mind.
To be informed of many things but nothing well
 No honor but a burden surely is.
A little many know of many things,
 Yet on the whole appear quite ignorant.
To know is hard, and also to retain:
 To learn is hard, and so it is to teach.
And I am all the more disturbed because
 No discipline can teach there is no death.[77]

These confused and senseless ruminations about the vanity of too much knowledge are certainly meant as a parody of the arguments of those who criticized the schools and the liberal arts. Indeed, the intended target may well be the Cistercians, upon whom Nigel Wireker heaps much scorn later on. It is certainly significant, too, that Brunellus next abruptly decides to give up his plans for an education and enter a monastery. Having failed to become learned, the old ass will try the religious life.

The sudden conversion of Brunellus is clearly intended to raise suspicions about monastic opposition to the schools. The reason he gives for choosing to become a monk was one often professed by those who entered the cloister after years in the schools. "To redeem my youthful years," he says, "it's right that I now should seek to save my life."[78] But the claim that he is trying to make amends for his misspent youth is hardly supported by the difficulties he has in deciding just which order to join. Surveying the options, Brunellus finds some orders (including the Cistercians) too lax, others too strict, and none quite to his liking. So he decides to become a reformer and to start a new order that combines the best of each: his monks will ride fine horses like the Templars, eat meat like the Cluniacs, take Mass only once a month like the Carthusians, wear luxurious tunics like the Premonstratensians, sleep without breeches like the Cistercians, and so on.[79] Pleased, Brunellus sets off for Rome to gain papal approval for his new rule. Nigel Wireker was obviously no less concerned about the vices and novelties widespread among monks than about those found among scholars.

The remainder of Brunellus's journey can be quickly summarized. On his way to Rome, he again meets the physician Galen, to whom he recounts the misfortunes he has suffered during the ten years since their first encounter. Brunellus criticizes every part of society, from the papal curia and kings to the entire laity. This long invective against the evils of the world is his last speech. Hardly has he finished when his former master, Bernard, appears to reclaim Brunellus after many years. As a warning to him, Bernard cuts off both his ears, mounts him, and rides the old ass all the way home to Cremona. The journey ends with Brunellus gaining not fame and fortune but humiliation and misery.

The *Speculum stultorum* is a funny and entertaining tale. But its author intended it to be understood also as a serious moral tract on the foibles of the day. In both the prologue and the epilogue, Wireker advises readers to search for the deeper meaning of the story of Brunellus and heed the "moral lesson" (*exemplum morum*) there. "Happy is the man," he writes, in words that echo Abelard's autobiographical letter of consolation, "who through the calamities of others is made cautious and is ruled by reason."[80] The lessons to be drawn from the calamities of Brunellus are hardly obscure, but Nigel took care to explain them fully in a letter of dedication sent with the presentation copy of *Speculum stultorum* to William Longchamp, bishop of Ely. Brunellus, he writes, represents "a monk or any religious person who lives in a monastery and who, like an ass, is obliged to bear heavy burdens in the service of the Lord." His search for a new tail stands for the ambitions these men have to become priors and abbots and to have lots of followers who "will proudly tail behind him wherever he goes."[81]

But monks are not the sole targets of his satire, as Wireker makes clear in explaining the significance of the time that Brunellus spends in Paris:

> Likewise, the ass who attends the schools of Paris but only wastes his time and money on the study of literature . . . signifies those who do not have minds trained or even capable of learning the letters of the alphabet, and yet show their learning both in the Old and New Testaments, read books they do not understand, and forget their titles as soon as they put them aside. They wish to be considered well educated by their diligent perusal of books rather than to know anything in the true sense of the word. These men seem to be educated until they betray themselves by their speech; and their learning, long hidden, appears as it really is. And yet it is most disgraceful and ridiculous for anyone not to blush to admit that he knows nothing at all when the truth of the matter is brought out. But there are many hypocrites today, and there is hardly a profession or order in the entire world where some hypocrisy is not found. Indeed, those in the schools make a pretense of knowing what they do not know. And those in religious orders wish to appear to be what they are not.[82]

For Nigel Wireker, excessive ambition, pretense, and hypocrisy are universal vices. They corrupt the schools no more or less than they do all the other institutions of society. Education is to be blamed, but it is still only one of the means abused by those seeking to gain fame and fortune.

In his other major satirical work, the prose *Tractatus contra curiales et officiales clericos*, written some twelve years after the *Speculum stultorum*, Nigel Wireker criticizes the schools directly for failing to meet the needs of the Church and society.[83] Again Paris is the object of his satire. With bitter irony he tells what happens when the pampered sons of the rich and powerful, who already have the income of several nonresident prebends and are also assured of further rewards through simony and nepotism, are sent to Paris to study. Not wanting to exhaust themselves or to reduce the time available for gentlemanly games, these students diligently avoid all serious and demanding subjects. Fortunately for them, there are numerous masters willing to allow such behavior and to write glowing reports home because they want to court the favor of these students and their parents. These students leave Paris at last having acquired more in the way of pretensions than useful knowledge of grammar or logic. Moreover, never having been taught the virtues of a good life, they are wholly devoted to vanity and luxury. But this in no way impedes the success of their careers. After a few years spent mainly in hawking and hunting, they become bishops, and all the Church is made to suffer for their ignorance and immorality.

Paris does not bear all the blame for poor education, however. Worse yet, according to Nigel Wireker, are conditions in Montpellier and Bologna. Young men who might have studied the liberal arts in Paris are increasingly attracted to Montpellier to study medicine, which has become a more certain path to fame and fortune in the service of the rich. Meanwhile, many scholars in Paris are giving up the liberal arts and rushing off to Bologna to study law because they envy the wealth of the physicians. At Bologna they then learn an obscure and multisyllabic language that enables them to manipulate the law to their material advantage. As a result, the legal situation has become so complicated that neither princes nor prelates think they can survive without the services of lawyers.[84]

Despite the vehemence of his attacks on physicians and lawyers, Nigel Wireker places the root of the educational problem elsewhere, in the excessive concern of the clergy and prelacy for secular, rather than spiritual, matters. Appointment and advancement too often depend on criteria other than learning and worthiness. With particular indignation, Wireker writes of bishops willing to ordain as priests men as ignorant as a "country bumpkin" (*rusticum laicum*).[85] His harsh criticisms of "the thoroughly uneducated and illiterate, who are clerics in title alone," make clear his strong belief in the importance of learning.[86] A cleric who cannot read is, in his view, no better than a soldier who cannot fight. It is possible to get a sound education at Paris and even at Bologna, but not enough clerics are willing to devote their time to study:

Such is the state of the clergy of our time that, while a few spend a very long time in Paris or Bologna or some other place devoted most lovingly and productively to the study of letters—and their devotion should be greatly commended—others are contemptuous of applying their minds to the study of letters, but search for other activities and are even willing to stick their hands in the deepest mud for a modest stipend. So much is the dignity of the clerical office debased today . . . that you will more easily find a ploughman than a priest skilled in his art, more quickly an industrious shepherd than a learned cleric.[87]

According to Wireker, prelates are no better educated, and the consequences of their ignorance are even more serious. Without a sound knowledge of Scripture, how can a bishop fulfill his essential duties of hearing confession and giving penance, preaching, setting a good example, defending the Church against evil princes, and providing justice in the cases that come before him? Above all, asks Wireker, "how will he be able to teach what he never learned?"[88] As long as most bishops are not properly educated, the prospects for the improvement of the rest of the clergy are poor. Still, Wireker concludes, many continue to excuse bishops from their spiritual and educational responsibilities on the grounds that their more important duties are to attend to public affairs, to manage estates and finances, and to serve kings, matters that require little formal education and no knowledge of Scripture. Under the circumstances, what hope could there be for reform or for a renewed commitment to learning? The *Tractatus* is not an optimistic work.

Like many other satirists who wrote so vehemently about the poor state of learning, Nigel Wireker was expressing the bitter disappointment of his own career. As a young man he had studied in Paris and, having acquired the title "master," on which he would subsequently pile such abuse, he had entered the service of Archbishop Thomas Becket. After Becket's murder and the dispersal of his learned court, Wireker's ambitions seem to have diminished. Converting to the monastic life, he entered the Benedictine community at Christ Church, where he remained until his death sometime before 1200.[89] Although his career took a different path from others who had been in Paris and also had gone into court service in England, such as Walter of Châtillon and John of Salisbury, Wireker's satires reflect many of the same educational attitudes. He complained from within the monastery about increasing specialization and professionalism and was saddened to see the schools corrupted by avarice and ambition as the rest of society.

As critical as he could be about conditions in the schools of Paris, however, Nigel Wireker's sympathies were clearly with those who studied diligently only to see sharp-talking lawyers, illiterate courtiers, and the lazy children of the rich and powerful receiving the benefices and positions that the learned deserved. Much like Walter of Châtillon, Wireker seemed to believe that the value of education would soon be realized if men trained in the arts and theology, rather than in law and medicine, gained advancement. That they did not was partly the fault of the schools and scholars themselves. Just as Brunellus had been put back into the service of his master, the schools would again have to serve society. But Nigel Wireker does not suggest how this change could be brought about. As a satirist, he was fulfilling his responsibility in pointing out society's problems; he left it to others to try to solve them.

THE PURPOSE OF SATIRE

The satirists of the twelfth century have often been misunderstood. They have been depicted either as rebels radically alienated from society and intent upon undermining established institutions and ideas or as amoral, even hedonistic, entertainers who wrote only to please or amuse their wealthy, and often remarkably tolerant, patrons.[90] With the probable exception of the Archpoet, the satirists who lamented the decline of learning were neither. Serious critics of society, they were conservative, rather than radical, in their basic attitudes. They looked back to a golden age when humane learning was valued and men like them, trained only in the liberal arts, had been rewarded with secure positions in society. All had attended the schools, most in Paris, at least for a time. Many were young scholars, often from modest backgrounds and diligent in their studies, who were genuinely concerned about the limited opportunities that awaited them when they left the schools. Others had completed their studies years before and were disappointed that their careers had not advanced as far as they had hoped. Usually no less critical of the schools than of the rest of society, these older satirists could be especially harsh in their attacks on the pretensions and ambitions of the younger generations of scholars.

But although their experiences differed, these satirists all saw themselves as defenders of learning. Satire was their common weapon against powerful adversaries—the well-born and successful, worldly prelates, monastic opponents of the secular arts, and, especially later in the century, lawyers and physicians—as well as against the growing corruption that was undermining the value of education. Lacking power and influence, and unsure that their voices would be heard, they resorted to the traditional tactics of the satirist: wit, mockery, irony, a fair amount of obscenity, and lots of exaggeration. Their rebellion lay only in their choice of literary style and satirical conventions, not in their ideas or values. While they were often writing to entertain and to gain the support of patrons, their humor and apparent frivolity were also intended to put a serious moral point across in a pleasant fashion.

Nigel Wireker gives the most explicit explanation of the purpose of this satire. Brunellus, he tells William Longchamp, "desires to criticize in a jesting manner those things that he knew could never be eradicated by harsh rebuke. For it is true that many diseases respond more readily to healing medicines than to cauterization."[91] Several centuries later, Alexander Pope explained the function of satire in a slightly different way when he wrote, "Satire heals with morals what it hurts with wit." The twelfth-century satirists were certainly intent upon both hurting and healing. Their biting invective and ludicrous exaggerations were none other than desperate attempts to point out the urgency of reform.

One final example will show just how powerfully the tools of satire could be used to draw attention to the cause. An anonymous satirist, writing in the late twelfth century, gives full flight to his imagination in treating the theme of the decline of learning:

> Learning that flowered in days of yore
> In these our times is thought a bore.
> Once knowledge was a well to drink of;
> Now having fun is all men think of.
> Today mere striplings grow astute
> Before their beards begin to shoot—
> Striplings whose truant dispositions
> Are deaf to wisdom's admonitions.
> Yet it was true in ages past
> No scholar paused from toil at last
> Nor shrank from studies the most weighty
> Till his years numbered more than eighty.
> Now boys you'd think were barely ten
> Throw off the yoke and pose as men,
> Nay, even plume themselves as masters:
> Blind lead the blind to swift disasters.
> Our birds unfledged must now take wing,
> Our donkeys tune the lyre and sing,
> Bulls dance in hall, and herald's calling
> Is mocked by knaves at the plow-tail bawling.[92]

This ludicrous exaggeration goes on as the satirist tells of a world turned completely topsy-turvy, where everything once valued is now held in total contempt. Despite its apparent fun and the frivolity of its ridicule, the lesson of the poem is quite serious. The ridicule is aimed directly at young scholars who are overly anxious to become masters. As forcefully as possible, the satirist depicts the serious social dangers of such pretensions and ambitions. His purpose is to shock his contemporaries into realizing what to him was the obvious absurdity of a state of affairs in which such behavior was tolerated. The satire is a cry of protest against a situation the poet found intolerable but did not know how to change.

Writing about the anti-Roman satirists of the twelfth century, Richard Southern argued that their satire is intelligible as an unwilling tribute to the growing power of the papacy and that it actually implies both their acceptance of the inevitability of the situation and their lack of any constructive alternative.[93] The same point can be made of the satirical reaction to the schools. Concerned about the decline of learning, these satirists had little confidence that the situation either within or outside the schools would improve. They lamented the end of a golden age in the past and saw nothing but bleak prospects for themselves in the future. Did their satires have any effect? Any direct influence would be difficult to prove. But their protests may well have increased the general awareness of the need for action and influenced those in stronger positions to play a direct role in the regulation and reform of the schools.

FIVE

The Humanists

THE SAME COMPLAINTS about the decline of learning and the same yearnings for a past golden age found in the writings of the satirists also characterize those of the "humanist" critics of the schools.[1] Like the satirists, the humanists were graduates of the schools whose education had been primarily literary and philosophical, rather than theological or professional. Well trained in the liberal arts, especially in grammar, they could write Latin with ease and, often, with eloquence. Classical allusions, quotations, and examples embellish their works, proudly flaunted as signs of their erudition and as authority for their claims and criticisms. Against adversaries both inside and outside the schools, the humanists vehemently tried to defend the liberal arts as the essential basis of all learning and as the training most valuable in preparing one to lead a virtuous life. It was the trends of increasing specialization and professionalism that most alarmed the humanists. As critics of the schools, they wrote of how both the rise of dialectic to its position of dominance in the arts curriculum and the pressure to specialize in the lucrative subjects of law or medicine were undermining the foundations of humane learning. As critics of society, they bitterly complained of how the advancement of lawyers and professional courtiers, instead of men well trained in the liberal arts, was doing serious harm to public life.

Sharing the same worries as the satirists about the impact of specialization and professionalism on their own prospects, the humanists were generally no more optimistic about the possibility of reversing these trends. And as we shall see, it was especially in times of the greatest disappointment in their careers and frustrations about their futures that the humanists looked back nostalgically at the great masters, sound learning, and wise rulers of the past. Of all the critics, it is the humanists who best reveal in their writings how the attitudes expressed toward education came to be influenced by the difficulties graduates had in advancing their careers while trying to remain faithful to the moral principles and values they had been taught in the schools. Because so little is known about the lives of most of the satirists, we had to try to surmise from their verse how much of their complaining about the decline of learning and criticism of the schools was related to their personal experience. The humanists' letters and treatises provide more direct evidence of the relationship between the anxieties some learned men increasingly felt about their careers and the concerns they voiced about the state of education.

Among the humanists, three—John of Salisbury, Peter of Blois, and Gerald of Wales—serve as especially good illustrations of the frustrations such men suffered and expressed. Their writings, which span nearly three generations, also show the continuity of humane ideals about the nature and purpose of education throughout a period of rapid change both within and outside the schools. Despite their different reputations, the careers of the three men were similar in several respects. Each studied in Paris in the middle decades of the century. They were masters who, after no more than a short time teaching, left the schools for careers as civil servants. From then on they kept in touch with intellectual developments in the schools either directly, by visits when on diplomatic missions or when out of favor at court, or indirectly, by corresponding with scholars resident in Paris. They were, as one historian has written, "en marge des groupes scolaires."[2] Most of their lives were spent in the courts of England during the turbulent reigns of Henry II and his two sons, where and when there were plenty of opportunities for ambitious men to advance their careers, if sometimes at the cost of their principles. They all belonged to the expanding group of what Beryl Smalley has called "intellectuals in politics."[3] Each of them was, if in different ways, torn between the schools and the court, between learning and politics, or, in John of Salisbury's words, between "the footsteps of philosophers and the trifles of courtiers."

For John of Salisbury, the most learned and idealistic of the three, and probably also the one least ambitious for himself, the frustration came from the difficulty of balancing the pleasures of study, which for him was a lifelong pursuit, and the demands of service at court. Although his career was not without its share of disappointments, he was successful in the end at both. Peter of Blois and Gerald of Wales were different. Only as they became more frustrated in their ambitions, as the positions they sought eluded them, did they turn to philosophy, partly for some small consolation in—and for an explanation of—their failure, but also partly in the hope that a demonstration of their learning would finally bring them advancement. Yet although they differed in their motives for writing and in the kinds of works they composed, the three humanists shared a set of experiences and perceptions that made them similarly concerned about the declining value of the learning they had acquired and harshly critical of the conditions, both in the schools and in the courts, that they held accountable for this decline.

JOHN OF SALISBURY

John of Salisbury has long been recognized as one of the most learned men of the twelfth century and regarded as one of the most appealing. Of relatively humble origins, he was born at Old Sarum around 1115, received his early education from a local parish priest, and then, at about age twenty, followed the path of other young men eager for learning to Paris, where he spent twelve years (1136-48) in study. The detailed account John gives of his studies in the *Metalogicon* (2.10) has already been mentioned,[4] but it requires closer attention. If perhaps not typical of the curriculum followed by young men in the schools, it certainly was exemplary of the serious desire for learning that motivated some of them.

When John arrived in Paris he began his studies at the school on Mont Ste. Geneviève, where Peter Abelard was again teaching dialectic after his troublesome years at St. Gildas. Thus he had the chance to learn this art from the greatest dialectician of them all. After Abelard's departure—"too hasty," complains John—he continued his studies on the Mont under Master Alberic and Robert of Melun, neither of whom he found entirely satisfactory as a teacher.[5] Two years of dialectic were enough for John, and he turned to grammar, which he studied under William of Conches for three years.[6] Sometime before or soon after these years (John's account is vague), he sampled the teaching of other masters of the liberal arts, including Richard the Bishop, praised by John as a grammarian but also said to have taught the quadrivium; Hardewin the German, John's principal instructor for these four subjects; and Thierry of Chartres and Peter Helias, from whom John says he learned rhetoric.[7]

Meanwhile, John took on some pupils himself, induced, he writes, by his "pinched finances, the appeals of his colleagues, and the advice of his friends."[8] John emphasizes his own reluctance and the influence of others here perhaps to avoid the charge, which he himself elsewhere makes against others, of being too anxious to teach. His account mentions the name of only one of his students (William of Soissons) and suggests that when teaching, John may have somehow been associated with the school of his fellow Englishman Adam of Balsham, on the Petit Pont. After three years of part-time teaching, John returned to full-time studies under Gilbert of Poitiers, whose lectures on logic and theology he attended until the master left the schools to become bishop of Poitiers in 1142. John continued his theological studies under Robert Pullen, until this master was made cardinal in 1144, and finally under Simon of Poissy, whom he found to be dependable but not up to the standards of his other theology masters. It is significant that although John, according to his own account, spent more than six years studying theology in Paris—enough time, even by the strict statutes of 1215, to qualify him to teach the subject[9]—he never makes any claim to be a theologian.

When John left the schools to enter public service, his career began propitiously. Bernard of Clairvaux wrote a letter on his behalf to Theobald, archbishop of Canterbury, praising the worthiness both of John's life and of his learning.[10] Instead of returning immediately to England, however, John entered the service of Eugenius III, probably during the pope's visit to Paris in the spring of 1147, and possibly thanks to the patronage of his former master Robert Pullen, then the papal chancellor. Although his *Historia pontificalis* gives an account of events during the years he spent in papal service, the exact nature of John's own employment remains unclear.[11] Nor is it clear when or why he left the papal court.

By 1154 John had returned to England and was serving in the modest but demanding position of secretary to Theobald of Canterbury. In this capacity he composed much of the archbishop's correspondence and frequently represented him on diplomatic missions, including at least three to Rome between 1155 and 1159. Apparently as a consequence of his activities on the first of these missions, John incurred the displeasure of Henry II and was nearly forced into exile.[12] After a few months, however, he was well enough restored to royal favor to be able to continue in the archbishop's service. Although Theobald's illness considerably added to the burdens of John's position, he somehow managed to complete three major works—the *Policraticus*, the *Metalogicon*, and the verse *Entheticus de dogmate philosophorum*—during the years before the archbishop's death in April 1161. It was once thought that John wrote these works during the period of enforced leisure when he was in royal disfavor. But it is now agreed that he wrote them while very much preoccupied with what he calls "the trifles of court life."[13] All three are dedicated to John's friend, the royal chancellor Thomas Becket.

There is a defensive tone in the introduction to the *Policraticus*, where John describes his situation as a man of modest origins struggling to live virtuously. Thomas Becket, he writes, had once warned him that his lack of ambition suited him poorly for life at court. John heartily agrees. "I scorn," he asserts, "the aspirations of the courtiers, and they mine."[14] Why, then, did he, who had been trained for "a far different sphere" and who knew himself to be more fit for the ranks of the philosophers than for the guild of courtiers, continue at court, where he had already wasted twelve years? This autobiographical question is the key to understanding John's purpose in writing. The *Policraticus*, subtitled "concerning the frivolities of courtiers and the footsteps of the philosophers," is not about two alternative callings or careers but about the difficulties a learned man faces in trying to combine public service with the pursuit of truth. Although John of Salisbury often wrote disparagingly of court life, he never willingly chose to leave it, nor did he deny ever that he was both a philosopher and a courtier. Throughout his career his model remained the philosopher-statesman, Cicero. His purpose was to follow Cicero by showing in word and in deed that philosophical principles were not inconsistent with court duties but, rather, vital to the proper exercise of them. As a philosopher and as a courtier, John believed himself to be in an ideal position to write knowledgeably and critically about both careers. He left it to those who read his treatise to judge what to accept and reject in each.

The *Policraticus* was not intended to be a theoretical work on politics but a practical and didactic treatise on governing. Using as his model the traditional form of the "mirror for princes," John of Salisbury addressed the more modern problem of the functioning of a court bureaucracy.[15] His principal concern was not the nature of the state but the responsibility of the men who exercised political power and influence—or, rather, the habits and vices that prevented them from properly fulfilling this responsibility. Above all, John blamed the political misfortunes of his time on courtiers who were unwilling, because of their own ambitions, and unable, because of their lack of learning, to distinguish right from wrong or to offer good counsel to the princes whom they served. His treatise was to be a lesson to princes that the situation would improve only when these unworthy and unlearned courtiers were replaced by soundly educated and virtuous men.

The *Policraticus* is a complex and diffuse work. John, busy with the demands of his office, found it difficult to distill the vast amount of material he had collected both during his education in the schools and from his experience at court. His arguments are often quite difficult to follow as he compiles examples, drawn from both classical sources and his own observations, and then digresses at length on some matter only marginally related to his main theme. Most of the work (Books 1-6 and 8) is a critical review of the private lives and public misdeeds of princes and courtiers. John satirizes every aspect of the behavior of the ruling elite of his time, from the frivolous pastimes of hunting, gaming, and listening to minstrels and actors to the excessive credence given in court circles to omens, portents, dreams, and astrology. But above all, John describes the court as a place where flattery alone wins favor and where the Epicurean delights of wealth, power, vanity, and lust are thought to be the only virtues.[16] No longer was it a place where a philosopher willing to speak the truth and to act for the public good was welcome. As a result, justice could be bought and sold, rulers were repeatedly counseled to act foolishly, and tyranny was advancing at the expense of liberty.

It is in Book 7 of the *Policraticus* that John of Salisbury turns his attention from the court directly to the schools. There he sees many of the same problems. Like courtiers, scholars have been blinded by their ambitions. Seeking to advance their careers, they no longer care to learn or teach the subjects that would best serve the needs and interests of society. As a result, scholars, who ought to be getting or providing a sound training in philosophy, have become no more accustomed than courtiers to following in the "footsteps of philosophers."

The fault, John concedes, is not completely theirs. As he explains in the opening chapters of Book 7, the ancient philosophers did not leave an easily identifiable or a completely satisfactory set of footsteps to follow. The heritage of philosophy does not consist of a single, undisputed definition of the good and a certain path of virtue but of several philosophical sects, each with a different idea of how to live well. Although all these sects did attempt to define and to seek the true good, some of them—in particular the Epicureans and Stoics—went dangerously astray because of their pride or rashness. Still, John insists, there is nothing wrong in examining the doctrines of any or all of the philosophical sects, but only "until, as a result of a comparison of views, the truth shines out as though from the clash of ideas."[17] Then one must wisely choose to follow the most virtuous path. Among the sects, John's personal preference was for the Academicians like Cicero who based their search for the truth on probable reason and did not try to resolve insoluble metaphysical questions. A philosophy that is essentially practical rather than speculative in orientation is the one best suited to serve the pressing needs of public life.[18]

Nevertheless, according to John, the mistake being made by scholars has less to do with which particular sects they choose to follow than with the general approach they take to the study of philosophy. Rather than carefully searching for truth by systematically examining the opinions of the ancient philosophers, they are selecting doctrines and models of conduct on the basis of whim alone. The primary blame belongs to the masters, whose excessive verbosity and useless disputations deceive rather than assist students in their search for truth. Some masters fail because they are too specialized and teach only one art. Others are no more successful in trying to teach a broad range of the arts. Whether specialists or generalists, most masters are merely trying to disguise their lack of true philosophical knowledge. Of the two, John believes that the generalists are, on the whole, more devoted to learning than the specialists but are still no more likely to make proper use of what they have learned.

There is more involved, then, in following in the philosophers' footsteps than choosing the right subjects to study. No less essential is how and why they are studied. This brings us to the key principle of John of Salisbury's educational thought. "Everything should be read," he writes, "in order that some of it, when completed, should be neglected, some condemned, and some of it studied only in passing so that it not be completely unknown. But above all, the greatest diligence must be applied to those things that train one for political life, by teaching either civil law or ethical principles, or to those things that attend to the health of the body or soul."[19] The advice to learn all echoes Hugh of St. Victor. But for John the true measure of all learning was whether it could be applied to improve public life. The obligation of the schools was to offer the broad philosophical training that would make such learning possible.

The *Policraticus*, unlike the *Metalogicon*, does not recommend a specific course of study; rather, it establishes more general guidelines for determining the value of what one studies. Here, John's primary concern is not to prescribe particular subjects, authors, or methods but to defend the practical usefulness of studying pagan philosophers. According to John, it is incumbent upon the Christian scholar to search for wisdom wherever it can be found, to read widely and critically in the works of pagan philosophers, and to make use of those ideas that conform to Christian revelation and that reinforce the virtues taught by the Bible and the Fathers. Reading only Christian writers may be, he admits, a safer and more cautious means of edification, but also studying the pagan authors, though potentially dangerous for the simple, can be very useful to the prudent reader who can be discriminating in his choice of examples.[20]

This idea of critical selectivity, however, is only his preliminary argument. John also defends the value of the study of philosophy in another way, one that sets an even higher standard or purpose. All true philosophy, which is by definition concerned with the pursuit of wisdom, must have as its goal the love for God, which, according to Christian teaching, can be fulfilled only in charity. Those writings that teach honesty, modesty, sobriety, and other virtues that serve to advance charity are true philosophy and are to be studied. On the other hand, writings that do not teach such virtues contain not philosophical truths but useless fables and inventions, and are to be ignored. Still, more is required than simply the ability to discriminate between the two. If one truly wants to follow the philosophers, John concludes, one must not only learn or teach these virtues, one must also practice them.[21]

This is how, ideally, philosophy should be studied and taught. It is not happening, he argues, because masters have become no more than "vain imitators of philosophers," unwilling to search for wisdom and unable to teach virtue. Fearful of betraying their ignorance, these masters seek only to appear wise by endlessly debating trivial questions in intentionally obscure language. So bad have conditions become that when a teacher has managed to make his lectures completely incomprehensible, he is almost certain to be regarded as a preeminent philosopher. One needs little learning to be a success, just the ability to ridicule, invent, and deceive. The more you talk the more learned you seem. These descriptions of the arrogance of masters are drawn as much from the satires of Juvenal as from John's own observations of the schools.[22] He gives little practical advice about how teaching could be improved. That is left for the *Metalogicon*. In the *Policraticus*, John's tools are parody and mockery.

A capable satirist, John cannot resist mimicking a scholastic debate in which ludicrous objections, irrelevant analogies, bombast, and ad hominem attacks are the means of proving a point. This leaves him open to the same criticism he makes of others—the important questions get obscured in a flood of words and examples. Amidst all this, however, John does make one important point about method, a point not found elsewhere in his writings but frequently made by other critics. Whereas in interpreting the Bible, he argues, one must penetrate to the deeper mysteries hidden behind the written word, when reading the philosophers one need only expound the literal sense. Those masters of the liberal arts who are unable to teach the meaning of these texts clearly and simply are either unqualified to teach or deliberately trying to retain their students for longer than necessary.[23]

There is little original in John of Salisbury's list of the personal qualities and physical conditions most conducive to philosophical training. His six keys of learning are identical to those discussed by Hugh of St. Victor—a humble mind, eagerness to inquire, a quiet life, silent scrutiny, poverty, and exile. Their common source, we learn from John, is Bernard of

Chartres.[24] But John's discussion of the six keys is a disappointment. Rather than using concrete examples from his own observations, he characteristically illustrates each quality with a full array of literary citations drawn from both classical and patristic sources. The effect is to make these ideals seem even more remote from actual learning conditions in the urban schools. John does add a seventh key: love and respect for one's teacher. But as appropriate and commendable a quality for students as this might be, its inspiration too comes from a literary source, not John's own perceptions of what was lacking in the schools.[25]

Book 7 of the *Policraticus* concludes with John of Salisbury directly examining why those in the schools have wandered so far from the footsteps of the ancient philosophers. In the past, John explains, all philosophers, of whatever sect, sought the highest good and were willing to endure all the necessary hardships in pursuit of wisdom. But today few are willing to do the same. The pervasive desire for immediate material gratification makes wisdom impossible:

> Who, indeed, studies philosophy in order that he may become wise? You will see many, if not actually pursuing philosophy, nevertheless imitating the philosophers in order to be wealthy and prosper in worldly goods. . . . Do not fear that someone should leave his native land and embrace poverty willingly in order to study, for philosophy is regarded as useless labor unless it attains the fruit of opulence. Curiosity motivates some to learn; vanity stimulated by pride motivates others to study in order that they might appear to be learned; the desire for profit inflames others. Rare is he who seeks the ways of wisdom with the feet of charity and humility in order that he might be taught and might teach. Everything is done for worldly pleasures or useless trifles. . . . Philosophy, meanwhile, is the chosen way for only a few, since other ways appear to be much more profitable. For as the saying goes, "The love of genius never made anyone rich."[26]

Blaming the decline of learning on the unworthy motives of curiosity, vanity, and desire for wealth (cupidity) is another commonplace theme of the critics of the schools, derived ultimately from Bernard of Clairvaux. And John's treatment of curiosity and vanity differs very little from Bernard's. What does differ is his assessment of the effects of cupidity on learning.

According to John of Salisbury, cupidity, far from offering an incentive to study, was becoming a disincentive, as it was increasingly obvious that there were more certain and less arduous ways of acquiring wealth than imitating the philosophers. Few still expected that attending the schools would bring them material rewards; service at court was now favored as a surer means to wealth. In this way, "the frivolities of the courtiers" had actually become an alternative and a rival to "the footsteps of the philosophers." Rather than recognizing the value of philosophy, most courtiers, blinded by their ambition and avarice, regarded learning as useless and had little but contempt for those who struggled in its pursuit. To John, this attitude was both a personal challenge and a social danger. All he could do was hope that the few enlightened men still at court, like Thomas Becket, would be inspired by the lessons of the *Policraticus* to use their influence on rulers to improve the situation.

The *Metalogicon* differs significantly from the *Policraticus* both in tone and in content. Though John drafted many parts of the two works concurrently, and though he completed the *Metalogicon* no more than a few months after the *Policraticus*, sending them both together to Thomas Becket, the *Metalogicon* seems to reflect John's mounting worry about the worsening tensions at court and the distressing course of political events.[27] Increasingly alienated from court life and burdened by administrative duties, he apparently found the opportunity to write about education and to reminisce about his more pleasant years in the schools a welcome relief from the larger political concerns that were so much more beyond his control or influence. Although John's fame rests much more on the political ideas found in the *Policraticus*, it is the *Metalogicon*'s discussion of the principles and methods of a sound education that better reveals his abilities as a critical observer and a systematic thinker. Education, as we have seen, was a subject that John considered of political importance. It was also a subject about which, he seems to have realized, concrete advice was both easier to offer and more likely to be heeded.

Like the *Didascalicon* of Hugh of St. Victor, to which it has often been compared, the *Metalogicon* was intended as a practical treatise offering guidance on both what and how to study.[28] Although similar in purpose, however, the two works differ considerably in scope. Whereas the *Didascalicon* attempts to survey all branches of learning, the *Metalogicon*, as a defense of logic, is concerned only with the first part of the liberal arts, the trivium. In principle, John of Salisbury was probably no more sympathetic to specialization than Hugh of St. Victor had been. But the difference in their two works is an indication that John, despite his own broad training in the liberal arts, was apparently willing to accept the practical necessity of some specialization.

The *Metalogicon* explicitly recognizes the preeminent place occupied by the logical arts in the expanding schools of the mid-twelfth century. The trivium had always been studied first, and for some time dialectic itself had dominated the arts curriculum. The recovery of previously unknown Aristotelian logical treatises—the *Prior* and *Posterior Analytics*, the *Topics*, and the *Sophistical Refutations*—and the introduction of this

"New Logic" into the schools were now transforming the way dialectic was being taught. The challenge taken up by John was to defend both this New Logic and the old trivium. As their defender, he believed that he was fighting against educational attitudes and trends that threatened not only the schools but society as a whole.

The threats again came from those in the schools who were excessively concerned about their own careers. According to John, these men were not only refusing to take the time necessary to study the trivium but also justifying their action with claims that were both false and dangerous. Their essential argument was that since the logical arts do no more than teach the rules of speech, and speech is a natural faculty, there is no reason to study them. For John, much more was at stake than the trivium's importance in the arts curriculum. Even if used merely as an excuse by scholars seeking to shorten their course of studies for more practical reasons, the argument had to be taken seriously and refuted thoroughly because of its serious social repercussions.

Calling the principal proponent of this position by the name of the malicious detractor of Virgil, John forcefully states what he believes to be the dangers of "Our Cornificius":

> Although he may seem to attack eloquence alone, he undermines and uproots all liberal studies, assails the whole structure of philosophy, tears to shreds humanity's social contract, and destroys the means of brotherly charity and reciprocal interchange of services. Deprived of their gift of speech, men would degenerate to the condition of brute animals, and cities would seem like corrals for livestock, rather than communities composed of human beings united by a common bond for the purpose of living in society, serving one another, and cooperating as friends. If verbal intercommunication were withdrawn, what contract would be duly concluded, what instruction could be given in faith and morals, and what agreement and understanding could subsist among men? Our Cornificius, ignorant and shameless assailant of the study of eloquence, attacks not one or a few men but all civilization and political life.[29]

This polemic certainly shows something of the scholar's tendency to exaggerate the importance of his subject. Perhaps it was his distance from the schools that led John to overreact to an argument others would simply have dismissed as dubious and to depict it as a threat not only to all learning but to the very foundations of civil society. Also, like the other humanists and the satirists, John of Salisbury did have the habit of exalting the claims of his own position and debasing the opinions of his opponents. All this makes it difficult to understand exactly what were the issues of dispute. Nor is it even clear whom John is referring to as "Our Cornificius."

As an explanation for his use of this pseudonym, John claims that he is trying to protect his adversary's identity—"in reverence for his Christian name"—and also to emphasize that his argument is not ad hominem but directed at a false and pernicious doctrine. Despite this avowal, he can hardly resist debasing his opponent's character. Taking obvious delight in making so long a list of vices, John refers to Cornificius's "bloated gluttony, puffed-up pride, obscene mouth, rapacious greed, irresponsible conduct, loathsome habits, foul lust, dissipated appearance, evil life, and ill repute."[30] Only after additional comments about drunken carousals and carnal excesses "that would shame even an Epicurean pig"[31] does John turn to the more pertinent questions of where and how Cornificius was educated. No wonder, John argues, that Cornificius leads others astray. He himself was badly taught, or rather "untaught," by masters who valued verbosity over eloquence and whose reputations were based on the new arguments they made at disputations of trivial questions rather than on how well they taught the writings of the ancient philosophers. In turn, students like Cornificius, following the bad example set by these masters, likewise gloried in their own inventions and, after only the shortest time at the schools, themselves became "brand-new masters" who perpetuated the problem. "Behold," John complains, "everything was made new: grammar was innovated, dialectic was changed, rhetoric was despised; and leaving established rules, they also invented new methods [*novas vias*] for the whole quadrivium."[32]

This emphasis on novelty had completely undermined the established methods of teaching the liberal arts. But it perfectly served the interests of those seeking to spend as little time as possible studying the liberal arts. Once they had succeeded in making the arts into nothing more than a "frying pan of verbiage" (*sartago loquendi*), Cornificius and his colleagues were pleased to find that their expectations about learning were fulfilled. They then quickly turned to other means of serving their ambitions. According to John, four careers especially appealed to these men. Some became monks (we are reminded of Brunellus). Others went off to study at Salerno or Montpellier, becoming physicians no more competent at medicine than they had been at philosophy. Many became the undeserving courtiers criticized in the *Policraticus*. And, worst of all, some—including Cornificius himself—entered the "vulgar and profane professions," willing to do any business, even to practice usury, in order to get rich. These "deficient philosophers" have thereby replaced the true trivium and quadrivium of the liberal arts with a new quasi-quadrivium—consisting of the religious life, medicine, civil service, and money-making—that better served their ambitions for wealth.[33]

Not content simply to leave the schools, the Cornificians had further disrupted education by making malicious attacks on those masters who tried to defend the arts. John claims that the careers of teachers as capable as Thierry of Chartres, William of Conches, Bernard of Chartres, and Peter Abelard had all suffered because of the time and effort they had expended refuting the insanities of the Cornificians. It had only been thanks to the excellent teaching of these masters that the arts had been able to withstand the challenge. When they failed against the arts, the Cornificians next had launched a more general attack on the schools. The account John gives of these conflicts is vague and confusing. Among those supposedly attacked by the Cornificians is included a group of theologians whose careers span the entire first half of the twelfth century, from Anselm of Laon and William of Champeaux to Hugh of St. Victor and Robert Pullen. Cornificius, previously said to have become a usurer, is now said to have entered a religious order and to have cultivated the friendship of other religious of good repute, including Cistercians, Cluniacs, and Premonstratensians, in order to gain their support for his attacks against the schools.[34]

All this suggests that Cornificius is intended to represent not a particular person but a collection of all the attitudes toward education that John found either distasteful or dangerous. As a moneymaker, Cornificius stands for those who placed worldly ambitions above wisdom; and as a monk, he stands for those whose attacks on the schools, although made under the guise of defending the faith, were expressions of their ignorance and envy. The followers of Cornificius are, likewise, not to be identified with a specific religious order or social group. Within their contemptible ranks John of Salisbury encompasses narrowly specialized masters as well as the modestly educated men in lucrative professions who have always been regarded with particular acrimony by self-proclaimed defenders of humane learning.[35]

The description of Cornificius makes John's view of the opposition clear. The arguments used to impugn the liberal arts and to oppose the study of logic should be regarded, he believed, as little more than the false opinions of unlearned men attempting to make excuses for their own ignorance, pretense, and ambition. However, two of the arguments attributed to the Cornificians were considered by him to be substantive enough to be taken more seriously. The first of these has already been mentioned: the argument that since the logical arts only teach the rules of speech and since speech is a natural gift that does not have to be taught, there is no real need to study them. The second argument justified not studying the logical arts of eloquence on the more theoretical grounds that they are not part of philosophy.[36]

The *Metalogicon* never refutes the second argument directly. The distinction between eloquence and wisdom, upon which the Cornificians based their argument, was one known and accepted by John. It had been introduced into the schools by his master, William of Conches. And to refute the Cornificians, John could simply have repeated William's argument about the importance and usefulness of the logical arts as the essential instrument of philosophy.[37] This argument is implicit in the principle that John uses repeatedly in the *Metalogicon* to defend the integrity of the arts: "Just as eloquence, unenlightened by reason, is rash and blind, so wisdom, without the power of expression, is feeble and maimed."[38] He believed eloquence was as essential as wisdom in educating men to improve society. But against the Cornificians, John thought it more appropriate to make a quite different case for logic. What, he cynically asks, could be more valuable than eloquence in acquiring wealth, winning favor, or gaining fame?[39] Given his view of the Cornificians' motives, John probably made this point with great relish.

Against the first objection, that speech is a natural gift one does not need to learn, the *Metalogicon* makes a more direct and concerted assault. John takes his weapons from two sources: the rich tradition of didactic literature, including the recent synthesis provided by Hugh of St. Victor in the *Didascalicon*, and the experience of his own twelve years in the schools. The former supplied the principles upon which to base his defense, whereas his own observations of changes in the arts curriculum enabled John to reinforce these principles in ways that made them much more applicable to the existing situation in the schools.

John bases his defense of logic primarily on the premise that, although the capacity for speech is natural, one must nevertheless cultivate it with formal study in order to be able to use it effectively. His argument can be summarized briefly. All learning consists of fostering the development of abilities or habits innate to humans. The arts came into being to teach the rules whereby, through study and exercise, these natural habits can become fully developed faculties.[40] After making this argument, which applies to all the arts, John awkwardly avoids the broader issue of the relationship among the various branches of philosophy by immediately narrowing his attention to the seven liberal arts. Although all the arts equally foster the development of natural abilities, the trivium and the quadrivium are rightly given precedence in education because they are the best preparation for all other learning. "Those to whom the system of the trivium has disclosed the meaning of all words or the rules of the quadrivium have unveiled all the secrets of nature," John writes, "do not need the help of a teacher to understand the meaning of books or to find the solutions of questions."[41]

This is the same argument for the preeminence of the liberal arts that Hugh of St. Victor had made. Whereas the Victorine master had tried to prescribe a viable program of studies for all seven arts, however, John of Salisbury recognized that the changed conditions of learning had made the full arts curriculum impractical. Even the most serious students did not have the time necessary to complete both the quadrivium and the trivium. And many—those he calls the Cornificians—were refusing to study the arts at all. Under the circumstances, it appeared challenge enough to John to make as strong a case as possible for the trivium.

Still, in limiting his defense to the trivium, John was certainly in no way retreating from the traditional principles of humane learning. This is especially clear in his discussion of grammar. In summarizing the technical rules of the art, he explicitly tries to demonstrate how grammar can be taught both to make students proficient in writing and speaking Latin and also to improve their moral conduct. There are, he contends, four requirements for learning grammar properly. First, the contents of the art should be clearly defined and should be studied in an orderly way. Second, classical authors and texts should be chosen for their moral as well as their literary value. Third, it should be recognized that studying the rules of the art is only the first step in education, not an end in itself. After study, the rules must be committed to memory, then meditated upon to deepen understanding, and finally applied to living virtuously.[42] According to John, those who go no further than learning the technical rules of an art, however expert they might become at them, are not properly educated. The fourth requirement is a qualified teacher. A diligent master is needed, one who is attentive to the needs and capacities of his students and who has a clear and effective method of teaching grammar.

It is to illustrate this requirement that John gives his often-quoted account of the teaching methods of the famed grammarian, Bernard of Chartres. The account is not first-hand. Bernard's career as a master had ended well before John had arrived at the schools. Nowhere is it clearer how much, even though he was aware of and receptive to many of the latest intellectual advances in the schools, John of Salisbury still yearned for the humane learning of the past, which he could only have heard about from the nostalgic recollections of his own masters. Given how little we know otherwise about the actual teaching of Bernard of Chartres, there is no way of determining for certain the accuracy of John's account. However, it seems likely that the description John gives of how Bernard taught grammar was inspired as much by what he disliked of conditions in Paris in his time as by what his masters had told him about Chartres in theirs.

Praising the teaching of grammar in the past, John paints an idealized picture of a quiet and peaceful classroom, far removed from the distractions of the world, where a diligent master feels no need to impress or to befuddle his students, where the students heed the master's exhortations and discipline, and where all work together harmoniously to improve both their learning and their lives. Bernard is described as patiently teaching his students the basic rules and advancing to the more difficult parts of grammar only when it was clear the students were ready, all the time following a set and careful sequence. He would select only the most useful authors, so that his students could read the assigned texts thoroughly without being distracted by superfluous material. The students would learn the rules of grammar by composing Latin verse and prose and by imitating classical models. There was little competition among students, who would meet daily to discuss and to criticize each other's work for their mutual benefit. Each evening, at a final meeting known as the *declinatio*, the day's lessons would be reviewed by using examples from the texts best suited to teach faith and virtue and to inspire good works. Instruction would end with the recitation of prayers and of a Psalm. Each succeeding day would incorporate what had been taught the one before until, within a reasonable time, the students had acquired an excellent foundation of Latin grammar and classical literature and would be well prepared to advance to the rest of the liberal arts.[43]

For John of Salisbury, the classroom of Bernard of Chartres exemplified an educational ideal that was orderly, sound, disciplined, and cooperative, and that taught students both excellent Latin and the principles of a good life. Such an education might have been possible in monastic schools, and even in the smaller cathedral schools, where one or two masters filled their classes with a few students eager to learn and unaware of alternative means of education. But, as John was sadly aware, it was hardly compatible with the atmosphere of the expanding schools of Paris, where masters competed for students and were willing to adapt their teaching to meet popular demand. Directly following his account of Bernard's teaching, John tells how his own grammar teachers, William of Conches and Richard the Bishop, who had tried to use the same methods, had been forced to retire from the schools when they found that students were more interested in those masters of the arts who "promised to impart the whole of philosophy in two or three years."[44] In John's view a good foundation in grammar, one adequate to support other philosophical pursuits, would require that much time alone. Thus, although he was aware of the pressures on masters teaching the arts in Paris, John strongly believed that unless the basic principles and methods of teaching grammar exemplified by Bernard of Chartres were restored, humane learning would be doomed and students would be condemned to the ignorance of the Cornificians.

But John of Salisbury was aware that the attitudes exemplified by the Cornificians were not the only, or even the primary, threat to the liberal arts curriculum. The dominance of dialectic itself was endangering the other arts, especially now that the demanding corpus of the New Logic had been introduced to the schools. Excited by the newly translated Aristotelian treatises, scholars were losing their interest in the Latin classics. In John's estimation, more scholars were studying dialectic than all the other arts combined. The popularity of dialectic itself was not the problem. Indeed, John insists, it is right that so many scholars should want to study this vital part of philosophy. The problem was that too many of them concentrated all their time and effort on that one art alone. These "pure philosophers," as he mockingly refers to them, disdained all other disciplines – grammar, physics, and ethics alike – and sought the truth in the rules of logic alone.[45] This excessive specialization in dialectic was, he believed, no less dangerous an internal threat to sound education than the external threat posed by the dilettantism and professionalism of the Cornificians.

According to John of Salisbury, two opposing tendencies were seriously impeding the value of learning. The Cornificians foolishly sought to spend no more than two or three years on all the arts. Equally foolish were the "Academicians," who spent not ten or twenty years but their entire lives studying the single art of dialectic. The results were the same. Like the Cornificians, the Academicians suffered from not having the solid foundation of classical studies essential to philosophical training. "Thus," John writes, "the Academicians become old men still occupied with boyish pursuits. They sift every syllable of what has been written, doubt everything, but never come to knowledge. Finally, they are converted to babbling; not knowing what they are saying or claiming, they concoct new errors. Either they do not know the doctrines of the ancient authors or they reject them as unworthy of being followed."[46]

John obviously did not spare the Academicians from the satire he used against the Cornificians. But whereas he believed that the dangerous attitudes and practices of the Cornificians should be completely eradicated, he viewed the errors of the Academicians primarily as a problem of methodology that could be corrected. Unlike the satirists, John of Salisbury was not unequivocally opposed to dialectic. Nor did he regard the art as an impediment to humane learning. With the guidance he had to offer on how to teach Aristotle, John believed that the study of dialectic could be reintegrated into a broad liberal arts curriculum. Those who specialized in dialectic without first acquiring a broad philosophical background were, he argues, misusing the tools of their art in two ways. First, unable to distinguish among various sources, they had no authoritative grounds upon which to choose one opinion over another or to determine which matters ought to be disputed. Second, having no understanding of the purpose of learning, the dialecticians expended all their time on subtle and trivial questions suitable only as school exercises. Seldom—and this, in John's view, distinguishes the Academicians from the Cornificians—were they misled by base motives so much as by the inadequacies of their own education.

These attitudes are most apparent in John's sharp yet sympathetic criticisms of the dialecticians at the school on Mont Ste. Geneviève. Both Alberic and Robert of Melun, the masters who succeeded Peter Abelard, are described as diligent scholars flawed by over-specialization. Alberic, John writes, had the fault of finding questions everywhere. Robert used his subtlety to answer each question in every possible way. Both were brilliant and, had some master combined their skills, he would have had no equal as a dialectician. But it was unfortunate that neither made better use of his acute mind and his diligence and that neither had studied grammar before dialectic or the quadrivium after. They would have been much better masters had they "followed in the footsteps of their ancestors as much as they applauded their own inventions."[47]

John also readily admits that after studying with these masters for two years, he himself had nearly made the same errors. Only after his infatuation with dialectic had faded did he realize the inadequacies of his education and recommence the study of grammar. Ten years later, returning to visit the schools on the Mont after having studied the other liberal arts and theology elsewhere, he saw that he had made the right decision. His former classmates were still bogged down, still disputing the same questions, and after a decade they had made very little progress toward solving them. "I was accordingly convinced by experience," says John, "of something that can easily be inferred by reason: that just as dialectic expedites other studies, so, if left alone by itself, it lies powerless and sterile."[48] What worried John was that some scholars, not out of purposeful negligence but out of unintentional ignorance, never acquired a broad enough foundation in the liberal arts to make good use of the potentially valuable tool of dialectic. The attitudes of the Cornificians put them beyond help, but these dialecticians only needed someone to reveal their errors to them and to give them some experienced guidance.

To offer such guidance to those studying dialectic, John reverses the argument he had previously used to defend the study of the trivium as a whole. Just as wisdom, to be useful, needs eloquence, so eloquence needs wisdom. Alone, dialectic is useless and an impediment to all progress in philosophy. Following William of Conches, John describes dialectic as a tool that must be applied to suitable material provided by the other disciplines in order to produce useful learning.[49] Scholars should, and must, study dialectic, but not to the extent that it prevents them from advancing to the other arts. Dialectic and the other arts of the trivium are only the essential beginning of a sound education. Students must study these arts thoroughly but in ways that help rather than hinder them in moving on to other parts of philosophy.

Still, John of Salisbury realized that it would do no good merely to state such principles without examining how dialectic was actually being taught in the schools and offering specific advice on how to improve the situation. His account of the grammatical instruction of Bernard of Chartres stands as the foil to the unflattering description John gives of the teaching of the dialecticians. The most obvious difference was in their attitude. Unlike Bernard, the dialecticians were more interested in showing off their own learning than in serving the needs of their students. Instead of advancing step by step, beginning with the simple aspects of dialectic and moving on to the more complex ones, they immediately entered into the debate over the question of universals.

In his lengthy discussion of the various opinions expressed on this question, John stresses that the competition in the schools and each new master's efforts to establish his reputation by making an original contribution were prolonging a debate that had become counterproductive to the teaching of dialectic.[50] He does not object as much to the differences of opinion—indeed, John asserts that there is little substantive disagreement among them—as to what the dialecticians' eagerness to assert opinions was doing to education. In three ways, they were making it nearly impossible to learn dialectic. First, by raising so difficult a question as that of universals in their introductory lectures, the masters were placing insupportable burdens on the frail shoulders of their young students. Second, from their very first lectures the masters were failing to follow the prescribed order of teaching. When they should have been lecturing on Porphyry's *Isagogue*, the introductory text, they were discussing matters not supposed to be raised until they came to Aristotle's more advanced logical writings. Third, instead of providing a simple introduction to Aristotle, the masters further confused their students by teaching opinions that contradicted Aristotle's doctrine and made his advanced writings even more difficult to understand.[51]

The attitudes and ambitions of the dialecticians were only partly to blame, however. Dialectic, John knew, had never been an easy subject to teach. The question of universals is raised at the very beginning of Porphyry's *Isagogue*, the introductory textbook of dialectic, and is never resolved. Thus even if they wanted to, masters could hardly avoid addressing this important philosophical issue in their early lectures. The recovery of the New Logic of Aristotle helped provide a satisfactory answer to this question, but it also raised new problems. How could Aristotle's position be reconciled with established doctrine? And, a more serious challenge to education, how could the study of these complicated texts, which could alone take years to master, be incorporated into the traditional liberal arts curriculum? These were weighty questions that could only be resolved by reforms in the way dialectic, especially the recovered writings of Aristotle, was taught. Dialectic, John believed, could be mastered without detriment to the other liberal arts only if studied in accordance with the principles of simplicity and orderliness.

John of Salisbury had learned from his own experience as a master that teaching often requires simplifying complicated and disputed matters. "It is my considered opinion," he writes, at the beginning of Book 3 of the *Metalogicon*, "that one ought to lecture on every book so as to provide the easiest possible understanding of what is written. One should not search for an occasion to assail students with difficulties, but everywhere generate facility."[52] To illustrate this point, John pays what might seem a rather underhanded compliment to Peter Abelard, with whom he had first studied dialectic. While praising the renowned dialectician for simplifying instruction so his students could advance expeditiously, John comments that this was probably the reason why Abelard subscribed to what he refers to as a "childish opinion" about universals.[53] This surprising remark exemplifies what every teacher knows, that the simplification of material, however necessary it might be for one's students, is not likely to please one's colleagues.

As for the order of study, there is little notable about John's prescription. Porphyry's *Isagogue* remained the introductory text, followed by Aristotle's own basic texts, the *Categories* and *On Interpretation*, which, together with Boethius's commentaries, made up the Old Logic. Only after mastering the more elementary aspects of dialectic were students to advance to the more complex texts of the New Logic and be taught, in sequence, the *Analytics*, *Topics*, and *Sophistical Refutations*.[54] John does do more than merely state the principle of simplicity and prescribe the order of study. Nearly half of the *Metalogicon* consists of a detailed commentary on the prescribed texts themselves, on how they should be taught, and on the specific aspects of each that the teacher should emphasize and the student should learn in order to advance in his understanding of dialectic.

Most of this part of the *Metalogicon* is too technical to be discussed here. What interests us is not so much how John thought each of Aristotle's logical writings should be taught as what he thought was more basically wrong with the teaching of dialectic in the schools. Unlike some critics, John did not attribute the difficulties to Aristotle but to the masters who misused and mistaught his logical texts. Two examples will suffice to demonstrate this point. The first concerns how masters were teaching the *Categories*, the most basic of the logical writings of Aristotle. Here, John complains that masters frequently went far beyond the elementary principles covered and "read everything into this little book" in order to impress their students. In one of those observations that make the *Metalogicon* so valuable a source of information about the schools, he tells how Adam of Petit Pont derided the masters who did this, even though he was aware of the pressures they were subjected to by their students. "He used to declare," John writes of Adam, "that if he himself were to teach logic with the simplicity of words and clear statement of opinions that it deserves, he would have no or few listeners."[55] In the case of Aristotle's more difficult logical writings, like the *Analytics*, John's criticism is different. When teaching these works, he argues, masters too often make the mistake of involving students in a useless confusion of nouns, verbs, and subtle intricacies, instead of selecting only those things necessary to provide them a sound grounding in the rules of dialectic. Again John cites Adam of Petit Pont, only this time in a less complimentary way. Adam's textbook, the *Ars disserendi*, gets so involved in the verbal intricacies of the *Analytics*, complains John, that his exposition is practically useless.[56]

This criticism is not completely fair to Adam, about whom John expresses unusually ambivalent opinions. But the two examples do serve well to demonstrate the standard by which he consistently evaluated the teaching of dialectic. To provide a thorough training in the art in reasonable time, a teacher had first to keep instruction in the elementary texts simple and then cover the more complex texts as concisely as possible. Although John of Salisbury recognized that the pressures competition placed on arts masters were difficult to resist, especially for those like Adam of Petit Pont who depended on student fees, he steadfastly refused to absolve them of the responsibility to teach what was basic and essential, not what was fashionable and popular.

The misuse of Aristotle was just part of the problem. The teaching of dialectic was also impeded by the misunderstanding of some of his logical writings and the mistrust of his authority. According to John, two of Aristotle's works were widely disparaged in the schools—the *Categories*, which was said to be too simple, and the *Topics*, which was dismissed as useless.[57] John's defense of these works echoes the educational principle stated in the *Policraticus*. All the works of Aristotle's logical corpus, he insists, if taught properly and in the correct order, are not only useful but also necessary to the development of eloquence. As for the two specific works, the *Categories* and the *Topics* receive much longer and more detailed attention than the other dialectical texts. Conservative resistance to the New Logic of Aristotle—which included the *Analytics* and the *Sophistical Refutations*, as well as the *Topics*—was another obstacle. According to John, some masters persisted in limiting their lectures to the Old Logic of the *Categories* and *On Interpretation*, the works translated and commented upon by Boethius. In their view, the use of other Aristotelian writings was not sanctioned by the authority of a Christian commentary. Moreover, they were concerned that the authority of Aristotle, who was known to have erred on doctrinal and ethical matters, might be dangerous even in logic. This is the earliest evidence of the charges that led to the condemnation of Aristotle's *libri naturales* in 1210. John's refutation of them is typical of the argument made repeatedly in defense of the secular arts and pagan authors. Usefulness is to be the criterion of judgment. Despite the errors Aristotle is known to have made on other matters, he simply has no equal as a logician. Aristotle, John concludes, "must be acknowledged as the teacher not of morals but of disputation, whose instruction is to advance young men to more serious philosophical pursuits."[58]

These comments on Aristotle illustrate John's general attitude about how pagan authors are to be used. Despite his insistence in the *Policraticus* that scholars should follow in the footsteps of their predecessors, John is critical of those who indiscriminately follow ancient philosophers down every path, wherever it might lead. The *Metalogicon* gives more practical advice about how to follow in these footsteps. Authoritative texts like Aristotle's logical corpus are essential guides to sound learning, but they are valuable only if used discriminately and taught properly. When using them, masters must follow the shortest route leading both to instruction in the liberal arts and to the edification of morals. All unnecessary digressions, especially those that might lead away from Christian doctrine, are to be avoided. In the *Policraticus*, John admits that it is probably safer to study only Christian authors and that the writings of pagans must be used selectively. In the *Metalogicon*, he goes further in limiting the study of the classics by stipulating that when the text of a "modern" author provides a simpler and better guide to a subject than an ancient one, it is to be preferred. The criterion for judging any work should be its practical usefulness, not its age.

In applying this principle both to classical and to contemporary learning, John of Salisbury shows himself to be neither unaware of nor unimpressed by the significant intellectual advances being made in his own lifetime. Although he is often critical of those of his contemporaries who take too much delight in their own inventions, he does not hesitate to praise other modern masters for their achievements. The prologue to the *Metalogicon* commends those masters of "noble talents, subtle searching, diligent studies, excellent memories, and copious words" whose opinions (*sententiae*) are to be preferred above those of the ancients.[59] Elsewhere, John harshly criticizes those who do not share his favorable estimation of modern masters. He condemns as "foolish and disagreeable" (*insulsus et ingratus*) those who regard a proposition as authoritative just because it is attributed to an ancient author when they would reject it out of hand if asserted by Gilbert of Poitiers, Peter Abelard, or Adam of Petit Pont—just because they are modern. Such men are more willing to accept the erroneous opinions of the ancients than the trustworthy ones of the moderns, John claims, not because they are genuinely committed to established authority but because they are envious of their contemporaries' achievements.[60] Clearly, however critical he was of the schools, John desired to distance himself from those he regarded as opponents of learning per se. However much he might allude to a golden age of learning in the past, he also understood the considerable intellectual advances being made in his own time.

The fullest discussion of the relationship between the learning of the past and of the present occurs in Book 3 of the *Metalogicon* when, writing of the difficulty of teaching Aristotle's *On Interpretation*, John states that modern masters need to add their own commentaries to make the work more understandable to their students.[61] He supports his argument with the authority of two of the most renowned masters of the twelfth century—the unlikely combination of Peter Abelard and Bernard of Chartres.

Abelard, we are told, was understandably sensitive to the resistance to new sources. John reports that he once heard Abelard make the observation—one with which he is in full agreement—that even though it would be easy for someone now to write a book on logic that would not be inferior in any way to books written by ancient authors on the subject, it would still be impossible, or at least very difficult, for such a book to gain approval as authoritative. Abelard also asserted that respect was owed to the ancients for the considerable achievements their genius and hard work left as a bequest to posterity. It is, John adds, because of this bequest that things to which so many ancients had dedicated so much of their lives and energies to investigate could now be easily understood by one man in a short time. Abelard serves as a powerful spokesman of the confidence John of Salisbury himself had in the potential of modern scholars to equal, and even to surpass, the knowledge of the past. "Our own generation," he continues, "enjoys the legacy bequeathed to it by that which preceded it. We frequently know more, not because we have moved ahead by our natural ability, but because we are supported by the strength of others and possess riches that we have inherited from our forefathers." At this point, John suddenly turns to Bernard of Chartres and introduces a metaphor that became a commonplace among the humanists. "Bernard of Chartres," he writes, "used to compare us to dwarfs perched on the shoulders of giants. He pointed out that we see more and farther than our predecessors, not because we have keener vision or greater height, but because we are lifted up and borne aloft on their gigantic stature."[62]

Perhaps John intended Bernard's authority to moderate the remarks attributed to Abelard. But his own confidence in the intellectual achievements of his age still comes through clearly. For all his apparent devotion to the learning of the past, John of Salisbury did not believe that following in the footsteps of philosophers meant being either subservient to the ancients or satisfied with what was already known.

The primary objective of the *Metalogicon*, and of those sections of the *Policraticus* concerned with education, was to demonstrate the need to remove the obstacles, both within and outside the schools, that were impeding the progress of learning. Although John of Salisbury found much more to criticize than to praise about existing conditions in the schools, he seems to have remained confident that knowledge would be advanced and society improved if education were reformed and if properly educated men were placed in positions of responsibility. With proper guidance, such as he was providing, sound education might yet be restored.

But there were other, more basic impediments to learning whose existence undermined this confidence. In one of the final chapters of the *Metalogicon*, John writes that eight obstacles seriously impede learning: the invincible ignorance of those things that human reason can never explain (such as the mystery of the Trinity); the frailty of the human condition; the brevity of life; the twin tendencies to neglect what is useful and to occupy oneself with what is useless; the conflicting opinions of authorities; sin; and, finally, the multitude and the immensity of the things that need to be investigated. Of the eight obstacles, John actually discusses only one. It is sin, he writes, that is the primary obstacle "to understanding those things that should be known." In particular, it is the sin of vanity that leads men to investigate matters beyond their reason, to be concerned with useless things, to invent opinions in order to advance their careers, and to waste their lives furthering their material ambitions rather than seeking the truth. Overcome by their vanity, men have lost the ability to distinguish between right and wrong. In his view, the problem plaguing the schools, no less than the courts, was fundamentally a moral one derived from the irremediable human fault of pride.[63]

Yet even at his most pessimistic, John remained steadfast in his belief that a sound education would effect moral reform, that training based on the solid foundation of the liberal arts, studied in accordance with the right principles and following the guidelines he offered in the *Metalogicon*, would prepare at least a few to lead useful and virtuous lives and to work for the improvement of politics and society.

After completing the *Metalogicon*, John of Salisbury did not survive much longer as a courtier. When his friend Thomas Becket was chosen to succeed Archbishop Theobald at Canterbury in 1161, John's personal prospects as well as his hopes for reform brightened. But the improvement was short-lived. John's previous difficulties with Henry II, his political ideas and social criticisms, and his outspoken support of the actions of Thomas Becket all combined to make him one of the first targets of royal anger in the growing dispute between the king and his troublesome archbishop. In 1163, months before the quarrel came to a head, John was removed from the archbishop's service by royal order, deprived of all his revenues, and forced into exile in France. Despite considerable efforts to regain Henry's favor, as he had been able to do relatively quickly once before, John of Salisbury found himself confronting what looked like a long period of unemployment.

Following Thomas Becket's advice, John made his way to Paris, with the intention of spending his exile studying and writing at the schools. As we have already seen from the letter he wrote back to the archbishop, Paris, despite all his criticisms and complaints, remained high in John's esteem.[64] After the demands of court life and the troubles in England, it is not surprising that John found Paris so appealing. But either because he did not have the financial resources to support himself—he complains, in his letter to Becket, of the high rents and long leases for housing—or because of the appealing invitation from his Benedictine friend, Peter of Celle, John did not remain in Paris as long as he had intended. Most of his six years of exile were spent at the monastery of St. Rémi, where the hospitality of Abbot Peter of Celle gave him the opportunity to study, maintain an active correspondence, and write up the notes from his years at the papal court into the *Historia pontificalis*.

Although John was intellectually productive, his letters during these years of exile tell of his dissatisfaction with a life of pure scholarship. He seems to have found little consolation in the peaceful study of which he had so often written wistfully while at court. He complains in a letter to Master Gerard Pucelle in 1166, midway through his exile:

> Of my own situation I can say nothing new, since nothing here is changed. . . . But we shall be able to be of more service to one another if we take pains to serve more closely that very philosophy to whose profession we have long been dedicated; that is, so that we might be executors of her commands rather than jugglers with empty words. True philosophy seeks, attends to, and gains real things, not words; and you have long known that I have never approved an opinion based on talk alone. Nor are mere hearers of the word, nor preachers of it, righteous in God's eyes, but only doers.[65]

In accordance with these principles, the exiled John tried to direct his learning where he thought it might do some good. For example, one of John's longest letters from these years advises the learned Henry the Liberal, count of Champagne, on how to read the Scriptures.[66] Not surprisingly, John also remained an outspoken critic of the foibles of his time, especially when they affected education. Of the expulsion of foreign scholars from France in 1167 he writes disapprovingly: "Wars and rebellions flare up on every side; Mercury's clients have been so harshly treated that France, the kindest and most courtly of all countries, has expelled foreign scholars."[67] And in a letter dating from the following year to Master Odo of Soissons, John echoes his previous complaints about teaching. Though there are numerous masters, he writes, few are truly learned or live in accordance with the principles they teach.[68]

In November 1170 John was finally able to return to England with Thomas Becket, only to be a witness to the archbishop's brutal murder at Canterbury the following month. After that shock he seems to have found it best to remain unobtrusively at Canterbury, even though his relationship with the new archbishop, Richard of Dover (1174-84), was not close and knowing that he could expect little in the way of advancement from Henry II. It was Louis VII, not Henry, who finally rewarded John's learning by making him bishop of Chartres in 1176. There, during the last four years of his life, John had the opportunity to employ his knowledge and to apply his principles actively in the administration of a wealthy and important diocese. The Chartres obituary praises the learned bishop for his defense of ecclesiastical privileges and for his social reforms.[69] As a fitting bequest, John of Salisbury left to Chartres cathedral his personal library, the impressive collection of classical, patristic, and contemporary works to which he had turned so frequently throughout his life to guide him both in his words and in his actions.[70]

PETER OF BLOIS

For the humanists a generation younger than John of Salisbury, the struggle for influence and advancement proved even more difficult. In the schools, the place of the liberal arts in the curriculum was increasingly challenged, not only by the dominance of dialectic and the appeal of law and medicine but also by the new academic discipline of theology. Theology took its method almost exclusively from dialectic and did not require the broad training in all seven arts that earlier scholars such as Hugh of St. Victor had regarded as necessary preparation for the study of Scripture. Outside the schools, in both secular and church courts, men who had little to commend them besides their humane learning must have seemed less employable than those with the more concretely useful talents of lawyers, whether civil or canon, physicians, and theologians. Considering themselves at a competitive disadvantage, the humanists had no choice other than to use their greatest skill, their literary eloquence, to attempt to prove the value of their learning and to undermine the position of their rivals.

Few were better suited in either training or temperament to do so than Peter of Blois (c. 1130–1212). The compilation of his own letters that Peter first made in 1184, when already in his early fifties, and that he continued to revise and circulate for nearly two decades can best be described as a blatant bid for literary fame. And fame these letters brought him. They remained models of epistolary style throughout the Middle Ages and Renaissance and were read with admiration for centuries after. But despite the literary success of his compilation, it failed to obtain for Peter what he most sought and thought he deserved—a secure, well-paying, and influential position in the English Church. However thankful he, as something of a humanist scholar, might have been for the recognition of posterity, Peter of Blois would have much preferred a more concrete reward from his contemporaries.

Although Peter spent the last half of his life in England, he was born at or near Blois about 1130.[71] As a young man, he was sent to Paris to study the liberal arts. There he was tutored briefly by John of Salisbury. Peter left Paris about 1150, succumbing to the attraction of law that was drawing so many young men to Bologna—a trend he would later write about in the most disapproving terms. He was back in Paris studying theology by 1155, when the great Peter Lombard was lecturing on his *Sententiae*. He was also teaching grammar probably, like John of Salisbury, in order to support himself financially while he continued his own studies. Next, perhaps because Paris offered little security to a master who lacked greater specialization, he moved to Tours, where the liberal arts remained more soundly entrenched in the curriculum of the schools. After teaching grammar and rhetoric for several years without attracting a patron, Peter seems to have become worried enough about his future prospects to take a risk. In 1167 Peter traveled to Sicily as a member of the entourage of a group of knights answering the desperate appeal of Queen Margaret, the French widow of William I. As regent for her young son and as a foreigner, Margaret was in a precarious position, and Peter no doubt found conditions at the court in Palermo far different from those in Paris. Amidst all the intrigues and dangers of Sicilian politics, Peter tutored the future William II and served as keeper of the royal seal. When a revolt against the French faction nearly cost him his life in 1169, he finally concluded that the risks of remaining in Sicily outweighed the chances that he might one day be handsomely rewarded for his services.

It is difficult to piece together Peter's movements during the first years after he left Sicily and when he was struggling to get his career back on track. Eventually, he did return to Paris, where he tried, again unsuccessfully, to attract enough students to his lectures on the trivium to support himself financially as a teacher. When teaching failed, he renewed his search for some important person to recognize his talents. In 1174, after short periods of service to the archdeacon of Salisbury and the archbishop of Rouen, he finally found a position at the court of Becket's successor as archbishop of Canterbury, Richard of Dover. At Canterbury, Peter had the chance to renew his acquaintance with his former tutor John of Salisbury, before he was elected bishop of Chartres. For the next few years, Peter appears to have been encouraged enough by his accomplishments to hope that his own career would turn out as successfully as John's. Never one to pass up any opportunity to make himself known where it might help, Peter dedicated two of his treatises to Henry II. By 1178 he had advanced to the influential position of chancellor to the archbishop. In 1182 he was given the archdeaconry of Bath. Little did Peter expect that he would rise no further. From then on, his career suffered one disappointment after another.

Peter's hopes for promotion were shaken first by the death of his patron, Archbishop Richard, in April 1184. Uncertain how this would affect his future, Peter spent the long months it took to elect a new archbishop compiling the first edition of his letters. The election of the Cistercian Baldwin of Ford, whom Peter had known since their school days in Bologna, allowed him to remain a member of the archbishop's household—but not, it seems, as chancellor. Whatever Peter's actual position at Canterbury, the next six years seem to have been especially pleasant ones for him: he had the confidence of Baldwin and his reputation was growing with the circulation of his expanding collection of letters.

While participating in the Third Crusade, Peter of Blois again found himself suddenly without a patron, when Archbishop Baldwin died in Syria in November 1190. Even more than in 1184, Peter despaired of his future, especially now that Henry II, whose favor he had so carefully cultivated, was also dead. Peter never again acquired secure and satisfactory employment. On his way back to England he spent some time at the court of Eleanor of Aquitaine, drafting letters urging the release of Richard the Lion-Hearted, then being held captive by his enemies in Germany. Peter's efforts on behalf of the king gained him an additional prebend, the deanery of Wolverhampton, but again he seems to have hoped for more. Save what appears to be only occasional service to a third archbishop of Canterbury, Hubert Walter, and a short time in the household of Geoffrey, archbishop of York, Peter passed the next ten years revising and adding to the letter collection, which remained his one success. He also began to turn his attention to religious subjects. In 1202 Peter exchanged the archdeaconry of Bath, which he had held as a nonresident since 1182, for the same position in London. There he passed his last ten years. Old and weak from the illnesses he had contracted in the East, and having finally lost all hope of further employment or advancement, Peter even gave up working on his letters, the labor of his love for nearly twenty years.

This sketch of Peter's career is an important key to understanding the nature of his collection of letters. At first reading, the collection seems to consist of the personal correspondence of an influential courtier and of copies of the official letters he drafted for the powerful men whom he served. In fact, it is a compilation of letters that were edited and reedited over a long period by a man who was uncertain about his future and trying to present himself and his literary skills in the best possible light. The collection was intended to provide models of epistolary style and moral lessons applicable to both personal conduct and political life.[72] There was no precedent for such a compilation. All previous epistolary collections, such as those of Bernard of Clairvaux and John of Salisbury, consisted of copies of actual letters that were compiled by disciples, not by the authors themselves, and that circulated with little or no editing. In contrast, Peter, in making his own collection, could—and, despite his frequent denials, did—rewrite the letters he chose to circulate. He also carefully selected the letters he thought best displayed his skills as a writer and best expressed his views of the events and issues of the time.

Richard Southern argues that Peter intended his collection to present, in an apparently haphazard way, a system for the conduct of human life.[73]

It is this purpose that makes the letters so valuable a source for attitudes about education. But it also means that they must be interpreted with caution. Like John of Salisbury, Peter of Blois wanted to prove that he was a learned man, worthy of advancement, who suffered because of the foibles of his time and the vain ambitions of his less soundly educated contemporaries. Although Peter did his best to imitate the older humanist, neither his learning nor his character proved equal to John's. The humane ideals defended by John of Salisbury find an echo in the letters of Peter of Blois, but they have a much hollower sound.

Probably the best place to begin to examine and to interpret the educational attitudes of Peter of Blois is the often-quoted letter written to the archdeacon of Nantes in defense of the liberal arts.[74] Two of the archdeacon's nephews had been committed to Peter's care when he was teaching, possibly still in Paris, about 1160. Reporting on their progress, Peter complains that the previous education of the older boy, William—of whose learning his uncle was apparently quite proud—had failed to give him a proper foundation in the liberal arts. "Omitting the study of grammar and of the classical authors," Peter writes of William, "he has hastened to the cunning of logic, where he has learned dialectic not, as he should, in books, but in notes and notebooks." The complaint echoes John of Salisbury—which is not surprising in itself. But as the letter goes on to describe the specific shortcomings of William's education in words taken almost verbatim from John's writings, one becomes more sceptical of the dependability of Peter's attitudes and observations.[75] Trying to assert the need for a thorough grounding in grammar and classical literature, Peter then lists a group of authors, all of whose works he claims, unconvincingly, to have read. The list is, again, taken directly from John of Salisbury.[76]

Despite the doubts raised by these two examples of what has been called plagiarism—but could be more generously described as literary embellishment—there is still sufficient evidence of Peter's essential sincerity in upholding the values and ideals of humane learning. He had indeed been trained in Latin grammar and style in the way the letter describes, by imitating classical verse and memorizing examples of elegant letters. His models probably included the epistles of Hildebert of Lavardin (or Le Mans), the modern master whose name heads Peter's long list of classical authors. As a teacher, too, Peter had taken some of John of Salisbury's principles to heart. He emphasizes that all the texts he used to teach grammar were not fables but true histories, which could inculcate morals as well as demonstrate literary style. Even though the actual words Peter uses in this letter were borrowed, exaggerated, and, worst of all, made to sound pretentious, they were still intended to embellish ideas Peter took seriously. Humane ideals were central to Peter's image of himself, however inflated we might judge that image to be. They were also vital in helping him to understand, and perhaps to justify, the failings of those who did not recognize and reward his talents.

It is clear from several other letters in the collection that Peter truly felt both obliged to defend the educational principles and standards inherited from John of Salisbury and threatened by the attitudes and ambitions of his contemporaries. A few examples of the more general advice and criticism Peter offers should be cited before we examine his particular concerns about the state of learning. In a strongly worded letter to a young student, a canon of Chartres called Simon, Peter writes at length of the importance of putting aside the concerns of youth for more mature and honest studies. Apparently intended to convince Simon not to be in a hurry to find employment after completing only four years of study, this letter, unlike the one to the archdeacon of Nantes, does not prescribe a specific course of studies. Instead, Peter merely urges Simon to remain at the schools, to accept the poverty of the scholar's life (a rhetorical flourish, as Simon, although presumably as a nonresident, still received the income of his canonry), and to delay his search for wealth in order to acquire wisdom.[77] In another letter Peter, in terms reminiscent of those John of Salisbury used against Cornificius, rebukes a young monk, his own nephew Ernaldus, for neglecting his studies in order to further his ambitions.[78] And just to mention one final example, the collection includes a very poignant letter chastising Bishop Jocelin of Salisbury for reneging on an agreement to have his two nephews tutored by Peter. Expressing all the bitterness of a teacher struggling with his finances, the letter makes an eloquent, though at times clearly ironic, case for the moral value of a sound education.[79]

Each of these letters expresses Peter's belief that learning was of essential importance in preparing for a useful and virtuous life. This view of education differs hardly at all from John of Salibury's. But Peter of Blois contributed his own criterion of evaluation. In his letters, he writes repeatedly that what is taught and learned must above all be "edifying for salvation" (*edificans ad salutem*). For Peter, a sound education could and should pay off in eternal, as well as temporal, rewards.

Such an education began with the study of the liberal arts, but it did not end there. Although Peter was more often critical of those who, out of excessive ambition for temporal rewards, never completed the arts curriculum, he also voiced his objections to those scholars who spent too much time studying these subjects. Peter does this most strongly in a letter to a renowned grammarian, Master Ralph of Beauvais. Writing in response to criticisms this master had apparently made of those who left their studies in the schools to serve in bishops' households, Peter expresses, in no uncertain terms, his views of those who studied the arts excessively:

> You [Ralph] reverberate the air uselessly with confused chatter, disputing frivolities constantly like a sailor. You still employ your talents on letters and syllables and teach only the most elementary principles. You are, I hesitate to say, a hundred-year-old boy, an old man still teaching the rudiments. It is shameful and burdensome for me to say that whereas all your colleagues have ascended the mountain of more eminent knowledge, you remain with the ass in the mire of denser understanding. Priscian, Cicero, Lucan, and Persius: these are your only gods.[80]

Judging from the harshness of his attack and the defensive tone of his letter, Peter took Ralph's criticisms personally. The letter continues with a highly glorifying account of the court at Canterbury. Peter writes of the court almost as a school, where learned men spend their time studying and disputing, not useless frivolities, but the most difficult questions of the kingdom. How different this is from the description of court life in the *Policraticus*!

Admittedly, the opinions Peter expresses in this letter may be too obviously self-serving to be taken seriously. But another of Peter's letters can be cited, this one written to his friend and confusing namesake, Master Peter of Blois. Our Peter, while praising the other for his eminence as a literary scholar and for his eloquence, urges him not to continue to study or to teach the liberal arts much longer. Compare the words used here with those he addressed to Ralph of Beauvais:

> School learning has lifted you to the highest glories of eminence. But when you ought to be a model of virtue and a mirror of honesty for others, you have led many into ruin through the scurrilous frivolities and useless falsehoods of the pagans. What are these vanities and inane fables to you? What are the mythical loves of the pagans for their gods to you who should be an instrument of the true God?[81]

Note that Peter, like John of Salisbury, measures the worth of the liberal arts by how much they serve to edify Christian faith and morals. But Peter emphasizes less what is actually studied than how long these studies endure. As "boyish" subjects, the liberal arts should be studied only in youth, then left for the more mature discipline of theology. For this reason, Peter is especially critical of his namesake, who has spent too long on classical literature, philosophy, and civil law and has "feared the sacred pages of theology." With a not unusual lack of accuracy in recalling the events of his life, Peter portrays himself as a model of someone who spent his youth studying the liberal arts and writing frivolous poetry but "at the other threshold of youth" turned completely from this vain learning to theology.

These criticisms of masters of the arts, which seem somewhat to belie Peter's reputation as a humanist, must be weighed against other letters in which he is no less vehement in defending the liberal arts against those who questioned their value altogether. For example, writing to an unnamed prior who was strongly opposed to the study of secular subjects, especially to the application of profane learning to the interpretation of Scripture, Peter attempts to make a strong case for the usefulness of both the liberal arts and civil law to Christian doctrine.[82] Although he again offers little specific guidance about what to study and avoids stating directly how the arts are to be applied to theology, Peter uses the same combination of authority and experience that John of Salisbury had used so convincingly in the *Metalogicon* to articulate certain principles about how the arts are to be studied and used. There is little original in the authorities Peter cites. His most notable citation comes when, arguing that one need take only what is useful from the works of pagan authors, he uses the story of the marriage of the foreign woman from Deuteronomy 21.11-13.[83] First invoked by Jerome, the passage was often cited in the sermons of Paris masters (which will be examined in the next chapter) to defend the study of the liberal arts. More interesting is what Peter says in this letter about civil law. After briefly mentioning that the Fathers approved of the subject, Peter writes defensively of his own efforts in Bologna to exhort the civil lawyers to attend, like him, only to those aspects of the law that were useful. He refused, he insists, to take part in disputing any legal question unless he judged it to be "edifying for salvation."[84]

The fact that this letter contradicts other accounts Peter gives of the time he spent studying civil law seems to undermine his defense of the liberal arts. We shall have to return later to the apparent ambiguities in Peter's attitudes to the liberal arts. But first, to broaden our perspective on Peter's expressed concerns about the state of learning, it will be necessary to examine two letters in which he is unambiguously critical of civil law and lawyers.

Despite the time he had spent studying at Bologna as a young man, Peter of Blois came to share the aversion felt by so many of his contemporaries to the legal profession. Nowhere is this aversion more clearly expressed than in Peter's letter warning an unnamed friend of the dangers of civil law and advising instead the study of theology.[85] Although probably first written soon after he himself had left Bologna, the letter was apparently revised considerably when Peter later edited his collection. Drawing upon what he claims to be his own experience, Peter gives a very unflattering account of his studies in Bologna. He had been attracted to civil law, not by the practical usefulness of the subject, but by its eloquent language and charming arguments. Only after he had fortuitously turned to the study of theology did he overcome his infatuation and begin to understand the superiority of divine over human law. Urging his friend to get on with the study of theology, Peter then launches into an attack upon lawyers. It is impossible, he argues, to study both civil law and theology or to be both a lawyer and a minister of Christ, not because there are inherent contradictions between human and divine law but because of the damage civil lawyers have done to their subject. "Today," he writes, "only avarice motivates the advocates of law, and the once venerable name and honorable profession of law has become cheapened by venality."[86]

The law, in Peter's view, had become completely corrupted by men who studied and used it only for their personal gain. Instead of serving truth and justice, knowledge of the law had been turned to unjust, but profitable, causes such as bribery, dissolving marriages, destroying friendships, and violating contracts. These criticisms of lawyers, suggesting a serious decline of their ethics, seem especially likely to have been added in Peter's later revisions of the letter. This also appears to be the case with his concluding argument that legal knowledge, as a gift from God, should not be used for profit. "The lawyer," Peter writes, "ought to freely give what he freely received, to advocate for the orphan and widow, for the public good and the liberty of the Church."[87] At least, Peter insists, lawyers should cease to seek immense fortunes and be content with modest, honestly earned salaries. How little complaints about lawyers have changed over the centuries!

Peter's obvious bitterness about the corruption of law—especially the very different account he gives of his own legal studies at Bologna—is probably not unrelated to the disappointments of his own career. It may even reveal some regrets, whatever his denials, that he had not continued to study civil law and joined the legal profession. But let us put aside for the moment the question of Peter's motives in order to examine his perspective more closely. Peter's life spanned a long and decisive period in the development of the schools, one that was marked by a great intensification in the specialization and professionalism against which earlier critics had railed. To someone like Peter who spent most of his career in court, the legal profession must certainly have seemed to be by far the likeliest path to success. Under the circumstances, it is hardly surprising that Peter would come to question whether law could any longer be integrated into the broad program of studies that had appealed to him in his youth. From the humanist perspective, law now appeared to be one of the most serious impediments to a sound education.

In another letter—this one to a certain Master Peter, a deacon serving at the court of Henry II who was planning to return to the schools[88]—Peter of Blois describes the choice of whether to study civil law or theology as nothing less than a decision between the vanity of the world and the truth of God. The two subjects, he argues, are irrevocably opposed. Again, Peter is uncompromising in his condemnation of the ambitions of lawyers. "There are only two things," he writes, "that strongly draw men to the study of law—the ambition for advancement and the desire for vain glory."[89] He chastises the legal profession for being dominated by men of pride, cupidity, ostentation, error, and destructiveness. An excessive array of scriptural citations makes this letter one of the longest in the collection. But Peter's basic argument is simply that theology is a useful and suitable subject, especially for a deacon, and that civil law is not. "Reject that science which leads to disaster," he recommends. "Seize that which is edifying for salvation."[90] What, we might rightly ask, has happened to the idea of the usefulness of all learning?

Peter of Blois can best be understood as a disappointed and uncertain humanist struggling to hold on to the ideas and values he had learned in the schools and about which he had written in his first letters. But however eloquently he might have tried to defend humanist ideals, the circumstances of his own life seem to have caused him some doubt about their viability. It was not just that his own education, broad but not deep, had failed to gain him the secure and prominent position for which he had hoped. He also seems to have come to recognize that the trend toward specialization in learning was irreversible and that it was as much a result of the rapid expansion of knowledge as it was of increased professionalism. The question was no longer how all subjects could be studied but which should be studied. Thus, although still following the principles of a sound education that John of Salisbury had articulated in defending the liberal arts, Peter emphasized the importance of choosing subjects that would be preparatory for, and remain subservient to, the study of theology. If that ideal was not new, what it meant in practical terms was. Some subjects—and law had now replaced dialectic as the most obvious one of concern—would better be avoided altogether in order not to impede or prevent the scholar from progressing to theology.

Like John of Salisbury, Peter of Blois accepted the need for scholars to specialize. However, in placing a greater emphasis on theology, Peter parted from John in what he saw to be the ultimate purpose of a sound education. Whereas John had hoped that clerics, educated according to the guidelines he had prescribed, would be better able to serve princes as courtiers and could improve political life, Peter was opposed to the presence of clerics, especially those trained in theology, in secular courts and to their involvement in political affairs. He might have countered Ralph of Beauvais by defending service at Canterbury, but he was critical of those who served at Westminster. In two letters to clerics at the court of Henry II, Peter rails against the dangers of political life—which he could well remember from his years in Sicily—and writes of his astonishment that anyone as learned as they could tolerate the annoyances of the king's court. Careful not to appear critical of Henry II, Peter argues that educated clerics could serve the king much better in churches than at court and that places in the royal household, which could be adequately filled by those who are "simpler," especially need not, and should not, be occupied by those trained in theology.[91]

For Peter of Blois the main criterion in evaluating learning had become how well it prepared men, not for political life, but for service to the Church. This goal, in his eyes, did not lessen the value of a sound education in classical learning and the liberal arts but restricted its duration and required that it be applied directly to the study of theology. Ideally, the liberal arts and theology would be part of an integral program of study completed without impediment or interruption. Writing to a former student just completing the arts curriculum, Peter strongly advises against the postponement of theological training. Delay, he warns the student, would weaken his intellect, induce sloth, suffocate virtue, increase pride, and lead him down the road to hell. Under the circumstances, it was urgent for him to get on with his studies while he was still capable of learning. Only after studying theology should he consider leaving the schools and then only to join the household of a bishop, where he would be able to put his education to use in the service of the Church.[92]

These ideas of the purpose of education are not wholly consistent with the seemingly more humanist attitudes Peter expresses elsewhere in his letters. Peter himself was probably not completely aware of how much his opinions had changed. His own experience must have embittered him about politics as it had about civil law. In the years when Peter, cut off from political life, was increasingly preoccupied with religious matters and corresponded more often with prelates and theologians, he may have been influenced by the new reform ideas emanating from Paris and later, under Innocent III, from Rome.[93] Still, his hopes for the future were, no doubt, tempered both by his personal disappointment over his career and by his apparent scepticism about the improvability of human nature.

In a letter to Cardinal Octavian written after 1190, Peter complains that illiterate men, wholly untrained in theology, are appointed to the episcopacy while learned men are overlooked. "In former times," he writes, echoing the familiar theme of the decline of learning, "the position of the wise was incalculably venerable, but today prudence is judged both vile and common."[94] But Peter was hardly sanguine that even learned bishops would improve the situation. In a letter written in his younger days in response to a certain master's complaints about bishops who rewarded their relatives instead of scholars, Peter bluntly charges hypocrisy. "You who now rage so against bishops," he writes, "will become a bishop, God willing, and you will, if I know you, then publicly rage against scholars. For those who have sweet tongues while in study sharpen them when they become bishops. . . . Surely, I know that when you are carried into the bishop's chair, the memory of the scholar's life will be carried out of your mind."[95] For Peter, there was no assurance that a scholar, however well educated, would as a bishop correct the abuses he had once so strongly condemned while in the schools. Few of his contemporaries would have been so honest.

Perhaps it was his honesty, as his most sympathetic biographer has argued, that kept Peter of Blois from attaining his ambitions.[96] Neither his harsh tongue nor his vanity could have endeared him to those who might have helped him. It also was probably no help that he was a Frenchman who, although resident in England for more than half his long life, never learned to speak the language of that country. Even if he had, however, he would likely have suffered from the increasing hostility the English were feeling toward foreigners.[97] Other than his skill as a letter writer and the literary renown that his collection brought him – that unfortunately came much too late in his life to make any difference in his career – Peter always had too little to offer. He had neither the good birth nor the powerful friends and patrons nor the practical expertise that might have assured his success.

But whatever the obstacles that stood in the way of his advancement – and he was hardly so completely self-deluded as not to have recognized them – Peter seemed to find comfort in rewriting his letters to explain his life not as a series of personal failures but as an example of the failings of his time. Throughout, he retained his humanist pretensions. Indeed, even after Peter turned his attention to religious matters and renounced his worldly ambitions, he continued to use the idea of the decline of learning to help to justify his own past.

Probably nowhere are Peter's pretensions better revealed than in the letter he wrote to defend himself against the quite accurate charges of a critic—whom he, again imitating John of Salisbury, calls Cornificius—that he could only compile opinions and cite examples from classical and patristic sources.[98] After marshaling a wide array of authorities and repeating, without acknowledgment, Bernard of Chartres's metaphor of dwarfs standing on the shoulders of giants, Peter states that he simply wrote too fast to have plagiarized.[99] By characteristically embellishing his defense with the classical example of Julius Caesar dictating four letters at a time—which he had to go no further than the *Policraticus* to find—Peter appears to prove himself guilty as charged.[100]

Such habits and pretensions have not gained Peter of Blois the sympathy of modern scholars. They also make it rather difficult to take much of what he says, including his criticisms of the schools and his complaints about the state of learning, at face value. Nevertheless, Peter's letters do contribute to our understanding of the significance of the educational ideas of those who, despite their distance from Paris, remained interested in developments in the schools.

GERALD OF WALES

Nearly as long-lived as Peter of Blois, and by far the most prolific of the humanist critics of the schools, was Giraldus Cambrensis, or Gerald of Wales (c. 1146–1223). His varied writings, which fill eight thick volumes of the Rolls Series, represent Gerald's efforts to portray himself as a man whose learning and experience qualified him to serve Church and king but who was denied advancement because of his society's disregard for his education and distrust of his nationality. Whereas Peter's personal aspirations remained rather vague, Gerald had one specific goal in mind all his life: to succeed his uncle David FitzGerald as bishop of St. David's and to gain metropolitan status for that see. Twice the goal seemed in reach but twice it eluded him, the second time after four long years of litigation. It was after this second defeat, in 1203, that Gerald turned his full attention to writing, as Peter of Blois had done in 1184. The first work Gerald completed was an autobiography, *De rebus a se gestis*.[101] Like Peter's collection of letters, Gerald's autobiography is a retrospective account of a career, the selective, and often even deceptive, rewriting of a past, in which the disappointed humanist author attempts to portray his life in the best possible light. An important source for information about the schools and for attitudes toward education, the *De rebus* is perhaps most valuable for what it reveals of the humanists themselves, of the frequent disparity between their learning and their pretensions, as well as of the close connection between the ideals about which they wrote so eloquently and the ambitions that they were never able to forget or to hide.

Before examining what Gerald of Wales says about the schools, let us first look at his life by following, though at a critical distance, the autobiographical account he gives in the *De rebus*.

Gerald was born into a prominent Pembrokeshire family of mixed Norman and Welsh ancestry. Despite his later claims, he was, in fact, only one quarter Welsh, but that one grandparent was the Welsh prince Rhys ap Tewdr (d. 1093). Gerald emphasizes that from his youngest years he had been identified as an advocate and champion of the Church. When he played in the sand with his older brothers, they would build castles and villages; he designed only churches and monasteries.[102] Called by his father "my bishop," not an unlikely destiny for the younger son of such a family, Gerald was sent to be educated at the monastery of St. Peter in nearby Gloucester. From there, having learned his Latin, he went to Paris sometime before 1165 to continue his study of the liberal arts. At the schools of Paris, Gerald was, according to his own immodest testimony, wholly devoted to the arts, an exemplary student whom masters cited as a model for the other pupils. He probably also taught the trivium, like John of Salisbury and Peter of Blois, while still a student. But Gerald, characteristically, makes the more exalted, and doubtful, claim that his teaching, especially in the art of rhetoric, was equal to that of the greatest masters in Paris.[103] After making such an apparently promising start for a career in the Church, Gerald returned to Wales in 1174 and immediately became embroiled in conflict.

Gerald's first stay in Paris, though devoted mostly to the study of the liberal arts, acquainted him with the reform ideas then being taught by the theology masters. He would not formally study theology until later, but he was already committed to a program of ecclesiastical reform. In Wales, Gerald zealously and, at times, ruthlessly promoted this program of reform, first under commission from Archbishop Richard of Canterbury and later as archdeacon of Brecon. Gerald's predecessor in this position was an elderly cleric who had long gotten away with keeping a concubine, until the young reformer had mercilessly had him deposed. His reform activities brought Gerald into conflict with many Welsh ecclesiastics, including the newly appointed bishop of St. Asaph's, his former colleague in Paris, Master Adam of Petit Pont, who had finally been able to retire from the schools in 1175 after decades of teaching.[104] But however unpopular his actions made him in some circles, Gerald still had the social connections to make him a leading candidate for bishop when his uncle died in May 1176. Although not quite thirty, and therefore below the minimum age for a bishop, Gerald was among the four candidates nominated by the cathedral chapter and, according to his own testimony, their preferred candidate. But the chapter had acted without royal approval. When Henry II received the nominations, he ignored the advice of Archbishop Richard and of other English bishops, who supported Gerald as the candidate ideally fitted to be bishop by both birth and education. Instead, the king pressured the chapter to elect the Cluniac prior of Winlock, Peter de Leia. According to Gerald, Henry II chose this Anglo-Norman monk as bishop to prevent any furtherance of St. David's claims of metropolitan status, which he feared, if established, might boost the cause of Welsh independence from royal authority. If so, the king no doubt acted wisely in not agreeing to the election of the ambitious young Gerald of Wales as bishop.[105]

At the time, this must have seemed no more than a temporary setback to Gerald. It also gave him the opportunity to return to Paris and continue his studies. According to his own account, Gerald accomplished a great deal in the three short years he spent in the schools. His intention had been to complete the study of the liberal arts so that, as he writes, "he might have power, upon the foundation of arts and letters, to raise high the walls of civil and canon law and above them to complete the sacred roof of theological learning, and finally to secure this triple edifice with bonds that time should not destroy."[106] Proudly, Gerald claims not only to have successfully completed this program of study but also to have become a renowned lecturer on the *Decretum* of Gratian, able to fill the largest lecture halls in Paris and to impress even the greatest masters with his knowledge of the law and his erudition. His audience, he boasts, often assumed he had studied in Bologna. But, despite his original intentions, he never did actually attend the law schools. Gerald first postponed his plans to go to Bologna in order to take over the law lectures of Martin of Anjou, when that Paris master was made a cardinal. Then, as he was having some problems receiving the income from his prebends, he found it necessary to leave Paris and return home.[107]

One historian has aptly called this account of Gerald's time in Paris "one of the most delightful specimens of his naive self-glorification."[108] It would have been nearly impossible for any scholar, however diligent, to accomplish all that Gerald claimed he did in less than three years. Nor is it likely that the fees Gerald would have received as a successful lecturer in law would have failed to support him adequately until his financial problems were resolved. Indeed, the lack of any corroborative evidence of Gerald's claimed renown as a teacher confirms that this really is an account of what Gerald, as an old man writing his autobiography, wished he had accomplished when younger. We do know, however, that during these years in Paris Gerald did attend the lectures of the leading theologians of the day, including Masters Peter Comestor and Peter the Chanter, and was strongly influenced by their ideas.[109]

For the period from 1179 until 1184, when Gerald entered royal service, his account of his career is rather obscure. No doubt he was preoccupied with seeking a means of advancement. Meanwhile, Gerald claims, Richard of Canterbury asked him to assume the administration of the diocese of St. David's because Peter de Leia had had so much difficulty with his chapter and clergy that he had fled Wales and sought refuge in an English monastery. How long this commission lasted is unclear, but it appears that Gerald, despite his animosity for Peter de Leia, did play a part in restoring peace between the bishop and the chapter.[110] Elsewhere, Gerald reports that in 1182 or 1183 he made his first journey to Ireland with his elder brother, Philip, to help his uncle, Robert FitzStephen, royal governor of the kingdom of Cork.[111] It was on that trip that he began to collect material for his histories of Ireland.

Only in recounting his reluctant decision, in 1184, to become court chaplain to Henry II does the *De rebus* again begin to provide a detailed account of Gerald's career. Gerald maintains that he entered the king's service unwillingly. Sounding very much the humanist, he explains that only Henry's persistent commands and promises convinced him that he had to leave the pleasant life of scholarship for the detestable life of the courtier. Whatever promises Henry made him were never fulfilled. Gerald complains that his ten years of loyal service to the king would have made him a great man had he not been Welsh.[112] Disappointment colors the account Gerald gives of his activities during these years. Despite his frequent complaints about the lack of rewards for learning, Gerald claims, paradoxically, that he refused several bishoprics, two in Ireland and two in Wales, because he desired to continue his studies and pursued them with almost ceaseless assiduity while serving at court.[113] More likely, Gerald had turned these down in the hope that St. David's would be offered to him again. There is less reason to doubt Gerald's claims that he wrote late into the night. All four of his works on Ireland and Wales were drafted during these years.

The self-flattering account Gerald gives of his efforts to publicize the first of these works, the *Topographia Hibernica*, when it was completed in 1187 is a wonderful example of his pride and self-aggrandizement. Rather than hiding the candle he had lit under a bushel, Gerald explains, he decided to let it shine by reading the book before the most learned audience in England, the clerics of Oxford. On each of three successive days he read one of the three parts of the book and then gave a magnificent feast: for the poor on the first day, for all the masters and their best students on the second day, and for the rest of the city's scholars, as well as local knights and prominent townsmen, on the third. Gerald describes the occasion as "a magnificent and costly achievement," one comparable to the public presentations of the ancient poets (whom he seems to have been trying to imitate) and never equaled in England before or since.[114] If Gerald did in fact give what might have been the first published public lecture series in Oxford, it would be interesting to know the scholars' reaction to him and his book. Still, to put Gerald's story in perspective, it should be noted that Oxford was hardly a Rome or an Athens, and would not even begin to rival Paris for several decades to come.

Gerald of Wales finally left royal service in 1194 or 1195, desiring to withdraw "from the vanity of the court to the calm and tranquil haven of the schools" and intending to recommence his theological studies in Paris.[115] Unhappily, he found that the renewed warfare between Richard I and Philip Augustus made travel from England to France difficult and dangerous. Instead of Paris, Gerald had to settle for the best school in England. He made his way, accordingly, to Lincoln, where Chancellor William de Montibus, himself a former student and master in Paris, was trying to make the latest ideas of moral and sacramental theology understandable to the English parish clergy.[116] William's teaching was simple, practical, and not very original, but it apparently satisfied Gerald. Still, during the years he spent at Lincoln, Gerald was probably less occupied with his studies than with preparing for the death of his old rival Peter de Leia, which he knew might provide his final chance for the bishopric of St. David's.

When Peter did die in July 1198, Gerald again headed the list of four candidates nominated by the cathedral chapter. This time, however, he was strongly opposed by the new archbishop, Hubert Walter, who, anxious to keep the Welsh Church securely subordinate to the authority of Canterbury, was attempting to convince the chapter to accept an English candidate. Little happened until the accession of King John seemed to clear the way for Gerald's election. In June 1199 the chapter of St. David's unanimously elected Gerald bishop and directed him to bypass the archbishop of Canterbury and proceed directly to Rome to be consecrated by the pope. While preparing for the first of the three journeys he would make to Rome, Gerald learned that the chapter of St. David's had received letters from Hubert Walter and from the royal justiciar stating that if they did not accept as their bishop Geoffrey, prior of Llanthony, the English candidate they had previously refused, he would be consecrated without their approval. For four years the case of the two rival bishops-elect languished unresolved before Innocent III. Finally, in April 1203, the pope quashed the claims of both, ordered the chapter to hold a new election, and stipulated that the bishop-elect was to be consecrated by the archbishop of Canterbury.[117] After all his efforts and expenditures traveling back and forth to Rome, Gerald recognized that the case had been decisively lost for both St. David's and himself. No longer interested in being bishop if it meant he had to be consecrated by the archbishop of Canterbury, Gerald accepted the election of his rival, Geoffrey of Llanthony, resigned the archdeaconry of Brecon, and returned to Lincoln. The final twenty years of his life were devoted wholly to scholarship.

The manuscript of Gerald's autobiography, his first project during these years, ends suddenly and inexplicably in the midst of the dispute over St. David's. Throughout his lengthy account of these struggles, Gerald unconvincingly portrays himself as an unwilling and scrupulous litigant, more concerned with the rights of the Welsh Church than with his own advancement. He claims, for example, that when he was first urged to approach Richard I about the vacant position, he refused to do so because on principle he believed that men should be sought for bishoprics, not seek them, and also because he preferred to continue his studies at Lincoln.[118] Only later, when summoned by King John and chosen unanimously by the canons of St. David's, did he give all his honest efforts to pursuing his rightful cause. Telling of his first trip to Rome, he likewise emphasizes that he did not, as was common practice, try to win his case by bribery. Instead he offered the learned Innocent III six of his own writings. "Others offer you pounds [*libras*]," Gerald says he told the pope, "but I offer you books [*libros*]."[119] Innocent III was so impressed with the books, Gerald boasts, that he kept them all at his bedside for nearly a month. After that, although he reluctantly gave the other five to cardinals, Innocent insisted on keeping the *Gemma ecclesiastica*, which he especially loved.

This is the typical persona that Gerald ascribes to himself throughout his autobiography and in his other writings. He is both a serious scholar and an active reformer, especially committed to defending the rights and liberties of the Welsh Church. Both his learning and his experience put him a cut above his contemporaries. These qualities were recognized by the truly great but not by those, like Hubert Walter, who did not appreciate the value of a sound education and who were often prejudiced against him because he was Welsh. It has been argued that Gerald's Welshness was never more than a convenient excuse for his failure to secure St. David's.[120] Gerald was three-quarters Anglo-Norman, and he willingly spent years in service to the English crown and Church. Although the author of important books on Wales and Ireland, he could not speak Welsh and expresses little esteem for what he generally characterizes as the barbarous, ever-rebellious Celtic nations. Still, Gerald's identification with Wales does seem to have grown stronger, at least temporarily, during his struggle for St. David's. Welshmen from all levels of society supported him at that time against what they had long regarded, and he came increasingly to regard, as English oppression. After 1203, however, Gerald was as disillusioned with the Welsh Church as with the English crown.

The other prominent aspect of the identity Gerald tried to establish for himself, and the one that concerns us more directly, was his commitment to scholarship. Here his claims are far more convincing. Although his autobiography obviously exaggerates his educational accomplishments, his fame as a scholar, and especially his eminence as a master, Gerald did devote much of his life to scholarship. In total, he completed seventeen books. Judging from the limited number of surviving manuscripts, most of them made remarkably little impact on his contemporaries. Nevertheless, Gerald's scholarly activities and pretensions are significant expressions of the educational and cultural standards against which he measured himself and others. There is a temptation to dismiss Gerald's frequent complaints about the decline of learning, his repeated criticisms of the ignorance of the clergy, and his calls for educational reform as no more than thinly disguised attempts to justify the failure of both his literary efforts and his career. Still, however annoying we may find his intellectual pretensions, Gerald's writings show the unmistakable influence of the learned masters of arts and of the theologians with whom he had studied in Paris. Despite his sometimes uncontrollable bitterness and defensiveness, Gerald of Wales was genuinely committed to using his learning and his experience to further the cause of reform in the schools, in the Church, and in society as a whole.

We can only glance at a few of Gerald's writings here. The best place to begin is the dedicatory prefaces Gerald added to the revised editions of the two histories of Wales, the *Itinerarium Kambriae* and the *Descriptio Kambriae*, which he presented to Stephen Langton sometime after 1213. The explicit purpose of each is to justify the time and effort he spent writing and rewriting these works. Gerald begins the preface to the *Itinerarium* by giving his own version of the now-familiar humanist idea of the decline of learning, its causes and consequences:

> Just as in our daily habits we are affected by new circumstances and by fresh ideas, so are the minds of men influenced by their various life-patterns. . . . Conditioned as they are by their different social backgrounds, men will devote themselves to pursuits of the most varied kinds. Young soldiers delight in bearing arms and waging war; lawyers take pleasure in putting on their gowns and arguing

cases; others strive anxiously to accumulate riches and see wealth as the supreme good. Some study Galen, others give all their time to Justinian. Those who aspire to honors frequent the court, and, as their reputations wax and wane, so their ambition, which is insatiable, can only leave them disillusioned. Some, indeed, but very few, find pleasure in the liberal arts. Among their number we can wonder at the logicians, who, when they have made some small progress, are so delighted with their studies that we watch them "pass their later years in the mazy labyrinths of dialectics with as much joy as if they were bearing down on the rocks where once of old Sirens sang."

Among so many different sorts and conditions of men, where are the divine poets? Where are the masters of the Latin tongue? Who nowadays in his writings, whether they be poetry or history, can hope to add new lustre to the art of letters? Who in our time, I ask, is building up a system of ethics, or, held firm for ever in the works he writes, recording for eternity deeds which are nobly done? In earlier times the man of letters stood on the topmost step of the hall of fame. Now those who devote themselves to study, which is toppled deep in ruin, or so it seems, and sunk in disrepute, are no longer there to be emulated, they earn no respect, on the contrary they are disliked and despised.[121]

The passage has force and originality. The combination of social observation, autobiographical reflection, and literary allusion, characteristic of Gerald's writing generally, here adds credibility to the treatment of themes that had become commonplace yet remained compelling. All of the usual enemies of the humanists are included—lawyers, physicians, courtiers, logicians. Gerald reserves his criticisms for the last two, charging that their occupations have the same attractions and failings. Gerald does not elaborate on this charge, but its meaning is clear: both service in court and the study of logic attract those who seek wealth and fame, keeping them from other, more useful activities and studies. This pairing of the court and dialectic suggests the connection the humanists saw between professionalism and specialization.

Yet Gerald goes on to make an important distinction between the two activities. Dialectic can be useful if studied in moderation. The courtly life, on the other hand, is completely useless, an irretrievable waste of time and, even for the ambitious, no more certain a means of gaining a reward than playing dice. Alluding only vaguely to his own years in court service, Gerald depicts himself as a man of letters no longer interested in pleasing princes or in gaining material rewards (although he is honest enough to admit that he would not refuse them). He is writing, instead, in order to please future generations and to gain immortality. Still, Gerald hopes that Stephen Langton will read and approve the works being sent to him. If not, Gerald writes, "then, indeed, the esteem in which literature was once held really has vanished, and my work must be left to posterity, in the hope that one day such honors may return."[122] Here it is especially clear how closely the humanists' complaints about the decline of learning were tied to their personal concerns about the lack of social recognition and material reward for their years of scholarship.

Gerald wrote two different prefaces for the *Descriptio*, each refuting a different criticism of his scholarly efforts. The first objection was that he had been misusing his learning by writing about unworthy subjects when he should be devoting his time to theology. Gerald justifies writing the history of his own country as an opportunity to contribute to the record of noble human deeds. Moreover, he says, it has always been his intention, once he had practiced his literary skills on such writing, to compose what he immodestly describes as "a great masterpiece upon a theme both sacred and sublime."[123] His scholarship thus perfectly exemplifies the principle of the arts serving their queen, theology.

The objection addressed in the second preface recalls Thomas Becket's concern about John of Salisbury's lack of ambition. Scholarly preoccupations, some had charged, had gotten in the way of Gerald's promotion. In his own defense, Gerald insists, unconvincingly, that he was never motivated by the desire for material rewards, but only by the love of letters. He would hardly be foolish enough to seek or to expect any gain in a time when princes are illiterate and do not value learning. The unprincipled life of the courtier is the way to affluence, but, he says, "I prefer my honest poverty to affluence which I do not want. What one owns must always perish, but what I have will live. Possessions pass away, but my skills live for ever. Fame I prefer to money, I would rather have glory than wealth."[124] Yet even fame eluded Gerald. He complains that the great men to whom he sent his writings had locked them away and never looked at them again. His hope rests on a final plea to Stephen Langton to read his history, recognize its merits, and prevent him from perishing into obscurity.

These prefaces, especially the second, are compelling in a way the letters of Peter of Blois never quite succeed in being. Gerald seems intent upon rewriting his entire life to deny the ambitions he had once had, to separate himself from every action and every person that had injured him, and to give himself one last chance of recognition and success. More than anything else, perhaps, the fact that he addressed his appeal to Stephen Langton reveals the aspirations that he, even in his last years, continued to nurse. The victorious archbishop represented what Gerald had wanted to be. A renowned master of theology, Langton had been elected to the primacy of England without ever courting the favor of kings, and then it had taken him years of bitter struggle against the king and English ecclesiastics to secure his rightful position. When he came to compare his own life to that of Stephen Langton, Gerald felt understandably defensive about the years he had expended both in royal service and on his secular writings.

The change is most apparent in his political treatise, *De principis instructione.*[125] When he began this treatise in the early 1190's, Gerald was still hopeful of gaining King Richard's support for St. David's. It was then intended to be a "mirror for princes," much like the *Policraticus*, teaching what makes a good ruler and warning of the dangers of tyranny. Not completed until the tumultuous final years of King John's reign, when Stephen Langton was in the thick of political affairs, the treatise became instead a harsh diatribe against the entire Angevin dynasty. Henry II, once considered a patron by the humanists, is portrayed as a tyrant indifferent to learning and hostile to the Church. His sons Richard and John fare no better. In contrast, Gerald has much praise for the Capetians, especially for Louis VII, the king who had made John of Salisbury bishop of Chartres. The French kings' policy of patronizing learning and of defending the Church served them well in gaining the esteem of the humanists.

Despite his defensiveness about his secular writings, Gerald seems to have accepted the fact that if he were ever to gain fame, it would be for his histories, not his theological works. Even after he completed his first major theological treatise, the *Gemma ecclesiastica*, which Innocent III supposedly liked so much, Gerald returned to revising his histories of Wales, writing his autobiography, completing the *De principis*, and editing his earlier works and letters. Although he often asserted that history should be written as the liberal arts should be studied, only by young men, Gerald himself did not conform to this principle. For example, in a letter to his friend and fellow humanist Walter Map about the superiority of theology, Gerald advises that the liberal arts be studied as quickly as possible because "we should apply our more mature years to more mature studies and especially to sacred Scripture, for whose majesty and profundity human capacity is hardly sufficient, even when given all its time."[126] But Gerald is far more convincing when, in a letter to William de Montibus, he criticizes scholars who, too anxious to prove themselves theologians and unable to come up with any original ideas, collect old and often outdated material from previous works and present them as their own inventions. In contrast, he contends, his histories offer new information that is useful in the present and will be valuable to posterity. Here too, however, after citing an array of classical and patristic sources to prove the value of writing history, Gerald reverts to the more cautious if less accurate defense that he has now put these youthful endeavors aside for theology.[127] Gerald never quite stopped wanting to have it both ways.

When he did turn his attention from history to theology, Gerald changed only his subject, not his style of writing. Both his major theological works, the *Gemma ecclesiastica* and the *Speculum ecclesiae*, are far more anecdotal and descriptive than methodical and analytical. Despite his apparently serious efforts to present the practical theology he had learned in Paris in a simple and popular way, Gerald found it easier to tell entertaining stories, which were often only remotely related to his theme, than to be systematic. Even when writing what was supposed to be theology, he could never cease emphasizing matters that bore directly on his own experience or that he hoped might raise his esteem in the eyes of posterity, if not of his contemporaries. This is clearly evident in Gerald's preoccupation with describing the unsuitability, particularly the ignorance, of the prelacy and of the clergy. His discussion of the adverse effects of appointing bishops who spent their careers in royal service gave him the chance to get back at his adversary, Hubert Walter, and in criticizing monks who became bishops he took a swipe at his two successful rivals for St. David's.[128] Nevertheless, Gerald's complaints about the lack of learning among the prelacy, even if they do sound self-serving, echo those of many other reformers.

Gerald of Wales had an annoying tendency to use correct principles in questionable ways. For example, Gerald is quick to charge that bishops who refuse to allow members of their chapters to take up temporary residence at the schools do so because "they know that it would be advantageous to have archdeacons and priests under them who are stupid, illiterate, immoral, and idle, and who would not dare to raise their heads against them, rather than honest, stout, and educated ones."[129] Other supporters of nonresidence for scholars made the same point, but somehow Gerald's sincerity and objectivity always seem suspect. In this case, he was writing to none other than his successful rival Geoffrey, bishop of St. David's, who had apparently refused to permit Gerald's nephew and successor as archdeacon of Brecon to leave the diocese to study at Lincoln.

If Innocent III really liked the *Gemma ecclesiastica* as much as Gerald boasts, it may be because he enjoyed well-told stories of clerical life—or, more likely, because he recognized that substantial portions of the book were a reworking of chapters of Peter the Chanter's *Verbum abbreviatum*.[130] Without any direct acknowledgment, Gerald excerpts extensive material from the Chanter's work. For the most part, Gerald's contributions are limited to the comments and anecdotes he adds to make "the gems of doctrine from the writings of the Church" – as he explains it in the preface – more accessible to the Welsh clergy of his archdeaconry.[131] It is on the issue of clerical ignorance that Gerald of Wales shows his greatest independence from Peter the Chanter. The *Gemma* is no less critical of the clergy's inability to understand or speak Latin correctly than it is of their ignorance of doctrine. According to Gerald, this limited knowledge of grammar and rhetoric impedes all other learning and makes it impossible for the clergy to fulfill their essential duties of teaching and preaching to the laity. To illustrate his point, Gerald cites more than twenty examples of simple but serious errors of grammar and punctuation made by priests and prelates of every rank, including archbishops, in their sermons, letters, and arguments before a court.[132] It is the kind of detailed evidence that Gerald relished as a historian. He expounds the grammatical errors with all the smugness of a proud Latin master. We are a long way from John of Salisbury's more theoretical concerns that the degeneration of speech was a threat to social life.

For Gerald of Wales, as for the other humanists, the problem was not so much that clerics and prelates were not being educated – the humanists were not unaware of the rising numbers of young men attending the schools – but that they were not being educated properly. Using a scheme he attributes to Ralph of Beauvais, the grammar master whom Peter of Blois criticizes so harshly, Gerald distinguishes between three types of scholars: (1) the "patchers" (*pannosi*), who gather only bits and pieces of the liberal arts, not really trying to learn anything, but wanting merely to appear learned; (2) the "superficially educated" (*superseminati*), who neglect the writings of the classical poets and philosophers and, after studying only the elementary grammar texts of Donatus and Cato, rush off to study law; and (3) the "solidly educated" (*massati*), who take the time to acquire a sound foundation in grammar and the liberal arts before advancing to other subjects. Only the last group, he insists, can be said to be "truly and formally learned."[133] The appeal of law is, again, seen as the most serious hindrance to learning. With the humanists' typical distrust of the motives of lawyers, Gerald complains that avarice and ambition alone could account for increasing numbers of young men studying civil law. There were now so many lawyers, Gerald adds, that a prediction that he had heard Master Mainerius make in Paris had come true. "The days will come," Mainerius had warned his students, "and woeful will they be, when the laws will obliterate the knowledge of letters."[134]

Most of Gerald's criticisms in the *Gemma ecclesiastica* are reserved for that other enemy of humane learning, dialectic. Again he prefers to relate anecdotes and cite authorities, rather than argue his point directly. After deriding certain clerics who returned to England from Paris and boasted of their learning in incorrect Latin, Gerald tells one story, perhaps for the first time, that would later appear frequently as an exemplum in the *sermones ad scholares*. In his version, a cleric who has spent five years in Paris is asked by his father what he has learned and he proudly claims to be able to prove logically that "four is eight, and six is twelve, etc." Later, at dinner, the clever father orders his son to prove that the six eggs they have been served are twelve. When the scholar uses the rules of logic to produce six more eggs, his father tells him he can eat those eggs and keeps the six real eggs for himself. The hungry scholar, Gerald concludes, is sent back to Paris again, "not to waste his time on the ensnaring subtleties of the logicians, but to exert all his efforts in learning letters."[135] The story is meant to embellish the same lesson that John of Salisbury had illustrated with the account of his time in the schools. Dialectic, Gerald argues, can be a useful tool when applied to the concrete problems that arise in studying other subjects, but when studied exclusively or excessively, it only traps scholars in a morass of trivial and insoluble questions that are of no practical use whatsoever.

There is little new in this argument or in the various classical and patristic sources that Gerald then quotes at length to defend the study of dialectic. He does differ from other humanists and comes much closer to Peter the Chanter, however, in making a strong case for dialectic's potential value to pastoral theology and to the practical needs of the ministry. Dialectic could be valuable in the training of clergy, but it was not being taught correctly. Instead of learning how to preach and to defend the faith, students of dialectic learned skills useful only in scholastic disputation. When he was studying dialectic himself, Gerald writes, an aged theologian had asked him a question that taught him a wise lesson:

> What use is the dialectic you torment yourself so much to learn unless you have a colleague with whom to dispute? And since dialectic involves disputation to defeat another, he will not be satisfied to debate in private. Thus, there will have to be a judge, and you would not want one who might be prejudiced in favor of your opponent. Then, too, you will want a learned crowd to witness the dispute, so that your art might appear publicly useful. I, however, even if seated alone in a corner reading my books, can extract the fruit of theological doctrine, either to edify myself or in order to edify others. And even if I am the only learned man in a large crowd of laity, I can recite a useful sermon on faith and good morals and talk continuously, not needing any discussion.[136]

The conclusion Gerald draws from this story applies not just to dialectic but to all other disciplines, including theology. "Just as speaking," Gerald writes, "is the instrument of, or the reason for, rhetoric and argumentation is the instrument of dialectic, so preaching is the instrument of theology."[137] Although awkwardly stated, the principle is clear: all learning should be judged by its practical usefulness. The liberal arts, as well as theology, should be taught in order to prepare clerics for the duties of the ministry. For a priest who must teach and preach, the ability to speak correctly and to make a logical argument are no less important than knowledge of doctrine. As far as Gerald was concerned, the leaders of the Church had no less of a responsibility to ensure that the clergy were taught the liberal arts properly than to oversee their instruction in theology.

The *Gemma ecclesiastica* was completed and presented to Innocent III in 1199. More than twenty years later, in 1220, when Gerald composed the preface for his second theological treatise, the *Speculum ecclesiae*, his concerns and attitudes had changed little. Again he addresses the theme of the decline of learning, this time documenting grammatical faults in – apparently (this part of the text is missing) – the Latin pronunciation and accentuation of the monks of Christ Church, Canterbury. If these faults are not corrected soon, he argues, they may spread to the rest of the English clergy, who have hitherto "long excelled in learning."[138] As in the *Gemma*, Gerald attributes the defects to the fact that even those who attend the schools generally receive an insufficient grounding in grammar before specializing in law or logic. Concerning the appeal of law, Gerald repeats, with only minor changes, both the prediction of Master Mainerius and the threefold scheme of Ralph of Beauvais. To these he adds a third anecdote: Master Martin, he says, when participating in a legal disputation in Oxford, often defended himself by attacking his opponents for having jumped too quickly from the rudiments of grammar to the complexities of Roman law.[139]

In the years since he wrote the *Gemma*, Gerald apparently came to see a closer connection between the errors of the dialecticians and other developments harmful to humane learning. After criticizing lawyers, Gerald writes:

> Another cause of the defect of letters is that these days scholars who study the trivium almost completely neglect the two most important disciplines: grammar, which teaches one to speak correctly, and rhetoric, which teaches one to speak elegantly and ornately. Instead they rush as quickly as possible to study logic, seeking the garrulous loquacity that will make them seem clever and keen. They are not even ashamed to become masters after only three or four years of study and to teach poorly to others the useless learning that they themselves have imperfectly mastered, so that they can boast of the proud title of master and still move on quickly to the lucrative sciences of law and medicine.[140]

In identifying the dialecticians with lawyers and physicians, Gerald was probably being more polemical than factual. Specialization and professionalism had long been paired as the twin enemy of the liberal arts. But they did not, in Gerald's view, bear the entire blame for the decline of learning. Princes were equally at fault because they no longer patronized the learned. Repeating criticisms he had made before, Gerald contrasts both ancient rulers, who bestowed honors and rewards on the great poets and philosophers, and more recent ones, who appointed bishops from among those well trained in the arts, to the ignorant and illiterate princes of his own day, who offered neither encouragement nor support to scholars.[141] Obviously even in the last years of his life, Gerald remained bitter about how little he had gained from his years of service to the Angevins.

Yet, although his criticisms remain much the same as before, Gerald displays a new, if cautious, optimism in the preface to the *Speculum ecclesiae*. "Perhaps," he writes with unusual hope, "literature might soon be restored."[142] Gerald sees two recent events as signs of possible improvements in the state of affairs from which he had so unfairly suffered and against which he had so actively struggled. Both are reforms affecting the schools of Paris. He cites first a mandate of Pope Honorius III, almost certainly the bull *Super speculam* promulgated in November 1219 and addressed to the masters of the University of Paris.[143] To bolster the teaching of theology and to counteract the appeal of the "lucrative sciences" of law and medicine, Honorius had decreed that masters and students of theology were to be allowed to receive the revenues from their benefices for up to five years while resident at the schools, he had extended the previous decrees prohibiting monks and the regular clergy from studying civil law or medicine to include the beneficed clergy of all ranks, and he had ordered that the teaching of civil law cease in Paris. Judging from the still-readable lines of the damaged manuscript, Gerald believed that the decree would benefit the liberal arts as well as theology. He hoped "that when they [clerics] are not allowed to make the leap from letters and syllables directly to civil law as accustomed, . . . they will turn to literature and to the liberal arts, and then, building upon this sound foundation, they will proceed to the study of canon law and theology, the disciplines most necessary to human salvation."[144]

Gerald's second stated reason for hope was that lecturing on "certain books ascribed by title to Aristotle, discovered in Toledo, and translated into Latin" had been prohibited in the schools of France. It is not clear whether he is referring to the action taken by the Paris synod of 1210 or to the statutes promulgated for the university by Robert of Courson in 1215, both of which stipulated that neither Aristotle's books on natural philosophy nor their Arabic commentaries were to be studied or taught in Paris.[145] In either case, Gerald is unexpectedly optimistic that the prohibition of these novel and dangerous works, which, as he correctly comments, had already led some scholars into heresy and of which many others had grown too fond, would motivate scholars to return to "saner, sounder, and more salubrious" subjects. There could be no clearer indication of how rapidly and widely these new works had disseminated than the fact that Gerald quotes directly from one of them, the translator's preface to the *De anima* of Avicenna.[146] Conviction, not ignorance, made Gerald hopeful that he was witnessing the restoration of the traditional liberal arts to the curriculum and the realization of some of his educational ideals.

It may be remarkable but it is hardly surprising that in his final years Gerald of Wales should be so concerned, as well as so knowledgeable, about what was going on in Paris. Like the other humanists, Gerald, after the disappointments of his life in England, had increasingly looked to the schools to provide the impetus – and, no less important, to the papacy to provide the leadership – for the reforms that might reverse the decline of learning. It is true that the specific actions Gerald applauds in the *Speculum ecclesiae* were intended to strengthen the position and the prominence of theology at Paris and were not concerned with the liberal arts. But Gerald, who followed developments in Paris closely, must have known and been reassured by the fact that the statutes the papal legate Robert of Courson had promulgated in 1215 had given the arts a secure place in the curriculum of the university. He must also have considered the effort to subordinate all other subjects, including the liberal arts, to theology – which he himself had called "the queen of the arts" – to be completely compatible with his humanist educational ideals. Perhaps, too, Gerald of Wales saw, from a distance, that both the curriculum and the organization of the nascent University of Paris embodied these ideals, and he was optimistic enough to think he might be witnessing the triumph of humanism.

The optimism of this long-lived humanist has caused us to jump ahead. The university, as Gerald of Wales seems to have partially understood, was being shaped not by abstract, and already rather outdated, ideals but by active efforts to translate some of these ideals into a specific and practical program of educational reform. While the humanists and the satirists were criticizing trends in Paris from a distance, other critics, who shared many of their concerns and ideals, were directly trying to rectify the conditions in the schools that impaired what they believed should be the true nature and purpose of learning.

SIX

The Moralists I: Preaching to Scholars

MOST OF THOSE who were educated in the schools left Paris when their studies were completed to pursue careers elsewhere. Sometimes they came back to the city for a short visit or, when unemployed, for a longer stay, as John of Salisbury had done during his exile. But however interested these alumni were in the schools, they seldom had better than secondhand knowledge of recent educational developments and even more rarely did they have an opportunity to influence scholars directly. The critics we have discussed in the last two chapters, the humanists and the satirists, viewed the schools from a distance both of time and space. The ideals they advocated would probably have been rejected as old-fashioned, and certainly as impractical, by subsequent generations of scholars—if, that is, their criticisms had actually been heard or read in the schools. Perhaps those trained largely in the liberal arts did lack the ability to translate their learning into action. Or was the problem, rather, as the humanists and satirists would certainly have argued, that very few of them ever achieved positions in society that would enable them to do so? In either case, it is almost certainly true that there were others much better situated, as well as better prepared, than the masters of arts to observe and to influence developments in the schools.

By the middle of the twelfth century it was the teachers of theology and their students who dominated intellectual life in the schools, who ensured the prestige of Paris as a great center of learning, and who, despite the competition from those in what were commonly called the "lucrative sciences," law and medicine, usually went on to have the most distinguished careers. Although far fewer in number than the masters of arts, the theologians had greater prestige in the schools owing both to the status of their subject and to the fact that their tenure was usually longer and, thanks to the increased availability of prebends for their support, also more financially secure. Among the theologians who taught in Paris during the formative years of the university, many were concerned not with speculative questions but with practical and moral matters, many of which bore directly upon education. Strongly committed to using their learning to solve the ethical problems of their contemporaries, clerical and lay alike, these men often began by addressing and attempting to rectify the conditions that existed in the schools. There, they believed, they were training those who could and should provide the leadership necessary to reform the rest of society. In Paris, not only did these theologians lecture their own students on standards of conduct, but they also frequently preached to other scholars and clerics, ensuring these standards a broader audience and following. When they or their students later rose to positions of prominence outside the schools, their educational training had prepared them to translate the moral principles they had learned and taught into a practical program of social reform.

Thanks to John Baldwin's important book *Masters, Princes and Merchants: The Social Views of Peter the Chanter and His Circle* (Princeton, 1970), we now know just how the teaching of an important group of Paris theologians, the associates and pupils of Master Peter the Chanter, helped prepare the way for the program of social reform, including regulation of the schools and improvements in education, that culminated in the great Lateran Council called by Pope Innocent III in 1215. Less well known is how the preaching of a group of clerics who can best be called moralists, most of whom were theologians trained in Paris and some of whom were members of the circle of Peter the Chanter, may have been no less important in shaping attitudes both within and outside the schools about the necessary reforms.

These were critics who had the advantages of being able both to monitor conditions in the schools closely and to address their criticisms directly to scholars. When preaching at or about the schools, these critics tended to emphasize the moral aspects of education – the social responsibilities of the learned, the suitability of the curriculum, the conduct of scholars, and the duties of masters – and it is primarily for this reason that I have chosen to call them "moralists." It is a label no less descriptive, however, of the tone than of the topics of their sermons. Preaching to exhort scholars to improve their own behavior, as well as trying to inspire them to assume an active role in reforming others, the moralists tended to exaggerate the seriousness of the faults in the schools and in society.

Thus, although these critics were often in a better position to observe the schools, their sermons do not necessarily depict actual conditions any more reliably than the writings of the other groups we have studied. As we shall see, the moralists made many of the same criticisms of the schools and spoke for many of the same ideals as the other critics.

But their more direct and recent knowledge of the schools did enable them to articulate these ideals in more practical and useful ways. Their more specific criticisms and more concrete recommendations reflect the influence, so well documented by Baldwin, of the efforts of the masters of theology in Paris in the second half of the twelfth century to apply general ethical standards to specific cases. In the moralists' sermons one first sees the ideas that were to provide the impetus for reform and the practical policies that were to become the basis for legislative action. The sermons show the moralists involved in the process of translating educational ideals into a viable plan of action and reform. Since they were often preaching at or near the schools of Paris, in what were the formative decades of the university, their criticisms and recommendations probably had an important impact on the attitudes and the actions of others who were trying to arrive at a consensus about how reforms should and could be implemented.

But it is also important, in weighing the evidence of their sermons, to realize that these moralists were active and influential not only as preachers. Among them were several of the most prominent masters in the schools of Paris as well as renowned scholars who were—or were to become—powerful churchmen. They include two bishops of the diocese of Paris and—most notable for their direct responsibility overseeing the schools—the chancellors of Notre Dame cathedral for most of the period between 1160 and 1210. The moralists' sermons represent the opinions and concerns of a group of critics that includes, if not the actual founders of the University of Paris, then certainly those who were in positions to play a major, perhaps even a decisive, role in the university's formation and development.

Sermons are a vast and important source of evidence that historians have only recently begun to examine systematically. The richness of twelfth-century sermon collections as a source of information about the schools was established by Jean Longère's monumental study of the preaching of Paris masters published in 1975.[1] Although his study was limited to a group of twelve preachers who were active between 1153 and 1215, Longère examined no fewer than twelve hundred sermons in more than a hundred manuscript collections. It would hardly have been possible, nor fortunately has it been necessary, for me to duplicate such a vast endeavor. With the benefit of Longère's efforts and those of other scholars to identify preachers and to catalogue their sermons, I have been able to concentrate on the main sermon collections of a larger group of sixteen preachers who are known (with one exception) to have been educated, to have taught, or to have resided in Paris during the formative decades of the university. Eleven of these preachers belong to the group of Paris masters and secular clerics studied by Longère. To these I have added three theology masters (Robert Pullen, Simon of Tournai, and Alexander Neckham) who were associated with Paris for a time; one other master (Geoffrey of Troyes) with no known ties to Paris but whose sermons I found to share certain concerns and attitudes with this group of critics; and, finally, one very learned and influential regular cleric (Stephen of Tournai) who, although not himself educated in Paris, observed the schools and preached to scholars as abbot of Ste. Geneviève.

In the sermon collections attributed to these preachers, I have found a considerable number of sermons addressed explicitly to scholars and many others on topics clearly intended for a learned audience. Although relatively few of these sermons can be placed or dated with precision, most of them, given what we know about the careers of their authors, must have been written or first preached in or near Paris prior to 1215. The sermons vary in both literary quality and historical value. Some preachers are very specific in their criticisms and recommendations; others address educational matters only in general terms that required little knowledge of actual conditions in the schools. In many cases, one hears only distant echoes of the opinions and attitudes expressed by other critics; other sermons better reveal how some of the moralists used their preaching to publicize more widely the ideas that they also lectured about in the classroom.

In the next chapter, a few of these sermons will be analyzed in detail. Mostly, however, I have chosen to examine the sermons collectively by theme rather than individually by author. Despite the differences in their sermons, the moralists shared a commitment to improve education and to reform the schools. As we shall see, the scholars and other clerics preached to by the moralists heard many of the same lessons repeatedly. How much this preaching actually affected educational attitudes or the conduct of scholars is impossible to determine. But because many of the moralists had means other than preaching to influence their contemporaries and some were in positions that enabled them to act directly to effect their principles and policies, their sermons provide evidence of clear importance to the development of the schools. Before examining this evidence, we must therefore look closely at who the moralists were and at the relationship between their preaching and other activities.

THE PREACHERS

Ranked according to the influence of the positions they held while in Paris, the most prominent of those who preached to the scholars were two theology masters who became bishops of the city, Peter Lombard (1158-60) and Maurice of Sully (1160-96).

Peter Lombard, the "Master of the *Sentences*," received his early education in his native Novarra. He was nearly forty when he arrived in Paris, via Reims, in 1134 with a letter of introduction from Bernard of Clairvaux to Abbot Gilduin of St. Victor. Although he apparently planned only a short stay at St. Victor, Peter, like so many others, found Paris impossible to leave, and he remained to study under Hugh of St. Victor and perhaps also to hear Peter Abelard's final lectures. Within ten years of his arrival, the Lombard was teaching at the cathedral school and had already established a reputation as an outstanding theologian.[2] In 1148 he was one of the prominent masters named by Eugenius III to examine the writings of Gilbert of Poitiers. Meanwhile, having become a canon of Notre Dame sometime before 1145, he rapidly advanced up the ranks of the cathedral chapter as subdeacon (1147), deacon (1150), archdeacon (1157-58), and, after a disputed and controversial election, as bishop, an office he held for less than two years before his death in July 1160.[3]

As a theologian, Peter Lombard was renowned primarily for his summa, the *Sententiarum libri quatuor* (completed between 1155 and 1157), which became the standard theological textbook for centuries, and to a lesser extent for his earlier glosses on the Psalms and on the Epistles of St. Paul. His preaching was far less distinguished than his teaching. Of his thirty-four extant sermons all appear to date from his years in Paris, some from his short time as bishop; most were probably preached at Notre Dame.[4]

Peter Lombard's successor as bishop, Maurice of Sully, was, by contrast, renowned for his preaching. Born about 1120 into a poor family in a village near Orléans, Maurice provides an example of the opportunities learning sometimes provided for social advancement. Able somehow to make his way to the schools of Paris, Maurice by the mid-1140's had established himself as a theology master and as a prominent member of the cathedral chapter. Like the Lombard, he steadily advanced in capitular ranks before being elected bishop in a disputed election. According to one account of the dispute, the final choice of the chapter was between Maurice and another theology master, and member of our group of critics, Peter Comestor. Louis VII decided that the Comestor, who was the better teacher, should continue in the schools while Maurice, who was both a better preacher and better suited for the active life of caring for souls, should be bishop.[5] It was probably the right choice. For more than thirty-five years, until he retired to St. Victor shortly before his death in September 1196, Maurice of Sully proved himself an excellent administrator and an ardent reformer.[6]

Best remembered for raising the funds for and beginning the construction of the great new Gothic cathedral, Maurice of Sully was no less committed to his pastoral duties. Throughout his long term as bishop he worked actively to reform the clergy by frequently making parish visitations and by holding regular diocesan synods and to improve the instruction of the laity by encouraging preaching. Most of his extant sermons are addressed to the parish clergy or to the laity. The primary collection is a compilation, in both Latin and French versions, of short sermons on simple matters of doctrine intended to provide the clergy with examples of how to preach to a lay audience. Only the preface, which is concerned with the qualities of the clergy, has much relevance to education. In fact, Maurice's sermons are generally notable for their lack of direct reference to the schools or to issues that might have concerned an audience of scholars.[7] Although he had himself been a prominent master and as bishop was vitally concerned to improve the learning of the clergy, Maurice of Sully did not choose, unlike some of his successors, to get too directly involved in running the schools. Preoccupied with his other duties as bishop, he was apparently willing to leave the immediate direction and supervision of the schools to the learned chanters and chancellors who served under him.

By the mid-twelfth century there were two officials in the chapter who shared responsibility for the cathedral schools. The "chanter" (*cantor* or *precentor*), whose primary duty as supervisor of liturgical services placed him in charge of the choir, usually assumed responsibility for only the most rudimentary education of the choirboys. Much more important was the "chancellor" (*cancellarius*), to whom the bishop customarily entrusted the general supervision of the cathedral library and schools. His jurisdiction extended over all the scholars in Paris, excluding those on the Left Bank, who came under the authority of the abbot of Ste. Geneviève.[8] Whoever wished to teach had to obtain a license (the *licentia docendi*) from him. Of the six canons known to have held the position of chancellor of

Notre Dame between about 1150 and 1209, five were former masters who can be included in this group of moralist critics: Odo of Soissons (c. 1153 or 1160 to c. 1167), Peter Comestor (1168-78), Hilduin (c. 1178 to 1193), Peter of Poitiers (1193-1205), and Prévostin of Cremona (1206-9).[9]

The exact dates of Odo of Soissons's chancellorship remain in dispute. It is generally agreed that he was an early student of Peter Lombard and began teaching theology himself at Notre Dame by 1145, after being granted a canonry "per regis benignitatem." He left Paris in 1166 or 1167 to enter the Cistercian monastery of Ourscamp, near Noyon. Odo may have become chancellor as early as 1153; more likely, however, he was appointed to that position by his former master Peter Lombard in 1159 or 1160. After his retirement, Odo complained to Alexander III that Bishop Maurice of Sully had reneged on a promise to choose one of his former students (probably Simon of Tournai) to succeed him as chancellor and had appointed Peter Comestor instead.[10] Odo himself advanced rapidly. Elected abbot of Ourscamp soon after his arrival, he was appointed cardinal-bishop of Tusculum by the pope in 1171. He died in Rome the following year.[11] Among the works attributed to Odo are a collection of *Quaestiones*, which may be representative of his teaching, and nineteen sermons. Some of the sermons are addressed to monks, but others were certainly delivered to scholars while Odo was still in Paris.[12]

Odo's successor, Peter Comestor ("the Eater"), was said by legend to have been born one of a set of learned triplets, his brothers being two other renowned masters, Peter Lombard and Gratian, the author of the *Decretum*. The dubious story might suggest that he, like them, was of Lombard origins. Little is known for certain about Peter Comestor's early life. He first appears in the historical record as scholasticus and dean of Troyes in 1147. However, it is likely that he had previously studied in Paris, probably at St. Victor under Master Andrew. He certainly had been a student of Peter Lombard and probably also that master's direct successor at the cathedral school. Comestor had been teaching theology in Paris for at least two years when he was nominated to succeed Peter Lombard as bishop. His successful rival, Maurice of Sully, may have sought to placate him by giving him the chancellorship when it eventually became vacant on Odo's retirement in 1168. Peter remained chancellor for about ten years. He resigned upon entering St. Victor a few months before his death in October 1178.[13]

While he was chancellor, Peter completed his major work, the *Historia scholastica*, which quickly became the standard textbook of biblical history. Other examples of his teaching include treatises on the Eucharist, confession, and penance; commentaries on the Gospels (the first such lectures by a Paris master known); a summa on the sacraments; and collections of *quaestiones* reported from his lectures.[14] Judging from the number of his surviving sermons, Peter Comestor must also have been a popular preacher. No fewer than 160 sermons have been attributed to him. Preached in Troyes and in Paris to a variety of named or identifiable audiences—including monks, canons, priests, prelates, synods, and scholars—they comprise one of the richest collections of the period.[15]

Virtually nothing is known about the early career of the next chancellor, Hilduin. Probably, like his predecessors, he had been appointed to the position after a period of teaching in the schools. His only known works are a total of fifty-nine sermons found in two manuscripts attributed to "Master Hilduin" or to "Master Hilduin, Chancellor of Paris."[16] Most of these sermons are addressed to monks, regular canons, and synods. But Hilduin, as we shall see, seldom let pass an opportunity to condemn the particular vices of his contemporaries, and the scholars in his audience, whose conduct he supervised as chancellor, frequently heard him preach against their vanity, lust, and ambition. We do have one other possible bit of evidence of Hilduin's concern for scholars. As chancellor he was consulted by Jocius of London, who in 1180 endowed the first hospice for poor scholars, a room in the Hôtel-Dieu, next to the cathedral, that subsequently became known as the Collège des Dix-huit.[17]

Hilduin was succeeded by Peter of Poitiers, whose tenure as chancellor (1193-1205) coincided with a stormier period in the history of the schools, one marked by frequent conflicts between town and gown and by increasing criticism of the moral conduct of scholars. A native of Poitiers or the Poitou, Peter apparently had a long career in the schools. In the 1150's he was a student of Peter Lombard and Peter Comestor, and in 1169 succeeded the latter as master of theology at the cathedral school. During his years of teaching he produced a wide variety of works, ranging from biblical history to speculative theology. But Peter of Poitiers never achieved the eminence of his masters. His major theological work, the *Sententiarum libri quinque* (c. 1175), is a systematic commentary on the Lombard's *Sententiae*. Although it shows evidence of Peter's considerable interest and skill in disputation, it lacks originality. As a preacher, Peter was especially attentive to the needs of his audience. Fifty-nine of his sermons survive, most dating from the years he was chancellor and most directed at the same variety of audiences addressed by his predecessors. When preaching to learned clerics, Peter never alluded specifically to the conflicts raging in Paris, but he was cautiously critical of the behavior of the scholars. The sermons reveal him actively promoting educational reform while trying at the same time to defend the schools from their harsher critics.[18]

The last of this series of chancellors, Prévostin (Prepositinus) of Cremona, did not directly succeed Peter of Poitiers. The chancellorship was briefly held by another theologian, Master Bernard Chabert (or Chobert), who within a year left Paris to become bishop of Geneva.[19] How Prévostin was chosen to succeed him is unclear. Although, like his predecessors, a renowned theologian, Prévostin had spent much of his career away from Paris. He held the position of scholasticus at the cathedral schools of Mainz from 1194 or 1195 until 1203, when his support for the losing candidate in a disputed archiepiscopal election brought him a stern reprimand from Innocent III and forced him to resign his position. When Prévostin reappears in the historical record, three years later, he is already chancellor of Paris and also, apparently, back in the good graces of Innocent III, since he is acting as a papal judge delegate on a mission in Chartres. Prévostin had certainly been in Paris before. He probably came to the city shortly before 1159 from his native Cremona to study with his fellow Lombard, Master Peter, and taught theology in the cathedral schools for at least several years before 1185. As a theologian, his most influential work was a four-book *Summa theologica* that added considerably to the tradition of Peter Lombard's *Sententiae*. In addition, he wrote several shorter summae and treatises for school or pastoral use and, as a product of active missionary work among the heretics in his native Lombardy undertaken probably between 1185 and 1195, a well-informed *Summa contra hereticos*.

Among the more than eighty sermons that have been attributed to Prévostin, at least sixty-one seem authentic. Most of them appear to be from the final decades of his life, and many can even be dated precisely to the years of his chancellorship, when he had frequent occasion to preach to laymen, monks, canons regular, secular clerics, or scholars in various locations in Paris. Prévostin was an effective and forceful preacher whose harsh criticisms of his contemporaries' behavior often border on satire. Perhaps it was his growing reputation as a preacher, as much as his previous success as a theology master in Paris, that gained him appointment as chancellor. Already quite aged when he returned to Paris, he apparently gave up the chancellorship sometime in 1209, probably to retire to one of the monasteries in the city, where he died in February of the following year.[20] Prévostin brought to an end a line of learned chancellors who rebuked the conduct of scholars in their sermons but still, as former masters, remained strongly favorable toward the schools.

Several of the moralists are Paris masters who, after varying periods of time teaching in the city's schools, pursued careers elsewhere, some becoming eminent churchmen. They are: Robert Pullen, cardinal and papal chancellor (d. 1146); Raoul Ardent (d. circa 1200); Simon of Tournai (d. 1201); Alan of Lille (d. 1202/3); Alexander Neckham (d. 1217); Stephen Langton, archbishop of Canterbury (d. 1228); and Jacques of Vitry, bishop of Acre and cardinal-bishop of Tusculum (d. 1240).

Of an earlier generation than the others, Robert Pullen became a theology master in Paris about 1140, after having taught at schools in both Exeter and Oxford. As the successor to Gilbert of Poitiers at the cathedral schools, he taught theology to his compatriot John of Salisbury, who describes him as "a man commendable both for his virtue and his knowledge."[21] While teaching in Paris, Pullen retained the income from the archdeaconry of Rochester, to which he had been appointed in 1134.[22] In 1143 he was summoned to Rome and made a cardinal. Within a short time he was serving as papal chancellor, a position he held until September 1146, when he either retired because of ill health or died.[23]

Robert Pullen seems to have owed his success completely to his reputation as a master of theology. As a speculative theologian, he drew together the advances of the school of Laon, the doctrines of Hugh of St. Victor, and the dialectical method of Peter Abelard to resolve the questions that had been disputed in the schools during the first decades of the twelfth century. Before leaving Paris he organized his lectures into a collection, the *Sententiarum libri octo*, which remained the most comprehensive and widely used summa of theology until Peter Lombard compiled his.[24] Pullen's sermons, like his *Sententiae*, were products of his teaching in the schools. Similar in both form and content to academic lectures, the sermons were apparently an integral part of the instruction Robert Pullen offered to his students as he prepared them for the practical application of their education.[25]

The great preacher Raoul Ardent (Radulphus Ardens) was active in the second half of the twelfth century. His extant works include, in addition to a vast collection of sermons, a major treatise on ethics entitled the *Speculum universale*.[26] There is no definite evidence that he either studied or taught in Paris, but his treatise shows the strong influence of Paris theologians, above all of Gilbert of Poitiers, suggesting that he spent at least part of his career in the schools of the city. Several manuscripts give him the title "master," and John Baldwin has argued that Raoul should be included among the members of the circle of Peter the Chanter.[27] It has recently been established that Raoul served as chaplain to King Richard I of England between 1190 and 1197.[28] The date of his death is known—September 12—but not the year.

Raoul's fame seems to have come from his preaching. In their clarity and directness, and in the diversity of audiences to which they are addressed, his sermons are surpassed only by those of Jacques of Vitry. Raoul was probably far more active and successful as a preacher than as a teacher of theology. It cannot be determined whether he wrote most of his sermons in Paris, while teaching somewhere else, or as an itinerant preacher. As we shall see, however, several of his sermons to learned audiences show an intimate familiarity with the moral and intellectual issues being debated in the Paris schools, and his explicit criticisms of masters suggest that Raoul Ardent shared the concerns of others, like Peter the Chanter and Robert of Courson, who were actively promoting educational reform.

Although only one example of his preaching survives, Simon of Tournai has been included in this group of critics because both his controversial career and his theological writings provide important evidence of conditions in the schools. Having received his early education in the cathedral schools of his native Tournai, Simon arrived in Paris before 1155 and became a student of Odo of Soissons. Simon was, probably, the unbeneficed provost Odo tried to have appointed his successor as chancellor, whom he supported financially for more than twelve years, and for whom he tried to secure a prebend from Alexander III.[29] We do know for certain that about this time Simon, thanks to the intervention of the pope, was provided with a canonry at Tournai. Contrary to a diocesan statute prohibiting nonresidence, he used his revenues as canon to support himself in Paris. When the bishop and chapter tried to deprive him of his prebend, it was another member of this group of critics, Stephen of Tournai, then abbot of Ste. Geneviève, who intervened on his behalf and asked the archbishop of Reims to allow Simon to remain at the schools.[30]

Simon of Tournai continued to teach theology in Paris until 1201, when, according to some unfavorable accounts, he was suddenly struck mute, because of either his presumption or his blasphemy. The extant evidence suggests that he must have been a popular but controversial master. The collection of his *Distinctiones* and his *Summa* are learned, systematic, and self-assured works in the tradition of Gilbert of Poitiers, and perhaps of Peter Abelard; they are also provocative in their use of the latest translations of Aristotle, which were just reaching Paris from Toledo. Like Abelard, Simon was a subtle dialectician and an ambitious theologian who tended to be immodest in his claims and intemperate in his language. This, and perhaps also his reputation for keeping a concubine, made Simon appear to some to be another Abelard and caused him similar difficulties throughout his long career in Paris.[31]

A native of Flanders, like Simon of Tournai, Alan of Lille entered the schools of Paris perhaps as early as 1136, after completing his basic studies at the well-known school of St. Peter in his native Lille. Other details of his education and career are more difficult to sort out. After studying under Thierry of Chartres and Gilbert of Poitiers, Alan taught theology for many years in Paris. Later in his career, while teaching probably at Montpellier, he was involved in the campaign against heretics in Languedoc. Some time shortly before his death in 1202 or 1203, Alan became a monk at Cîteaux.[32]

Renowned as a poet, philosopher, theologian, preacher, and polemicist, Alan of Lille became revered as the "Doctor Universalis." The chronology of his writings, now slowly being established, suggests that for much of his teaching career Alan lectured on the liberal arts as well as theology. His theological summa, the *Quoniam homines* (1160-65), and perhaps his *Regulae theologicae* are earlier than his major literary works, the *De planctu naturae* (c. 1165-82) and the *Anticlaudianus* (1182-84). But from the mid-1180's Alan seems to have turned his attention increasingly from speculative theology and the arts to moral and practical theology. His polemical work against heretics (*De fide catholica contra haereticos*), penitential guide for confessors (the *Liber poenitentialis*), and manual on preaching (the *Summa de arte praedicandi*), and most of his vast collection of sermons all date from the last twenty years of his life, when, although already quite aged, Alan was actively promoting reform in Paris and in southern France.[33]

Alexander Neckham spent most of his teaching career in his native England, but he had been trained and had also taught in Paris. The chronology is uncertain. Neckham was a master at Dunstable in 1183; at St. Alban's, where he was born and first schooled, in 1184; and at Oxford after 1190. It seems likely that he was in Paris twice. His first stay was probably in the 1170's, when he apparently attended the school on the Petit Pont and studied the liberal arts at least briefly under his fellow Englishman, Master Adam of Balsham. The second was just before he became the first Paris-trained theologian to teach in Oxford. During this second stay in Paris, Neckham somehow managed to study not only theology but also both canon and civil law, and even some medicine, while at the same time supporting himself by teaching grammar and rhetoric. Sometime before 1202 he retired from teaching and left Oxford to enter the Augustinian abbey at Cirencester. As abbot, after 1212, he served frequently as papal judge delegate and was present at the Fourth Lateran Council.[34]

The range of Alexander Neckham's scholarship is greater than that of even Alan of Lille. His writings include grammatical handbooks, poetry, natural science, biblical commentaries, and speculative theology. He was also a renowned preacher. He seems to have preached most of his sermons during the years he was teaching at Oxford. As we shall see, he was generally less critical of the state of learning than his contemporaries in Paris.[35]

As a renowned theologian who became a powerful archbishop, Stephen Langton was a near approximation of the ideal churchman envisioned by the reforming masters in the schools. Langton, a native of Lincolnshire born c. 1155, spent more than thirty years studying and teaching in the schools of Paris. Having distinguished himself both as a master of arts and, from the 1180's, as a master of theology, he was summoned to Rome early in 1206 and made cardinal-priest of St. Chrysogonus. Before the end of the same year, Innocent III had convinced a delegation of monks from Canterbury, in Rome appealing the disputed election that had followed the death of Hubert Walter in July 1205, to elect Langton as their new archbishop. The events of his subsequent career are well known and need only be briefly reviewed. Because of the opposition of King John, Langton was not able to enter England nor assume his duties as archbishop until 1213. Then after two remarkable years struggling for reform and to restore the rights of the English Church, he was suspended from his office by Innocent III for his support of the rebellious barons and defense of the Magna Carta. As a result, he spent three more years in exile. Finally, in 1218, he was able to return to England, where he spent the last ten years of his life actively involved in both ecclesiastical and political affairs. He visited Paris at least twice during this period, first in 1221 on a papal commission to help resolve one of the earliest disputes between the university and the bishop of Paris.[36]

Stephen Langton earned his scholarly reputation by both his teaching and his preaching. As a biblical scholar, Langton not only wrote commentaries on nearly every book of the Bible but also established what became the standard order and division of the books and chapters of the Vulgate.[37] Less known are the collection of *Quaestiones*, which represent his disputations as a teacher of practical theology.[38] Stephen Langton was famous in his own lifetime above all as the preacher with "a thundering tongue," and more than three hundred sermons are attributed to him in medieval manuscripts. Most of the sermons now considered authentic were preached while he was a master in Paris.[39] No other Paris master was as successful as Stephen Langton in fulfilling the established duties of lecturing on Scripture, disputing theological and moral questions, and preaching.

Although Jacques of Vitry spent far less of his career actually in Paris than Stephen Langton, he is in many respects as important a figure in the history of the schools. Born into a wealthy bourgeois family in the region of Champagne sometime between 1160 and 1170, Jacques studied in Paris, probably under Peter the Chanter, and was licensed to teach sometime before 1193. Judging from the account of Paris he gives in his *Historia Occidentalis*, Jacques probably spent most of the next two decades in the city. Unfortunately, the details of his life are obscure until 1211, when he joined a community of Augustinian canons at St. Nicholas in Oignies, near Cambrai. There he became a supporter of the lay religious movement led by Mary of Oignies, one of the founders of the Beguines. Jacques was commissioned in 1213 to preach against the Albigensian heretics and in the following year to preach for the new crusade to the Holy Land. His renown as a preacher gained him election as bishop of Acre in 1216. He spent the next nine years in the East and was an eyewitness to the disappointing events of the Fifth Crusade in Damietta (1218-21). Weary of the worsening situation in the East, he returned permanently to Europe in 1225. Gregory IX accepted his resignation as bishop and appointed him cardinal-bishop of Tusculum in 1229. For the final eleven years of his life Jacques was an active member of the papal curia.[40]

More than four hundred sermons survive from Jacques's long career as a preacher. In his final years he organized them into four major collections to serve as models for preaching. One of these, the *Sermones vulgares*, is the first major collection of sermons "ad status"; it includes seventy-four sermons addressed to more than thirty different groups.[41] In both form and content, Jacques's sermons reveal the influence of his theological studies in Paris. None of his contemporaries, however, equaled Jacques in his ability to apply the moral theology taught in the schools to the particular concerns of a congregation or to enliven sermons with illustrative stories that were both relevant and entertaining. As we shall see, his sermons to scholars and to other learned audiences are especially direct and detailed in their criticisms of the state of learning in as well as outside of the schools. Among Jacques's other writings, the second of his major historical works, the *Historia Occidentalis* (completed c. 1225), is also a valuable source of information about conditions in Paris in the important decades around 1200.[42]

Also included in this group of critics are two other preachers, Geoffrey of Troyes and Stephen of Tournai. All that is known of Geoffrey is that he held the position of dean of Troyes about 1200. In one of the primary manuscripts of his sermons he is referred to as "Master Geoffrey of

Troyes," but it is uncertain where he taught. That he had ties to the schools of Paris is strongly suggested, however, by the contents of his sermons and by the fact that examples of his preaching are often included in the sermon collections of Paris masters.[43] In contrast, Stephen of Tournai probably never studied or taught in Paris, but he did have occasion to preach to scholars as abbot of Ste. Geneviève from 1176 to 1192. His sermons will be considered separately from those of other critics in this group not because his ideas about education differed all that much from theirs, but because, whereas the other moralists were committed to trying to reform the schools from within, Stephen called for intervention from the outside.

THE ART OF PREACHING

For all the members of this group, preaching was a central activity of their careers as masters, ministers, or prelates. They devoted great care to the composition of their sermons, and either they or their disciples carefully recorded and collected what they regarded as the best or most suitable of these sermons to be used as models for other preachers. The vast collections of sermons dating from the late twelfth and early thirteenth centuries, so many of which originated in Paris, are an expression of the vitality and the reforming zeal that came out of the expanding schools. Preachers addressed increasing numbers of these sermons to lay audiences, trying to tailor their lessons to the social and moral concerns of the laity. It is now recognized that Paris masters were at the forefront of a revival of popular preaching: they were setting precedents for the later evangelism of the learned Franciscans and Dominicans. Jacques of Vitry proved himself an especially perceptive historian when he wrote that the preaching of a group of Paris masters, from which he modestly excluded himself, signaled the beginning of "the renewal of the Western Church."[44]

Yet although the preachers were giving increased attention to popular audiences, the vast majority of the sermons in their collections were still preached to clerical audiences at the schools, in houses of regular clergy, or at synods of diocesan clergy. These sermons represent the more practical side of the education offered in the schools, the efforts of the masters to prepare their students, as well as other clerics, for the active ministry by teaching them both sound doctrine and the right moral values. Paris masters had come to regard such preaching as an essential part of the process of training an elite of learned clerics who would themselves, in turn, use sermons to instruct the simple parish clergy and the laity.

According to the expectations of the day, preaching (*praedicatio*) was as much of a duty for the master of theology as reading or lecturing (*lectio*) and disputation (*disputatio*). The master himself was expected to preach, as well as to teach others how to preach. In his widely used treatise, the *Verbum abbreviatum*, the influential Master Peter the Chanter set the following standard for the theological curriculum in the schools:

> The practice of studying the Bible consists in three exercises: reading, disputing, and preaching. . . . Reading is like the foundation or basement of what follows, since through it the others are prepared. Disputation is like the wall in this study and building, since nothing is fully understood or faithfully preached unless first chewed by the tooth of disputation. Preaching, which the others support, is like the roof, sheltering the faithful from the heat and the wind of the vices. One must preach after, not before, reading Holy Scripture and investigating doubtful things through disputation.[45]

Because of the importance the masters themselves attributed to their preaching, their sermons are as significant as evidence of the teaching that went on in the schools as are their collections of *quaestiones* and *disputationes*.

Some of the sermons addressed to learned audiences, especially those of the earlier preachers like Robert Pullen, are indistinguishable from academic lectures. Often they are no more than biblical commentaries that are said to have been "preached." But preaching was increasingly being distinguished both in purpose and in technique from other aspects of teaching.[46] Probably as a result of the concerns of some masters to take on a more active and direct role in the reform of the laity, preaching was reoriented and redefined. It came to be seen as a distinct form of instruction with its own rules and methods. By the 1170's teaching the "art of preaching" had been established as an integral and essential part of theological training in the schools. To teach the rules of this art, theology masters made use of the occasions of their own preaching to scholars, they compiled examples of their sermons as models for addressing various audiences, and they produced a considerable number of preaching manuals and guides.

Among the late-twelfth-century guides to preaching, Alan of Lille's *Summa de arte praedicandi* provides the best summary of these masters' ideas about the nature, importance, and techniques of preaching. Alan begins, in typical scholastic fashion, by defining his subject. "Preaching," he writes, "is the manifest and public instruction of morals and the faith, devoted to the education of men and proceeding from the footpath of reason and the fountain of authority."[47] This states concisely both the importance and the purpose of preaching. Alan's definition shows the strong influence of Peter the Chanter's view of the relationship of preaching to other aspects of teaching. The idea that preaching must proceed from reason and authority is another way of stating the Chanter's principle that one must know (from *lectio*) and understand (from *disputatio*) Scripture before attempting to teach others. Alan's emphasis on the public nature of preaching also reflects the increased effort among masters to make the sermon a more effective instrument of instruction. Whether addressed to lay audiences or to clerics, sermons came to be viewed as a means of taking the theoretical learning of the schools and making it applicable to the practical needs of contemporary society. Above all, effective preaching was seen as vital in promoting moral reform and spiritual renewal. In the struggle against the spread of heresy, it was a potentially powerful instrument that would have to be refined and, as the masters were also aware, controlled.

After defining preaching, Alan of Lille goes on to make an important distinction between it and teaching in the schools. As a public activity, preaching must provide clear and simple moral lessons suitable for a large and diverse audience. In contrast, the formal teaching of the classroom (which Alan calls *doctrina*) must advance the knowledge and understanding of a more select group of students.[48] Preaching is therefore distinguished in three ways: it is addressed to a general audience, it is simpler and clearer in form, and it is concerned primarily with moral, rather than doctrinal, matters. According to Alan's original definition, preaching does include instruction in both faith and morals, and his *Summa* stipulates that the preacher should know and use both speculative and moral theology. But in recommending specific books of the Bible to preachers, Alan chooses the Gospels, Psalms, Epistles of Paul, Proverbs, and Ecclesiastes, because they are especially useful for "moral instruction." The other books, he advises, should be used cautiously.[49] Likewise, in his discussion of exemplary themes and subjects, as in the model sermons to various audiences with which the treatise concludes, Alan of Lille's emphasis is on moral instruction, on the vices that obstruct and the virtues that open the way to eternal life.[50]

As we shall see, this emphasis was characteristic of the sermons preached by these masters both to lay and learned audiences. Whatever their particular interests as teachers of theology, their principal concern as preachers was to provide guidance for the improvement of moral conduct. As a result, Paris masters became the leaders both in developing new techniques of preaching and in raising the standards for preachers. To be effective at promoting moral reform, they understood that sermons had to do more than imitate patristic homilies or repeat general platitudes. Preachers would have to make their sermons more suitable to their audiences. Peter of Poitiers advised preachers to compose their sermons with four specific factors in mind: the location, the time, the type of audience, and its size.[51] Others emphasized that the preacher should be brief and simple, and limit rhetorical flourishes and classical allusions—especially when addressing laymen. Preaching was not, they advised, an occasion to show off one's learning. Even the most conscientious masters sometimes had difficulty heeding this type of advice.

The greatest advances in preaching method came with the adoption and rapid diffusion of two homiletic techniques. The first was the increased use of illustrative stories or exempla to retain, or at times regain, the attention of the audience and to demonstrate more concretely and simply the moral lesson being taught. The second innovation was the practice of selecting themes to suit not just the day of the liturgical year but also the social composition of the audience, that is, preaching *ad status*. The development of these techniques, the exemplum and the *sermo ad status*, seems to have been originally inspired by the effort to preach more effectively to the diverse groups of laity found in late medieval society. But preachers also found them useful when addressing the various ranks and orders of the clergy, including scholars.

The use of exempla was not an innovation. The preachers who developed this technique recognized that it was a well-established means of Christian moral instruction soundly rooted in Scripture. If they thought they needed an authority to defend the use of an exemplum, they could—and often did—refer to Gregory the Great's dictum that people are moved to love God and their neighbors more by examples than by words.[52] What was new was the attention the use and selection of exempla received in the schools. Paris masters impressed upon their students the value of a properly used exemplum. In one of his school commentaries, Stephen Langton finds in the unlikely passage of Judges 3.31 ("Samgar son of Anath slew of the Philistines six hundred men with a ploughshare") an opportunity to lecture on the value of exempla in preaching to the laity:

> See! This makes clear that a preacher should not always use polished subtle preaching, like Aod's sword, but sometimes a ploughshare, that is, rude, rustic exhortation. Very often a popular story [*exemplum vulgare*] is more effective than a polished, subtle phrase. Aod killed one man only with a two-edged sword, Samgar six hundred with a ploughshare; so, whereas the laity are easily converted by rude, unpolished preaching, a sermon to clerics will draw scarcely one of them from his error.[53]

Following this advice in his own preaching, Langton typically used exempla only when addressing popular or mixed audiences, not for clerics.

Alexander Neckham describes the use of exempla in a different way. Exempla, he says in one of his sermons, are means whereby a preacher can "refresh" his audience.[54] Although speaking in this sermon specifically of preaching to the laity, Neckham—and here he differed from Langton—also regularly used exempla to refresh his more learned audiences at Oxford. Among the moralists, Jacques of Vitry seems to have been most convinced, and to have convinced his contemporaries, of the general value of exempla. He included them in his sermons to all groups. To suit the needs of the occasion and the audience, he drew on the ever-widening variety of sources of anecdotal material that was available to learned preachers of the time: biblical history and saints' lives, classical literature and history, mythology and legend, natural history and animal fables, popular folklore, and travelers' tales of the wonders of the East. But what makes the exempla found in the sermons of this period particularly interesting to the historian is the extent to which the preachers, and again Jacques of Vitry is preeminent, claimed to be drawing from their own experiences and observations.

Many of Jacques of Vitry's sermons include exempla that seem to tell of actual events, conditions existing in the schools, or the state of learning. But like the stories of the satirists, these exempla must be treated with some caution. Even when there may be some basis of truth in the story, the particulars were often changed to suit the occasion. Take, as an example, the story of the conversion of Master Sella, which Jacques recounts in one of his sermons to scholars:

> Likewise it happened in Paris that a certain student, wearing what seemed to be a cope made entirely of parchment and covered completely with tiny writing, appeared on the day after his death in the presence of his former master. When the master, called Sella, asked the student about the cope and the writing that covered it, he replied: "These writings burden me so much that they weigh more than if I carried on my head the tower of that church." (And he pointed to the church of St. Germain des Prés, not far from where they stood.) "These writings," he continued, "are the sophisms and the curiosities on which I spent my days. I cannot express to you verbally just how greatly I suffer under this cope, but I can show you by having you feel a drop of my sweat." At that, the master extended the palm of his hand to catch the drop, and the heat pierced him as violently as if it were a very sharp arrow. Immediately, the master departed from the schools of logic and entered the Cistercian order, quoting the verse: "I leave croaking to frogs, the morning to ravens, and empty things to the vain. / I am awakened from logic, which does not fear death." For the rest of his life his hand remained pierced and, when I was in Paris, he was living at the schools showing the hole in his hand to everyone.[55]

It is a good story, and Jacques tells it with skill. There is, moreover, probably some basis of truth to it. The two lines of verse were written by Serlo of Wilton, a renowned poet and grammar master who taught in

Paris and, perhaps, Oxford in the mid-twelfth century. Serlo later entered first the Cluniac and then the Cistercian order, spending his last years (between 1171 and 1181) as abbot of the Cistercian house of Aumône, near Chartres.

There are numerous other accounts of the conversion of this Master Sella (or Serlo), which vary in detail but not substance. The earliest and longest version places the story in Oxford, rather than Paris, identifies the student as a cleric named Richard, and makes no mention of Serlo's having a hole in his hand.[56] What Jacques, and several later preachers, did was take a story that was apparently already well known among scholars and monks and change the details to suit their moralizing purpose. A few changes could make the same story fit a variety of lessons. Jacques of Vitry's purpose was to criticize those scholars who spent all their lives studying the arts, especially logic. In contrast, Stephen of Bourbon, a renowned Dominican preacher of the next generation, uses the exemplum—which he dubiously claims to have first heard preached by Peter the Chanter—to illustrate the need to fear death. His account does not even bother to mention the subject taught by the master.[57] The final embellishment Jacques gives to the story—that Master Sella was still residing in Paris and showing the hole in his hand during Jacques's student days in the 1180's—is, given what we know of Serlo of Wilton's life, pure fiction. Nor is it essential to making the moral of the exemplum any clearer. Such personal references were often included in exempla to lend credence to a story. There is no guarantee, we should be duly warned from Jacques's literary embellishment, that even when a preacher does refer to his own experience in the schools, he is accurately recounting actual conditions or events.

To some extent, the same warning applies to the use of *sermones ad status* as historical evidence. The purpose of this new technique of preaching was to speak more directly and concretely about the problems, needs, and concerns of the social group or groups being addressed. However, rather than speaking directly from their own knowledge, preachers came to depend more and more on the rapidly growing collections of model sermons and preaching handbooks and manuals available to them.[58] Fortunately, this is less of a problem with the preachers studied here. Preaching in the formative years of the new technique, they had little choice other than to draw upon their perceptions of actual social conditions. It was their successors who used the collections of their *sermones ad status* as models. The sermons that this group of Paris masters and reformers addressed to scholars are far different in content and purpose from the *sermones ad scholares* preached when the university had become a well-established and venerable institution. Delivered in the formative years of the university, these sermons were part of a concerted effort to urge educational reform and to influence, in a concrete and direct way, the development of the schools. Although not free of the moralization and exaggeration about academic life that would characterize thirteenth-century preaching, the sermons of these masters reveal much more about actual conditions in the schools and the efforts to reform them.

Before turning to the sermons themselves, we need to consider one additional aspect of the revitalization of preaching: the increased concern about the qualifications needed to be an effective preacher. To the Paris masters, teaching the art of preaching involved both practical training about how to give a sermon and moral direction about how to live. In the sermons they addressed to their students and other clerics, in the preaching manuals and handbooks they composed, and in the model sermons they collected, the masters emphasized that effective preaching depended as much on the moral qualities of the preacher as on his verbal abilities. They systematically examined the questions of who should preach, of what educational and moral standards should be set for the preacher, and of how preaching might be controlled.[59]

Preaching, as the requirements Peter the Chanter set for the study of theology clearly indicate, was viewed as one of the duties of the learned. It was also seen as an important responsibility that should be assumed only by clerics who were of sound doctrine and exemplary conduct. In the protheme of one of his sermons, Jacques of Vitry states the requirements for preaching with especial succinctness: "He is said to be a wise man who knows, teaches, and does what is good. It is these three things God strictly requires of every preacher: knowledge, teaching, and good conduct or a good life."[60] Other masters repeat essentially the same requirement in a variety of ways. Most often the emphasis is on the need for a preacher to lead a good life, especially because the laity, as some of them knew from their experience combatting heresy, were more likely to listen to a preacher with a reputation for holiness. "Of little weight is preaching," Stephen Langton tells an audience of clerics, "that good work does not commend."[61]

Despite all the effort they put into developing and diffusing the rules and techniques of the new art of preaching, the masters frequently warned their students against thinking that their rhetorical skills or eloquence alone could make them good preachers. Eloquence, they emphasized, could add to the effectiveness of a preacher only if he was also wise and virtuous. Even then, according to Alexander Neckham, the true eloquence of effective preaching was inspired by God, not by the vain verbal ostentation learned by studying rhetoric in the schools.[62] Raoul Ardent, who had an especially exalted view of the duty of a preacher, warns clerics not to presume that learning and eloquence are sufficient in themselves. Unless God inspires the preacher and opens his mouth, he will certainly not be able to preach effectively.[63] Ardent also speaks for the other masters when he insists that the "office of preaching" (*officium praedicationis*) is not just a duty but an honor to which one must be called directly by God, as Aaron was, an honor that no one should presume to usurp on his own.[64]

In emphasizing the idea of preaching as a special vocation, Raoul Ardent was especially concerned about those who were preaching not to instruct others but to serve their own ambitions or to make money. There was good reason for this concern about the motivation of preachers. In the schools, preaching, like teaching, was widely recognized as a means of acquiring fame. Among the moralists themselves were several whose careers benefited greatly because of their renown as preachers. Hoping to advance themselves, preachers competed to attract large audiences and to gain popular acclaim.[65] On the other hand, many great theologians—according to Alexander Neckham—quit preaching and entered the cloister because audiences only wanted to hear pleasing words, not to be exhorted to improve their conduct.[66] Judging from the moralists' frequent criticisms of "false preachers" (*pseudopraedicatores*), however, there must have been many others who, motivated by ambition and avarice, were quite willing to try to please, rather than to instruct, their audiences. Still, the desire for glory and popular acclaim was thought to be not nearly as pernicious as the desire for money. Accepting payment for preaching was regarded as a form of simony equivalent to selling other spiritual offices or functions. Some, like Raoul Ardent, took a very hard line on the issue, insisting that after his sermon the preacher should collect money neither for himself nor for any other cause. Others were less strict, arguing that it was not simony to request money from an audience if the preacher had no other income or sought to support some worthy cause.[67] But the masters who debated and discussed this issue all agreed that the opportunities to gain materially from preaching were endangering the cause of reform and the struggle against heresy.

Perhaps because the masters were addressing their criticisms primarily to clerics already educated or still at the schools, they tended to emphasize the harm done by worldly and immoral preachers, even more than by unlearned ones. Hypocrisy, not ignorance, often becomes the principal obstacle to reform. Geoffrey of Troyes speaks with particular force about the ineffectiveness of those preachers whose actions do not match their words. "More often they," he says ("they" being "modern clerics") "are striving to appear not to be great. They preach great things, but do not do them. They reproach others for their vices, but do not overcome their own. What they preach in their sermons, they destroy in their actions."[68] As we shall see, the moralists raised many of these same criticisms and concerns when they discussed studying and teaching within the schools. Scholars, whether the clerics being trained for the active ministry or the masters responsible for training them, were exhorted to uphold standards that were as demanding morally as they were intellectually.

THE PLACE OF SCHOLARS IN SOCIETY

When the moralists took up the task of exhorting the scholars of Paris to improve their behavior, there were no clear and ready standards to which the scholars could be held accountable. Most of the large numbers of students and many of the masters congregated in the city belonged to no one established group or organization. Very few of the scholars were formally enrolled in or employed by the cathedral schools of Notre Dame. Fewer still were attached to one of the religious houses, whose schools had been closed to outsiders and whose members were now usually prohibited from pursuing studies outside the cloister. All the scholars in the city were still regarded as clerics. But their clerical status no longer meant what it had when the vast majority of students had been training for the diocesan clergy under the close supervision of the bishop and the cathedral chapter. With the increased employment opportunities for educated men outside the Church, many students, even though they were generally accorded the same legal privileges as the tonsured clergy while they were at the schools, did not belong, or aspire, to even the lowest grade of minor orders. To be sure, most of those studying theology were destined for the priesthood and prelacy, and some masters were already ordained. But these scholars were greatly outnumbered by those preparing for secular careers at the schools and studying the liberal arts or the lucrative subjects of law and medicine. Clerics by legal status but usually lacking the accountability or the obligations of the clergy, scholars collectively represented a new and distinct social group, one that did not fit neatly into existing moral categories.

The questions this situation raised were not simply theoretical. The concentration of large numbers of young students and masters on the Ile de la Cité and the Left Bank of Paris posed serious problems of control and discipline.[69] The clerical status of scholars, it was generally agreed, gave them immunity from secular jurisdiction, but it was not certain which ecclesiastical authority had responsibility over the moral conduct and the spiritual life of the young students and their masters. Since most of them came from outside the diocese, it was difficult for the bishop of Paris to use the same sanctions to control scholars as he could use over the diocesan clergy. Nor was it clear what standards were to be used to judge the conduct of scholars. Were they, or were they not, subject to the same standards and regulations as the rest of the clergy? This question long remained unresolved.

In the absence of any effective sanctions that could be used against scholars, preaching remained the one means available to address the problem of discipline in the schools. Scholars had to be exhorted to good behavior. The *sermones ad scholares* were part of the effort to define and to establish suitable criteria for judging the conduct of those at the schools. We certainly have reason to doubt that exhortation alone had very much of a direct influence on the behavior of scholars. The moralists themselves frequently complain of how little their words were heeded. But however slight their immediate impact on the conduct of students and masters, these sermons were important to the schools in other ways. The regular preaching of the moralists at the schools did convince some scholars of their moral obligations and social responsibilities as the educated elite. At the same time, by frequently preaching about the value of education to other audiences, the moralists helped these scholars gain recognition and support for their cause. Both among the scholars themselves and among those who had influence over them, the moralists helped to build a consensus for the reform and regulation of the schools.

Although the moralists did not all agree on the specific standards that should be set for scholarly conduct, they collectively had a very exalted view of the place of scholars in society and of their prominence among the various orders in the Church. They often spoke of the social importance of scholars in symbolic terms. Jacques of Vitry uses an especially vivid image when, taking the common idea of the Church as a human body, he equates the schools with the primary senses: the eyes, which "minister spiritual light to the whole body," are the doctors of theology (and, no less significant, the preachers); the nose is the faculty of arts; and the ears are the students.[70] Hilduin uses a different image to a similar end. Adopting the familiar biblical metaphor, he compares the diverse orders of the Church to the people found in the rooms of a great mansion. Those who study theology work in the refectory, the room where the rest of the household comes to be fed.[71] In each image, scholars—specifically theologians—are especially prominent. Their role in the Church is to minister to the needs of others, whereas the role of monks and other contemplatives is more passive—in one variant of Jacques's image they replace students as the obedient ears of the body, and in Hilduin's sermon they remain sleeping in the bedchambers of the great mansion.

There is a distinct resonance in these sermons of the continuing debate over the question: Which is the higher form of spiritual life, the active or the contemplative?[72] From the end of the eleventh century the canons regular and the reformed monastic orders had debated this question, often bitterly. At issue had been the relative merits of their lives and their respective places in the spiritual hierarchy of the Church. The increased prominence of school-trained secular clerics in ecclesiastical affairs had then posed a new challenge to both the monks and the canons regular. In response, as we have seen, members of both groups had become outspoken opponents of the schools. By the middle of the twelfth century the disagreement between monks and canons regular about the merits of their respective vocations was generally less vehement than their agreement that the cloistered life they had in common was superior to the lives led by those in the schools. When the moralists took up the defense of scholars in their sermons, they deliberately used much of the same language and many of the same arguments their two groups of rivals had previously used against each other. It was a subtle but in the end effective way of disarming some of the opponents of the schools.

One of the arguments that could be used against both monks and canons regular was that scholars were no less involved in the contemplative life than those who resided within the cloister. For example, in one sermon Chancellor Hilduin speaks in terms of two different types of contemplatives: the cloistered are contemplatives devoted to prayer (*oratio*), the scholars contemplatives devoted to study (*lectio*).[73] Hilduin simply divides prayer and study, the two primary activities of contemplation, to distinguish between what he insists are equal, though distinct, types of contemplatives. In other variations on the idea, a less rigid distinction is made between the activities of the two types of contemplatives. Two masters, Peter Comestor and Peter of Poitiers, argue that study and prayer are common to both types but that scholars do more studying and the cloistered do more praying.[74] In a sermon probably by Stephen Langton, this same idea is taken a step further. Not only do scholars and the cloistered differ in the attention they give to study and prayer, but their meditation is also fundamentally different:

There are two kinds of contemplatives, the cloistered and scholars; but since contemplation consists in three things—study, meditation, and prayer—the cloistered are more frequently devoted to prayer, and the scholars more frequently to study and meditation. Also, the meditation of contemplatives can be divided in two. Some meditation strains itself to reach the heavenly court, to the state of the republic of that supreme city, and to the understanding of the incomprehensible mysteries of God, which cannot be understood in any other way; and this meditation is more familiar to the cloistered. The other meditation is occupied with divine law, and this is more suitable to scholars.[75]

The emphasis in this sermon is on the different social roles of the two types of contemplatives. Whereas the cloistered, who are seeking their own salvation, pray and meditate in search of a personal understanding of the mysteries of the faith, scholars, who are preparing for their social responsibilities as active leaders of the Church, must study and meditate upon divine law so that they will be able to direct human affairs in accordance with its dictates. Although their lives and their purposes differ, both groups are contemplatives.

Other favorable comparisons were also made between those in schools and in cloisters. Prévostin does not argue that scholars are contemplatives but preaches that both scholars and contemplatives (by which he means both monks and canons regular) share the three special spiritual tasks of reciting the Psalms, study, and meditation, as well as the four tasks (fasting, keeping vigil, praying, and working) that are common to all the faithful.[76] It became customary for masters, when preaching on either Canticle 3.11 ("Egredimini filiae Sion") or Zachariah 9.9 ("Exsulta satis filia Sion"), to compare the merits of scholars and contemplatives as the special children of Sion.[77] In general, the purpose of the comparison was not to emphasize the differences between the various forms of life, as the polemical literature of the monks and canons regular had long done, but to try to reduce the rivalry by arguing for their essential compatibility.

Yet although it was not uncommon for the masters to include scholars in the spiritual company of both monks and canons regular, some recognized that there was, at least potentially, a much closer affinity between scholars and the canons regular. This affinity was expressed in various ways. Both Peter Comestor and Hilduin state that scholars and canons regular share the common heritage of St. Augustine. Addressing the community at St. Victor on the feast day of St. Augustine, Peter Comestor, still at the time a master at the schools of Notre Dame, preaches:

Augustine, just like a pregnant mother, has two breasts, a left one and a right one. At the left sit scholars of theology nourished with a form of doctrine; at the right canons regular nourished with a form of life. These two breasts are the exposition of Scripture and the rules of canonical life. He is therefore our teacher [as] he is your founder.[78]

The imagery is awkward, but the intention is clear. That Peter Comestor saw a close affinity between scholars and the canons regular is hardly surprising. He had probably spent his first years in Paris at St. Victor during the time when the abbey's school was still thriving and open to outsiders. Throughout his career as master and chancellor at Notre Dame, he remained in close touch with the Victorines. And he chose to die as a member of their community. Peter is no doubt sounding a personal note when he refers in this sermon to the presence of canons as the "consolation of scholars." More puzzling, perhaps, is the use of the same theme by Peter's successor as chancellor, Hilduin, who had no known ties to St. Victor. When preaching on the same occasion some years after Peter, Hilduin similarly, but less awkwardly, described Augustine as the common spiritual father of three groups of clerics: scholars, to whom he gives instruction; secular clerics, whom he reformed; and canons regular, for whom he established a special rule of life.[79]

Both Peter Comestor and Hilduin seem to have wanted to use the opportunity of preaching at St. Victor to do more than merely express their personal admiration for the life of the canon regular.[80] By emphasizing the common heritage of scholars and canons, both chancellors may well have been attempting to counter the prevailing tendency among the Victorines to close their school and to distance themselves from the new intellectual developments in Paris. Ideally, for Peter Comestor and Hilduin, the canons regular and the scholars should regard each other not as rivals but as potential partners in leading the reform of the Church. Their sermons probably came too late to have a significant impact on the attitudes of the Victorines, but they did point in the direction that the new religious orders, led by the Dominicans, were to follow within a few decades.

When it actually came to discussing the relative merits of the lives of scholars and those in the cloister, the moralists' ideas and attitudes varied considerably. To some the cloister seemed an appealing alternative to the schools. In a sermon preached probably at the Parisian abbey of St. Germain des Prés, Peter Comestor favorably compares the cloister to the schools. The stability of life in the cloister, he argues, makes it possible for monks to concentrate completely on divine things. Outside the cloister, the instabilities of daily life severely limit the attention scholars can give to them. Peter urges the monks not to let the apparent attractions of the schools tempt them to leave the cloister.[81] Perhaps it was because Peter himself, despite his success as a master, never found the stability and security that would have enabled him to devote himself completely to his biblical scholarship that he ultimately left the schools and retired to St. Victor. Similarly, Alexander Neckham, another master who eventually entered the cloister, when preaching to monks often contrasted the turbulent life of the schools to the tranquility of the cloister and the perfection of the religious life.[82]

Peter of Poitiers, on the other hand, used terms that were more favorable toward the schools. In a sermon for the feast of St. Martin of Tours, he speaks of the "paradise of contemplation" being divided into a "scholastic paradise," where truth is sought, and a "cloistered paradise," where virtue is sought. The ideal, in this chancellor's view, would be an environment that combined the two paradises, where Scripture could be studied within a cloister-like setting, tranquil and remote from human affairs, where only true doctrine would flow from masters' mouths, and where there would be peaceful discussion, not disputation, among students. In such a setting one could achieve both the truth of the schools and the virtue of the cloister.[83] This ideal of learning is essentially the same as that envisioned by Hugh of St. Victor decades earlier, when the schools of Paris were just beginning their great expansion and the school of St. Victor was still prominent among them. Peter of Poitiers, as we shall see, was not the only late-twelfth-century reformer who hoped that the kind of discipline and order once found at St. Victor could be revived to temper the turbulent activities of the thousands of students and masters now resident in the city.

Those moralists who compared the schools to the cloister and saw education as, ideally, a form of contemplation tended also to emphasize the idea of learning as a form of withdrawing from the world to pursue truth. In the tradition of Hugh of St. Victor, they thought of study as the first step on the path to individual spiritual perfection. Much more commonly found in the sermons of the moralists is a view of learning that emphasizes the social benefits of education and that recognizes the essential role of the schools in training clerics for the active life of ministering to the laity. Even some of the same language is used in these sermons.

For example, Hilduin uses the idea of scholars and the cloistered as two types of contemplatives in a way far more favorable to the schools and to the social role of scholars. Those who live in the cloisters, he says, are the males who grow up spiritually strong and who become well able to resist the temptations of the world. Scholars, in contrast, are the females who live in the world and who are weakened by their social obligations and by their responsibilities tending to the spiritual needs of others. But this, Hilduin emphasizes, does not diminish the status of scholars. Switching to the imagery of a familiar biblical story, he argues that although the cloistered, like Rachel, might be more beautiful, scholars, like

Lia, are far more fruitful.[84] Robert Pullen makes a similar point in his *Sententiae*. Using the term "contemplation" in a narrower sense, he insists that the contemplative life might be greater in its spiritual dignity and private merit but that the active life is superior in its fruitfulness and social value.[85] Here Pullen is writing of the difference between the cloistered religious and the secular clergy. But in the sermons he preached at the schools, Pullen often speaks of the importance of regarding contemplation and action not as rival forms of spiritual life but as the two requisites for the perfect life.[86] Pullen is, in fact, borrowing the argument that the canons regular had long been using to claim their superiority to both monks and secular clerics.

Other moralists were to follow Robert Pullen in proclaiming this combination of the contemplative and active life as the ideal for the scholar. When masters like Raoul Ardent and Stephen Langton preached to clerics about the value of contemplation, they were not telling them to enter the cloister but urging them to attend, or to remain at, the schools to prepare for the ministry.[87] The most excellent spiritual life, they held, was achieved by priests and prelates whose education in the schools had prepared them to fulfill their responsibilities. For these moralists, combining the contemplative and active lives meant being devoted both to learning and to moral reform. This ideal could be achieved only by those who were first suitably trained in the schools.

When preaching about this ideal, the moralists, again borrowing a theme from the canons regular, often echoed Gregory the Great. "No one ventures," Gregory wrote in his *Regula pastoralis*, "to teach any art unless he has learned it after deep thought. With what rashness, then, would the pastoral office be undertaken by the unfit, seeing that the government of souls is the art of arts?"[88] This theme occurs in sermons addressed to audiences both outside and within the schools. In each case the purpose is to emphasize the importance of formal learning as preparation for the active ministry. In sermons to prelates, the moralists used Gregory's authority to exhort those charged with choosing the priests and appointing the clerical officials who would minister to the laity to select only clerics who had been suitably educated. They hoped ideally for a time when nearly all prelates and clerics would have trained for their pastoral duties in the schools. But they realized that to improve the quality of the clergy and reform the Church they would need the cooperation of the many prelates who had spent their early careers in the cloister or at court. Mindful of the opposition to the schools, the moralists were tactful about proclaiming the importance of education when preaching to those outside the schools. In their sermons for these occasions, they chose their arguments and their authorities carefully. St. Gregory's words suited this need especially well.[89]

The same words were effective in preaching to scholars, but for a different reason. When, for example, Master Geoffrey of Troyes called the care of souls "an arduous and laborious task, the art of arts, the discipline of disciplines," he was intentionally using a vocabulary familiar and meaningful to students and teachers.[90] It is a language especially well suited to encouraging scholars to study, not in order to acquire knowledge for its own sake or, even worse, to serve their personal ambitions, but to prepare themselves for the care of souls. The true test of learning will be how well they are able to fulfill the arduous responsibilities of this, the "art of arts," not how well they master the rules and techniques of the academic arts or disciplines. Geoffrey was urging scholars to complete their studies and get on with the important pastoral duties for which they had, or should have been, trained. By calling the care of souls the "art of arts," Geoffrey, like other moralists, was choosing a vocabulary that could be used in sermons both to convince those outside the schools of the importance of learning and to persuade those within the schools to understand the pastoral obligations their learning imposed upon them. Let us now look more closely at both aspects of this preaching.

THE PROBLEM OF CLERICAL IGNORANCE

Clerical ignorance, it has recently been argued, did not become a major preoccupation of reformers until the late thirteenth century, when the supply of educated men began to exceed demand and university graduates became increasingly anxious about their ability to acquire a good living. Since the general educational level of the clergy had, by any objective standard, improved significantly, this concern has been interpreted as evidence of the graduates' efforts to advance their own interests rather than of their genuine commitment to reform.[91] Can this same argument be applied to the moralists, who were among the first reformers to give prominence to the issue of clerical ignorance?

Probably not. Among the moralists, the most outspoken critics of the illiterate clergy tended to be the most successful masters. They did not emphasize the moral benefits of a sound education only while teaching at the schools. Through their later careers as eminent churchmen they found—and they complained—that the continued advancement of insufficiently learned clerics and prelates was the greatest obstacle to reform and spiritual renewal. Stephen Langton is perhaps the best example. His considerable achievements as archbishop lend his frequent criticisms of ignorant priests and prelates particular authority. In one sermon, at the end of a long exhortation on the clergy's responsibility to teach the laity, Langton sternly warns that clerical ignorance is "exceedingly damning and damnable." Like an untaught teacher, he preaches, an unlearned priest is an abomination (*quasi res monstruosa*).[92] Similarly Alan of Lille, who knew of the problem directly from his experience trying to combat heresy in southern France, uses very harsh terms to criticize priests whose ignorance was so great that even the laity found them offensive.[93] And Jacques of Vitry came to believe that admitting uneducated men to the priesthood was no less grave than breaking the canonical prohibition against ordaining those who were of obvious ill repute, illegitimate or physically deformed.[94] To these moralists, who were certainly aware of the notable strides being made by graduates of the schools, progress was simply not happening fast enough. What worried them was not declining opportunities for the learned but the vanishing opportunity to advance the reform of the Church and society.

However remarkable the achievements of Paris-trained masters seem in retrospect, the reformers of the time were acutely aware that many clerics were still acquiring good livings and advancing their careers in the Church without having to spend years studying in the schools. The long-criticized practices of simony and nepotism still remained ready means for wealthy or well-connected young men, regardless of their learning, to obtain the most places and rise to the best positions. More often than not, this system must have worked to the disadvantage of the scholar who had spent long years studying and teaching at the schools. Simony, nepotism, and clerical ignorance are often criticized together in the sermons of the moralists. By 1200 they had become the common enemies of the reformers both within and outside the schools.

To some moralists, however, simony and nepotism were not the only factors working to the detriment of both the learned and reform. Some charged that learning and the schools were actively discriminated against, that either from envy of those more learned than themselves or from fear of the reform ideas emanating from the schools, some prelates were deliberately withholding places and advancement from scholars.[95] We must avoid confusing these serious accusations with the more obviously self-serving complaints of the humanists and satirists about the decline of learning. Resistance to the schools remained a strong factor in the Church at the end of the twelfth century. Despite all the apparent successes of scholars, there were still men in prominent places who were suspicious of scholastic learning and contemptuous of the claims of the learned. The moralists worried that, even if not a direct threat to the schools—which enjoyed both the local support of the bishop and the distant support of the pope—this opposition did jeopardize the prospects for reform, which required the more general support of bishops and prelates. How could the problem be solved?

The moralists blamed the situation on the attitudes of the scholars themselves as much as on those of their opponents. In their sermons to scholars, they frequently point out the socially harmful consequences of boasting about learning or being condescending toward the less educated. They considered the arrogance of the learned clergy as dangerous to reform as the ignorance of the unlearned clergy. Some moralists, in fact, quite deliberately balanced their attacks against the ignorance and simplicity of the clergy with warnings to scholars not to misunderstand or overestimate the value of education. The training of the schools, they argued, made a cleric more learned and in some ways, perhaps, more effective in teaching and preaching to the laity, but it did not necessarily make him a better or a holier man. They often reminded scholars that Christ had chosen his disciples from among simple and uneducated fishermen, not from among the learned. "The Lord selected the simple and the dumb, not philosophers," preaches Hilduin, admonishing scholars not to let pride be their damnation.[96] Raoul Ardent harshly criticizes proud masters for their scorn and mockery of the illiterate. When preaching to the laity, he complains, masters confound rather than instruct their audience by arrogantly showing off their intellectual skills. They should be more mindful of the example of Christ, who was patient with his disciples and taught the simple in simple words.[97] Jacques of Vitry was more concerned with the condescending attitude of scholars toward priests and bishops who made grammatical errors. An exemplum in one of his *sermones ad scholares* tells the familiar story of how the simple hermit Antony proved that he was wiser than the learned philosophers who had ventured into the desert to trick him. The lesson is stated clearly. As the philosophers came to recognize the great wisdom of Antony, concludes Jacques, so should scholars realize that some uneducated priests and bishops, whatever their difficulties with the rules of grammar and their lack of eloquence, might yet teach others all that is necessary for salvation by the clear example of their good lives.[98]

These examples served to warn scholars that if they were too arrogant, mocked the laity, and publicly criticized less learned clerics, they would likely alienate both the people whom they should be concerned to instruct and the prelates whom they needed as patrons and allies. Such examples also reminded scholars that learning brought with it the increased expectation of, as well as responsibility for, good conduct. The moralists saw learning as a privilege that made the educated more accountable than others for how they lived their lives. "It is less harmful not to know the way of the truth," warns Geoffrey of Troyes, "than to return after knowing it."[99] Odo of Soissons states with especial clarity a moral principle often found in sermons to scholars: "We read that where there is a greater gift of knowledge, there is a more serious peril of blame; to whom more is given, from him more is expected."[100] The gift of knowledge increased the scholar's moral responsibility both to himself and to the rest of society. This principle embodied an educational ideal. It also reflected the moralists' more practical concerns about the opposition to the schools. As scholars themselves, they were sensitive to the fact that the behavior of those at the schools was subject to close public scrutiny. At a time when they were making exalted claims about the importance and value of education and trying to gain increased public support for the schools, the moralists understandably worried about the damaging effects of charges of hypocrisy or immorality among the learned. Raoul Ardent wisely advises learned clerics, particularly those in prominent positions, to avoid even the shadows and likenesses of bad conduct in order to prevent scandal.[101] There was a certain urgency to the calls on scholars to improve their attitudes and conduct.

No one was in a better position to understand the damage scholars were doing their own cause than Peter of Poitiers. During his tenure as chancellor, Peter confronted the serious problem of the worsening relations between the scholars and the townspeople of Paris. Although generally outspoken in voicing his strong support for the schools, he did not hesitate to blame scholars for the tensions in the city. There were, he complains in a sermon for the feast of St. Martin, too many young men who came to Paris, not to learn but rather to enjoy the social freedom and to act in ways they would not dare to elsewhere. This immoral conduct, Peter warns in one version of the sermon, "inflicts shame upon masters and other scholars, scandalizes the laity, and renders the entire clergy odious to them."[102] In another sermon to a synod of priests, Peter offers a vivid example of the mistaken conclusions that might be drawn from the vices of a bad cleric. "Some simple, stupid layman," he warns, "says, 'So you think it is a sin to lend money for interest, to keep a concubine, or to gloat over food and drink? If it were, my priest, who is prudent and discreet, would never do it. If it is a sin, he should be charged like me. Indeed, I would never have done such things if I had not seen them done.'" But a priest or cleric who set a bad example could do much more serious harm than simply confuse or mislead the laity. Peter goes on to warn that such misconduct could actually undermine the authority of the clergy:

Indeed, what is even worse than that, because of one such priest, all others, even good ones, become suspect. It will be said: "Look at what this man is like, how disgraceful he is, and how he was discovered to have done such shameful and evil things. Do you think that all the others are not just the same? Certainly they are." He who slanders does not separate or distinguish the bad from the good. They do not say that bad priests do such things, but that all priests do. Indeed, it is quite natural for all the illiterate to hate the learned; so, because of the vice of one, all are condemned.[103]

Peter of Poitiers was no doubt speaking from his experience as chancellor. Voiced by a man in his position, such concerns were likely to have been taken seriously. Peter may well have made the same warning to scholars as he did here to a synod of priests. It is important, then, to try to understand the significance of what he says about the laity's contempt for the learned clergy.

The concern that Peter of Poitiers voices in this sermon is quite different from the frequent laments of other critics about the decline of learning or the contempt for the learned. The humanists and the satirists usually complained about the unfavorable attitudes not of the laity as a whole but of the lay elite, that is, of those who could – and who were thought once to have been willing to – patronize the learned. Such complaints, as we have seen, were often the expression of disappointed scholars who found the rewards for learning limited and advancement slow in coming. In contrast, those like Peter of Poitiers, whose careers were more secure, apparently realized that the learned had made, and were continuing to make, considerable strides. The schools were expanding. Their graduates held prominent positions in the courts of both princes and prelates. In northern France and in England, where what was probably a large majority of Paris graduates resided, the general level of education among the prelacy, and even among the clergy as a whole, must have noticeably improved – though this probably also had the effect of making the situation elsewhere look worse. When the moralists cried out against clerical ignorance, they were expressing their concern that despite the improvement, education was still not widely enough available. Additional financial support was needed for the schooling of poor clerics destined to be parish priests and for the fees of the masters to train them. Only a better-educated clergy could combat the increasing dangers of dissent and heresy and minister to the changing spiritual needs of the laity.

Since Paris was seen as the primary place where this learned clergy was to be trained, the conditions in its schools were an important issue. Instead of setting an example of high moral standards for the rest of the clergy and laity, however, Paris masters and students were doing serious harm to the advancement of reform – especially by their public profligacy. The often arrogant behavior of scholars was also depriving the schools of both needed support and potential influence. For the sake of their own ambitions, no less than of the needs of society as a whole, scholars would have to realize the responsibilities entailed by their status as clerics and by the gift of knowledge, cooperate to improve conditions in the schools, and strive to use their education to serve the public interest more actively and effectively. The moralists were confident that if they could somehow succeed in exhorting the masters and students of Paris to improve their behavior, they would be removing a serious obstacle to the cause of reform. Once the schools were reformed, the rest of the clergy and the laity would follow the example set by the learned.

THE IDEAL OF LEARNING: 'DOCERE VERBO ET EXEMPLO'

To understand the criticisms directed against scholars by the moralists, we must first examine their ideal of the learned cleric. It was their strong sense of the obligations of the schools to the rest of society that shaped the moralists' views of what should be taught and learned. Whether preaching to audiences of scholars or to synods of priests, they repeatedly emphasized the importance of the kind of learning that would prepare the cleric to teach others both by his word (*verbum*) and by the example (*exemplum*) of his life – or to express it another way, to be exemplary both in how he lives (*vita*) and in how he teaches (*doctrina*).

There is little original in the moralists' formulation of this educational ideal. As Carolyn Bynum has convincingly established, "docere verbo et exemplo" was the defining idea of the instructional treatises of the canons regular.[104] However, though their formulation was the same, the moralists meant something quite different. The canons regular, as Bynum's study of their treatises shows, did not emphasize public teaching or preaching but the edification of others by living well within the cloister. In contrast, when the moralists spoke of the need "docere verbo et exemplo," they were specifically referring to the public responsibilities of the pastoral life, above all to the importance of example in supporting the word of the preacher. This difference helps explain what the moralists saw as the primary purpose of the schools. Although young men were no longer studying only, or even mainly, to prepare for the priesthood, the standard against which the moralists measured the behavior of all scholars was that of the good pastor or preacher. They defined the essential role of education not, like the humanists, to be that of preparing men to live good lives but to train them for the pastoral duties of the priesthood and prelacy.

This emphasis is most evident in *Evangelistis evangelizare*, the sermon with which Bishop Maurice of Sully began his manual on preaching. Learning (*recta scientia*), Maurice says, is one of the three requirements of the priesthood, and the one that prepares the way for the other two, a holy life (*sancta vita*) and frequent preaching (*predicatio continua*). In order to guide both their own lives and those of the laity whose care is entrusted to them, priests must receive an education that provides "the perfect knowledge of divine law [and] the capacity to distinguish between truth and falsehood, good and bad, right and wrong."[105] Maurice lists the specific works that priests must know to accomplish this purpose: a sacramentary, lectionary, and computus, the canon of the Mass, a penitential manual, the Psalter, a manual of sermons for Sundays and feast days, and a collection of saints' lives. This assortment of liturgical texts and practical manuals is certainly well suited to the simple parish priests for whom Bishop Maurice compiled his preaching manual.

No moralist found it necessary to recommend such basic writings in sermons addressed to more learned clerics. But others were usually no less emphatic about the importance of learning divine law and about the practical purpose of knowledge of Scriptures.[106] The theology these moralists wanted taught in the schools was not speculative but practical. Thus Stephen Langton distinguishes, in his sermon *Qui descendunt mare*, between the meditation of the cloistered, who speculate on the mysteries of God, and that of the scholars, who seek to understand divine law.[107] The scholar is to be educated not, like the monk, for his own knowledge or his personal salvation but in order to teach others how to be saved. The moralists' emphasis on the public value of education constituted a new and different argument for the superiority of theology over all other disciplines. They argued for the supremacy of theology not primarily in theoretical terms—as did the Victorines—but in practical terms that stressed the fundamental importance of knowledge of Scripture to the pastoral life and to preaching.

Whether addressing the clergy generally or preaching at the schools, the moralists said little about how exactly the Scriptures were to be studied. Their emphasis was on the purposes of learning, rather than on the means. In their sermons, the value of learning is always closely tied to the responsibility to live and teach well. The study of Scripture is essential, first of all, because it prepares the cleric to lead a good life by teaching him moral precepts and by inspiring him to do good works. The moralists repeatedly reminded their clerical audiences that study could be fulfilled only by action. The fullness of knowledge of divine law, Jacques of Vitry insists, is found "not in the book but in the heart; not in reading but in loving."[108] "It is not enough to read or to hear the Scriptures, one must also demonstrate knowledge in the fruit of good works," advises Peter of Poitiers.[109] Geoffrey of Troyes similarly argues that the virtue of studying Scripture comes only through demonstrating one's knowledge in good works.[110] These good works benefit not only the cleric himself but also the rest of society. By living according to the precepts of the Scriptures and by doing good works, the cleric teaches the laity in the most effective way, by the example of his life.

The moralists had high expectations of the potential influence of secular clerics who were prepared by education to lead exemplary lives. Preaching on chapter 7 of the book of Numbers ("Factum est autem in die qua complevit Moyses tabernaculum," *Num.* 7.1), Peter Comestor argues that the candles that enlighten the tabernacle at night symbolize, not contemplatives occupied with prayer or those satisfied only to study Scripture, but clerics who by the shining example of their honest lives enlighten those in the darkness of sin.[111] Jacques of Vitry expresses the influence of the clergy's good conduct in a more direct way: "The life of the clergy is the book of the laity."[112] When elaborating on this theme, the moralists usually based their case on one or the other of two closely related arguments: that examples teach better than words or that if the life of a cleric is contemptible, his preaching, however learned and eloquent, will not be heeded.[113] In no sense should such arguments be interpreted as denying the importance of education. The moralists were committed to having the schools educate more of the clergy and provide sound training in theology. But they were equally concerned that the clerics demonstrate the value of this learning through their conduct after leaving the schools. For the moralists, as for the humanists, learning divorced from moral action had little value.

In addition to preparing the clergy to live well and to teach others by example, the study of theology obliged them to teach by the word, that is, by preaching. The moralists emphasized two points about this responsibility. They insisted first that no cleric should presume to teach others before he himself had been taught doctrine. Peter Comestor warns that a priest should not be ignorant of what he is supposed to teach others, "for it is indecent that he who sits in the chair of Moses should have yet to learn in order for him to teach."[114] Robert Pullen insists, more specifically, that no one should dare assume the duties of the priesthood unless he knows the truth of the Catholic faith, has been taught in the schools, and has scrutinized Scripture.[115]

The moralists' second, and by far the greater, emphasis is on the obligation of the properly educated cleric to commit himself to teaching others. Maurice of Sully's third requirement for the priesthood, after learning and living well, is continuous preaching. "Both pertain to the priest," exhorts Robert Pullen, "to do and to teach, since should he do and not teach, he does not complete his office."[116] Other moralists, such as Peter Comestor, invoke the learned cleric's duty to speak out against sin and to urge good conduct.[117] Jacques of Vitry argues that it is no less a sin to be learned and unwilling to teach others as it is to be unlearned and want to teach.[118] Clearly, the moralists were as concerned about the failure of the learned to use their knowledge to instruct and to reform the laity as they were about clerical ignorance. In their sermons they not only urged the expansion of the educational opportunities for the clergy but also exhorted those already at the schools to prepare themselves to assume the duties of the ministry and to accept their obligations to teach others.

Alan of Lille, in an Advent sermon harshly critical of the state of the clergy and especially of the corruption of the prelacy, speaks of another school, that of the ministry of Christ. "Christ," Alan preaches, "came to school that he might instruct us. . . . He came to a double school, to the school of doctrine and to the school of life, whence it is said of him, 'Jesus began to do and to teach' [Acts 1.1]. In the school of doctrine, he taught verbally; in the school of life, by example."[119] This was the model of the teacher that the moralists held up to all the clergy. It was also the ideal against which they judged what was being taught in the schools. As we shall see, the personal qualities that they required in masters and students, as well as the guidelines that they recommended for teaching and learning, followed directly from their belief that the primary purpose of the schools was to prepare young men to assume the responsibilities of Christ's school, the active ministry.

SEVEN

The Moralists II: Promoting Reform

AS EXALTED as their educational ideal might seem, the attitudes of the moralists cannot be dismissed as being either uninformed or unrealistic. Among the moralists were the renowned theologians whose teaching made Paris so great a center of learning and the undisputed queen of theology. However much these masters complained of the appeal of other subjects, they found their own classrooms filled with students anxious to hear their lectures on Scripture and theological disputations. Certainly, at least some of these students shared their masters' expectations about the purpose of their education and willingly trained for the active ministry.

Following these masters as they move from the classroom to the pulpit, we can be equally certain, given the reputations many of them had as preachers, that they often spoke before large audiences eager to hear their words, if not necessarily to heed their lessons. When, in their sermons, they criticized scholars, we should remember, they were talking to their own colleagues and students. When they complained of conditions in the schools, they were speaking about matters they knew well, having spent much of their careers there. And when they promoted reform, they were making recommendations they were prepared to act upon as masters in positions of influence and authority. Having now placed the moralists in the pulpit and learned something of them and their perspectives, we are ready to listen to the criticisms they make in their sermons and examine their proposals for reform.

QUALITIES FOR LEARNING AND TEACHING

Let us begin with the most fundamental question addressed in the sermons: What makes a student able to learn or a teacher qualified to teach?

For the moralists, as we have seen, the primary purpose of the schools was to train men for the active ministry. Consistent with this view of the purpose of education, they insisted that scholars needed to have suitable moral attitudes and qualities of mind and likewise that the schools needed to establish suitable standards of behavior and conditions of study. Not all the moralists emphasized the same qualities in their sermons. This is a reflection partly of variances in their preaching styles and partly of differences in their particular concerns. However, despite the considerable variation in the specific qualities they prescribe, a common set of certain persistent moral values and educational principles seems to have shaped the attitudes of the moralists, as it had those of other critics we have studied.

A sermon of Peter Comestor, a member of the first generation of the moralists, is a good place to begin to demonstrate the persistence of common themes and ideals. Preaching on the feast of St. Nicholas, the patron saint of scholars, Comestor chooses as his main theme the qualities requisite for learning. "The first entrance to wisdom," he says, "is humility. Hear what the philosopher said when asked what was necessary for study: 'A humble mind, eagerness of seeking, quietness of life, silent scrutiny , poverty, and a foreign land.'"[1] The philosopher's advice should sound familiar by now. It is the same passage quoted by Hugh of St. Victor in the *Didascalicon* and attributed to Bernard of Chartres by John of Salisbury in the *Policraticus*. Given Peter Comestor's known ties to St. Victor, one should hardly be surprised that his explication of the passage closely follows that of Master Hugh. This humility, he tells his audience of scholars, entails three qualities: not despising any writing, not being ashamed to learn from anyone, and not being condescending toward those less learned. A generation later, when Stephen Langton discussed the qualities necessary for the study of Scripture in his inaugural lecture as master of theology in Paris, he too emphasized the importance of humility. To improve their learning, scholars should eschew their contentious disputations and ornate language and, instead, demonstrate greater humility before both God and other men.[2] The particular practices Langton was criticizing are different from those deplored by Peter Comestor, but the ideal of humility is essentially the same. In his lecture Stephen Langton calls also for four other moral virtues: purity of life, simplicity of heart, concentration of mind, and gentleness. These four qualities, though not identical to those prescribed by Bernard of Chartres, certainly reflect the same general educational values and demonstrate the continuing influence of these values in the schools.

One would expect Peter of Poitiers, who as chancellor of Notre Dame was directly responsible for the schools, to be much more explicit than other moralists in prescribing qualities and standards of conduct for those engaged in study. His most detailed treatment of this subject comes in a sermon preached on the important feast day of St. Martin of Tours (November 11). Taking the theme of Luke 12.37–38 ("Beati servi illi quos, cum venerit dominus, invenerit vigilantes."), Peter compares the life of St. Martin to the four vigils that the good servants must keep. He then elaborates on his theme by introducing a series of distinctions:

> The first vigil is contempt for the world; the second, mortification of the flesh; the third, the desire for virtue; and the fourth, the desire for heavenly goods. Each of them has its hours. The first has three hours: honors, wealth, and pleasure. . . . The second vigil, mortification of the flesh, is divided into three hours: the first is frequent fasting; the second, manual labor; and the third, keeping watch. By these three luxury is expunged, pride weakened, and wantonness, the mother of vices, is slain. . . . The third vigil, the desire for virtue, also has three hours: the first is pure prayer; the second, shedding tears; and the third, giving alms. . . . Similarly, the fourth vigil, which is the desire for heavenly goods, is divided into three hours: the first is forgetting temporal things; the second, contemplating only eternal things; and the third, the destruction of the body.[3]

These distinctions serve to structure a discussion of virtues and moral qualities that seems, at first sight, as applicable to a lay audience as to a clerical. Perhaps on another occasion they were used for this purpose. In this sermon, however, Peter of Poitiers applies each quality directly to scholars – specifically, to theologians. The first vigil, he explains, teaches that "we should labor at Scripture not for the favors of the world, nor for secular honors, but so that, understanding them, we might do the will of God and advise others to do the same."[4] The second vigil shows the importance of living soberly and chastely, both for one's own well-being and, no less important, to avoid bringing shame upon other scholars. It is here that Peter, as discussed above, decried those scholars who come to Paris ostensibly to seek learning but really to gain the liberty to satisfy their sexual desires. This may be the chancellor's most overt reference to what he saw as the actual problems in the schools, but his discussion of each vigil offers concrete suggestions about how scholars could improve their lives and learning. According to Peter, the third vigil teaches that scholars should alternate their study with prayer, observe the canonical hours, give alms, particularly to poorer scholars, and not envy or disparage other scholars or masters. Finally, the fourth vigil teaches scholars to avoid useless questions and mundane subtleties, to keep within the limits established by authority, and to shun profane novelties and false opinions.

Other than Peter of Poitiers, the only moralist to discuss the qualities required for learning in such detail is Jacques of Vitry in his sermon *Cum esset Iesus annorum duodecim*. Unfortunately, direct comparisons cannot be made, because Jacques does not refer specifically to conditions in Paris. Nor is this sermon addressed to the same type of audience. Still, as we shall see, what Jacques has to say is relevant to our subject.

Jacques's theme, of course, is the often-told story (from Luke 2.42) of Jesus leaving his parents at the age of twelve and being found questioning the doctors in the Temple. According to Jacques, the story teaches a fourfold lesson: (1) we must relinquish childhood and child-like things when we reach the age of reason; (2) just as Jesus left his parents, so must we leave the world and pursue salvation by serving God; (3) we should attend the schools when young; and (4) we should obey our parents.[5] Discussing the third lesson, Jacques's first point is to emphasize that Jesus did not venture into the Temple to teach but instead to question the wise doctors. "By his example," Jacques preaches, "Christ teaches us that we should frequent the schools of wisdom and open our ears to the wise, and that we should question and inquire about those things of which we are ignorant." To become a "true scholar in the schools of true wisdom," he continues, requires nine qualities. These begin with (1) goodness, purity both of heart and of body, since, he says, "wisdom will not enter a malevolent heart and will not dwell in a body subject to sins." Also necessary as preparation for wisdom are (2) discipline and (3) skill. The six other qualities are more specific conditions and attitudes essential in the actual process of acquiring wisdom. The first three have to do with the relationship between master and student: (4) the master should not be reluctant to use the "rod of discipline" on his students; (5) the student should be humble, not contradict his masters, and believe what he is taught; and (6) the student must both fear and revere his master. The next three qualities concern how and what the student should learn: (7) the student must love the schools, be fervent in his studies, and be diligent in learning his lessons; (8) he should never be ashamed to ask about what he does not know or understand; and (9) he should not be "a curious investigator," seeking to know things beyond the powers of his intellect, but should study only what is useful.[6]

Jacques's nine qualities make an eclectic and odd list. They are certainly far more suitable for boys just beginning their studies of grammar than for the more mature scholars of theology, to whom other moralists addressed their sermons on this subject. Indeed, judging from the substance of Jacques's other three lessons, the sermon was obviously addressed to a general audience containing more young boys and their parents than scholars. In Jacques's mind, however, some of these nine qualities were no less vital for those more advanced in their studies. The final three requirements—in particular, the advice to limit study to what is useful—can each be found in his *sermo ad scholares, Cum egrediemini.*[7] So, too, can the emphasis on moral goodness as a necessary prerequisite for the rest. And the subjection of students to authority and to the discipline of their masters was one of the primary objectives of the reformers of the Paris schools.

All the moralists agree on four prerequisites to learning: humility, a pure and virtuous life, discipline or zeal, and disregard for worldly pleasures, secular honors, and material possessions. Implicit in these requirements is the idea of study as a form of contemplation, as a spiritual life pursued outside the cloister but requiring many of the same qualities. To detach themselves from worldly concerns, scholars do not, and need not, withdraw into the cloister. Instead, they exile themselves in a foreign land and, like the members of religious orders, voluntarily accept poverty. Peter Comestor explicitly compares scholars to monks and commends them for being willing to accept poverty, hunger, thirst, cold, and threadbare clothing in order to become wise.[8] In another sermon to scholars, he explains that leaving one's family and native land enables one to escape worldly entanglements and to experience the less comfortable living conditions that help develop the discipline needed for learning.[9] Jacques of Vitry, in a sermon to pilgrims, speaks no less positively about the virtues of exile. "Because of its delights and distractions," he explains, "scholars do not learn as well in the place of their birth as in foreign lands, which is why they frequently travel abroad and dwell most happily in alien places."[10]

Given what we can surmise about the living conditions most foreign scholars found in the expensive and overcrowded city of Paris, this may have been only making a virtue of necessity. When Peter of Poitiers, who knew the conditions in the city better than the others, tells, as he does in his sermon *Beati servi illi*, of the mental and physical anguish scholars suffer when they are forced to live in horrible rooms and to survive on poor meals far away from any family or friends, he is not describing what he regards as ideal circumstances for learning.[11] Peter wanted material conditions in the schools to be improved and urged his audience to give alms to poor scholars. But no less than the other moralists and, like them, very much in the tradition of Hugh of St. Victor, Peter of Poitiers believed that one learned best in an environment that emphasized intellectual rigor, physical discipline, and complete separation from worldly concerns. The educational ideal remained closer to the monastic cloister than to the academic ivory tower.

Like those prescribed for scholars generally, the qualities the moralists stipulated for the masters who taught at the schools were a combination of general educational principles, practical requirements, and standards of behavior. When the moralists preached that teachers should instruct both by their words and by the example of their lives or that they should be suitable both in how they live and in what they teach, however, they often spoke so generally that it is unclear whether their words were addressed specifically to the masters in the schools or to all the clergy. Seldom does one find a sermon that discusses how these requirements are to be attained, practiced, and judged explicitly enough to establish that the intended audience consisted of scholar-teachers. Even in *sermones ad scholares*, the practical skills needed to teach in the schools usually take second place to the moral qualities expected of all the clergy.

A good example is one of the sermons Master Robert Pullen delivered to an audience of clerics studying theology. Preaching on the text of Matthew 21.1 ("Tunc Iesus misit duos discipulos"), Robert comments: "Many of you wish to become masters, and yet few of you are to be masters. Whence of the many disciples who traveled with him the Lord sent only two, signifying that few among the many are worthy of the office of master. Likewise, there were two in order that he might point out the two things necessary to each master, namely, knowledge for teaching and virtues for living well."[12] Most of the sermon exhorts the students to follow the example of the martyrs and confessors in struggling to live virtuously among the evils and temptations of the world. Although he discourses at length on the virtues needed to be a good master, Pullen says relatively little about the knowledge needed to teach well. His advice to his audience is, in fact, quite general. They should study Scripture in order to be able to extract what is beneficial to teach others, and they should avoid the confusions that often come from concentrating on the writings of the philosophers and pagan authors.

Raoul Ardent's prescription for a good master also emphasizes moral qualities, but it includes more specific standards for his conduct. To the usual formulations of "vita et doctrina" he adds two other requirements: "The perfection of a master is contained in these four things: first, that he be true in purity of life; second, that he be true in knowing the law; third, that he not be concerned for some thing, that is, that he not be distracted by curiosity for temporal things; and fourth, that he not accept payment." According to Master Raoul, few are actually able to attain this perfection in their teaching. The latter two qualities are especially lacking. Even those masters who do seem both to live morally and to teach truthfully are more preoccupied with worldly concerns and ambitions than they ought to be. And rather than criticizing the rich, as the learned ought to do, even the most virtuous masters flatter them and accept their money.[13] Such high ideals, as Raoul Ardent himself seems to have realized, were quite unrealistic. They required a degree of scholarly concentration and personal self-denial, even asceticism, that far exceeded the desires, if not the abilities, of most masters in the schools. Few were willing or able to make such a commitment to perfect teaching. Judging both from the frequent criticisms of masters and from the careers of those we know something about, most masters seem to have expected that teaching would be financially as well as intellectually rewarding and that after their success in the schools they would move on to lucrative and prestigious careers outside of them. Such ambitions, combined with the competitive atmosphere of intellectual life, were hardly conducive to Ardent's ideal of the perfect master uninterested in any material gain from his learning and teaching.

Even those moralists whose own careers were to fulfill, and perhaps encourage, these expectations emphasized qualities far more suitable to the sheltered life of the schools than to the tribulations of a life spent in political or ecclesiastical service. Stephen Langton, stating the requirements for teaching Scripture in his inaugural lecture, places the usual qualities of knowledge and a good life—"scientia et vita" is his formulation—at the top of his list. To these he adds two of the same qualities he had prescribed for students of Scripture: humility and gentleness. The former, he explains, prevents the teacher from becoming presumptuous and thereby making his eloquence and wisdom useless, while the latter, by keeping him modest in word and in action, enables him to teach others effectively.[14]

Discussing the qualities of a good life, Langton uses the adjective *idoneus*, the word ordinarily used in defining the qualifications necessary to obtain the license to teach (*licentia docendi*) in the schools. For example, Alexander III's bull *Quanto gallicana*, which aimed to end the practice of charging a fee to grant the license, stipulated that it was to be granted freely to all "suitable and learned men" (*viri idonei et litterati*).[15] What did the pope mean by "suitable"? How were those responsible for granting the *licentia docendi* expected to judge whether a candidate possessed this quality? The use of *idoneus* by Langton and other moralists to describe masters or ministers makes it clearer what was meant by "suitable." In Langton's inaugural sermon, *idoneus* is used as a synonym for honest living.[16] Raoul Ardent preaches that a "worthy ministry" (*ministerium idoneum*) requires a good life, a good reputation, and good preaching.[17] Jacques of Vitry lists four necessary qualities for "worthy ministers" (*ministri idonei*): purity of life, honesty, learned preaching, and diligence.[18] Each of these moralists uses *idoneus* to mean primarily personal worthiness, that is, living virtuously. But when applied to the ministry the adjective also carries, or at least implies, the broader meaning of the cleric's suitability to teach publicly, in the sense of having both the necessary learning and verbal skills as well as the good reputation that will make his words effective. Thus, according to the standards set by these moralists, judging the suitability of a scholar seeking the *licentia docendi* would require an evaluation of his life and his reputation, no less than of his learning.

To suggest a more specific rule for judging a cleric's fitness to teach, Raoul Ardent and Jacques of Vitry each cite the example of Christ, who did not assume the active ministry until he had reached the age of thirty. Preaching on the same theme on which Jacques of Vitry had based his discussion of the qualities necessary for learning—"Et cum factus esset annorum duodecim" (Luke 2.42)—Master Raoul explains that the example of Christ questioning the doctors in the Temple should be understood as a lesson that men should begin learning at an early age but delay teaching until they are more mature. "That Christ sat in the Temple in the midst of the doctors and heard and questioned them," he says, "provides an example to boys and to adolescents that they should go to church, hear teachers, and question them about doctrine. But this must be remembered . . . it is recorded that our savior heard and questioned when he was twelve, but did not teach publicly until he was thirty." Ardent also cites the examples of Ezechiel, who did not have visions until he was thirty, and of canon law, which prohibited the ordination of priests younger than thirty. No one, he concludes, should presume to be a master or preacher before reaching that age. "And you, stupid and proud," he berates the overly ambitious clerics in his audience, "before you even know how to be a student, seek to begin to be a master!"[19] Jacques of Vitry makes a similar argument for delaying teaching. Like Christ, who remained in obscurity as the son of a carpenter for thirty years before beginning his ministry, Jacques insists that no one should become a priest or preacher "unless of manly age" (*nisi virilis aetatis*).[20]

Although the lessons of both sermons are intended for ministers generally, not specifically for masters in the schools, they reflect the concerns often expressed elsewhere by these and other moralists that many masters were too young either to have acquired enough wisdom or to have proven themselves worthy to teach publicly. Something had to be done about these "ignorant and unbearded youth" whose ambitions to teach, charged the moralists, stemmed either from their foolish presumption about how smart they were or from their sinful desire to become famous and wealthy. To solve this problem, the establishment of an age requirement for teaching came to be seen as an obvious and relatively simple means of reform.

Finally, although the moralists insisted that no scholar should assume the office of teacher lightly or presume to teach without meeting all the necessary requirements, they were no less emphatic in arguing that it was the duty of the learned to share their knowledge with others—and, first of all, among themselves—willingly, freely, and without envy. In their sermons they stated repeatedly the principle that knowledge without generosity is useless. Not to teach what one has learned is the worst kind of avarice, the moralists argue, because, unlike all other possessions, knowledge increases in value when it is shared. "Wisdom is a noble treasury," preaches Jacques of Vitry, "since, when it is shared, it grows. He who has wisdom and does not endeavor to use it publicly is guilty of avarice."[21] Jacques criticizes scholars who seek to gain an advantage over their colleagues by not publicizing their ideas. "He who does not wish to share wisdom because of envy," he warns, "acts against the nature of wisdom, which wishes to be common to all."[22] Peter of Poitiers also expresses his concern that scholars should openly exchange their learning. Preaching on the text "Maria unxit pedes Iesus" (John 12:3), he exhorts, "You, everyone who is in this society of scholars, if you freely share the good that you receive from above with your colleagues, if you show yourself ready to serve others, loving, kind, tractable, and humble, all will agree that you are fragrant, and you will be the choicest ointment."[23] Each scholar should be committed to comforting others, to teaching those less learned, and to sharing his knowledge both verbally and by writing, freely and without envy. As chancellor, Peter certainly knew how much the competitive conditions in Paris were detrimental to producing such virtuous practices among scholars.

To masters—who were openly competing for fame, for students who could and would pay for their lectures, and for social advancement—the moralists held up the ideal of a community of scholars openly sharing their learning with each other and willingly teaching others with no regard for temporal benefit or gain. According to the moralists, the acquisition of learning required exile, poverty, concentration, and total withdrawal from social affairs. When this education was complete, scholars were then expected to assume the responsibility of teaching others both in and outside the schools. Despite the expenses and hardships of their years of study, scholars were to have no concern to benefit materially from their learning. To most it must have seemed a pretty lofty ideal. And the moralists themselves, even the most idealistic, were well aware that the principles and standards they were proposing were quite remote from the actual situation in the schools, where more practical goals motivated both students and teachers and more mundane qualities were admired and rewarded.

EDUCATION FOR THE WRONG REASONS: CURIOSITY, VANITY, AND SIMONY

In Sermon 36 of his commentary on the Song of Songs, Bernard of Clairvaux had charged that those who sought learning were too often motivated by the desire to know, by the ambition to be known as learned, or by the expectation that their learning would bring them money and honors. The moralists held these same three motives largely responsible for the serious shortcomings of the learning and teaching at the schools. Instead of studying in order to gain the knowledge needed to live well and to teach others, scholars were corrupting education with the vices of curiosity, vanity, and simony. The first step toward reforming the schools was to change the reasons young men were choosing to study and to teach.

The moralists' criticisms of the motives of scholars often recall the words of St. Bernard. Two examples will suffice to illustrate these similarities. The first, from a sermon addressed to students of Scripture by Robert Pullen, a contemporary and an acquaintance of Bernard of Clairvaux, is filled with Old Testament imagery:

> Not all who join themselves to Lia and Rachel will be saved. Indeed, many of them will be delivered to eternal suffering, since they do not study Scripture in order to be just but in order to appear learned. Only those who study in order to uphold their knowledge in good behavior does the bridegroom introduce to the wine cellar [Cant. 2.4]. . . . The wine cellar is Scripture. Not all are introduced by the king. Indeed, many are introduced by either vanity, curiosity, or simony. Certain ones attend to Scripture that they might know, which is curiosity; others that they might be known, which is vanity; and certain others that they might sell, which is simony, since they work not for the praise of God but for the glory of men or for worldly gain.[24]

Preaching several decades later of the failures of both the cloistered religious and scholars to fulfill their spiritual duties as contemplatives, Prévostin of Cremona follows St. Bernard even more closely:

> They [*viri contemplativi et scolastici*] study that they might know, that they might be known, and that they might sell, not that they might be edified or edify others. They study that they might know, which is curiosity. They study that they might be known, and it is vanity. They study that they might sell, and it is simony. They do not study that they might be edified, which is prudent humility, nor do they study that they might edify others, which is brotherly love.[25]

The formula was not applied only in sermons. In the *Historia Occidentalis*, Jacques of Vitry complains that nearly all the scholars in Paris were studying because of curiosity, vanity, or simony.[26] The repetition of this theme is perhaps more indicative of the persistence of established educational ideals than of the actual conditions in the schools. Despite all the changes brought by the rapid expansion of the schools, the criticisms of the motives and conduct of scholars remained essentially the same.

Of the three disapproved motives for study, curiosity received a disproportionate amount of the moralists' scorn. "To study in order to know," as this motive was defined, is wrong for several reasons. Curiosity causes the minds and the eyes of scholars to wander from important studies, seducing them away from the contemplation of the truth to material concerns, carnal thoughts, and secular occupations. As a warning against curiosity, Peter Lombard cites the biblical story of Dinah (Gen. 34). Just as Dinah left home to see the women of foreign lands and was seduced by Prince Shechem, so the human mind, when curiosity leads it from divine contemplation to worldly concerns, becomes corrupted by the devil.[27] God's command to Abraham, "Egredere de terra tua" (Gen. 12.1), was also used to warn scholars about the connection between curiosity and carnal desires. Thus, for example, Robert Pullen preaches, "The land of man is the desire of his flesh. Man exits from the desires of his flesh if he wishes to come to the desirable land. It follows 'et de cognatione tua.' That family is curiosity. For whosoever labors for the desires of the flesh must be curious about many things."[28]

Curiosity, it was thought, resulted in inconstancy, which, whether sexual or intellectual, interrupted the concentration of mind necessary for serious study. Moreover, as their choice of biblical texts reveals, the moralists saw a close connection between this inconstancy and instability, between mental curiosity and physical wandering. Commenting on the text of Genesis 12.1 in another sermon, Pullen directly equates the land that Abraham was ordered to leave with the curiosity of the mind that causes men "to run now to this and now to that as if through diverse stretches of land."[29] The moralists' solution to this curiosity of mind was physical stability. Scholars who remained in one place would find it easier to concentrate on useful studies. Presumably, too, this arrangement would allow for closer supervision of both their learning and their conduct. These moralists were hardly favorable to the romantic image of the wandering scholar.

Other moralists were more concerned with the dangers of curiosity specifically when it was the motivation for studying Scripture. Raoul Ardent complains that the curiosity of teachers of Scripture (which he compares to the obstinacy of the Jews) makes them far too ready to ask questions but too slow to do anything useful with what they know.[30] In one of his sermons to scholars, Jacques of Vitry warns that "many scholars because of curiosity and false knowledge are corrupted and made abominable in their studies. . . . Many, indeed, from curious and excessive questioning will fall into heresy, and disputing about the Creator or Creation beyond measure and above the powers of their abilities, they will deviate from the truth."[31] Jacques recommends that students of Scripture refrain from investigating those matters that cannot be known. They should heed the warning given by Paul in Romans 12.3—"Non plus sapere quod oportet sapere, sed sapere ad sobrietatem"—and not discuss things beyond the reach of human reason. Elaborating on the same passage in one of his Sunday sermons, Jacques explains how the "vanity of curiosity" can destroy learning in three ways. First of all, curiosity can lead to presumption. The curious scholar becomes too proud of his wisdom and contemptuous of those he should use his wisdom to teach, and as a result he scandalizes others by his bad conduct. Second, curious scholars can fall into heresy by taking the rational investigation of the mysteries of the faith beyond the limits established by the Church Fathers. Third, curiosity can also have the adverse effect of keeping the scholar from theology altogether by making him too interested in the secular arts and in useless questions about the natural world.[32]

Learning in order "to be known," the second motive that concerned the moralists, was likewise blamed for decreasing the usefulness of education. Raoul Ardent was especially critical of the effects of this vanity on teaching. Many vain masters, he complains, lecture only to show off their knowledge and their disputations confuse rather than help their students.[33] It is pure presumption, he warned repeatedly, that motivates so many young men to presume to teach others before they have been sufficiently educated themselves.[34] Raoul was concerned about those who, like Brunellus and Geta in the satires, vainly sought the title "master" in order to further their ambitions. Explaining Christ's admonition to his disciples, "Vos autem nolite vocari Rabbi" (Mat. 23.8), he contrasts the vain master to the good one:

> It is one thing to be called rabbi, another to wish to be called rabbi. To wish to be called rabbi is to be ambitious and vain. Both the good and the bad are called master. But it is not pleasing, and by no means beneficial, for the good master to be called master. For when a good man hears himself called master, he understands the need to be in fact what he is said to be in name. Hence he strives and labors in words and by his example to show himself a true master to others. But it is pleasing to the perverse master if he is called master. For when he hears himself

called master, he believes himself to be better than others and, consequently, he is incited not to improve himself but to become even prouder.[35]

Whereas Raoul Ardent was concerned about the effect of vanity on the ability of a master to teach what is useful, Jacques of Vitry worried that it impeded true learning. The vain scholar who boasts of what he knows fails to realize that God is the source of all his knowledge. Praising himself rather than God, he will never succeed in learning either truth or virtue. As a remedy for vanity, Jacques reminds scholars of the need to combine humble prayer with their studies.[36]

Study undertaken in order to benefit materially, the third disapproved motive, was considered a form of simony equivalent to selling an ecclesiastical office or charging for a religious service. The moralists often repeated the principle that as a gift of God, learning should be freely shared and generously offered. The practical implications for teaching did not need to be stated: masters obviously should not require fees from their students. This was the principle behind Alexander III's prohibition against charging fees for granting the *licentia docendi*. But there was still the controversial issue—much debated in contemporary summae—of whether it was also simony for masters to accept fees from their students. Inexplicably, the moralists do not address this issue in their sermons and there are surprisingly few criticisms of masters who profit from student fees.[37]

On the other hand, the moralists frequently criticized the simony of those masters who sought to profit from their learning or teaching in other ways. Odo of Soissons cynically describes the schools as being filled with men hoping soon to be rewarded for their learning with well-paying and prestigious positions. No less damning than their ambition, in Odo's estimation, is their hypocrisy. These scholars want everyone to think that they are exhausted from long hours of hard study when, in fact, they are kept awake worrying whether they will become deacons, provosts, bishops, or royal courtiers.[38] Studying for material advancement was thought to affect education adversely in two ways. First, the desire to have a more readily marketable education led scholars to study medicine and, especially, law rather than theology. Both Peter of Poitiers and Jacques of Vitry explicitly attribute the large numbers of law students to their ambitions for a lucrative career.[39] But theology also became corrupted because many of those who studied or taught that subject were just as much concerned about their career prospects. Scholars of theology, complains Peter Comestor, have become so anxious to gain prestige, wealth, and favor that they hasten through the Scriptures without understanding them.[40]

The moralists' criticisms of curiosity, vanity, and simony reflect their strong belief that one should learn, not out of self-interest or even the desire to edify oneself, but in order to use knowledge to teach and to help others. These selfish motives accounted not only for the personal mistakes and misconduct of scholars but also for the more general failure of the schools to provide learning useful to society. Like other critics, the moralists recognized that the reasons why young men sought an education had a determining influence on what, as well as on how, they studied. The moralists seem to have realized, however, that little could actually be done to change these reasons for study. Despite their preaching, curiosity, vanity, and simony would continue to attract young men to the schools. But the moralists did believe that something could be done to change what these young men studied and how they lived while in the schools. When they preached on these other matters, the moralists were doing more than exhorting. They were promoting ways of reforming the educational curriculum and of regulating academic conduct.

PHILOSOPHICAL IDEAS AND CONCEPTS

Before examining the moralists' specific recommendations and proposed reforms for the schools, we should briefly consider some of the more general educational principles and the philosophical ideas and concepts discussed in their sermons. Sermons are, of course, better suited for moralizing than for the systematic treatment of such philosophical issues as the nature of knowledge or the relationship of faith and reason. Even in the sermons of masters known to have strong philosophical or speculative interests, like Alan of Lille and Peter of Poitiers, one should not expect to find very substantive discussions of such issues. Rather, as we shall see, when they and other preachers do raise these issues in their sermons, they tend to simplify and to moralize them. It is not unusual to find a preacher taking strands of thought from a variety of sources, monastic as well as scholastic, and weaving them together effectively to support his theme. A few examples will be adequate to illustrate this aspect of the moralists' preaching. My purpose here is not to try to establish the sources or the inspirations of the moralists' ideas and themes but to demonstrate how they used some of the same philosophical principles found in the writings of other critics to promote educational reform.

One theme that is frequently discussed in the sermons is the nature of knowledge. Several moralists take definitions of knowledge from either philosophical or spiritual writings to support their arguments about the purposes of learning and the relative value of different subjects of study.

Here again some found the monastic vocabulary especially rich. For example, they borrowed the idea of knowledge (*scientia*) as one of the seven gifts of the Holy Spirit, especially popular in the spiritual writings of the Cistercians, and used it to defend the study of the secular arts. For the Cistercians, the seven gifts – fear, piety, knowledge, fortitude, counsel, understanding, and wisdom – stood for the seven stages of the life of contemplation. Modifying this idea to suit their purpose, the moralists redefined knowledge as practical learning about how to live well in the world and how to administer worldly affairs. This knowledge, they argued, is important to the scholar preparing for the active life. Important, but not sufficient, for knowledge is only the third of the seven steps to wisdom. Thus Peter Comestor, preaching about the seven gifts, reminds his audience that even the pagan philosophers were able to reach this level of understanding. The Christian philosopher, he insists, should not be satisfied with this knowledge but should strive for the greater gift and the higher wisdom of understanding God.[41]

Preaching about the nature of knowledge, Jacques of Vitry also uses an idea drawn from the monastic tradition, one strongly reminiscent of William of St. Thierry's view of learning. In several sermons he takes the distinction between knowledge (*scientia*) and wisdom (*sapientia*) a step further, speaking of the difference between intellective and affective reflection, between knowing in the mind and loving in the heart. Like the Cistercians, Jacques argues that one needs both, but, for him, having both means combining the practical knowledge necessary for the active life with the wisdom of the contemplative life. Instead of the individual monk's spiritual ascent, Jacques emphasizes the scholar's need to have both knowledge and wisdom, both intellect and affect, to be able to teach others. Theologians, Jacques advises, must have wisdom in their words and in their actions as well as in their hearts.[42] For him and for the other moralists, the inferior wisdom of knowing how to live in society and how to provide for material needs was as essential a goal of education as the superior wisdom of knowing and loving God. By discussing the nature of knowledge in these terms the masters could thus both defend the importance of studying the secular arts and remind scholars of the higher goals of their learning.

When monastic formulations of the nature of knowledge were used in the moralists' sermons, the lesson could be rather oblique. Easier both to analyze and to understand are those sermons in which the moralists addressed the same issue by employing the device of *distinctiones*. Preaching on the feast of St. Augustine, Peter Comestor takes the text "Fili, mel invenisti, comede quod sufficit" (Prov. 25.16) and distinguishes among types of knowledge as honey found in four different places. He acknowledges Aristotle ("the philosopher") as his source for the first three divisions: theoretical knowledge ("mel sub faciem agri"), practical knowledge ("mel in truncis"), and sophistical knowledge ("mel latens in casulis"). The fourth – which, he notes, "the philosopher did not know" – is evangelical knowledge ("mel de petra"). Elaborating on this distinction, the Comestor speaks of four kinds of scholars: the philosopher learns about the secrets of nature (theoretical knowledge), the political man (*politicus*) about the conduct of worldly affairs (practical knowledge), the heretic about the death of the soul (sophistical knowledge), and the Catholic about eternal happiness (evangelical knowledge). Next he distinguishes among the effects of the four types of knowledge: the first kind of learning leads to pride, the second tortures the mind, and the third kills the soul; only the fourth vivifies. Thus, he concludes, only evangelical knowledge offers true wisdom; the three other kinds of knowledge offer only the appearance of wisdom.[43] The lesson is clear: it is the Scriptures, rather than the secular arts, that should be studied. After making this elaborate set of distinctions, the Comestor directs his words to scholars of the theoretical and practical arts:

> You err, my sons. You think yourselves learned when you divide theoretical knowledge into intellectible, intelligible, and rational, i.e., into theology, philology, and physiology, or that which concerns God, that which concerns spirits, and that which concerns bodies. You think yourselves prudent when you separate practical into private, domestic, and political. You admire the torrent of Cicero's eloquence, the famed exhortations of Socrates, the swollen words of Demosthenes, who enlivened events with vivid language. You labor over the complexities of Aristotle, obscure matters that he discusses so briefly that it is as if he had hardly treated them at all. In all these matters, wisdom might be eloquent [*facunda*], but it is fruitless [*infecunda*].[44]

There is, as this passage demonstrates, an element of parody in this sermon. While criticizing scholars of the secular arts for thinking that they can find wisdom by asking obscure questions, making elaborate distinctions, and using eloquent language, the famed master shows off his own philosophical training, familiarity with the scholastic method, and eloquence.

Peter Comestor seems to have found this rhetorical device more effective in getting and holding the attention of scholarly audiences than other techniques of preaching. In a sermon for the feast of St. Nicholas, the patron saint of scholars, for which the text is "Qui non humiliaverit se sicut parvulus iste, non intrabit regnum caelorum" (Mt. 18.4), Peter divides knowledge in six, corresponding to six breasts, and speaks of the historical origins of each in terms of the six days on which the breasts lactate. The first is the knowledge of man's damaged free will taught to Adam and Eve by the serpent (*paralogia*); the second is the knowledge embodied in the mechanical arts that were invented in Egypt (*scenologia*); the third is the knowledge of natural causes that the pagan philosophers acquired through their reason (*physiologia*); the fourth is the revealed knowledge of the Bible (*theologia*); the fifth is the erroneous knowledge of the heretics (*cacalogia*); and the sixth is the valuable knowledge gained by the disputations of the Fathers (*pantologia*). The Comestor then compares these six branches of knowledge to different kinds of milk: the serpent's milk is poisonous and cannot be drunk; the Egyptians' milk is bitter and, to be used, must be flavored or mixed; the spoiled milk of the philosophers must be refined, so that what is liquid can be used and what is waste destroyed; the curdled milk of revealed knowledge is soft and sweet and can be swallowed whole; the milk of heretics is watered down and useless; and the pure milk of the Fathers is especially nourishing. The primary lesson of the sermon concerns the value of the sixth kind of knowledge (*pantologia*), which, he concludes, "subdues cacology, explains theology, despoils physiology, tempers scenology, and crushes paralogy."[45] By arguing for the superiority of *pantologia*, which can best be understood as the equivalent of scholastic theology, the Comestor is again urging scholars to study Scripture. At the same time, what he calls *physiologia* and says should be done with the milk of the philosophers seem to be intended as a defense of the usefulness of knowledge of the liberal arts to the study of Scripture.

The moralists usually raised the issue of the relationship between faith and reason in their sermons only in order to criticize scholars who refused to believe an article of faith because it seemed contrary to reason or could not be proved by the rules of logic. The arguments and definitions they used on these occasions were those commonly made in the schools, abbreviated and simplified to suit the audience and genre. Two principles were emphasized. The first defined the essence of faith: the essential merit of faith is that one believes what cannot be known. The second stated the limits of reason: many revealed mysteries are contrary to natural law and thus beyond the power of human reason to understand.

Warning against over-dependence on human reason in one of his *sermones dominicales*, Jacques of Vitry gives a clear definition of the difference between faith and knowledge:

Faith [he preaches] is called voluntary certainty greater than opinion and less than knowledge. It is said to be voluntary in order that faith might have merit. It is a certainty, since he who believes does not doubt. Indeed, he is prepared to die for his faith before he would forsake it. We should, therefore, believe in the traditions of the Church and in the authorities of the holy Fathers more firmly than we believe in our own sense.

After thus exhorting his listeners, Jacques goes on to speak of the merit of faith:

Faith is said to be more than opinion since to believe is more than to think and less than knowledge since it is less to believe than to know. Faith, indeed, would have no merit if it could be proved by causes or if human reason gave us experience of it, for then it would not be faith but knowledge.[46]

In another sermon, defining faith in somewhat different terms as "the spontaneous comprehension of the truth of invisible things," Jacques admonishes his audience to understand that "faith is not subordinate to human reason but beyond it."[47]

Discussing the relationship between faith and reason, Raoul Ardent makes a distinction between two kinds of reason that recalls William of St. Thierry's emphasis on the "reason of faith":

The reason of nature is one thing, the reason of faith another. It is indeed the reason of nature that if a woman conceives she has slept with a man, and that if someone is God he cannot die, and that if he is a man he cannot walk upon water, etc. It is truly the faith of reason that he who is the author of nature is not subject to nature but can do things contrary to reason and to the laws of nature, such as be born of a virgin, make the eternal temporal, the immortal die, and a man walk upon water.[48]

Ardent's use of this distinction was an attempt to provide a simple argument against the scepticism of those who found it difficult to believe miracles and to accept fundamental articles of the Christian faith—including the doctrine of the Trinity, as he comments when making the same distinction in another of his sermons[49]—because they could not be rationally explained.

Scepticism, the reluctance of the learned to accept or to teach articles of faith that could not be explained by reason, seems to have been a persistent problem in the schools. Peter Abelard explained that he wrote the treatise *De unitate et trinitate Dei* (c. 1120) because his students had insisted that "nothing could be believed unless it was first understood, and that it was absurd for anyone to preach to others what neither he nor those he taught could grasp with the understanding."[50] Raoul Ardent was not the only moralist to echo Abelard and complain about this scepticism. Such concerns are especially prominent in the sermons of masters who taught theology in Paris in the middle decades of the century. Peter Lombard criticizes "worldly philosophers" who advance "inane arguments" that the Virgin Birth was impossible and that God could not have died on the cross because such things are contrary to the laws of nature.[51] Robert Pullen blames this scepticism on "the grammarians and dialecticians or the philosophers," who have so much confidence in the secular arts and in philosophy that they contest and resist matters of faith, including the humanity of Christ, which they find contrary to reason.[52] Like Pullen, Peter Comestor is convinced that this attitude results directly from the excessive confidence that the "wise of the world," who study only the secular arts, place in reason.[53] Those who heard these great masters preaching on this subject would certainly have understood that they were not denying that reason and dialectic could further the understanding of Scripture and help resolve theological questions. The issue was where to establish the limits. But on this the sermons of these masters offered surprisingly little practical guidance.

Peter of Poitiers, the one moralist of the later generation to discuss this issue, does offer some specific guidelines on the relationship between faith and reason. Again, the immediate concern is the demand for rational explanations of the most profound mysteries of the Christian faith, in this case of the Incarnation and the conception of Christ. Like Raoul Ardent, Peter of Poitiers begins by making a series of distinctions about reason:

> Some things are from reason, some according to reason, some beyond reason, and some contrary to reason. From reason are necessary things, according to reason probable things, beyond reason miracles, contrary to reason impossible things. The first and the last are not included in faith. Those things that are from reason are known and are, therefore, not subsumed under faith, since "faith consists in things hoped for and asserted, not perceived" [Heb. 11.1]. Those things that are contrary to reason cannot be believed, since they do not sustain reason. The middle two, however, do submit to faith. In the first instance, faith is aided by reason and reason is perfected by faith, since those things that are believed are according to reason. In the second case, faith is not aided by reason but reason by faith, since reason cannot grasp what faith discerns. Yet one is moved by something other than reason to worship in faith what he cannot understand. These things are made known by divine revelation, and reason is not effective in them; but should reason contest these things, it is to be castigated.[54]

There are two ways in which Peter's scheme provides a much clearer role for reason than does Raoul Ardent's distinction between the "reason of nature" and the "reason of faith." First, the distinctions include a category for those matters of faith consistent with probable reason, that is, for things that cannot be proved by reason but can be explained and understood by applying the rules of logical analysis to them. This category of beliefs "according to reason" encompasses that area where theological and philosophical knowledge overlap, which was already, and would remain, the established territory of the scholastic theologian. Second, Peter defines the mysteries of faith, such as the Incarnation, not as "contrary to reason," as does Raoul Ardent, but as "beyond reason." The clear implication is that even in these matters, there is definite, if limited, scope for reason. Here, especially, faith must have primacy over reason, but within the limits of revealed truth, reason can help clarify and explain what is believed.

No other moralist sermonizes as systematically about the relationship of faith and reason as does Peter of Poitiers. Others often went no further than to criticize scholars who were excessive in their questioning, who subjected the profound mysteries of the faith to the test of reason, or who, like Abelard's students, seemed to deny the essential primacy of faith. Perhaps these moralists realized that there was no obvious solution to the problem of scepticism as long as theological questions were being publicly debated in the schools—and this practice was hardly something that the moralists, many of whom were or had been theology masters, thought should cease or be controlled by external authorities. Other than proposing some qualifications for those who would be allowed to teach theology, their solution was to appeal to the scholars themselves to realize their errors and reform their attitudes.

There is a third theme that should be briefly mentioned, that embodied in the message of the Delphic oracle, "Know thyself." In twelfth-century monastic writings this idea of the importance of self-knowledge as the essential key to all understanding had become closely associated with the theme of contempt for the world.[55] In the monastic tradition, these ideas had expressed the need for reform more often than resignation. In the schools, they were similarly used to promote reform. However, whereas the lesson of the monastic reformers had been to teach their brethren to denounce all worldly pursuits and to withdraw completely from the corrupting influence of temporal affairs, the moralists sought to encourage scholars to realize the limited value of the secular arts and to turn to the study of theology.

Alan of Lille's sermon *Homo natus de muliere* provides the best example of how this theme could thus be used. Criticizing scholars for spending too much time studying the secular arts, Alan gives a gloomy summary of the miseries of human life from birth to death reminiscent of Innocent III's popular treatise *De miseria humane conditionis.*[56] It is human error, Alan says, the misuse of reason, that is responsible for this miserable condition. By looking into himself, fallen man can discover the nature of his weakness and rediscover the image of God in which he was originally made. By realizing the importance of turning his intellect from the secular arts to the study of Scripture, he will not only learn to differentiate between truth and falsehood, good and evil, the eternal and the transitory, but he will also receive the grace necessary to choose the former. Varying his treatment of the same theme in another sermon, *Memorare novissima tua*, Alan exhorts scholars to concentrate not on the books of secular learning but on three more important "books": the "book of knowledge," which is written in Scripture; the "book of experience," which is written in the human body; and the "book of conscience," which is written in the human heart.[57] Again, the point is that attaining self-knowledge and realizing the transitoriness of life and the vanity of worldly things will lead the scholar to learning that is more useful and enduring.

Alan of Lille was not the only moralist who found the ideas of the misery of life and the imminence of death effective and not too lugubrious when preaching about the study of the liberal arts. Peter of Poitiers also uses the theme in his sermon *Quasi modo geniti infantes*. Rather than spending all their time studying the trivium and the quadrivium Peter urges scholars to learn about themselves:

> Most praiseworthy among all knowledge is to know oneself, to consider what man was, what he is, and what he will be. What was he? Most vile sperm. What is he? A vessel of excrement. What will he be? Food for worms. Not a single king had a different birth. For all, there is one entrance into life and the same exit. We come into the world naked; we leave naked. We carried in nothing; we take away nothing. Only mercy will be the companion of the dead. . . . One should not confide in strength, nor in youth, nor in wisdom, nor in money. The strong man dies just as the weak, the young just as the old, the learned just as the unlearned, the rich just as the poor.[58]

Peter's lesson is not that the secular arts should not be studied at all, only that scholars must not devote all their ability and time to them. For Peter, as for Alan of Lille, self-knowledge is the means whereby scholars of the arts can gain a better perspective on the limited value of their studies. Awareness of the imminence of death should incite them to move on to the "science of truth" (the study of theology) as soon as possible. But he is not denying the value of the arts, if studied within limits. "I do not judge these arts themselves to be wicked," preaches Peter of Poitiers, "only the men who keep studying them when they ought to move on."[59] We have come across this idea in the sermons of the moralists before. Now it is time to examine what they thought the limits on the study of the liberal arts should actually be.

RECOMMENDATIONS FOR STUDY: THE LIBERAL ARTS AND THEOLOGY

A prominent concern in the sermons of nearly all the moralists was the growing number of young men interested in studying either the liberal arts alone or the more lucrative subjects of law and medicine. When preaching, they sometimes distinguished so sharply between the value of these subjects and of theology that they seem to be, like the severest monastic critics, condemning the study of the liberal arts, medicine, and law outright and denying them even a limited and subordinate place in the curriculum of the schools. Certainly the hostility often expressed against physicians and lawyers makes one question if these masters could accept as their colleagues those who taught medicine or law. Attitudes toward the liberal arts varied and criticisms could sometimes be as strong, but no moralist went so far as to deny the possible value of the arts when studied for the right reasons and under the right conditions. The occasional excessively virulent attacks on students or on teachers of the arts seem to be more often a matter of rhetorical technique or even an outburst of some personal antagonism than a true expression of conviction.

For some of the moralists, it is necessary to depend upon works other than their sermons to interpret their criticisms of the liberal arts. Alexander Neckham provides a good example of how a dependence upon sermons alone can lead to the misinterpretation of a moralist's attitudes. Among the sermons Neckham almost certainly preached at Oxford, one, *Cantate Domino canticum novum*, is an attack on the craze for novelties that is especially critical of students and teachers of the liberal arts. Neckham seems to deny completely the value of studying anything other than the Scriptures. "Foolish is every page," he tells his learned audience, "on which the sweet name Jesus is not read."[60] Preoccupied on this occasion with the problem of excessive innovation in the schools as well as in society as a whole, Neckham seems to have felt the need to be far more negative than usual about the study of the liberal arts. Most in his Oxford audience, however, were probably well enough aware of Neckham's renown as a teacher of the trivium and quadrivium, as well as of theology, to realize that he was not condemning the study of the liberal arts per se. And all we have to do is recall that his often-cited scientific treatise, the *De naturis rerum*, is an introduction to a commentary on *Ecclesiastes* to establish that Neckham fully believed in the value of knowledge of the liberal arts to the understanding of the Bible. Neckham's sermon thus has to be understood, as he must certainly have intended it to be, as an attack not upon the arts themselves but upon the harmful novelties advanced by those who studied them out of vanity and curiosity. "The arts are commendable," he writes in *De naturis rerum*, "but those who abuse them are worthy of condemnation."[61]

Among the other moralists, only his much older contemporary Alan of Lille had a greater reputation than Neckham as a teacher of the liberal arts. Neither as a teacher nor as a writer did the *Doctor Universalis* express any doubt about the value of secular learning. The greatest and most famous of his literary works, the long allegorical poem *Anticlaudianus*, gives the liberal arts a prominent role in the shaping of "the good and perfect man."[62] When preaching to scholars, however, Alan of Lille was often harshly critical of those studying the arts. For example, in a sermon on the text "Ve vobis qui transitis" (cf. Lam. 1. 12, Mat. 23.13*ff*), Alan explains that through these words "God speaks to us wretched clerics; he speaks of our inane and frivolous studies; he speaks of us who relinquish theology and run to inane and transitory sciences, who desert the heavenly science and run to inane philosophy."[63] Alan uses a variety of familiar images throughout the sermon to express the difference between theology and philosophy: fruitfulness of the Promised Land versus the arid desert of Egypt, the saving waters of the Jordan versus the dangerous currents of the Nile and Euphrates, crossing the river of life in a wooden boat versus using a boat made of papyrus, a lavishly fruitful tree versus a tree devoid of branches, leaves, and fruit; and so on.

But amidst all this invective and negative imagery, Alan states explicitly that he is not criticizing the arts themselves, only how they are being studied:

> I am not saying that God condemns the natural sciences, which were instituted by him and admirably ordained by him himself as the attendants of theology, as the handmaidens of heavenly philosophy. He does not condemn the nature of the art but the delay of the idle. For there are certain gray-haired men in the liberal sciences, aged novices in theology, who give the flower of their youth to natural science and only the waste of old age to theology. But according to Avianus, the liberal arts must be greeted only in passing, that is, after they have led us to the doorway of theology, to the door of the heavenly queen, they must be left behind in peace.[64]

Thus, although seemingly intending at the start of the sermon to inveigh against all secular learning, Alan actually ends up defending the value of the liberal arts as the handmaidens of theology. In what was to prove a popular formulation of this relationship, he claims, "The Egyptians are to be despoiled in order to help the Hebrews."[65] But Alan emphasized that this despoiling was to be done only "in passing" (*in transitu*). Stating this concern in a more original way, Alan advises his fellow clerics that rather than fixing their feet in the arts, they must use the arts as a bridge to theology.[66]

Other moralists shared Alan of Lille's concerns about how the liberal arts were being studied. Peter of Poitiers is especially critical of those who exhaust their abilities seeking to know "the complexities of argumentation and the deceptions of sophistry, who explore the secrets of the heavens, the movement of the stars, and the courses of the planets."[67] Robert Pullen identifies grammar and dialectic as subjects especially likely to distract and to detain the attention of scholars.[68] Chancellor Prévostin complains that instead of studying Scripture, scholars are preoccupied by law and other vain subjects.[69] Both Peter of Poitiers and Prévostin, like Alan of Lille, pair their criticisms with statements favorable to the study of the arts. "I do not judge the sciences themselves to be faulty," notes Peter of Poitiers, "but, rather, those men who, when they ought to pass on, delay."[70] And Prévostin comments, "I do not say that the study of the arts is not necessary in order to prepare the way, . . . but *all* the studies of these scholars are of vain things."[71]

Whereas some moralists worried only about scholars who spent too much time on the secular arts, others, like Hilduin, believed that the theologians were no less prone to excesses and errors. In the sermon *Christus oris nostri*, Chancellor Hilduin complains that just as students of the liberal arts were debating useless sophisms and superfluous questions instead of focusing on the permitted books of the philosophers, so students of theology were far more interested in "the confusing perplexities of causes" and in Gratian's *Decretum* than in advancing, as they should, in their understanding of Scripture.[72] Hilduin was not alone in recognizing that reform was necessary in the theology curriculum as well as in that of the arts.

Of the moralists, only Peter Comestor and Jacques of Vitry preach in more specific terms about how the liberal arts should be studied. Peter Comestor's views about the value of the arts were generally more positive than Jacques's. In a sermon for the feast of St. Augustine, a frequent occasion for preaching about learning, the Comestor uses the image of a bow to speak of the relationship between secular knowledge and Scripture:

"His bow remains strong" [Gen. 49.24]. The bow of Augustine is knowledge. The wood of this bow is secular knowledge; the string is evangelical knowledge. Augustine was expert and fully erudite in both. The hard and dry wood of secular knowledge is curved by the string of evangelical knowledge. But note that the inner part of the wood is not bent or curved by the string of evangelical wisdom, only the two extreme ends. The inner part is the truth and the foundation of the liberal arts, the learning of which is not bent or curved by the teaching of the Savior, but which endures and perseveres straight and whole as if quite necessary for the study of Scripture. The wise of this world, however, possessed in their wisdom only the two ends.[73]

Unfortunately, neither here nor in any other sermon does Peter Comestor explain just which aspects of the liberal arts constitute the unbent part of the wood, the secular learning necessary for the study of Scripture.

But elsewhere Peter does say more about those aspects of the arts that should be avoided. In *Converti me ad viam*, a sermon clearly intended for an audience of scholars, he warns that "the fictions of poets, the unseemly arguments of the sophists, and the pompous opinions of the philosophers" can be especially detrimental to those preparing to interpret Scripture and should, therefore, not be studied.[74] In another sermon, *Super tribus sceleribus*, he reproves scholars who subject articles of faith to the logical subtleties of philosophical disputation. It is permissible, he argues, to use the "images" (*phantasmas*) of the liberal arts to explain doctrine but not to go so far as "to attack Scripture sophistically."[75] Although Peter Comestor provides little indication in his sermons of just where he would have drawn the line, his own biblical commentaries stood as models for other scholars to follow.

Jacques of Vitry's sermon to scholars, *Cum egrediemini*, offers by far the most comprehensive discussion of the study of the liberal arts. It is difficult to compare this sermon to those of other moralists both because of this comprehensiveness and because of its late date. Even assuming that the version we have was first preached about 1200, when Jacques was teaching in Paris, the sermon reflects intellectual conditions far different from those known to Peter Comestor and to other moralists who discuss the arts. By 1200 the influx of new translations of Aristotle and of Greek and Arabic scientific works had altered the trivium and the quadrivium beyond recognition. The liberal arts were to be considered the foundation of higher knowledge throughout the formative years of the university. But the impact of the new learning, especially Aristotle's books on natural philosophy, the *libri naturales*, forced many concerned scholars to rethink and redefine the relationship between "philosophy," now used to mean only the liberal arts, and theology.[76] It is in the context of this new debate about "philosophy" that we must examine the attitudes Jacques's sermon expresses about the study of liberal arts.

As one of the two sermons to scholars included in Jacques's collection of *sermones ad status*, *Cum egrediemini* was apparently intended to provide a comprehensive set of guidelines for preaching to a scholarly audience. This makes the sermon difficult to summarize, but certainly important enough as a source of attitudes about learning to merit consideration in some detail. After an unusually long, elaborate, and obscure protheme—which can be discussed better after the rest of the sermon—Jacques explains his choice of the text of Exodus 3.21-22:

"When you do leave, you shall not go away empty handed. But each woman is to ask her neighbor and her guest for articles of silver and gold and for clothing, and you are to despoil Egypt." By these words, the Lord especially teaches scholars how the Egyptians should be despoiled in order to enrich the Hebrews. According to this text, we are allowed to study the books of the pagans at the appointed time, so that we might know the valuable from the worthless by taking the useful things from their words and rejecting the useless.[77]

To illustrate the applicability of this lesson to the curriculum, Jacques starts, appropriately, with the first art of the trivium, grammar. He praises it unequivocally as "the foundation and beginning of speaking, the art necessary to all other disciplines." But his praise of grammar is combined with a warning. Jacques first exhorts scholars not to be critical of less learned bishops and priests who make grammatical errors. "Learned and eloquent men," he advises, "should not scorn the ignorance of their simple brothers, whose unguent teaches all things necessary to salvation."[78] Having made the point that a good life and sound doctrine are far more important than good grammar, Jacques then turns to the issue of how the art should be studied to make it most useful. The items God commanded the Israelites to take from the Egyptians, he explains, symbolize the three things that can be gained from the proper study of grammar: the articles of silver stand for eloquence and correct pronunciation; those of gold are the useful and edifying moral lessons found in classical writings; and the vestments represent the virtues—such as chastity, contempt for the world, and piety—exemplified in the lives of the good pagans. More practically, Jacques recommends that grammar masters choose only books that combine training in correct Latin with useful moral lessons or information preparatory to the study of theology. As examples of such works, Jacques lists the writings of Cato, Theodulus, Avianus, Prudentius, Prosper, and Sedulius Scotus, as well as the *Physiologos*. Above all, he recommends the verse parts of the Bible itself. "Since such books are sufficient both for the exercise and for the art of grammar," he asks his audience, "why should one teach or learn those other curious books called 'historiographies' or those verses of the poets that might incite vanity or lust?"[79] Jacques gives no specific examples of these works or authors, perhaps lest mere mention of their names excite the curiosity of some of the scholars in his audience. Rather, he concludes his discussion of grammar by demonstrating—in a proud display of his knowledge of Lucan and Ovid—how classical sources can be used to teach both virtuous conduct and the rules of Latin grammar.[80]

From grammar Jacques moves on—not, as one might expect, to discuss the other arts of the trivium—but directly to an attack upon the *libri naturales*. Although he again states the principle that it is permissible to take from the "philosophers" anything fitting to the Christian cause,

Jacques's criticisms make it clear that he thought the newly discovered works of natural philosophy contained little fitting or useful knowledge. Scholars seeking to learn from the philosophers should study only the "wholly catholic and moral" *De consolatione philosophiae* of Boethius, he insists, and not waste their time over the "many false and vain things" asserted by other philosophers, such as Plato, who believed that the planets were gods, and Aristotle, who claimed the world was eternal. "Hence," he warns, "we must beware of those books they call 'natural' lest, from too much questioning, we err in the faith. The Christian faith holds many things that are beyond nature or contrary to it."[81]

There is nothing exceptional about Jacques's reaction to the *libri naturales*. Like many of the more conservative theologians in Paris, he worried about the dangers of the intrusion of natural philosophy into theology and insisted upon the disjunction of natural knowledge and revelation.[82] To illustrate the danger, Jacques cites two examples, neither of them original, of how scholars were being misled by natural philosophy to advance opinions directly contrary to Christian doctrine. Some scholars, he warns, have become "so infected by the *libri naturales*" that they will not accept as true anything inconsistent with natural reason and thus even refuse to believe the mystery of the Incarnation.[83] Other scholars, convinced by the astronomical writings of the philosophers that the stars and planets determine human actions, deny the doctrine of free will.[84] The *libri naturales* are not only misleading and dangerous, Jacques concludes, but also wholly unnecessary for Christians. Since everything important to know about natural philosophy can be found in Scripture, there is simply no need for anyone to spend his time studying these works. Scholars should thus concentrate on more vital and less dangerous matters. "All of man's life," admonishes Jacques, "is hardly sufficient to learn those things we can learn without danger and curiosity."[85]

What, then, should be studied? According to Jacques, the safe and useful studies include the trivium but not the quadrivium:

> We can safely hear those secular sciences, such as grammar, dialectic, and rhetoric, that prepare the listener for the science of piety. It is otherwise for the sciences of the quadrivium, which although they contain truth, do not lead to piety. . . . Geometry, arithmetic, and music have truth in their sciences, but this is not that science of piety. The science of piety is to know and to read Scripture, to understand the prophets, to believe the Gospel, and not to be ignorant of the apostles.[86]

Jacques's reversion here to the familiar terminology of the seven liberal arts might be simply a convenient way of bringing this part of his sermon to an end. It is thus unclear how much significance we should attribute to the distinction Jacques makes between the trivium and the quadrivium. Although willing to concede that the quadrivium does contain some truth, he seems to disagree with other moralists, like Alexander Neckham, who thought that these arts could be useful to understanding Scripture.

Jacques's negative attitude to the quadrivium undoubtedly resulted in large part from his concern about the impact that the newly translated texts of Aristotle and his Arabic commentators were having on the curriculum in the schools. This new learning, not the quadrivium, was clearly his primary concern in this sermon. But the evidence of his other sermons does suggest that Jacques also had some doubts about the value of the traditional liberal arts curriculum. Even when he admits that grammar and the trivium can be useful and are generally safe, as he does here, Jacques usually also emphasizes the need for a great deal of caution. Even the best of the pagan writings, he advises in one of his Sunday sermons, should be read rarely and borrowed from as little as possible.[87] Since he was preaching on this occasion to scholars, Jacques expresses his view of secular learning more obliquely. To warn them against becoming preoccupied with the study of the liberal arts, he uses exempla such as the well-known story of the angel's reprimand to Jerome for spending too much time reading Cicero, the frequently retold legend of the conversion of Master Sella, and an otherwise unknown story of how Bernard of Clairvaux, on a visit to the schools of Paris, used a logical trick to defeat the logicians at their own game.[88] It should be noted that each of the exempla concerns the study of the arts of the trivium.

In the second part of his sermon, Jacques turns from the arts themselves to speak more generally about how secular learning should be used. Again, he begins his remarks by commenting on a text often used in connection with secular learning, this time Deuteronomy 21.11-13:

> "If someone from among the sons of Israel wishes to marry a beautiful woman captured in battle, he should bring her to his house, shave off her hair, cut her nails, and take off her clothing." Morally, this can be understood to refer to any sentence taken from a book written by the pagan philosophers, which, if it pleases us because many aspects of it are found to be in harmony with truth, we can, by cutting away what is superfluous, convert the rest to our use.[89]

Shaving the woman's hair, he explains, symbolizes the need to refrain from studying the "vain subtleties and presumptuous opinions" of the philosophers; cutting her nails means avoiding the vanity of these philosophers, who glorified themselves rather than God and who used their knowledge for temporal gain; and removing the clothing of the captive woman symbolizes stripping from the useful knowledge found in pagan philosophy all superfluous ornamentation and useless verbiage. Scholars must take such a cautious and critical approach even to the best writings of the pagan philosophers, because all of them, in their vanity, concealed their wisdom beneath a superfluity of words. Many pagan writings are better avoided altogether. These include the "fictions of the poets [*figmenta poetarum*], who through the delights of their fables excessively incite the mind to sexual excitement,"[90] the writings of astronomers, and above all, the medical books of physicians (*physici*). The last are especially dangerous because they frequently make false promises of cures and also because their remedies often call for practices contrary to Christian ethics.[91]

After illustrating the dangers of these subjects with several especially effective and vivid exempla, Jacques abruptly changes the terms of his argument. "With all diligence," he preaches, "we must distinguish between the fruitful and the unfruitful sciences, and we must choose only the former." These are, Jacques explains, giving a surprising but familiar list of disciplines,

> ethics, which can be applied to our moral formation, economics, to managing our family, and politics, to serving the multitude; rational or theological science, which concerns the divine and those things remote from the senses that intelligence distinguishes and discerns; natural science, which investigates the nature of things; and dialectic and rhetoric, which prepare the way to natural science and to theology.[92]

It seems odd to inject this quadripartite, Aristotelian division of philosophy into the sermon at this point. Moreover, the list of fruitful sciences appears to contradict Jacques's earlier criticism of the study of the quadrivium and the *libri naturales*.

Yet with no further comment, Jacques simply goes on to introduce a second, tripartite division, attributed to Origen, between moral, natural, and inspective philosophy. Only in drawing his conclusion does Jacques resolve this apparent contradiction. To learn these three branches of philosophy, he explains, we need study no text other than the Bible. The writings of the pagan philosophers are completely unnecessary. The only author needed is the wise Solomon, whose books provide a complete knowledge of philosophy: Proverbs teaches moral philosophy; Ecclesiastes, by showing the vanity of the Creation and the need to concentrate on knowing and loving the Creator, teaches everything useful about natural philosophy; and the Song of Songs teaches the essential lesson of inspective philosophy, which is that only eternal things should be valued and contemplated.[93] In this clever way, Jacques returns to his earlier point that Christian scholars can find in Scripture virtually everything they need to know, not just about natural philosophy, as he had suggested before, but about virtually every branch of knowledge. Only for students or teachers of the preparatory arts of the trivium do classical authors seem to retain any possible value. And even here relatively few authors or texts should be used. Above all, the misleading and dangerous *libri naturales* should be avoided altogether.

Given all the restrictions Jacques wishes to impose, there seems to be very little of real value remaining to be despoiled from the Egyptians. And what there is can and should be taken quickly. Jacques's lesson is a call to scholars to give precedence in their studies to theology, rather than to philosophy, to spend their time at the schools learning Scripture, not reading the pagan philosophers. The sermon concludes with exempla warning against those vices for which the moralists so often berated scholars: curiosity and vanity.[94] For Jacques of Vitry, nowhere was the influence of these vices more evident than in the growing interest in natural philosophy in the schools.

I have left the protheme until the end, not because it expresses a different view of the relationship between the liberal arts and theology, but because in it Jacques offers scholars a spiritual alternative to the traditional seven liberal arts. From his opening words, Jacques makes it clear that he believes the study of the secular arts has little to offer to theology. "What," he asks, quoting Jeremiah 23.28, "has the straw to do with the wheat?" The secular arts teach only fables; Scripture alone teaches the art of good living. Thus, he argues, it is theology that should truly be called the liberal art, since it alone "liberates" (*liberat*) the soul from evil. Scholars should not be as much concerned with the liberal arts taught in the schools as with another set of arts far more vital to their lives.[95]

There follows a series of exhortations:

> Good is that logic that teaches us to distinguish between truth and falsehood. . . .
>
> Good is that grammar that teaches correct writing and speaking. . . .
>
> Good is that rhetoric that teaches us to speak aptly and effectively in persuading others.

Although these names and the definitions correspond to the trivium, Jacques is talking about something quite different from the arts curriculum in the schools. This is made clear by the biblical citations that he adds to each of these three exhortations. For example, he explains that writing correctly inscribes mercy and truth in one's heart (Prov. 3.3), and that speaking correctly prevents any evil word from passing one's lips (Eph. 4.29). When Jacques comes to the quadrivium, the definitions themselves clearly differentiate the arts he is prescribing from those taught in the schools. As he continues:

> Good is the geometry that teaches us to measure our bodies in order that we might consider our beginning and our end. . . .
>
> Good is the arithmetic that teaches us to consider the number and the paucity of our days. . . .
>
> Good is the music that teaches us to consider the harmonies and sweet song of the celestial spheres. . . .
>
> Good is the astronomy that teaches us to consider the heavens and the virtue of those stars that shine in the vision of God.[96]

Rhetorically this is very effective. Jacques often used his prothemes to display his mastery of the *ars praedicandi*. The spiritualization of the liberal arts served to introduce the theme of the sermon. Having so eloquently exhorted scholars, Jacques could then begin to instruct them about this higher learning.

The idea of a spiritual equivalent to the seven liberal arts is not unique to Jacques of Vitry. It is also found in two somewhat different versions of a sermon on the theme of Christ's miracle at the marriage of Cana (John 2.3: "Vinum non habent"), both probably by Prévostin.[97] The anonymous version of this sermon, which is addressed to an audience of scholars and contemplatives, includes a lengthy dialogue between Christ and his mother on the subject of learning. When Mary mentions the lack of wine, Christ launches into a long attack on those who study the secular arts instead of his "truly liberal" arts:

> "Some of them study the arts they call liberal—beautiful in name but less so in actual use—and they neglect my arts, which are truly liberal since they liberate man from eternal death. I have my grammar, my dialectic, and so forth.
>
> "My grammar teaches correct reading, correct writing, and correct speaking. He reads correctly who continuously contemplates my works in order that he might shape his life according to mine. For each of my actions ought to be a textbook for the Christian. He writes correctly who inscribes my mandates in his heart. . . . He speaks correctly who does good things in my honor, so that others, seeing him, will follow his good example and the Heavenly Father will be glorified.
>
> "Dialectic teaches how to distinguish truth from falsehood. But my dialectic teaches that I alone am the truth and that whatsoever else is sought is falsehood.
>
> "Rhetoric teaches persuasive speech. My rhetoric consists of continuous meditation on divine things, so that what my dialectic teaches rhetoric then firmly establishes after longer investigation.
>
> "Arithmetic teaches counting. Oh, what good arithmetic he studies who contemplates the facts that his months on earth are numbered, that he cannot know when his determined end will come, and that his years will be swept away like a cobweb [Ps. 89.9] unless he is on guard. . . .

"Geometry teaches how to measure the earth. But he studies true geometry who measures his own body and considers its beginning, middle, and end. He considers that his birth was unpure, his life is laborious, and his death will be perilous unless he is freed by me.

"Music teaches harmony. Oh, what good music he has who is satisfied that his sensuality be in harmony with his reason and his flesh with his spirit.

"Astronomy concerns the stars; but he truly knows astronomy whose life [*conversatio*] is focused on heaven, who seeks to free himself from the concerns of this world in order to find eternal life."[98]

These seven arts are, essentially, a more elaborate version of those prescribed by Jacques of Vitry in the protheme to *Cum egrediemini*. Like Jacques, Prévostin was exhorting his audience to give priority to a spiritual curriculum that is far more important than that of the schools. Whereas Jacques explicitly exhorts scholars studying the liberal arts to move on to theology, Prévostin wants everyone, whether in the schools or the cloister, who places too great an emphasis on learning, whether in the arts or other subjects, to think instead about improving his life and saving his soul. Both moralists concur, however, in granting no more than a very limited value to the study of the liberal arts.

The moralists were as ambivalent about classical authors and pagan philosophers as they were about the usefulness and value of the liberal arts. The limited admiration they express for the learning or for the virtuous lives of the pagans is usually qualified by a warning or criticism. *Cum egrediemini* is, in this respect, a typical sermon. Jacques of Vitry exhorts scholars to follow the classical authors in being chaste, unworldly, and pious, then warns them against the errors that result from following Plato and Aristotle.[99] Peter Comestor likewise cites philosophers as models of chastity and disinterest in wealth but warns that more often they teach useless and harmful things, because they had false ideas about the highest good.[100] Urging a cautious approach to the *Timaeus*, Alexander Neckham mentions the legend that Plato had been taught by Isaiah, who had himself been taught by Moses. Even though he seems to have known the true story of the Creation, however, "unhappy Plato" perverted much of this knowledge into error.[101]

Other moralists point to the unsound motives of the pagan philosophers. According to Raoul Ardent, although it might seem that many pagan philosophers, because of the sacrifices they had made in their lives, had carried their cross, they had done so not in imitation of Christ or for the love of God but for the vanity of their philosophical beliefs.[102] Geoffrey of Troyes concedes that a few pagan philosophers did come to know something of the majesty of God. But presumption, rather than devotion, was the result; because they failed to admire and to praise God, their understanding remained obscured.[103] Finally, Robert Pullen notes that as punishment for their arrogance, Christ passed over the philosophers and chose his first disciples from among simple fishermen.[104] In each case, the Christian scholar is admonished to realize the importance of avoiding the same pitfalls.

Several of these same admonitions about repeating the errors of the pagan philosophers also appear in a sermon of Peter of Poitiers. Preaching on the text "Beatus et sanctus qui habet partem in resurrectione prima" (Apoc. 20.6), Peter explains how the philosophers erred in their search for happiness:

> Happiness [*beatitudo*] is promised first of all. And who should not seek happiness? Indeed, as the philosopher says, all men desire to be happy. However, they strive for happiness in different ways. The pagan philosophers, although they lacked faith in Christ, did not lack morals and they sought the highest good. . . . Nevertheless, many went astray disputing about happiness. Intent upon exploring the secrets of nature and esteeming their own words, the pagan philosophers thought happiness lay in the knowledge of causes. "Happy is he," one of them said, "who can know the causes of things" [Virgil, *Georgics* 2.490]. But the Apostle condemned this opinion when he chided those who seek to explain the courses of the stars and the numbers of the elements according to the laws of physics, and who spurn God, the author of all these things, whom to know is the ultimate pleasure. If this knowledge of causes should be praised, how much more should the architect of them all be praised?[105]

Peter is not criticizing the motives of the pagan philosophers – indeed, he grants that it is commendable to seek knowledge of the highest good – but their failure to realize the true source of their knowledge.

In another sermon, *Gratia Dei sum*, Peter explains that the fundamental mistake the philosophers made was not to understand the importance of God's grace. Even those who came to know something of the majesty of God still arrogantly attributed this knowledge to their own abilities rather than to divine grace. Peter singles out Aristotle for special reproach: "What value is it, Aristotle, for you to be concerned with the summits of the heavens and the depths of the earth" he asks, "when you do not know about your creator?"[106] The question suggests Peter's concern with the role the *libri naturales* were coming to play in the curriculum of the schools during his chancellorship. But his point has as much to do with the purpose as with the substance of learning. Like the pagan philosophers, scholars are foolishly seeking learning only in order to advance themselves in the world. By criticizing the pagan philosophers, Peter of Poitiers alludes to a problem other moralists addressed more explicitly: the failure of scholars to understand that knowledge, as a gift from God, is to be used for purposes other than vain self-aggrandizement.

Although the moralists who discuss the pagan philosophers in their sermons generally cite them as examples of the misuse of knowledge, not all express identical opinions about the source and value of the philosophers' learning. Sermons for the feast of Epiphany provide an especially good opportunity to see the differences in the moralists' approach and attitude. Explaining the words "Ecce Magi ab oriente venerunt Ierosolymam" (Mt. 2.1), the moralists usually emphasized that *magus* does not mean "magician" but "philosopher," and then discussed the nature of the knowledge of the three Magi. For example, Raoul Ardent begins with the etymology: "These are not called Magi as magicians but as wise men, for those whom we call philosophers the Chaldeans called magi."[107] The three Magi, he explains, were philosophers, but they were superior to all others because their knowledge came directly from divine inspiration, not from the exercise of human reason. Other moralists repeat Raoul Ardent's etymology but interpret the knowledge of the Magi differently. Alan of Lille and, surprisingly, Jacques of Vitry say that the great wisdom of the Magi came from their knowledge of natural philosophy as well as from divine inspiration.[108] Peter Lombard and Hilduin, in their sermons for the Epiphany, express attitudes more critical of the usefulness of secular learning. Both emphasize that the Magi were true philosophers who sought knowledge, not in the earthly philosophy that deceives but in the heavenly theology that alone reveals the mystery of God.[109] The Magi, Peter Lombard insists, were not philosophers at all, but theologians.[110]

Many of the moralists, like Peter Lombard, draw a clear distinction in their sermons between philosophers and theologians. Philosophers study secular writings and depend upon human reason; theologians study Scripture and are inspired by divine grace. The moralists usually say more about the shortcomings of the sources and methods of philosophy than about the actual techniques theologians should use. Surprisingly little is found in their sermons about how Scripture should be taught or learned in the schools. Even those moralists from whom one would expect some useful guidance on the subject, such as Peter Comestor, often go no further than to warn against excessive disputation.[111] Jacques of Vitry has much less to say about the study of Scripture than about the liberal arts. His sermon to theologians, *Comede volumen istum*, largely concerns how knowledge of Scripture is to be used, rather than how it can be acquired. He offers only a little basic advice on the latter. It takes a great deal of hard work, he says, to interpret the obscure passages of the

Bible, and he recommends that scholars begin with the literal or historical sense before seeking to understand the allegorical.[112] When, in his sermon *Et lectulum Salomonis*, Robert Pullen comes to the subject of the order in which the Bible should be read, he merely comments that the Old Testament should be studied before the New.[113] Alan of Lille is the one moralist who offers any specific advice on how to teach theology. In a sermon to masters, Alan recommends that the established order of scriptural exegesis be followed: that masters teach first the literal, then the tropological, and finally the allegorical sense.[114] No other moralist had any more to say on the subject.

In an article about the medieval ideal of the theologian, Jean Leclercq comments that the thirteenth- and fourteenth-century sermons that he uses as sources contain more about what theologians should be than what they should do, more about their conduct than their techniques.[115] This is no less true of the sermons of this group of moralists. Rather than preaching about the methods that should be used in studying or teaching Scripture, they generally focus on the qualities that theologians should possess. For example, in his inaugural sermon as master of theology, Stephen Langton claims that the account of the Israelites being nourished in the desert by manna (Exod. 16.13-22) contains seven lessons for scholars who seek to study Holy Scripture.[116] First, just as the manna was sent down from heaven at night to feed the Israelites in their time of need, so Scripture is given to illuminate the human race in the darkness of their sins. Second, the fineness and flakiness of the manna, Langton explains, symbolize the subtle complexity of Scripture, which can be understood only by those with acute minds. Those proud scholars who think Scripture too easy for their attention are just like the Israelites who failed to understand what the manna was. Third, that the manna fell on the desert like snow means that the study of Scripture should subdue carnal desires. Fourth, just as the Israelites collected manna in the morning, so Scripture should be studied in youth and not left until old age. Fifth, just as the Israelites were only able to gather the manna they could use, so scholars are not to be avaricious with their knowledge. They should learn not to gain positions or favor but in order to live well and be saved. The greater the understanding that is acquired, the more it should be exhibited in good works. Sixth, the melting of the manna by the sun symbolizes the vital role of divine grace, without which no understanding of Scripture is possible. Finally, the delicious taste of the manna suggests the richness of the uses to which those who study Scripture properly can put their learning. "When the word of God," Langton concludes, "is crushed by the millstone of reading, ground by the pestle of disputation, and then cooked in the pot of the mind by assiduous meditation, 'it teaches, corrects, reproves, and trains' [2 Tim. 3.16] and thus, like oil, it feeds, refreshes, lubricates, and illuminates."[117]

Other than this allusion to the need to combine reading, disputation, and meditation, the sermon makes no mention of the actual techniques to be used in studying Scripture. Langton's concern was, apparently, not to explain *how* theology should be studied, but to show that it *should* be studied. As he prepared to assume his position as master at the cathedral school, Langton could be confident that the right kind of theological instruction would be available, at least in Paris. But his sermon reveals more than just a master's confidence in his own teaching. Langton—no less than most of the other moralists—seems convinced that those scholars who recognized the importance of theology, who understood the obligations their learning imposed, and who depended upon divine grace for guidance would be successful in their studies.

The moralists, it seems, were generally far less concerned about the errors that theology students might make than about the number of scholars who did not care about theology at all. They attributed much of this negligence, as we have seen, to the desire for material gain, which other subjects, especially medicine and law, satisfied. But there was another reason that some scholars avoided theology, one no less disconcerting and potentially far more serious. Some scholars, apparently, argued against the need to study theology on the grounds that literary and philosophical texts were more demanding intellectually and therefore required more, not less, attention than Scripture. Stephen Langton, as the second lesson of his inaugural sermon, warns against thus underestimating the Scriptures. Peter Comestor uses mockery to express his contempt of these scholars:

> There are some learned men who esteem their own tongues and say that Holy Scripture is not a science and it is not literature. They insist nothing is a science unless, by knowing certain trifles of information, like the numbers of hairs on a head, one is able to argue whether something is probable or improbable, or investigate the causes of things according to the rules of philosophical reasoning, or discourse according to the rules of rhetoric. They ask, "What science is it to know that Abraham had two sons, that Noah was saved with seven animals, and other things of this sort? This is the knowledge of fables, not literature. What science is it to know the number of Abraham's oxen, or of Sebeon's asses, or of Job's camels? This is the knowledge of money changers; it is not literature."[118]

Likewise, Peter of Poitiers speaks out against those "haughty listeners" who detest Scripture and ask blasphemous questions about episodes of sacred history. "Scripture does not have one worthless tittle," he exclaims indignantly.[119] And Raoul Ardent, as usual getting right to the core of the matter, turns the case against the proponents of the secular arts. Those "secular philosophers" who think Scripture plain and obvious, he comments, are unable to understand what a great and useful profundity of knowledge is hidden beneath the apparently simple words of Scripture. Instead, they foolishly spend their time studying the books of the secular arts, never realizing that amidst all the multiplicity and obscurity of verbiage, there is no useful knowledge at all.[120] Robert Pullen, Peter Lombard, and Jacques of Vitry similarly preached in defense of the richness and profundity of Scripture.[121]

Judging from the persistence of this issue in the moralists' sermons, so disparaging a view of Scripture may have been shared by more than a few masters in the arts faculty. But although seriously concerned about the problem, the moralists seemed certain that they knew both its cause and its solution. Those who condemned Scripture were acquainted with only the literal and historical meaning of the text. If these scholars could be persuaded to leave the secular arts behind and to begin the study of theology, they would soon come to understand the rich, profound, and useful knowledge hidden within Scripture. Again, however, the moralists did more general exhortation from the pulpit than actual explanation to scholars about how they should proceed in these studies.

LIFE IN THE SCHOOLS

The sermons of the moralists do not say much more about scholarly life in general than they do about the methods of teaching the liberal arts and theology. Sometimes, however, a moralist will illustrate his sermon with what appears to be an important detail about conditions in the schools or make a specific recommendation about an aspect of academic life. This practice is most common among those moralists who used exempla to support their arguments. It will hardly be a surprise, then, that the sermons of Jacques of Vitry are by far the richest source of such details and recommendations. Before we consider this material, a few words of caution will be necessary. As we have already seen, the sermons are generally far more reliable as expressions of the educational attitudes and ideals of the moralists than as sources that accurately describe what was happening in the schools. The moralists sometimes based their descriptions on outdated information, they exaggerated and simplified, and, perhaps most often, they altered the facts just enough to sharpen their criticism. Yet as long as we bear these cautions in mind, the comments made by the moralists add an important and often vivid dimension to our knowledge of life in the schools.

The sermons tell us, for example, something about the arrangements made for the education of young boys. Several moralists preach about the obligation of parents to provide for the education of their children. Jacques of Vitry stresses that this instruction should begin at an early age, since younger boys are both easier to teach and more impressionable.[122] In contrast, Peter of Poitiers, speaking about the need for scholars to develop self-discipline, comments on how difficult it is to educate children by recalling his own youth. "When we were boys and still under the rod of our teachers," he says, "we did not have an appetite for discipline, nor did we like letters, so we fled from the school and were flogged. Indeed, we so dreaded our teachers that we were prepared to kill them had our strength and age been sufficient to do so."[123] (This was an example likely to have struck a responsive chord in the many scholars in Peter's audience who had also received their early education from teachers who did not spare the rod.) The moralists also expressed different opinions on the kind of an education parents should desire for their children. Peter Comestor argues that their foremost obligation is to provide for religious instruction.[124] Stephen Langton several times complains of parents – or, in one case, of uncles – who are more concerned that the education of those under their care bring them wealth or social advancement than that it teach them doctrine.[125] On the other hand, Jacques of Vitry expresses a much more practical view in one of his sermons to boys and adolescents by urging parents to educate their sons in either the liberal or the mechanical arts so they will have the means to support themselves when they become adults.[126]

Only one moralist addresses the important question of how students should select their teachers. According to Jacques of Vitry, masters were often chosen for the understandable reason that they were previously known to the student or his family. More surprising is his suggestion that some masters, probably seeking to establish their reputations as teachers, actually paid students to attend their lectures. Jacques approves of neither practice. Instead, he admonishes students to be diligent in always seeking out the most learned and experienced teachers.[127]

Jacques fills his sermons with such practical advice. Conceding the need for specialization, he admonishes students to try to learn a few useful things well rather than to study everything.[128] In support of the policy of restricting the educational activities of monks and clerics, he recommends that monks should not teach even young boys,[129] that members of the military orders study theology but not the secular arts,[130] and that all clerics, even those in minor orders, be prohibited from studying civil law as well as from handling any secular legal matters, unless – in a typical concession to practicality – they are ordered by an ecclesiastical superior to become involved in such a case for the benefit of the Church or for the poor.[131] Finally, on the question of where the instruction was to take place, a subject about which we know so little, Jacques insists that teaching, like anything else involving payment, should not be done within churches.[132] Teaching space was probably a serious problem in Paris, but the only other moralist to mention the issue in a sermon was Peter of Poitiers, who criticizes masters who teach theology in public places.[133]

Jacques of Vitry's sermons and exempla offer insights into other aspects of scholarly life in Paris that are worth a brief mention. First, Jacques tells us that, along with ambition, the reason so many students were motivated to study canon law was that the decretists began their lectures at a later hour than other masters, so these students did not have to get up as early.[134] In the exempla, students are also portrayed doing things that were probably normal facets of life in Paris: begging for alms,[135] throwing dice with the stray cats of the city,[136] and harassing the less learned.[137] In addition to the stories of conversion of Master Sella and of how the king was unable to keep the popular Peter Abelard from teaching, other of Jacques's exempla also tell of the lives of Paris masters: the difficulties a certain Master Renaldus de Monte had with his students because he could not control his stammering,[138] and the concerns of a retired theologian excessively anxious to learn how his reputation stood in Paris.[139] We can perhaps learn something also of the varying motives of Paris students from the story Jacques tells of three Flemish brothers who came to the schools. One of them wished to become a Paris master, the second a Cistercian monk, and the third an actor and jongleur. Each, according to Jacques, achieved his goal.[140] A final exemplum tells of a successful lawyer who, after becoming a monk, lost every case he argued for his monastery – suggesting the problems that sometimes confronted learned men who sought refuge in the cloister. Jacques concludes from this exemplum that many more men who had been trained in the schools would enter the religious life if they did not fear that their orders would pressure them to continue to teach or practice just as they had before their conversions.[141]

THE CONDUCT OF SCHOLARS

The moralists, it should now be apparent, aimed three principal criticisms at scholars in their sermons. Each reflects the moralists' high ideal – but also their narrow view – of the nature and purpose of learning. First, they expressed their disapproval of those scholars who regarded education as something other than preparation for the active ministry, and of those whom they considered unlikely to use the learning they acquired either to improve their own lives or to teach others to do the same. Second, they accused many of their contemporaries in the schools of being motivated by curiosity, vanity, or simony, all of which they regarded as vices thoroughly incompatible with true and useful knowledge. Finally, believing in the intellectual preeminence of theology, they were strongly critical of scholars who either studied the liberal arts beyond the point where they might be valuable preparation for theology or who chose subjects, such as law or medicine, likely to be of more material benefit. Although these were their three most persistent criticisms of the schools, the moralists also voiced concern about some more specific aspects of scholarly conduct and behavior no less in need of reform.

Because they considered educational reform and moral renewal inseparable, how scholars lived was as important an issue to the moralists as what they studied. Judging from the frequent complaints found in the sermons of the late twelfth century, the conduct of scholars both in and outside the classroom had become a bothersome problem. No one had a better reason to be concerned than Peter of Poitiers. As chancellor during especially turbulent years in the history of the schools, he seems to have intensified his preaching when all other means to influence scholarly behavior had failed. Addressing scholars on the feast of St. Nicholas, he speaks passionately of how vice was impeding learning:

> We must take care lest, although we daily receive the dew of divine eloquence, we become a dry and arid land. If our learning is fruitless we will indeed be like that condemned and accursed land that is burned by fire. The condemned land is he who is inflated by human ambition, who seeks human praise, who envies, who disparages, and who destroys his body, which was consecrated to God in baptism, by whoring and sodomy; he who does not consider that wisdom will not enter a malevolent soul nor abide in a body subdued by sin. These are the vices that particularly belong to scholars.[142]

Peter mentions four vices—ambition, pride, envy, and lust—which he was certainly not alone in regarding as the characteristic weaknesses of scholars.

Ambition and pride are essentially equivalent to two of the three motives—simony and vanity—repeatedly blamed for attracting unsuitable young men to the schools and especially to the study of law and medicine. These vices were thought to harm the schools in other ways as well. According to Odo of Soissons, the schools were becoming filled with insincere students who adulterated all studies by their desire to learn only what they found convenient.[143] The masters who taught these students were no better. Ambition and vanity were typically blamed for the poor teaching of masters who were unqualified or simply too young.[144] According to Jacques of Vitry, however, learned men often refused to teach because other professions better satisfied their ambitions for wealth. If they did teach, it was only for as long as teaching seemed to be advancing these ambitions.[145] Moreover, as Jacques warns in another sermon, such ambitious masters were likely to be far more interested in showing off their eloquence, subtlety, and new ideas than in teaching their students something useful.[146]

The vanity of scholars was also thought to be a primary cause of the jealousies and rivalries that disrupted academic life. But those moralists, like Peter of Poitiers and Jacques of Vitry, who were the keenest observers of the schools regarded envy as the vice most endemic to scholars—as it has always seemed to be. As an example of pride and envy, Peter of Poitiers in a sermon for Ash Wednesday tells the timeless story of a scholar of relatively humble birth who is pleased with his own achievements but envious of his colleagues who have had an easier life. The scholar ruminates: "What a man I have become by my efforts alone, without any help at all! By studying and working, I have reached this pinnacle of knowledge. This great position, which even the sons of the nobility can hardly ever attain, I of humble birth have acquired by my worthiness alone!"[147] For Peter, even more serious than this scholar's envious attitude toward others is his failure to recognize that his abilities are not his own but gifts of God, and that divine grace is essential for learning.

Peter does, on other occasions, say more about envy's effect on conditions in the schools. For example, in his sermon for the feast of St. Martin, Peter complains about envious scholars who do not know how to praise their own teachers without attacking and destroying the reputations of other masters.[148] Worse still, in his estimation, is how the envious are always deprecating the achievements of colleagues who are more successful. In his Ash Wednesday sermon, Peter speaks with apparent familiarity about this practice: "I see someone who was once equal or perhaps even inferior to me in learning to whom God has granted such understanding that he is now far superior to me. I begin to envy him and, without reason, start to detract from whatever he does."[149] This example, like his others, suggests that Peter of Poitiers still remained primarily concerned with the harm envy did to the individual scholar.

In contrast, Jacques of Vitry characteristically emphasizes the social consequences of envy and warns scholars that their envious behavior is disrupting teaching and undermining peace and order in the schools. In the *Historia Occidentalis*, Jacques describes Paris as a city plagued by competition among masters and by rivalries among the various factions and nations in the schools.[150] His sermon to scholars, *Si videris sensatum*, gives a similar account of the situation but focuses on the harmful activities of envious masters. According to Jacques, it was envy that caused most of the dissent, rivalry, and conflict in the city's schools. Masters, who themselves failed as teachers because of their limited skills and learning, took to reviling others, particularly the masters who were most successful in attracting students to their lectures. Jacques claims he witnessed some masters trying to steal students, even to kidnap them, from other schools.[151] In their effort to appear equal to the greatest teachers, says Jacques, others simply made ludicrously false assertions in the hope of deceiving students into thinking they were hearing something important. With the concluding exemplum of his sermon, Jacques contemptuously compares such scholars to an envious frog who, desperately trying to puff himself up as large as an ox, bursts into bits.[152]

Envy may have been the most tenacious vice in the schools, but it was the scholars' lust that caused the greatest revulsion among the moralists. Paris had already acquired its reputation as a city of sexual license. According to Peter of Poitiers, more than a few young men claiming scholarly status had come to Paris not for the teaching available in the city's schools but for the whoring available in its many brothels. When he speaks about the harm the outrageous behavior of these scholars did both to the schools and to the Church, Peter cannot control his anger:

> What is more unseemly for a man than to simulate the cause of discipline and to enter this city of scholars not to study but to serve the desire of his flesh? Foul behavior that no one would even dare to think about in his native land or among his family and neighbors, here, among strangers and people from everywhere, he dares to do openly. He impales the good reputation of scholars, withdraws from the service of his Church, and wastes the alms of Christ that support him by living in lust with whores![153]

Believing themselves free to do anything they pleased, scholars indulged not just in fornication but also, as Peter laments elsewhere, in other unspeakable sexual vices.[154] Prévostin, Peter's successor as chancellor, tells of the complaints he heard about scholars from the prostitutes of Paris:

> What can I say of the arts scholars who nightly march with arms, break into the homes of young women, and treat them violently? And what of the things of which whores daily make complaint? Some complain that they are beaten by scholars, others that their clothes are torn off, still others that their hair is shorn off, and even more complain of conduct of which it is too shameful to speak![155]

At the time Prévostin was preaching, the arts students had apparently acquired the reputation for wildness that they were to keep for several centuries. By the early thirteenth century, learning and lust had become the trademarks of the city. According to Jacques of Vitry, both trades were often conducted in the very same building. Masters had their schools upstairs from the whores' brothels.[156]

Given the pleasures and distractions of Paris, there was some question as to how willing or able students were to acquire sound learning. Not all the moralists agreed on this matter. Some were sympathetic to the austere conditions under which many scholars seem to have struggled. According to Peter Comestor, scholars did their best to acquire wisdom even though often hungry, thirsty, cold, and underclothed.[157] Peter of Poitiers, who could be harshly critical of scholarly misconduct, also sympathetically describes how many scholars put in long hours of study while suffering both the physical and mental anguish of poor living conditions, an inadequate diet, and exile in a foreign land, far away from family and friends.[158] Others, while not denying that scholars spent a great deal of time studying, questioned the usefulness of their efforts. Robert Pullen describes scholars as working night and day on dialectical disputations and sophistical arguments, instead of on useful subjects. They strive to entangle their colleagues in sophistries but not to disentangle themselves from sin.[159] Geoffrey of Troyes compares grammarians and other arts scholars to beasts of burden. They do work assiduously, he concedes, but because they never use their learning to improve their lives, it remains little more than an onerous burden on their backs.[160]

Again, it is Jacques of Vitry who presents the most negative view of the schools. In *Si videris sensatum* he describes at length the various tactics students use to remain at the schools for as long as possible without studying. Some attend the schools only in the winter and leave in the summer; others change masters frequently, wandering from school to school without ever completing a book or hearing a full set of lectures; and still others go to class only enough—usually no more than once or twice a week—to retain their nonresident status as scholars and to be able to receive the income from their prebends. According to Jacques, these insincere students generally prefer the lectures of the canon lawyers, because they start later in the day. They also—like the logician in the satire *Hora nona sabbati*—make a great show of always carrying a weighty collection of books, which they of course never read.[161]

In another of his *sermones ad status*, this one for boys and adolescents, Jacques similarly complains of those who attend the schools without any real interest in learning:

> Certain boys go to school and do not wish to learn, but they remain illiterate and wild. . . . These are the ruined and ribald who do not wish to apply their minds to study. Instead, they pay money to their masters to be able to wander from the schools and also pay others to write their verses.

But this time Jacques holds the masters in the schools more to blame than the students, as he continues:

> Both those who write the verses and those who have them written are equally damned. The same punishment should be given to those students who pay to wander and to those who accept their money. Indeed, the masters' sin is greater since they willingly corrupt their students and abandon those whom they ought to coerce.[162]

The situation Jacques describes here probably applied more to the basic instruction in grammar that young men received at smaller schools before they went to Paris. But in the schools of Paris, given the apparent poverty of many scholars and the intense competition among masters, it is certainly likely that rich students uninterested in learning were able to find other students more than willing to accept money to do their work or masters happy to accept fees while demanding no more than minimal attendance at their lectures.

THE NEED FOR REFORM

As we have seen, the sermons of the moralists criticize those at the schools for a full range of errors and sins – from pursuing learning for the wrong reasons to inappropriate social behavior and moral conduct, from wasting their time studying subjects other than theology to not studying at all, and from taking up teaching too quickly to being unwilling to use their knowledge either to improve their own lives or to teach others. Although the concerns of the moralists differed, as did their criticisms and recommendations, they all agreed on one fundamental point: that the schools would have to be reformed in order to serve the needs of the Church and of society more effectively.

The moralists expected a great deal from the schools and from education. They were unprepared to concede, as other critics often seemed willing to do, that the unsatisfactory conditions in the schools were a consequence of external forces and social pressures about which the learned themselves could do little. Rather, by emphasizing the failure of the learned to meet their social obligations, the moralists held the schools more responsible for conditions in society than the other way around. This is especially evident in the frequent criticisms of the educated clergy that are made by the moralists preaching later in the twelfth century. Raoul Ardent, for example, reproaches the learned, as the eyes of the Church, for their failure to guide the rest of the body. "We, the priests and teachers of the Church," he charges, "who ought to be the light of the world, . . . are more smoke than fire."[163] Hilduin, in his sermon *Asperges me domine*, complains that vanity, avarice, simony, and lust have become so widespread among clerics that hardly a single one of them seeks to know or to serve God. Although this sermon is addressed to the clergy generally, Hilduin explicitly criticizes scholars in each branch of learning: grammarians, logicians, and astronomers (who together represent the arts), physicians, civil lawyers, canon lawyers, and theologians.[164] In another sermon, Hilduin complains that scholars no less than the two other kinds of clerics, the regular and the secular clergy, are setting bad examples for the laity.[165]

Other moralists used language especially appropriate to the schools to advise the learned clergy of their responsibility to the laity: their lives are the book from which the laity learn how to live. In a sermon to secular canons, Jacques of Vitry says, simply and directly, "The life of the clergy is the book of the laity; whence today the laity sin because their book is corrupt."[166] In the sermon *Novate nobis novale*, Stephen Langton uses another image to admonish the clergy. "Today," he says, "priests are just like lay people. No, in fact, the clergy is worse than the laity, since we, who ought to be a mirror and an example to others, are held in derision by everyone." Speaking, most probably, with scholars particularly in mind, he continues: "Indeed, the common vices of the laity are not sufficient for us; instead, we come up with new crimes and devise extraordinary worldly pleasures. We may wish to appear subtle in the exposition of Scripture, but we are far more subtle in inventing sins."[167]

These sermons suggest disappointment more than disgust—the disappointment of men who expected much more from education, who had hoped that the schools would provide a learned elite that could lead the reform of the rest of the clergy as well as of the laity. The image of the clergy as the book of the laity had a particular significance to these masters. It points directly to the failure of the schools to provide the clergy with the kind of learning that would make them capable of—or, for that matter, interested in—meeting their social responsibilities.

As critical as the moralists could be of the schools, they were often just as harsh toward those who refused to support scholars, the prelates who would not give them prebends and the princes who would not give them places at court. They were sensitive to the difficulties under which many in the schools struggled to continue their studies. The poverty and substandard living conditions of scholars are sympathetically described in some sermons. But these conditions are usually accepted as the dire facts of academic life. Several moralists suggest that those who have means should give alms to poor scholars.[168] Only one expresses actual outrage that while some members of the clergy—and, we may infer, not very learned ones—parade around in rich clothing, poor scholars in Paris are dying of hunger and cold. Worst of all, he laments, no one seems to care about these scholars.[169]

Most of all, the moralists were concerned that opportunities and advancement were being denied to the learned, often through no fault of their own. Raoul Ardent simply bemoans the fact that masters are not believed or respected anymore, giving little indication of why the change happened or what should be done.[170] Peter of Poitiers, preaching as chancellor, is clearly willing to place the blame squarely on the schools when he tells scholars it is their scandalous conduct that is causing the laity to feel contempt for the clergy.[171] More often, however, the moralists attributed the problem not so much to any of the faults or failures of scholars themselves but mostly to the hostile attitudes of those outside the schools. In one of his commentaries, Stephen Langton remarks that if every master whose words had scandalized someone were to stop lecturing, few would be left to teach in the schools of Paris.[172] Alan of Lille echoes the satirists and humanists in complaining that masters are losing their places in court to those who can offer greater wealth and status. "Once masters were held in the highest honor," he laments, "but now they are thought foolish and silly!"[173] As critical as Alan of Lille could be of scholarly misconduct, there is no suggestion here that he blamed the masters themselves for the diminished regard for learning.

According to several moralists, it was primarily the hostile attitudes of other clerics and of prelates that impeded the progress of learning and reform. Robert Pullen gives an especially bitter account of the discouraging problems scholars had to face as a result of the envies and fears of less learned clerics and prelates. "Of all those whom the earth sustains," he begins, "there are not a few wretched men who have no goodness themselves and who, when they hear of it in others, do not love but envy them."[174] According to Pullen, these opponents of learning make every effort to deter others from going to the schools. They argue against the value of studying theology, they urge delay, they falsely dispute what is being taught in the schools, and finally, when they have failed and the clerics they opposed return from the schools with ideas of reform, they virulently attack these young scholars for presumptuously proposing changes contrary to established customs.

Both Stephen Langton and Jacques of Vitry tell similar stories of parish priests and prelates fearful of reform striving to hinder scholars from preaching or teaching. Just as the high priest of Bethel opposed Amos (Amos 7.10-13), so do evil churchmen send the learned reformers away without giving them any chance. Stephen Langton speaks with particular force about this problem, perhaps inspired by personal experience:

> *And Amasius said to Amos:* "*Thou seer*, you prophet and learned doctor who threaten us so terribly in your preaching, *go, flee away to the land of Juda*; leave my bishopric or my parish, go back to your studies at Paris; *eat bread there and prophesy there*; keep your teaching and preaching to Paris."[175]

Robert Pullen, Stephen Langton, and Jacques of Vitry all suggest that the advancement of scholars was held up most not by secular rulers but by other clerics, envious of their learning and fearful of their ideas of reform. According to Langton, the story of Amos teaches that prelates are often more wicked and more resistant to learning or reform than princes. But whatever they considered the primary source of the opposition to the schools, the moralists recognized it as a serious obstacle to the progress of learning and reform and one that would likely remain whatever efforts there might be to improve the conduct of scholars within the schools.

What, then, did the moralists suggest those in the schools could or should do? Jacques of Vitry perhaps cannot be taken as typical, and he probably rewrote his sermons with the advantage of hindsight years after he left Paris, but he does provide a helpful insight into how the moralists thought the situation could be rectified. In addition to his general criticisms of scholarly contention, misconduct, and immorality, Jacques at times examines more specifically how such behavior is an obstacle to reform. For example, in a sermon to theologians, Jacques warns that the apparently justifiable, beneficial, and harmless practice of holding several prebends or benefices to support their theological studies could have adverse effects on both the regard for learning and the prospects for Church reform. According to Jacques, clerics who were criticized for pluralism and nonresidence frequently defended themselves by pointing out that prominent theologians and other reputedly learned men were allowed to acquire and hold multiple prebends and offices while at the schools.[176] The lesson Jacques hoped his learned audience would draw from this remark is obvious. Even those scholars who saw themselves as reformers sometimes, however unwittingly, behaved so as to impede their cause.

Like Jacques of Vitry, most of the moralists recognized that just as the eyes of the laity were focused on the clergy, so the eyes of the clergy were focused on those at the schools, especially on those in Paris. Given the educational preeminence of the city, what happened in Paris was noticed and might well have an impact throughout the Church. Though great improvements and advances could emanate from the schools, far more harm could be done by misconduct there than elsewhere. The moralists were seriously—and, it would seem, rightly—concerned that all their claims for the importance of education and all their efforts to increase the influence of the learned would be undermined so long as the schools remained unreformed and unregulated. If, in their view, little could probably ever be done to change the hostile attitudes of those who opposed scholars out of envy or fear, it was still imperative that those who were more sympathetic to learning not be turned against the schools by well-publicized examples of scholarly misconduct and immorality. For this reason especially, scholars had to be taught to view their education as no less a responsibility than a privilege. To the moralists it was apparent that in order to assume a greater role in leading the Church and in reforming society, scholars would have to prove the value of their education not only by demonstrating what they knew and could teach but also by conducting themselves in accordance with the highest moral standards and ideals. How was this reform to be brought about? Without explicitly denying the possibility of external influence or involvement, the moralists seem generally to have assumed that the responsibility and the impetus for the necessary reforms in education would have to come from within the schools themselves.

STEPHEN OF TOURNAI'S CALL FOR ACTION

Among those known to have preached regularly to Paris scholars and clergy during the formative years of the university, Stephen of Tournai offers a perspective significantly different from that of the other moralists. Unlike them, Stephen had never been a student or a master in Paris, and he watched and commented upon developments in the schools from the independent but influential position of abbot of Ste. Geneviève, from 1176 to 1192. Although he was not directly involved in the schools, however, Stephen's sermons and letters show that he took a serious and, more importantly, a generally sympathetic interest in what went on educationally in the city. He had been a canon regular for more than twenty years before coming to Paris, but both his very learned background and his extensive experience in worldly affairs enabled him to understand the increasingly vital role of education in the Church and in society as a whole. Consequently, Stephen of Tournai came to share many of the concerns and attitudes of those with closer ties to the schools. Like the moralists who were masters or chancellors, the abbot of Ste. Geneviève preached in the hope that his exhortations might help further the cause of educational reform. His views about what needed to be done to improve the schools were also similar to theirs. But in the end, for Stephen exhortation was not enough. Whereas the other moralists continued to promote reform within the schools and to wait for the scholars themselves to act, Stephen of Tournai ultimately saw the need to call upon the pope to intervene and take action.

Stephen of Tournai provides a notable example of the difficulty of trying to categorize the critics of the schools on the basis of their education or careers. Although a canon regular, he had been educated entirely at secular schools. Before entering the Victorine abbey of St. Euverte in Orléans sometime around 1155, Stephen had been educated first in the schools of his native Orléans, when that city was still at the height of its fame as a center for the study of classical literature and the *ars dictaminis*. He had also studied both canon and civil law at Bologna.[177] Of the other moralists, perhaps only Alan of Lille and Alexander Neckham had been as broadly trained in the secular arts. Moreover, Stephen of Tournai had acquired some fame for his erudition. In addition to his sermons and letters, he wrote at least one significant work of secular poetry, an allegorical poem on education similar to Alan of Lille's *Anticlaudianus* and to Godfrey of St. Victor's *Fons philosophiae*, composed while he was a student in Bologna, and an influential *Summa* on Gratian's *Decretum*, compiled after he had entered St. Euverte.[178] As a capable and highly regarded canonist, Stephen was consulted on legal matters throughout his career. He was frequently called upon to serve as a papal judge delegate and was also sent on several diplomatic missions by Philip Augustus. Like many masters who served the king, Stephen was rewarded with a prelacy. As bishop of Tournai from 1192 until his death in 1203, he worked diligently to reform the clergy and the laity of that large, wealthy, and politically important diocese.[179]

It was as bishop of Tournai, probably several years after he had left Paris, that Stephen wrote his well-known letter to the pope describing conditions in the schools and asking for papal intervention. There is, unfortunately, no clear internal evidence of the letter's precise date or of its intended recipient—it could have been Innocent III or his predecessor, Celestine III (1191–98). Given what we know of the difficult relationship between Stephen and Pope Celestine, however, it is far more likely that he would have delayed his appeal to Rome until his conflict with the papacy had been resolved, which did not happen until some months after the election of Innocent III, and when he could be more confident that his concerns might find a sympathetic ear.[180] The letter, then, was probably written sometime after 1200 and sent to Innocent III, just as he had begun to take a more active role in overseeing the schools. It also seems likely that Stephen was spurred to write not because he thought conditions had changed significantly since his days in Paris—as we shall see, the criticisms he makes in his letter differ little from those he had made earlier in his sermons—but because he was optimistic about the prospects for reform under the new pope. Stephen characteristically resorts to considerable invective in describing the need for reforms, but the sense of urgency in his letter is tempered by a note of confidence, suggesting that he believed it was an opportune time for papal intervention.

Stephen begins his letter by comparing the situation in the schools to a disease that, although it spreads only gradually, might, if not cured in the early stages, prove incurable later. He is writing to the pope, Stephen emphasizes, not because he himself wishes to assume the role of a censor of morals, a judge of teachers, or a debater of doctrine but to bring the situation to the attention of someone with the strength to act. "We merely wish," he claims, "to point out the illness [*quod dolet*] to your holy paternity, to whom God has given the power to uproot errors and the knowledge to correct them."[181] According to Stephen, the illness gravely affects each of the three major subjects of study in the schools: theology, canon law, and the liberal arts. In theology, a constant stream of new doctrines, summae, and commentaries are being produced by masters anxious for the applause of their students and for personal glory. The most profound mysteries of God, the Incarnation and the Eucharist, have become subjects of frequent public disputation. "The indivisible Trinity is cut up and disputed over in the streets [*in triviis*], so that now there are as many errors as teachers, as many scandals as classrooms, and as many blasphemies as public squares."[182] In canon law, masters willingly forge or invent decretals when established canons do not suit the cases they are advocating. The liberal arts have likewise fallen into servitude to those who seek personal gain from their learning. Beardless and long-haired adolescents teach in the arts schools instead of well-educated and experienced masters. They ignore the rules of the arts and study *summulae* filled with useless sophisms instead of the authentic books of the philosophers. Stephen adds a lament for the decline of the arts that is reminiscent of the satirists. "Philosophy," he writes, "cries that her garments are torn and disordered and, modestly concealing her nudity by a few tatters, neither is consulted nor consoles as of old."[183]

Having begun his letter by reminding Innocent that the papacy alone has both the ability and the authority to act, Stephen closes by urging the pope to do so: "All these things, Father, desire the hand of apostolic correction, that the disorder of teaching, learning, and disputing might be rendered into due form by your authority, that the word of God might not be cheapened by vulgar handling, that it might not be said on the street corners, 'Behold, Christ is here' or, 'Behold, he is there,' and that what is holy might not be given to dogs and pearls be trodden by swine."[184] An eloquent and compelling call for action, it is the letter not, as often claimed, of an ardent opponent of the new learning but of a prominent churchman who throughout his career had taken a lively interest in the schools. Although we have no certain evidence that his letter had any influence on the pope, we do know that the action Stephen of Tournai was calling for was not far off.

Other than this appeal to the pope, the only other commonly cited evidence of Stephen of Tournai's attitudes to learning and the schools are seven other letters, published among the founding documents of the University of Paris.[185] These include a series of four letters concerning the education of two nephews of the archbishop of Lund who entered Ste. Geneviève during Stephen's years as abbot, recommendations on behalf of Masters Simon of Tournai and Peter the Chanter, and a letter absolving the abbot of St. Germain des Prés from responsibility for the murder of a scholar that took place in 1192. Although they do concern the activities of Stephen's career that were, perhaps, most directly pertinent to the history of Paris, these letters represent only a few of the many occasions on which he acted to support the schools or to promote the cause of learning. The vast collection of more than three hundred of his letters includes numerous examples of the efforts Stephen made, primarily during his years in Paris, to protect scholars while in study or to assist them in gaining promotion in the Church.[186]

As bishop of Tournai, Stephen found himself both distant from the schools and preoccupied with political and religious conflicts, but he still did what he could to further education. Scholars were specifically excluded from the strict residency rules that he imposed upon members of his cathedral chapter in 1196. Those allowed a cleric to leave Tournai only to go on a pilgrimage, to obtain medical treatment, or to study.[187] A series of statutes promulgated in the following year and clearly intended to improve the cathedral schools include specific procedures for the selection and the supervision of the scholasticus. A prebend was provided to support the cleric who held the position, and he was strictly prohibited to be absent from the chapter for more than twenty days.[188] This legislation is quite consistent with reforms suggested by those both in and outside the schools as means of improving the general level of learning among the clergy. If there is little exceptional or particularly outstanding about any of these acts, they do collectively present a picture of an influential churchman who must be judged a patron and supporter of the schools.

The audiences to whom Stephen of Tournai preached during his years as abbot of Ste. Geneviève must often have included large numbers of Paris students and masters. As a famed canonist and a prominent abbot, Stephen was someone scholars would likely respect, and as an eloquent preacher, he was also, no doubt, quite effective in making his concerns and ideas heard. Stephen's major criticisms of the schools are not significantly different from those of other preachers. Like them, he was concerned, first of all, about the poor qualifications of many masters. It was not only in the arts faculty, according to Stephen, that inadequately trained adolescents had usurped the positions of qualified masters. In the sermon *Iesus christus ieri* he makes a complaint, similar to that in his letter to the pope, about impudent young scholars, not yet soundly educated in the arts, who have even presumed to teach theology.[189] Suggesting a possible solution to this problem in another sermon, Stephen, like other moralists, cites the example of how Christ did not assume the ministry until he was thirty. This example, he insists, should be heeded by those who usurp the places both of teachers and of prelates when still uneducated and too young.[190]

Stephen is less sure about what can be done to improve the arts themselves. In his letter to the pope Stephen complains about masters who do not follow the rules of the arts or use the established authorities to teach them. Preaching in Paris, he speaks more often about the related problems of scholars who study the profane arts excessively and never advance to theology. Here, too, his words often echo those of the other moralists. In one sermon Stephen rails against those, especially monks or canons, who consume their time studying the figments of poets, the opinions of philosophers, the rules of Priscian, the flourishes of rhetoric, the perplexities of Aristotle, the theories of Euclid, and the conjectures of Ptolemy. "The arts called liberal," he advises, "can sharpen the intellect for the study of Scripture, but according to the Philosopher, they must be greeted in passing. . . . Reading the books of the pagans does not enlighten, but darkens, the mind."[191] On another occasion Stephen warns that philosophical knowledge is like a mountain torrent: it runs swiftly but quickly ceases and soon dries up.[192] Almost with scorn, he elsewhere compares scholars who, having contempt for the apparent simplicity of Scripture, spend their lives studying the figments of the poets and subtleties of the philosophers to those who persist in drawing their water from the turbulent river of Egypt instead of from the gentle and more nourishing pool of Siloam, where the blind man was made to see.[193]

Addressing the issue of how the arts should be studied in the sermon *Iesus christus ieri*, Stephen of Tournai—like Jacques of Vitry in *Cum egrediemini*—uses the image of the captive woman from Deuteronomy 21.11-13. The scholar studying the profane arts, Stephen explains, is like a soldier who has captured an alien woman and wishes to marry her. Just as the soldier must cut the woman's hair and nails to make her suitable for marriage, so the scholar must cast away the useless and deadly aspects of the secular arts to make them suitable for study. The marriage takes place when the scholar employs the moral precepts and virtuous examples found in secular writings for his own edification and for the instruction of others. Just as, after the marriage, the woman produces both sons and daughters, so knowledge of the secular arts, when used in preaching, can be both helpful in exhorting the laity and fruitful in converting them to Christ.[194]

Although Stephen of Tournai was aware of the impact the *libri naturales* were having on the study of the arts, he seems to have been worried less about this new learning than about the more general problems of the unsupervised teaching and unregulated curriculum in the schools. In his letter to the pope, Stephen complains that instruction in theology has become "a workshop of confusion." In his sermons he suggests that there is a direct connection between the flaws in the arts curriculum and the confusion in theology. Without any clear standards of instruction or any effective means of control in the schools, the excesses and errors perpetrated by the masters of the arts were being carried over to the study of theology.

In *Iesus christus ieri* Stephen explains in some detail how the arts masters' vain questioning and useless disputation, here called the "two associates of secular learning," result in the kind of inane, insoluble, and incomprehensible questions about the most profound mysteries of faith that were being raised and disputed in the schools.[195] Instead of accepting the authority of the Fathers, he complains in another sermon, scholars dispute matters of doctrine as freely as if they were speaking of the teachings of Plato or Aristotle.[196] Preaching to scholars on another occasion, Stephen gives an especially vivid warning to overconfident young scholars. Like the young man in Proverbs 7, who, after wandering safely through the streets all day, is easily deceived and led off by a whore as soon as night falls, the scholar who thinks his own opinion is all he needs to interpret Scripture might find that some plain and simple matters pose few difficulties, but other, more obscure and difficult sentences will soon lead him into error and heresy. (The image used here of the freely wandering scholar is significant and one to which we will return.) In this sermon, Stephen blames the situation on theology masters, whom he criticizes for their unintelligent exposition of Scripture in the classroom.[197] In other sermons, as in his letter to the pope, Stephen places a greater emphasis on the harmful and dangerous influence of masters who dispute matters of faith publicly. In fact, the one actual regulation of the schools that Stephen of Tournai proposes in his sermons is the prohibition of all public disputation about doctrine.[198]

Such a prohibition, as Stephen of Tournai himself seems to have realized, might reduce the danger that heresy and schism would emanate from the schools, but it would hardly improve the confused state of learning within them. For him, as for most critics favorable to the schools, this general confusion within the schools was the more serious and difficult issue, because it was a direct consequence of the curiosity, vanity, and ambition of scholars. But Stephen is much more explicit than other moralists in suggesting ways of improving the situation.

For Stephen of Tournai the image of the young man wandering through the streets all day and then being easily seduced by a prostitute in the evening was symbolic of the conditions that adversely affected learning in the schools. When preaching about intellectual curiosity or the vanity of scholars, he almost always uses images of actual physical movement or wandering from place to place. Other moralists, as we have seen, sometimes drew a connection, if only an implicit one, between physical instability and intellectual inconstancy when warning scholars against being too curious.[199] Stephen seems to see the connection as suggestive of possible reforms in the schools. This impression, which one gets from several sermons, is perhaps clearest in *Cum esses iunior*. Addressing a Paris audience on the feast of Sts. Peter and Paul, Stephen explains:

> The freedom of wandering [*libertas vagandi*] is divided in two: the movement of the body through different places and the movement of the mind through different images. The curious wander with their eyes going from place to place, kingdom to kingdom, city to city, province to province. . . . Those fickle and unstable in mind also wander, imagining themselves to possess treasures, fields and buildings, cities and castles. . . . Of these it can truly be said: "The lord knows the thoughts of men since they are vain." This freedom of wandering in the mind through different images tires and impedes scholars in their studies and the cloistered in their prayers.[200]

This language, like the image, offers a revealing insight into Stephen of Tournai's thinking about the schools. Looking out over the city of Paris from the more stable and regulated environment of the abbey of Ste. Geneviève, Stephen could quite understandably have concluded that there was far too much freedom in the schools—not only, or perhaps even primarily, in the texts or subjects that were being studied but also in the wider sense that the general conditions of academic life there were subject to little order and restraint. The problem would persist, he seems to have concluded, as long as there was neither a set curriculum of study nor any established means of controlling extracurricular activities and, most of all, as long as the scholars remained free to come and go at will. To improve learning would require, first of all, establishing greater stability within the schools.

But, judging from what he says in his sermons, Stephen seems to have doubted that stability alone would be enough. There was physical stability within the cloister and yet, as he complains in the passage from *Cum esses iunior* quoted above, the monks' minds still wandered freely from their prayers. Additional reforms would obviously be needed to improve concentration in both the cloister and the schools.

In one of his major sermons, *Sapientia vincit malitiam*, composed for the feast of Ste. Geneviève and preached to an audience that included both scholars and canons regular, Stephen describes something of what he envisions these changes to be. First drawing an explicit parallel between heresy in the schools and hypocrisy in the cloister, he warns that the distracting allure of wealth and worldly delights is what causes both problems.[201] There is, he explains, a fourfold evil that impedes wisdom. Avarice preoccupies the mind with the desire to acquire money and possessions; ambition, with the hope of dignities and honors; vanity, with the worthless entertainments of games, spectacles, fables, and songs; and pleasure, with the enticements of drink, food, and sex. Against each vice, however, wisdom opposes a certain remedy: avarice it counters with voluntary poverty; ambition, with humility; vanity, with stability; and pleasure, with seriousness of purpose (*gravitas morum*).[202] Stephen here was repeating the call for moral reform that other critics had long been making to scholars. In fact, the remedies he prescribes are no different than the moral qualities that others had repeatedly proposed as the ideal conditions for learning. But as articulated and acted upon by Stephen of Tournai, these ideals point in the direction of the developments that were to transform educational conditions in Paris in the decades following the formation of the university.

In *Sapientia vincit malitiam* Stephen also speaks in the significant and now familiar terms of the need for the clergy to combine instruction in two schools, the school of doctrine and the school of discipline. They are to prepare for what he refers to as "the double duty" of seeking both truth and virtue.[203] This was an obligation Stephen took seriously as abbot of Ste. Geneviève. During his years in Paris he gave diligent care and attention to the members of his order who came to the city seeking an education. While not allowing them to study in the secular schools of the city, Stephen sought to ensure that these clerics would receive an education within the cloister that was intellectually equivalent but morally sounder.[204] The presence of such a thriving school at the abbey of Ste. Geneviève represents, in one sense, a continuation of the Victorine educational tradition in Paris. But its greater significance might well have been as the institutional model that other religious orders would later follow in establishing their own houses of study in the city.

This, no less than his appeal to the pope, makes Stephen of Tournai an important figure in the history of the schools of Paris. But in assessing his influence, we must not overlook the impact of his preaching. Though the letter he wrote to the pope stands out as the most direct call anyone is known to have made for the external regulation of the schools, Stephen of Tournai probably deserves no less recognition for his earlier contribution, as a prominent critic and eloquent preacher, toward shaping a consensus within the schools that made educational reform possible through the co-operative efforts of the nascent university and the papal legate, who was sent to Paris, apparently, in response to a growing appeal for action.

CONCLUSION

The Formation of the University of Paris

THE FORMATIVE YEARS of the university of masters and scholars in Paris fall between the 1150's and the end of the first decade of the thirteenth century. Unfortunately, this period in the history of the school is much more obscure than either the preceding decades, when the teaching of Abelard and his contemporaries attracted so much attention, or the years after 1210, when Paris masters and scholars again found themselves frequently embroiled in conflict. It is also the period that historians of the university have most generally neglected. Although not difficult to explain, this lack of attention poses a major obstacle to the understanding of the development of the schools. Paris in the second half of the twelfth century does appear, in retrospect, to have been less exciting intellectually than it was in the days when masters like Peter Abelard and Gilbert of Poitiers first attracted scores, perhaps even hundreds, of students to the schools. Likewise, Paris was experiencing a period of relative tranquility; there was little of the serious conflict within the schools or between scholars and external authorities that provides so much evidence for the subsequent history of the university. However, what did happen in Paris during this period cannot simply be overlooked, for the particular educational conditions of the time are fundamentally important to understanding how the university came into being and how the critics of the schools influenced its development.

First of all, there is the undisputed fact of the continued expansion of the schools. Even if the masters of the second half of the twelfth century were less distinguished and their teaching less original and stimulating (and this is debatable), they continued to attract students to Paris in ever-increasing numbers. The city never lost the preeminence as a center for the liberal arts and for theology that it had acquired earlier. And although Paris was never as celebrated as a place to study law as Bologna or as a place to study medicine as Salerno or Montpellier, instruction in these subjects was also available at the city's schools.

Young men from throughout Europe came to Paris to study these subjects. According to Jacques of Vitry, conflict was rife because of the varying temperaments and rivalries of the young men who gathered together in the city from places as diverse as England, Germany, Normandy, Picardy, Burgundy, Brittany, Lombardy, Rome, Sicily, Brabant, and Flanders, as well as from the Ile de France.[1] Stephen Langton, commenting on the book of Judges, compares the conquered city of Cariath Sepher to Paris, where so many diverse nations are gathered.[2] The truly international character of the schools has been confirmed by a recent statistical analysis of the geographical origins of masters teaching in Paris between 1179 and 1215. More than three-quarters of the masters known by name came from areas outside the French royal domain, the study revealed, including the neighboring provinces of Normandy, Picardy, and Flanders as well as the more distant lands of Provence, Spain, Italy, Denmark, and, above all, England.[3]

The scholarly population of the city remains largely a matter of conjecture, but between three and four thousand students by the year 1200, or somewhat more than one-tenth of the total population of the city, seems a reasonable figure.[4] That many students needed a considerable number of masters. Although the most recent study has been able to identify by name only forty-seven masters (including eleven in the arts, ten canonists, two physicians, and twenty-four theologians) who were actively teaching in the Paris schools between 1179 and 1215, the actual figure of masters regent at any one time must be much higher.[5] One sensible conjecture, based upon Innocent III's effort in 1207 to limit the number of theologians teaching in Paris to eight, estimates a total of at least 148 masters (one hundred in the arts, twenty each in law and in medicine, and eight in theology) regent at the schools in the early thirteenth century.[6] In fact, to judge from the frequent complaints about academic competition and from the charges that some masters actually hired students to attend their lectures, there may even have been, at times, too many masters teaching in Paris.[7] Whatever the actual numbers, there can be little doubt that Paris had a considerably greater concentration of students and masters, as well as a greater diversity of studies, than any other city. In the second half of the twelfth century, Paris secured its place as the thriving educational center of western Europe.

This would never have been possible had not conditions in the city remained highly favorable to learning. As the largest urban concentration in northern Europe and as a major commercial center, Paris could comfortably sustain a large population of scholars. By 1215 the walled area of the city was more than four times the size of Chartres, whose schools had once rivaled those of Paris.[8] One indication of the wealth of Paris is the fact that the city provided more than 14 percent of the total revenues in the royal budget of 1202–3.[9] Perhaps more directly beneficial to scholars, the rapid growth of the markets of the Champeaux on the Right Bank and their enclosure, early in the reign of Philip Augustus, in two great pavilions known as Les Halles meant that food remained plentiful and, judging from the infrequency of complaint, probably reasonably priced.[10] Lodging, however, does seem to have been a problem. When John of Salisbury returned to Paris in 1164, he marveled at the abundance of food in the city but complained about the long leases and the high rents.[11] Expensive housing was also an issue on the minds of masters. Peter the Chanter argued that students who asked excessive rents of their colleagues should be excommunicated.[12] And Stephen Langton mentions how landlords on the Left Bank tried to cheat students.[13] The decree of 1127 that had prohibited canons of Notre Dame from renting rooms to scholars within the cathedral close was reissued with a stronger sanction during this period, which must have made finding suitable housing even more difficult.[14]

Thus, though Paris does seem to have been able to accommodate a steadily growing population of scholars, there was some overcrowding, especially on the Ile and on the nearby Left Bank, the areas where most of the schools were. Perhaps this crowding explains why some masters had to hire lecture halls located inconveniently (for them, at least, if not for their students) upstairs from brothels.[15] The tensions caused by rapid growth might also explain the problems that soon arose between town and gown. Sometime before 1192 there occurred the first of the bloody conflicts between scholars and the residents of the Bourg-St.-Germain that were to be a recurrent feature of Paris life in the thirteenth century.[16] And although the famous tavern brawl of 1200, involving a group of German students, ultimately won scholars royal support in gaining recognition of their clerical privileges from the people of Paris, the initial response of the city's provost and leading citizens, who attacked the German hostel and killed several students, suggests that town-gown relations might have already been severely strained.

But judging from the unimpeded growth of the schools, scholars seem not to have been much discouraged or deterred by these problems and disturbances. They probably were found to be minor inconveniences compared with the great advantages Paris had to offer as a center of learning. No doubt, too, the reputation of the city as a "paradise of pleasures and garden of delights," in the disapproving words of Jacques of Vitry,[17] only added to its appeal. For all the townspeople's hostilities and the moralists' reproaches, Paris continued to offer the freedom and security so favorable to education. As in the days of Peter Abelard, masters were free to establish their own schools and students equally free to move from one school to another. In the second half of the twelfth century, this freedom seems to have owed less to the split jurisdiction between the chancellor of Notre Dame and the abbot of Ste. Geneviève—which had helped Abelard and which would in the thirteenth century again provide a haven for scholars on the Left Bank—than to the generally favorable and hospitable attitudes of ecclesiastical authorities in Paris to learning and the schools.[18] During this period, the scholars who congregated in Paris could usually count upon the sympathy and support not only of the king and the pope but also of the bishop and the chancellor of Notre Dame. These authorities did not struggle against the schools but, instead, nurtured their growth. The university of masters and scholars originated in a period not of conflict and revolt but of cooperation and generally harmonious relations between the schools and the external authorities.

The university in Paris grew; it was not founded. Though this common assertion is true, it has often obscured the important role of external authorities in the development of the schools. There is a useful and valid distinction to be made between the origins of universities such as Naples and Toulouse, which were later founded *ex privilegio*, and those of both Paris and Bologna, which developed *ex consuetudine* or, as some historians would have it, "spontaneously."[19] But, as Jacques LeGoff has argued, "the 'spontaneously born' universities arose out of situations in which the attitudes and needs of public authorities and the forces they represented always played a fairly large role."[20] What was sudden and spontaneous was the expansion of the schools, not the development of the university. For this, the support, the recognition, and the cooperation of external authorities were needed. Neither the king, nor the pope, nor any diocesan official planned that Paris should become a major international center of education, but any one of them could have acted to make conditions in the city less favorable to scholars and to impede the advance of learning. The conflicting interests among these authorities, as well as between some of them and the university, would later become serious enough to drive scholars from the city if only temporarily. But before

1210 there is little evidence of conflict. In the formative decades of the university of masters and scholars, the interests of the schools and of external authorities seem generally to have coincided. How the actions and policies of these external authorities—the king, the pope, and diocesan officials—contributed to the origins of the university is a subject that requires much closer examination than it has hitherto received.

THE ROLE OF THE KING

Let us begin by reconsidering the role of royal patronage in the history of the schools. The Capetians gained much praise and prestige for their support of learning, perhaps even more than they actually deserved. Despite what Walter Map says about Louis VII's promotion of clerics, recent studies have shown that relatively few masters became bishops in France during his reign (1137-80), as well as during that of his son, Philip Augustus (1180-1223). In fact, although the number increased steadily, not until the reign of Louis IX (1226-70) did the percentage of masters among the French episcopacy begin to compare favorably with the English.[21] Similarly, the French kings seem to have directly employed relatively few masters, compared to the Angevin kings of England.[22] Better at public relations than their English rivals, the Capetians seem to have secured their reputation as patrons of the schools less by the numbers of scholars whom they favored than by the visibility of those whom they did promote or employ. Having Peter Lombard or Maurice of Sully as the bishop of Paris, appointing John of Salisbury bishop of Chartres, and using masters on important diplomatic missions to Rome were policies that served the royal interests well. By being so prudent in their appointments, Louis VII and Philip managed to avoid the criticism that both Henry II and John of England received from scholars in royal service who did not advance as quickly or as far as they believed they should.

There is some irony in the fact that the English kings, who made much greater use of masters, were abused by the disappointed Master Gerald of Wales, while the French kings, who were much more deliberate in advancing the learned, won the praise of Master William the Breton.[23] Here is another example of how the caution and austerity of the Capetians served the French monarchy so well.[24] By steadily, if slowly, increasing the employment of scholars, the kings gained for themselves both gratitude and prestige. And, perhaps more fortuitously than intentionally, they also kept attracting young men to the schools in Paris from throughout Europe with expectations that the learning they acquired might win them promotion in the French court or Church.

The presence of the king in Paris was no less of an asset to the schools than the presence of the schools was to the king. The schools gave the king prestige; the king gave the schools safety and security. The royal projects to defend and improve the city—the new walls, paved roads and squares, and covered markets—benefited the schools directly, even if undertaken for other purposes. For example, there certainly were good military reasons for enclosing Mont Ste. Geneviève and the adjacent Left Bank area within the city's walls, as Philip did in 1209 at considerable cost to the royal treasury, but these new walls also added to the security of the masters and students who resided there. It may even be that the walls helped secure the unity of the nascent university corporation by physically tying the interests of the scholars on the Left Bank to those of their colleagues on the Ile de la Cité.[25] More obviously beneficial to scholars was the endowment, apparently under the auspices of the Capetians, of the first two foundations for poor clerics in Paris. The Collège de St. Thomas du Louvre was founded in 1186 on the Right Bank near the new castle and endowed, with the explicit approval of Philip II, by Count Robert of Dreux, Philip's uncle and Louis VII's brother.[26] The Capetian connection with an earlier foundation, the Collège des Dix-huit (1180), is indirect, but probably no less significant. Located in the Hôtel-Dieu on the Ile near the cathedral, this foundation for eighteen poor clerics was endowed by a pious and wealthy English merchant, Jocius of London, who had been granted considerable protection and commercial privileges by Louis VII.[27] Such foundations, although quite small and able to provide beds and minimal stipends for only a few scholars, were nevertheless important in keeping the schools of Paris accessible to poor clerics without benefices or other means of support.

One reason, perhaps, that the schools appealed to the Capetians was that the fame of Paris as a center of learning added to the monarchy's prestige without drawing on the royal treasury. In fact, the monies expended by three to four thousand masters and scholars must have been an important source of revenue to the citizens of Paris and in turn, through taxation, to the king. But the presence in the city of so many scholars, the vast majority of them from outside the royal domain, was a mixed blessing. Paris, as the chosen capital of the Capetians, was vital to the defense of the realm. Thus, in 1167, when Louis VII found himself at war with Henry II—who was angry that Thomas Becket had found asylum in France and who was seeking to consolidate Angevin continental territories—Louis took the action, so lamented by John of Salisbury, of expelling all foreign scholars from France.[28] Louis most probably ordered the expulsion—which was apparently never actually effected—out of fear that the presence of so many English students and masters in Paris might hinder the defense of the city.

A more chronic problem was the disorder and lack of discipline among the city's heterogeneous collection of young scholars whose studies and extracurricular activities were subject to no direct supervision. The intense rivalries among students of diverse nationalities and the fierce competition among masters must often have burst into violence, requiring the intervention of the royal provost to restore peace to the schools. And we have no reason to doubt the truth of the moralists' assertions that scholars often treated the prostitutes of the city with violence. On the other hand, Peter Abelard was probably not the only scholar to be physically assaulted by the vengeful relatives of a young woman. Otherwise, we know surprisingly little about relations between scholars and townspeople. We can only assume that there were the usual tensions and disputes that occur in a town with a large student population. Other than the famous riot of 1200, the only other serious town-gown brawl recorded is that between the residents of the Bourg-St.-Germain and scholars adjudicated by Stephen of Tournai in 1192.[29] But other incidents no less troublesome to local officials must have occurred. Peter the Chanter suggests that King Philip received so many complaints about the conduct of scholars that he even considered evicting them from the city.[30]

When, however, in the wake of the riot of 1200, masters suspended lectures and threatened to leave Paris, Philip instead granted the famous charter guaranteeing scholars the legal privileges of clerics and assuring them of continued royal support. This charter and the events leading up to it are well enough known not to need discussion in any great detail. The whole affair began with a minor, probably commonplace, altercation between a foreign student's servant and a tavernkeeper, perhaps over payment for the wine the servant had been sent to purchase. Unwilling to tolerate the abuse of his servant, the student, a certain Henry de Jacea, the archdeacon and bishop-elect of Liège, and other German clerics wrecked the tavern and beat its keeper. The incident quickly aroused a citywide uproar, with the citizens demanding that the guilty students be arrested. The royal provost, Thomas, led an armed group of citizens in an assault on the German hostel, and several students, including Henry de Jacea, were killed.

This was a matter that the masters of the schools could not overlook. Concerned, undoubtedly, that their clerical privileges might be jeopardized if they did not act, the masters—how many there were and how they were organized is, unfortunately, obscure—suspended their lectures, demanded redress from the king, and threatened to leave the city. Philip acted swiftly and harshly. Although he did not, as the masters had requested, have Thomas whipped in the schools "more scholarium," he ordered that all the offenders, including the provost, be arrested and imprisoned for life. Those involved who fled the city during the inquest were to be pursued throughout the kingdom and brought back to Paris for the same punishment. In the meantime their houses, vineyards, and gardens were to be destroyed. The provost was given the option of trial by the ordeal of water. If thereby proven guilty, he was to be hanged; but even if he cleared himself, he was to be banished from Paris and the realm. Thomas never took this option. According to the best narrative source of the incident, the *Chronica* of Roger of Hoveden, the provost spent a long time in the royal prison, then was killed while trying to escape over the walls.[31]

In contrast to the severe punishment suffered by the provost and his accomplices, no direct action seems to have been taken against any of the student perpetrators who survived the riot. The citizens of Paris must have regarded Philip's actions as a clear demonstration of the monarchy's strong support for the schools. But these actions apparently did not satisfy the scholars of the city. Before the masters would consent to recommence their lectures, they requested from the king, as a guarantee for the security of scholars in the future, a written confirmation that the customary privileges of their clerical status would be recognized both by royal officials and by the citizens of Paris.

The detailed provisions of the royal charter granted on this occasion were probably the result of lengthy negotiations between the representatives of the king and of the schools. But in the end the scholars seem to have gotten most of what they wanted. First, the citizens of Paris were required by oath to swear both to respect and to enforce the *privilegium canonis*, the canonical privilege protecting a cleric from bodily harm. They were all bound to report any crimes they saw a layperson commit against a scholar, to help arrest the assailant, and to testify at the royal court about the crime. The provost was also empowered to conduct inquests in cases involving assaults on scholars and to bring suspects to trial before the royal justices. Second, the king recognized the scholars' immunity from secular jurisdiction, the privilege known as the *privilegium fori*, or "benefit of clergy." Both scholars and their chattels were protected from seizure by civil authorities. "Neither our provost nor our justices," reads the charter, "should lay hands on a scholar for any offense whatsoever." Only in the case of an especially serious crime could a scholar be arrested, and even then he was to be taken without force, unless he resisted, and immediately handed over to an ecclesiastical court. If the provost arrested a scholar at a time when the cognizant judges could not be found, he was to be placed in custody at the residence of another scholar (*in aliqua scolaris domo*), not in jail, until he could be delivered to an ecclesiastical court. Finally, to assure scholars that these privileges would be generally recognized, Philip decreed that the provost and the people of Paris were to affirm all the provisions of the charter by oath in the presence of scholars (*in conspectu scolarium*). Each succeeding provost was likewise to be required, on the first or second Sunday after his appointment, to swear in good faith to respect those privileges before a gathering of scholars (*coram scolaribus*) in one of the churches of Paris.[32]

This was certainly an important victory for the scholars of Paris. But to understand the origins of the university it is necessary to be clear about what the royal charter of 1200 did and did not do. King Philip did confirm and sanction the special status of scholars in the city. Addressed specifically to scholars and explicit in stating that its provisions did not apply to the canons of Paris,[33] the charter did more than simply recognize the clerical privileges of those at the schools. Scholars had become an acknowledged group within the city, with their own rights and privileges, which were similar in kind to but distinct in form from those of other clerics. However, although the charter did distinguish scholars from other clerics, it was not in any way a formal recognition of the existence of a university or legal corporation.[34] No more than the *Authentica "Habita"* Frederick Barbarossa issued for Bologna in 1155 or 1158 should Philip's charter be considered the foundation deed of a university. The privileges were granted to scholars and the provost and people of Paris were to swear their oaths before assemblies of these scholars; there was no mention whatsoever of a guild or corporation of masters. This does not diminish the importance of the charter. William the Breton was certainly right in emphasizing the importance of the "freedom and the special privileges" that the king had thereby given to scholars in Paris. Such a clear expression of royal favor must have greatly added to the scholars' sense of security. It was also the first step in the forging of the close alliance between the university and the French monarchy, which would become so important politically later in the thirteenth century.

William the Breton attests that scholars were not unappreciative of what the king had done for them. According to the royal chronicler, when Philip marched into Paris after his great victory at Bouvines in 1214, scholars were especially prominent among those who greeted him, and their celebrations—with sumptuous feasts, singing, and dancing—lasted for an entire week, during which, presumably, classes were canceled.[35] This, no doubt, was also one of the many occasions on which it became apparent that the royal charter had not resolved the problems of disorder in the schools, especially that of how to discipline troublesome students. Criminous clerics and conflicts between town and gown remained issues of concern in Paris. In 1210 Philip had, in fact, issued a new decree on clerical privileges, one which listed the specific crimes that justified the arrest of clerics by civil authorities. These crimes included homicide; adultery; rape; assault and battery with sticks, stones, or pointed weapons; and housebreaking.[36]

Were Paris scholars actually committing such crimes? Unlike the charter of 1200, the decree of 1210 did not apply specifically either to scholars or to the city of Paris but, rather, to clerics throughout the realm. Still, judging from the moralists' descriptions of conditions in Paris, it does seem likely that the decree was intended to clarify and to strengthen the authority of civil officials over the large and often unruly scholarly population in the city. Thus, while willingly conceding to scholars the privileges and immunities they demanded, the king also seems to have insisted on his right to provide for the maintenance of public order—a state no less essential to learning than to the other vital activities conducted in the capital of his realm. Having set clear guidelines for royal officials, Philip must have been assured that the ecclesiastical authorities would establish effective means to exercise their jurisdiction over the schools, as well as to control and to discipline troublesome scholars. This policy served both royal interests and the scholars quite well. With the protection of the king, scholars were able to enjoy the security and stability of Paris without sacrificing their freedom or autonomy.

THE ROLE OF THE POPE

The distance of the pope was perhaps no less important than the proximity of the king in accounting for the development of the university in Paris. As Paris became the preeminent place in western Europe to study theology, the subject of primary importance to the papacy, it was probably advantageous to scholars that Rome was so far away. This distance from the one external authority whose claims to jurisdiction could not have been readily dismissed served to protect the schools from the direct control or supervision of teaching that would have seriously impeded both the intellectual and the institutional development of the university. This is not to suggest that the papacy itself was either hostile to the new learning or opposed to what was happening in the schools. In general, the popes were sympathetic to the work being done in the schools, and their policies usually benefited scholars. The active support provided by such popes as Innocent III (1198-1216) and Gregory IX (1227-41) has rightfully earned them, from some historians, the title of true founders of the university and chief guarantors of its freedom.[37] Nonetheless, during the truly formative years of the university, the schools of Paris may have owed their freedom and autonomy as much to the practical limitations that distance imposed upon the papacy's involvement in their internal affairs as to the positive actions the popes took on behalf of scholars. Because of the distance from Paris to Rome, the scholars of the city found they could call upon the popes, when necessary, to defend their interests and to secure their freedom from local authorities without ever having to worry that they would in turn have to submit to the control of the papacy.

This factor takes on a special importance when one looks back at the earliest episodes in the history of the relationship between the papacy and the schools of Paris. Some Paris scholars, in the latter part of the twelfth century, may still have recalled that Innocent II had condemned Peter Abelard as a heretic in 1140 and ordered his writings burned, and that eight years later Eugenius III had presided over the council at Reims where Gilbert of Poitiers had been placed on trial.[38] In each case, we know that the pope acted upon the instigation of Bernard of Clairvaux and in opposition to many both within the papal curia and in the schools. After the death of the powerful Bernard in 1153, such intervention in the teaching of the schools became less likely—especially with the election of popes who had themselves been trained in Paris and were thus less likely to be unfamiliar with or suspicious of the new methods that theologians were applying to questions of doctrine.

But papal intervention in what was taught in the schools did not cease altogether. In 1164, during his exile in France, Alexander III, who had himself probably been a student of Peter Abelard, called together in Sens a large assembly of masters and learned men—one source gives the inflated number of 3,000—where he condemned certain theological questions, apparently including several disputed sentences of Peter Lombard on Christology, and charged the bishop of Paris, Maurice of Sully, to prohibit them from being taught in schools throughout France.[39] Again in 1170, Alexander ordered the archbishop of Sens to convoke a meeting of his suffragan bishops and of other prudent men in Paris to condemn the Lombard's false doctrines and to warn the masters of the schools not to teach them in their theology lectures.[40] These actions must not have been completely effective, since in 1177 the pope ordered his legate, Archbishop William of Reims, to convoke a meeting of the masters of the schools of Paris, Reims, and other nearby cities to condemn the same errors.[41] Significantly, after this bull we have no further evidence of papal intervention in what was taught in the schools, whether direct or indirect, until 1215. During these decades, scholars seem generally to have been free to teach and to learn whatever they wished.

How does one account for this apparently more liberal papal policy toward the teaching in the schools? Certainly, a major factor must have been the significant changes that took place within the theological faculty of Paris in the last decades of the twelfth century. Many of the positions previously occupied by speculative theologians were now held by more practical theologians, like Peter the Chanter and his associates, whose instruction on moral problems and practical issues so much better suited the needs and interests of the papacy as it sought to reform the Church. The popes seem to have realized that these theologians were their natural allies. Moreover, it is also significant that until the time of Masters Amaury of Bène and David of Dinant, the new threats of heresy and dissent that worried the papacy arose outside the schools, in places far from Paris. Finally, Alexander III's difficulties in enforcing the prohibition against the erroneous sentences of Peter Lombard may have convinced the popes that what was to be taught in the schools could be regulated only with the support of the masters themselves. Indeed, masters did play a prominent role at the Paris synod that, in 1210, condemned fourteen heretics and prohibited, for the first time, the teaching of the *libri naturales* in the schools of the city.[42]

Whatever the popes' motivations, their apparent change of policy facilitated the forging of the close alliance between Paris masters and the papacy that was so important to the later history of the university. From the 1170's on, any lingering doubts about cooperation with Rome seem to have been steadily overcome with the emergence of a papal educational program that aimed at protecting scholarly privileges and providing financial support for those in study, and, no less significantly, that espoused the same principles and ideals as those masters promoting reform within the schools. Although intended to encourage the expansion of education throughout the Church, the papacy's new educational policies proved especially favorable to the already thriving schools of Paris. No doubt, too, it was the benefits they had derived from these policies that encouraged the masters and scholars of Paris to seek the support and assistance of Rome when they began to have difficulties with the local authorities.

The first step in the emergence of this papal education program involved the protection of scholarly privileges. Between 1170 and 1172, in response to an appeal from a group of students who had clashed with a priest of the Bourg-St.-Remi, Alexander III rendered a judgment strongly favorable to the immunity and freedom of scholars. According to the papal bull, the priest, having been publicly reproached and derided by some students for dancing during a Sunday procession, had led a group of his parishioners in an attack on the schools, during which several students had been physically assaulted. The next day, without informing the archbishop, the priest had excommunicated all the students involved. Agreeing with the scholars that both actions had grievously violated their freedom, the pope ordered the abbot of St. Remi and the dean of Reims to hold an inquest into the actions of the priest and his accomplices. If it was found that the priest had conducted himself as the students charged, he was to be severely punished and allowed no recourse of appeal. In addition, anyone who had laid hands on students who were clerics was to be excommunicated and not to be absolved until he had rendered satisfaction to those injured and presented himself before the papal curia.[43] The students were tacitly exonerated of any blame for the incident. To protect them from further injury, the pope ordered that no one should "dare to molest these scholars against their liberty in any way, as long as they were prepared to submit to the jurisdiction of their masters."[44] This judgment in favor of the students of Reims was to become a precedent for the principle, important in the later history of the schools of Paris, that the primary jurisdiction over the conduct of students lay in the hands of their masters, not of local ecclesiastical authorities.

More immediately beneficial to the schools of Paris were those papal actions intended to support scholars financially and to increase educational opportunities for the clergy. Here, again, it was Alexander III who established important precedents. He is the first pope known to have intervened to help individual scholars in need of financial support. For example, in 1174 he secured a prebend at Ste. Geneviève for Master Mainerius, another former student of Abelard.[45] Four years later he granted Master Gerard Pucelle the right to retain all the income from his English benefices for four years if he returned to teach at the schools and also restored to him certain German revenues he had lost during the papal schism.[46] And, in the last months of his pontificate, Alexander requested an unnamed cathedral chapter to give a prebend to a certain Master Theobald to study theology in the schools for two years.[47] Such actions could benefit no more than a few masters deemed especially worthy of support. To provide a more general stimulus to education, Alexander III also initiated two other important policies. One required each cathedral church to set aside a prebend to support a master who would teach the clerics and the poor students of the diocese without charge. The other prohibited chancellors or any diocesan officials from requiring a fee in return for issuing the *licentia docendi* to a qualified master.[48]

Much has been written about these policies, especially about the importance of the gratuitous license to the growth of the schools and to the development of the university. It has been argued that Alexander's legislation on the *licentia docendi* removed a major obstacle to the expansion of the number of independent masters and schools in Paris and also established an early precedent for papal control of the university.[49] Such claims for the practical effects of the legislation are debatable. Despite the papacy's determined policy against charging for the license, the chancellors of Paris continued to collect fees at least until 1215. In 1174, less than four years after issuing a decree (*Quanto Gallicana*) prohibiting the practice in all the dioceses of France, Alexander III conceded to Peter Comestor, then chancellor of Paris, the right to collect moderate fees for the license.[50] There is little evidence that the masters objected. As long as they themselves could collect fees from their students, it seems unlikely that paying a moderate fee for the *licentia* imposed much of a burden on them.

Indeed, the true import of the papal legislation prohibiting diocesan officials from charging for the *licentia docendi* may be not that it removed a financial obstacle preventing some scholars from becoming teachers but that it challenged the idea that anyone should profit from teaching. If, as the pope decreed, chancellors could not require fees from masters, then, by implication, neither should masters require fees from their students—a practice that was no less customary in the schools and that would have been even more difficult to eradicate. Ultimately, of course, theologians and canons did find the means to justify the payment of student fees to masters.[51] But whatever concessions had to be made to practicality, the principles upon which Alexander III based his policies remained well-established ideals. By equating charging for the *licentia docendi* with selling spiritual offices and services, the pope was espousing the principle, dear to the moralists, that knowledge, as a gift from God, should be freely shared.[52] The complementary policy of reserving a prebend in each cathedral chapter to support a master was the practical means of realizing this ideal of free education.

Another recognizable principle was implicit in these policies, this one having to do with the purpose of learning and the obligations of the learned. It was not enough that knowledge should be shared for the mutual benefit of those at the schools. The objective was to improve the Church as a whole. The wording of the decree against charging for the *licentia docendi* issued at the Lateran Council of 1179 states that any official who exacted a fee was rightly to be deprived of his benefice since "he who sells the license to teach strives to impede the progress of the Church."[53] Despite its obvious benefits for scholars, the papal educational program set a high standard for evaluating the schools. It also established an important precedent, one that would later be used to provide justification for papal intervention in the university. Alexander III's policies clearly showed that the papacy was prepared to support the interests of the schools. But no less evident in them was the expectation that, in return, the schools were to serve the interests of papacy.

Until the pontificate of Innocent III, there is virtually no evidence of further direct papal involvement in the affairs of the schools. A bull of Pope Celestine III (1191-98), which ordered that all civil cases involving clerics in Paris (*clerici Parisius*) were to be judged in the bishop's court according to canon law, may have been primarily intended, as some historians have argued, to support the claims of those in the schools to immunity from secular justice.[54] However, unlike Alexander III in his decree for Reims, Celestine III does not specifically mention scholars. For the scholars of Paris, the far more important recognition of their special privileges was that granted by Philip Augustus in 1200.

Not until several years after the royal decree did the papacy act to distinguish the rights of the scholars of Paris from those of other clerics resident in the city. In 1208, when the papal legate, Cardinal Gualo, imposed strict reform measures on the clergy of the Paris diocese, he added a decree explicitly addressed to masters and students. All other clerics and monks were thenceforth to be liable to immediate excommunication if they lived with women, committed simony, were not tonsured, did not wear the garb of their orders, or were involved in business transactions. But scholars who were guilty of the same transgressions were first to be collectively admonished by their masters and merely threatened with excommunication. If their misconduct persisted, they were then to be summoned individually before the schools, warned by name, and given no more than a short time to reform. Only then, if they continued to resist, were scholars to be denounced as excommunicates to the chancellor and to be treated as such until they were formally absolved by the bishop or, in his absence, by the abbot of St. Victor.[55]

Like Alexander III's decision for Reims, this decree placed primary jurisdiction over students within the schools, in the hands of their masters. At the same time, the masters were to share that authority with the chancellor, who imposed and enforced sentences of excommunication, as well as with the bishop and the abbot of St. Victor, who alone among local prelates possessed the power of absolving excommunicated scholars. Subsequent papal legislation would reaffirm and strengthen this delegation of authority over scholars.[56] This, then, was an important step in the reform and regulation of the schools. An apparently satisfactory means had been found to discipline the scholarly misconduct and immorality that had so concerned the critics. Moreover, a precedent had been established by the papacy's recognition of the special status of scholars in Paris and its confirmation of their essential right to govern their own affairs.

This was but one of many actions beneficial to the schools undertaken during the pontificate of Innocent III. Not only did this Paris-educated, activist pope expand upon the policies of his predecessor Alexander III in protecting scholarly privileges and providing benefices for prominent masters.[57] He also took new initiatives in seeking to further the cause of learning. Innocent offered increased patronage to scholars and, in return, expected their increased service to the papacy and the Church. After the conquest of Constantinople in 1204, for example, the pope called upon the masters and scholars of Paris to go to Greece to reform the study of letters (*litterarum studium reformare*) and to aid the Latin emperor in restoring obedience and devotion to the Roman Church.[58] Though the promise of material rewards probably did more than a sense of obligation to the pope to motivate scholars to respond to this appeal, the mutual interests of both were served. Throughout most of the early history of their relationship, scholars and popes, as Beryl Smalley has put it, formed a mutual help society.[59]

Innocent III's first direct intervention into the affairs of the schools came in November 1207, when he ordered the bishop of Paris, Odo of Sully, to restrict the number of masters actively teaching theology to no more than eight. There is no clear evidence of why Innocent decided to impose the restriction at this time. It seems highly likely, however, that he was responding to the concerns raised by Stephen of Tournai and other critics that unqualified and inexperienced masters were teaching theology in the schools. But the bull makes no mention of a direct appeal from Paris. It merely states that the pope was acting on the prudent authority of those in his presence (*consideratione prudenter inducti auctoritate presentium*). Paris, Innocent explains, should have enough theological masters to provide for the needs of the Church but not so many that regard for the office of theologian would be lessened and instruction unskillfully discharged. The restriction was not intended to be absolute; it was clearly seen as a means of controlling the quality more than the quantity of masters. The bishop could allow the number to be exceeded if, in his judgment, great need or utility (*multa necessitas vel utilitas*) should require it.[60] To the prominent masters already teaching in Paris, whom Innocent celebrates for their knowledge, the bull must have offered some practical security as well as a definite indication that they could count on support from the papacy in their efforts to reform the schools.

It is perhaps suggestive of the favorable response of Paris scholars to this restriction and to the disciplinary procedures established by the papal legate, Cardinal Gualo, that the next time the pope became involved in the internal affairs of the schools he did so in response to a direct appeal from the masters themselves. At issue on this occasion was the right of Paris masters to reform and to regulate their own activities. The problem had arisen when certain young masters of arts (*moderni doctores liberalium artium*) had deviated from what were apparently already established norms in what they wore, in the order in which they gave their lectures and disputations, and in refusing to attend the funerals of their deceased colleagues. To prevent such violations of custom in the future, masters of the faculties of theology, canon law, and the arts had unanimously elected eight deputies to write statutes on these matters and had agreed to require all masters to swear to submit to them. At least one arts scholar, a certain Master G., had refused to take the oath and, after ignoring three summonses to appear before the university of masters (*universitas magistrorum*), had been expelled. Sometime later, however, this master had decided to take the oath and, having made amends for his original obstinacy, requested readmission to the body of masters. As the original statutes had not provided for this contingency, the masters had been uncertain whether they had the authority to readmit Master G. and had appealed to Innocent III for his judgment on the matter. The pope's decision was that if Master G.'s amends had satisfied the masters, they could readmit him to their body (*consortium in magistralibus*) by their own authority.[61]

Ex litteris vestre, the papal decree issued in 1208 or 1209 to decide this case, is our only source for these events, which were so important to the early history of both the internal development of the university and the relationship between the university and the papacy. It provides the earliest evidence of the masters of Paris – and, notably, the masters of each of the three primary disciplines – functioning together as a single guild or corporation. Moreover, it shows the papacy tacitly recognizing the essential right of the masters to make and to enforce their own statutes as well as to exercise control over the membership of their society.

RELATIONS WITH LOCAL AUTHORITIES

The issuing of the decree *Ex litteris vestre*, marks an important milestone in the history of the university. By 1209 Paris masters had already developed a strong enough sense of corporate identity to act as a group. The nascent university had also received the first confirmation from the papacy of its corporate and independent status. Having reached this milestone, we must pause to ask how and why these developments had come about and, especially, to reexamine the question of the role of local authorities in the early history of the university. Can the argument be sustained that the masters had organized themselves and sought recognition from the papacy in opposition to the chancellor or to the bishop of Paris?

Certainly it is significant that *Ex litteris vestre*, the decree that contains the earliest evidence of masters acting together and seeking the support of the papacy, was issued to resolve a conflict within the nascent corporation, not a dispute between it and external authorities. In this case the masters turned to the pope to settle a legal question, not, as they would later, to defend their rights and autonomy against the chancellor or bishop. Indeed, until 1212, when a conflict between the masters and Chancellor John of Candeilles broke out over the granting of the *licentia docendi*, relations between the schools and the diocesan officials of Paris seem to have been generally harmonious. Admittedly, the documentation tells us little about the concrete relations between scholars and local authorities before these disputes arose. But it seems highly likely that as long as the bishops and chancellors of Paris were men who had themselves studied and taught in the schools, they shared common interests and maintained close ties with their former colleagues. As we have seen, the moralists who preached as bishops or chancellors had essentially the same criticisms of the schools as other masters. Whereas diocesan officials in other cathedral cities often sought to restrict the growth of the schools, those in Paris who oversaw education directly supported scholars and encouraged the expansion of the schools.[62] As bishop, Maurice of Sully did act to keep scholars from living within the cathedral close. But it is far more significant that, throughout his long pontificate, he allowed masters to teach freely everywhere in the city.

Perhaps most beneficial to the schools was the policy, initiated by Maurice and continued by his successor, Odo of Sully (1197–1208), of appointing prominent Paris masters from the theology faculty to the chancellorship.[63] As chancellors, these learned men seem to have served the interests of both the bishops and the schools well. In 1207 Odo of Sully issued a decree requiring that future chancellors swear upon their election to remain resident in the city.[64] Although we do not know what specific concerns motivated this action at this time, the decree's reference to the importance of a resident chancellor to the community of scholars suggests that the bishop now thought it necessary to provide for the more regular supervision of the schools by the cognizant diocesan official. It is unlikely, however, that scholars felt any cause for alarm. The incumbent holding the office was Master Prévostin, the last—although, of course, this was not known then—of the long series of learned chancellors, stretching as far back as Odo of Soissons more than fifty years before, who had so sympathetically watched over the growth of the schools.

Although these chancellors retained control over the *licentia docendi* and, thus, over who could become a master, there is no indication that they ever used this authority either to restrain the freedom of the masters or to impede the expansion of the schools. If anything, to judge from the complaints of the critics about unqualified masters, the chancellors may have often granted licenses too liberally. At the same time, though we know from their sermons that the chancellors frequently decried the motives and the conduct of scholars, we have no evidence that they used their office to restrict what was being learned or taught. These chancellors seem to have worked with and through their former colleagues in trying to influence the schools, not against them. The interests of the chancellors, as well as of the bishops who appointed them, did not conflict with those of most of the leading masters teaching in the schools; their educational ideals and objectives essentially coincided. Thus the schools of Paris developed and masters first organized to form the university not in opposition to local authorities but under the generally favorable and supportive supervision of the bishop and the chancellor.

After 1209, when Prévostin retired from the chancellorship, the situation changed considerably. Neither Prévostin's successor as chancellor, John of Candeilles (1209-15), nor Odo of Sully's as bishop, Peter of Nemours (1208-19), was nearly as benevolent toward the scholars of the city as their predecessors had been.[65] It was their attempts to increase diocesan supervision over the schools and to limit the autonomy of the nascent corporation of masters that brought about the first serious conflict in the history of the university.

The primary issue of contention was the chancellor's continuing control over the granting of the *licentia docendi*. Although papal decrees clearly stipulated that licenses were to be freely granted to all "worthy and learned" men who wished to teach, it was apparently left up to the chancellor to judge the qualifications of a candidate. As long as the chancellor and the masters of the schools had common interests and could agree on the criteria for granting the license, this regulation did not pose a problem. There is no evidence of any disputes over issuing the license during the tenures of the learned chancellors up through Master Prévostin.

John of Candeilles, in contrast, appears to have been set upon using his control over the license to increase his authority over the schools. We learn from complaints made by the scholars of Paris that before granting a license, John regularly exacted an oath of fidelity and obedience from the candidate and sometimes also required payment of a fee. Although charging fees for the license violated previous papal decrees more directly, the practice of exacting oaths from candidates was a far more serious abrogation of academic freedom and a greater threat to the autonomy of the nascent corporation. Not surprisingly, given papal support for their rights in the past, the masters and scholars of Paris appealed directly to Innocent III. At issue was not only the changed requirements for receiving the license but also the chancellor's abuse of his judicial authority over scholars. Apparently, John had adopted a policy of arresting and imprisoning scholars for even minor offenses and then, we are told, inspired less by zeal for justice than by greed, of fining them before their release. In a forceful bull issued in January 1212, Innocent made his indignation clear. "When I studied in Paris," he wrote, "I never saw scholars treated in this way."[66] And he ordered the bishop of the neighboring diocese of Troyes to censure John of Candeilles unless he immediately ceased these practices.

Confronted with the threat of censure and with such a strong indication of the pope's support for the scholars, the chancellor had little choice but to submit the matters in dispute to arbitration. It still took more than a year, however, for the six arbiters, three from each side, to reach a satisfactory agreement. Not until August 1213 was the bishop of Paris able to announce the results of what he referred to as their "long deliberations." Thenceforth, no chancellor was to require an oath of fidelity or obedience or to impose any other obligation upon a candidate before granting the *licentia docendi*, nor was he to demand a monetary fee or any other form of compensation. In addition, strict limitations were placed upon the judicial authority of the chancellor. Clerics were to be incarcerated only in cases of evident necessity; even then, they were to be handled carefully and released as soon as possible. When serving as judge in a case, the chancellor was expressly forbidden to levy a fine on any scholar for injuring another person, whether cleric or layperson, even if the injured party was the chancellor himself. However—and here was a loophole—the chancellor could order a scholar to pay compensation directly to the injured party.[67]

These restrictions applied to all future chancellors no less than to John of Candeilles. John alone was also required to agree to follow a special procedure for granting the license. As long as he held the office, it was to be the masters themselves, not the chancellor, who were to judge the qualifications of a candidate. The procedure stipulated that, in the faculties of theology, law, and medicine, the chancellor could not refuse the license to a candidate approved by a majority of teaching masters. In the larger faculty of arts, the determination of worthiness was to be made by a panel of six masters, three nominated by that faculty and three by the chancellor. The membership of this panel was to change every six months. Any time the chancellor rejected a favorable judgment by one of the faculties, the candidate was to be licensed by the bishop. On the other hand, the faculties were not given complete control over the certification of those masters who would teach in Paris. The agreement allowed John of Candeilles to license candidates in each faculty without the prior approval of the masters.[68]

The conflict was thus settled by a compromise. And as with all compromises, its terms were fully satisfactory to none of the parties involved. As long as the chancellor could license masters at his own discretion, the faculties were denied independent control over their membership. But with the support of the papacy, the nascent university had taken another major step in establishing its autonomy. It was also during this conflict, probably, that the university first received formal recognition of the important legal right of electing its own proctor or procurator to represent it in litigation.[69] In the settlement of their first dispute with the chancellor, the masters and scholars had been treated by the pope as a legal entity, as a corporation.

It was a victory in principle for the university, but one that still left the specific matters of contention unresolved. The procedures established for certifying candidates to teach applied only to John of Candeilles, not to his successors. And the issue of the chancellor's discretionary authority over the license would figure prominently in the subsequent struggles of the university. The bishop of Paris, Peter of Nemours, had taken care to reserve his future rights over the schools. To his confirmation of the decision of the arbiters, he had added a proviso stating that the chancellor agreed to the terms of the settlement "saving in all said things our jurisdiction and the authority of the Church of Paris."[70] Five years later, in 1218, Peter and his new chancellor, Philip of Grève, would initiate a bold new effort to assert this jurisdiction and to try to reestablish their authority over the masters and scholars of Paris by challenging the right of the university to make its own statutes and to require that its members swear to observe them.[71] By then, however, the masters had been functioning as an independent guild for more than a decade. They had also learned that they could count upon the papacy to guarantee their freedom and their corporate autonomy.

The bitter conflicts and prolonged litigation between the university and local authorities after 1218 lie outside the scope of this study. Given the persistence with which the bishop and chancellor then tried to assert control over the masters and scholars of Paris, the university might well have been crushed or permanently driven from the city if it had not had the full support of the papacy. It was not until after the two-year dispersion of the university, from 1229 to 1231, and the issuing by Pope Gregory IX of the important bull *Parens scientiarum* (April 1231), still rightly regarded as the Magna Carta of the university, that the masters and scholars of Paris won the decisive victory for their corporate autonomy and freedom.[72]

Still, as much as these conflicts with local authorities helped strengthen the corporate identity of the masters and scholars of Paris, they do not explain the origins of the university. Indeed, the university predates them. A guild of masters had already formed in Paris before John of Candeilles became chancellor. His licensing policies were opposed not by individual scholars nor even by a temporary association of masters, but by a nascent corporation of masters prepared to act to further their collective interests. This corporation had been formed not because the masters had needed to defend their freedom from local authorities but because they had been determined to reform and to regulate the schools.

This brings us back to the events of 1208 and 1209, when we have the first indication of Paris masters acting together as a corporation. Unfortunately, the statutes written by the eight elected deputies and sworn to by all the masters do not survive. However, we do know from the papal decree tacitly confirming their authority that these statutes concerned the wearing of suitable clothing, the scheduling of lectures and disputations, and attendance at the funerals of deceased colleagues, all matters of some importance to the identity and functioning of an emerging guild of masters. After this successful first step in regulating their own affairs, further efforts at corporate action by the Paris masters seem to have been impeded by the dispute with the chancellor over the *licentia docendi*. Understandably, this would remain a central issue in the early years of the university. To be able to reform and to regulate the schools, the guild had to have control over the approval and certification of those who would teach in Paris. Though the settlement reached with the chancellor in 1213 did not completely resolve this matter, further conflict had at least been postponed, and the masters, generally pleased with what they had achieved so far as a corporation, must have had good reason to feel encouraged about the prospects for further reform, especially if supported by the papacy.

Two years later, under the authority of the papal legate, Cardinal Robert of Courson, a set of statutes was established for the masters and scholars of Paris that went well beyond those tacitly approved by Innocent III in the bull *Ex litteris vestre* of 1208 or 1209. These statutes, which do survive, constitute the key document in the early history of the university. Not only do they embody the first formal and explicit recognition of the corporate rights of the masters and scholars of Paris, but they are also the best source for understanding just how the university was conceived.

ROBERT OF COURSON AND THE STATUTES OF 1215

The statutes of 1215 were not a systematic set of rules imposed upon the university by an external authority.[73] The papal legate who promulgated them was no stranger to the schools of Paris, nor was he unfamiliar with the concerns and the interests of the nascent corporation of masters. Prior to becoming cardinal in 1212, Robert of Courson had for twelve years or longer been a prominent master in the schools and a highly influential member of the theology faculty.[74] Although definite evidence is lacking, there can be little doubt, given both his professional prominence and his frequent service as a papal judge delegate, that Master Robert had played a major role in the early episodes of the university's corporate history. His appointment as a cardinal and his duties as papal legate to France (from April 1213) removed him physically from Paris, but they did not sever his well-established ties with the corporation of masters he had helped to form. When, in the final months of his legateship, the cardinal returned to Paris with a special mandate from Innocent III "to reform the schools and to provide for their future tranquility,"[75] he was prepared to work with his former colleagues to secure their previous corporate achievements and complete the program of internal reform and regulation they had begun during the years when he was a master.

Both by training and by conviction, Robert of Courson was ideally suited to be a leader in reforming the schools. As a master of theology he had proven himself particularly skilled at reconciling the principles advanced by those who debated moral issues on a theoretical level with the more concrete and practical questions raised by everyday life. Robert's only extant work is a *Summa* known by its opening words *Tota celestis philosophia*, which he wrote during the last years of his teaching career in Paris (1208–12). John Baldwin has called Courson's *Summa* "the final product of the school of Peter the Chanter."[76] And before discussing Robert of Courson's own teaching, it is necessary to say something more about this school, which also included among its members several of the moralists – most notably, Stephen Langton, Raoul Ardent, and Jacques of Vitry – and also the humanist Gerald of Wales.

During a long and distinguished career of teaching in Paris, Master Peter (d. 1197), the chanter of Notre Dame, inspired a group of his colleagues and students to turn their attention from the more speculative and metaphysical qustions that had previously dominated theological instruction to issues of practical morality and social reform. Though primarily interested in matters of more general social significance, these masters by no means ignored what was happening around them in the schools. In their lectures and disputations they specifically discussed many issues of particular importance to the state of education. Their summae contain many *quaestiones* dealing with controversial curricular matters, such as the value of the liberal arts, restrictions on the study of civil law and medicine, and the limits and purposes of theological disputation; with the sensitive problems of educational finance and providing for the economic support of scholars, including the very topical issues of whether fees should be charged for the *licentia docendi* or for attending lectures and of whether scholars should be exempted from the prohibitions against pluralism and nonresidence; and, above all, with the question of who had the authority and jurisdiction to deal with the pressing problem of deportment and discipline in the schools. John Baldwin gives a fairly comprehensive survey of the masters' treatment of these questions,[77] and there is no need to review their opinions here. What Baldwin's study shows is that for several decades prior to the promulgation of the statutes of 1215, a group of Paris masters had been actively trying to resolve some of the complex practical problems and difficult moral issues raised by the state of affairs in the schools. It was the scholarship and teaching of these masters that had made many of the educational reforms called for by the critics possible to legislate as the university's first statutes.

The choice of a former master who had been involved in these activities to draw up the statutes for the university was both a logical and a fortuitous decision on the part of Innocent III. Moreover, even in comparison to other members of the circle of Peter the Chanter, Robert of Courson had, as a teacher, been especially methodical and practical in his approach to questions pertaining to the schools. Consider, for example, how he dealt with the important issue of academic fees in his *Summa*. As we have seen, most critics of the schools felt that it was wrong to teach for profit or for advancement, because knowledge, as a gift from God, should not be sold, and they often supported this opinion by citing Matthew 10.8: "Freely you have received, freely give." But although this principle was widely accepted in theory, it conflicted with the financial needs of those masters who lacked prebends. How, then, could a theologian trying to establish a practical policy on fees reconcile the lofty educational ideal with the very real needs of his unbeneficed colleagues in the schools?

Courson approaches the problem by systematically applying the principle—that knowledge should not be sold—to the different professional circumstances of arts masters and of theologians. Treating the arts first, Courson begins by distinguishing between teaching such rudimentary subjects as grammar and foreign languages or geometry and arithmetic, which he compares to exercising a mechanical skill like weaving or carpentry, and, on the other hand, providing instruction in those liberal arts that teach a student ethics. It is not permissible to charge for the latter, he concludes, since the knowledge involved pertains to morals, but a master can contract for his services in teaching the former just as a farmer charges a predetermined price for plowing a field. In the case of theology, no justification for fees could be made on the basis of what was taught since the theologian's responsibility was only to teach moral and spiritual doctrine. So, instead, Courson makes a second distinction, this one based on the different financial circumstances of masters. If a theologian has no other means of support, Courson then argues, he can request fees from his students to provide for his material needs. However, unlike masters of arts, who could require students to pay in advance for attending their lectures, masters of theology should accept money only after completing their lectures and then only from those willing and able to pay.[78]

This solution was perhaps more satisfactory to masters of arts—even if somewhat demeaning of their professional status—than to masters of theology. It was also consistent with the policies already in effect aimed at restricting the number of theologians teaching in the schools and at providing them with adequate prebends. As this example from his *Summa* shows, Robert of Courson, even as a teacher, had been determined to consider actual conditions and to introduce existing policies into his scholastic disputations.

However, as papal legate to France—commissioned both to preach the crusade and to prepare for the ecumenical council Innocent III had summoned to meet at the Lateran in the autumn of 1215—Robert of Courson found that reforming society was not a simple matter of implementing the policies he and his colleagues in the schools had already worked out. In June 1213, soon after his appointment as legate, he briefly returned to Paris to preside over the first of the many diocesan synods that he would convene in France over the next two years. No formal action involving the university was taken on this occasion—the masters had still not resolved their conflict with John of Candeilles—but several of the decrees promulgated did bear directly on matters pertaining to the schools. First of all, the council renewed the decree, first issued at the Council of Reims in 1131 and later repeated at the Lateran Council of 1139 and at the Council of Tours in 1163, that prohibited monks and the regular clergy from leaving their cloisters to study medicine or law.[79] Moreover, this policy was taken two steps further. Although there remains some question about how broadly the restriction was intended to apply, the council apparently extended the prohibition to forbid members of religious orders from attending the schools, not only if intending to study medicine or law but for any reason whatsoever; they were to be educated exclusively within the cloister. Those religious already at the schools were given two months to return to their cloisters.[80] In addition, for the first time, the restrictions on the study of medicine and law were extended to the secular clergy. The council ruled that if a parish priest obtained the permission of his bishop to attend the schools, he was to learn theology, which would help him serve the spiritual needs of his congregation, and was not to study the "secular sciences" of law or medicine.[81] On another, quite unrelated matter—but one that bore no less on life in the schools—a decree was promulgated prohibiting all public prostitutes from residing within the city of Paris.[82]

The policies embodied in these decrees were probably greeted with general approval by Robert of Courson's former colleagues on the theology faculty. However, they were probably far less pleased with the strict decree promulgated at the council against pluralism. While teaching in the schools, Courson had justified the holding of multiple benefices in cases when one was insufficient in value to support a cleric or when the pope explicitly permitted some distinguished cleric to retain several benefices for the public good (*propter publicam utilitatem*). In his *Summa* he specifically cites the example of his own master, Peter the Chanter, as a pluralist for whom such an exception had, appropriately, been made. Nevertheless, repeating a concern also expressed by Jacques of Vitry, Courson had duly warned that making such exceptions for prominent masters could set a bad precedent for the rest of the clergy.[83] It was perhaps his increasing awareness of this problem that motivated him, as legate, to support a decree prohibiting pluralism without exception.[84] This strict policy was modified two years later at the Lateran Council. That council's decree against pluralism made an explicit exception for masters by allowing learned men to hold more than one benefice "when reason demanded it."[85] It is not unlikely that objections raised by Courson's former colleagues to the pluralism decree he had promulgated in Paris in 1213 had something to do with this change.

After his initial successes at the first diocesan councils he convened at Paris and then at Rouen (February-March 1214), Robert confronted increased resistance, hostility, and, finally, well-organized opposition as he took his reform program to other parts of France. Neither his personality nor his policies proved popular. Several contemporary chroniclers complain about the unfairness of Robert's judgments and the severity of his actions against the French prelacy and clergy.[86] According to William the Breton, not only had the legate done more harm than good by his indiscriminate preaching of the crusade, but his indiscreet criticisms of the clergy in his sermons to the laity had caused so many scandals and local disputes that the entire French clergy (*clerus universus*) and the king had together lodged a complaint against his conduct before the pope.[87] Although such accounts may exaggerate Robert's unpopularity, we do know for certain that his harsh actions against usurers antagonized Philip Augustus.[88] Responding to appeals from France, Innocent III had found it necessary, on at least three occasions, to intervene to moderate Courson's actions or to annul his decisions.[89] Resentment against the legate finally became so great that, when he called another council to be held at Bourges in May 1215, the French prelacy unanimously refused to attend and the council never took place.[90]

It was in the wake of these difficulties and soon after the humiliating experience at Bourges that Robert of Courson returned to Paris in the summer of 1215 with his special papal mandate to reform and to regulate the schools. It was fortunate for both his own later reputation and the future of the university that Robert was given this final opportunity to exercise his legatine commission. His reform efforts elsewhere in France may have failed, but in Paris he achieved an enduring success. Many of his other decisions and judgments were rescinded or overturned by the papacy within a few years, but the statutes he promulgated in August 1215 long remained authoritative as the founding privileges and decrees of the university.

Two factors contributed to this success. Having apparently learned that it was little use trying to impose a program of moral reform on an unwilling clergy and prelacy, Robert worked closely with the masters and scholars to reform the schools. The statutes state explicitly that he had sought "the counsel of good men," which no doubt means that Robert had formulated the decrees in consultation with his former colleagues, especially with those on the theology faculty.[91] Moreover, the time seems to have been ripe for reform in Paris. A sizeable group of masters both agreed about what needed to be done and were willing to cooperate with the papal legate to establish written policies that the university would thenceforth enforce independently.

The striking lack of orderliness in the statutes of 1215 has never been satisfactorily explained. It may be that Robert of Courson, still trying to resolve the disputes resulting from his previous legatine actions and decisions and also needing to get to Rome before the Lateran Council opened in November, had only a limited time to negotiate with the masters and to formulate the decrees. He seems to have wisely decided to concentrate his efforts on establishing policies only in the areas where there was already substantial consensus among masters about what ought to be done or on confirming existing practices and customs consistent with the stated objectives of reforming and tranquilizing the schools. In many cases, this simply involved renewing previous decrees and privileges. But the statutes also regulated some important aspects of the schools that, up to then, had remained uncontrolled though not uncriticized. Despite their apparent disorder and lack of unity, the statutes, considered as a whole, do address most of the principal concerns of the moralists and of the would-be reformers of the schools.

Given the frequent criticisms about the harm being done to teaching by young and inadequately trained masters, it is not surprising that priority was given to establishing minimum qualifications for teachers of both the arts and theology. No arts scholar was to be allowed to lecture until he had reached the age of twenty-one and had studied the arts in the schools for at least six years. Theology teachers had to be at least thirty-five and had to have studied for a minimum of eight years, including five years of faithful attendance at lectures on theology. In his *Summa*, Robert of Courson had especially emphasized the importance of maturity in those teaching theology and canon law.[92] The legate's particular concern about this matter may explain why the decree set an age requirement for theologians that even exceeded the recommendation of moralists, such as Jacques of Vitry and Raoul Ardent, that no one under the age of thirty should teach or preach publicly.

Nor were age and length of study the sole prerequisites for teaching. In theology, no one was to be allowed to lecture or to preach unless he was also of approved life and learning (*nisi probate vite fuerit et scientie*).[93] Since no specific procedure was stipulated, this evaluation was presumably to be performed by the theology faculty itself. For the arts faculty a similar qualification was decreed, which required that a master not be tainted by any disgrace (*non sit respersus aliqua infamia*). In this case, the statutes specify that a candidate was to be examined according to the procedure that had been agreed to between the chancellor and the scholars in 1213, that is, by the appointed examining panel of six masters.[94] As a further requirement before beginning to teach the arts, a candidate for the license had to promise to lecture for at least two years; this obligation was to remain binding unless the master was later able to make a reasonable cause for an exemption either publicly or before the examiners. Judging from the criticisms the arts faculty had attracted, this requirement was doubtlessly intended not to relieve a shortage of masters but to provide a greater degree of stability within the schools.[95]

The regulation of the arts faculty also extended to what was and was not to be taught. John of Salisbury would have been quite pleased had he lived to learn of the arts curriculum prescribed by the statutes. The entire corpus of Aristotle's logical writings, both the Old and the New Logic, as well as one or, preferably, both of the two parts of Priscian's grammar (the first sixteen books were known as *Priscianus maior* and the last two as *Priscianus minor*), were to be covered in the ordinary lectures of the masters of arts. On feast days, in place of these lectures on dialectic and grammar, masters were to schedule lectures only on rhetoric (the third book of the *Ars maior* of Donatus, known as the *Barbarismus*, and the fourth book on the *Topics* of Boethius were the specified texts); on Aristotle's *Ethics*; and on the arts of the quadrivium, for which no specific texts were prescribed. Presumably, these less technical subjects were considered somewhat less demanding and thus more likely to appeal to students on days when many distractions would be competing with lectures.

This curriculum, if hardly as ambitious as that prescribed by Hugh of St. Victor, does stipulate that instruction was to be offered at the schools in each of the seven traditional liberal arts. On the other hand, the arts faculty was prohibited from teaching Aristotle's writings on natural philosophy and metaphysics and their commentaries (i.e., the *libri naturales*), as well as the heretical works of David of Dinant, Amaury of Bène, and a certain Maurice of Spain. This decree simply renewed the ban that had been promulgated five years earlier, at the council in which Robert of Courson had participated as a regent master.[96] In contrast to these detailed prescriptions and proscriptions for the arts faculty, only one rule was imposed on the theologians: they were not to begin to lecture before tierce (or 9 A.M.). This rule was probably intended to enable masters of arts to attend lectures in theology after completing their own, a policy consistent with the principle that the study of the arts should be propaedeutic to theology.[97]

No less important in reforming the schools than the regulation of masters and the curriculum were the new rules concerning scholarly conduct and deportment. To curb the excessive drinking and feasting that had made scholars open targets for the satirists, the decrees prohibited large banquets either at the time when a master began to teach or when a student was examined. These customary celebrations were to be limited to a few friends or colleagues. Scholars were urged instead to increase the donations of clothing and other items usually offered on these occasions, especially to the poor. (One is reminded by this decree of the moralists' concern for the needs of poor scholars.) Excesses in clothing were also prohibited. When lecturing, masters of arts were to wear a simple black round ankle-length cope, a pallium, and plain shoes without pointed toes. No similar stipulations were made for the clothing of masters of theology, presumably because most of them, already in orders and usually beneficed, would be subject to established requirements on clerical dress. To provide for the tranquility of the schools, decrees were also promulgated on two specific issues we know to have been causes of serious contention. First, rights to a meadow in the Bourg-St.-Germain, known as the Prato clericorum or the Pré-aux-Clercs, about which scholars had previously clashed with residents and with the abbey of St. Germain, were confirmed to the university.[98] Then, to lessen the conflicts among scholars over the city's scarce lodging and classroom space, about which we have heard so many critics complain, it was stipulated that no one was to occupy a room without seeking, whenever possible, the previous tenant's consent.

The decrees providing for the discipline of scholars and for the governance of the schools largely restated and reinforced existing legislation. Consistent with Alexander III's judgment of the case involving the scholars of Reims (1170-72) and with the decrees promulgated by Cardinal Gualo (1208), Courson placed students under the legal jurisdiction (*forum*) of their masters.[99] To enforce this rule, he explicitly decreed that no student was to remain in Paris unless he was willing to submit to the authority of a specific master.[100] The independence of the masters was protected by the renewal of the decree of 1213, which stipulated that neither the chancellor nor any other official could require a monetary payment, oath, or other precondition before issuing the *licentia docendi*.

The right of masters to legislate and to enforce their own statutes, tacitly recognized by the bull *Ex litteris vestre* in 1208 or 1209, was also now formally confirmed. The decrees gave the masters and scholars the authority to establish obligations and regulations (*obligationes et constitutiones*) sanctioned by sworn oaths and agreed penalties. These, Courson stipulated, could be binding both between the university and others – for example, in the matter of what to do if a scholar was murdered, mutilated, or seriously injured and the case was resolved unjustly, or in setting rents for lodgings – and between the masters and scholars themselves, in such matters as establishing rules for academic dress, the burial of colleagues, or the scheduling of lectures and disputations. Courson probably listed these specific subjects of legislation not to set limits on self-governing authority of the university but to encourage masters to exercise their responsibilities over those matters that he knew had previously caused the disruption of learning. Seemingly by way of both justification and exhortation, Courson added that this right was to be exercised so that "the university [*studium*] might not be dissolved or destroyed."[101]

Finally, there can be little doubt that in promulgating these statutes,

Robert of Courson was seeking to strengthen the corporate identity and autonomy of the nascent university that he had, as master, been involved in forming. Significantly, on no matter are the statutes more detailed than in establishing procedures pertaining to the death and burial of a member of the university. When a student of the arts or of theology died, all the masters were to attend the funeral, but in two shifts so that, presumably, classes would not be disrupted. On the other hand, when a master of either faculty died, all masters were to attend the funeral and to keep vigil together, and, on the day of the burial, all lectures and disputations were to be canceled. Such funerary practices, no less than the making and enforcing of their own decrees, were vitally important to the ability of the masters and scholars of Paris to function and to be recognized as a single corporate body.

Perhaps most important to the future autonomy of the university, however, was the procedure established by Robert of Courson for the enforcement of the decrees. Anyone who intentionally violated the prescribed rules and regulations was to be excommunicated unless, within fifteen days of his transgression, he had amended his action by appearing before the entire university of masters and scholars (*coram universitate magistrorum et scolarium*) or before some smaller group appointed for such cases by the university (*coram aliquibus ab Universitate constitutis*).[102] It made no difference in the procedure, apparently, whether the rule violated applied only to a single faculty or to all masters and scholars. Jurisdiction, in both cases, rested within the university as a whole, in the several faculties acting together as a single corporate body.

This procedure was, of course, nothing new. The Paris faculties had been cooperating and functioning as one guild since before 1208. In this sense, the university had already existed for some time when Robert of Courson promulgated these statutes. Even if they were not the foundation charter of the university, however, Courson's statutes were the decisive document in confirming the corporate rights, strengthening the corporate identity, and securing the corporate autonomy of the already formed "university of masters and scholars of Paris." After 1215 there could be no doubt that the future of learning in Paris would depend upon the collective will of the masters and scholars of all the faculties acting together as an essentially autonomous and formally recognized guild. The university had been decisively established.

CONCLUSIONS

What conclusions about the origins of the university can be drawn from this history of events up to 1215? First, it should be clear that the statutes promulgated by Robert of Courson served a dual purpose. They fulfilled both a program of educational reform long urged for the schools and provided official papal recognition of the corporate rights of the university that had been formed seven or more years before, when the masters of Paris had acted independently to attempt to regulate their own affairs. In an important sense, then, the statutes can be understood as a summary of and a conclusion to the period of corporate development during which Paris masters from the various schools and faculties had first come together to function effectively and to be regarded as a single guild.

Still more important, however, is what these events suggest about how and why this corporate development took place. It was hardly inevitable that masters teaching different subjects in the various schools of Paris should join together to form one guild, instead of several. What could have motivated masters of the faculties of arts, medicine, law, and theology to overcome their intense competitiveness and antagonism in order to advance their mutual interests in a single corporation? The usual explanation—that the masters needed to join forces as they struggled to assert their freedom and to gain autonomy from the chancellor and the bishop—is not sustained by the evidence. We know from the decree *Ex litteris vestre* that the masters of theology, law, and the arts had formed a corporate body several years before the first serious conflict with the chancellor. Moreover, save for the dispute with John of Candeilles, relations with local authorities caused no apparent difficulties for the masters until after 1215. During the formative years of the university, the masters were not opposed but were actively supported by diocesan authorities, many of whom had themselves once studied or taught in the schools. The corporate origins of the university of Paris cannot, therefore, be explained as a negative or self-protective response to external conflict or opposition, or, even, to the threat of encroachment. Nor is it satisfactory to point simply to what has been called the corporate instinct or spirit—or the "mouvement associatif"—of the twelfth century.[103] The concurrent development of urban communes, trade and craft guilds, commercial associations, and religious confraternities no doubt helps explain why the masters might have felt compelled to associate together, but it does not answer the question of why they formed one university instead of several more narrowly defined or specialized guilds.

A single corporation including masters from all the faculties and schools in Paris could not have been formed without the prior development of a professional consciousness of some common values, objectives, and ideals. Various views have been advanced to explain the development of this professional identity among scholars. It has been suggested that the university was formed by scholars whose shared love of knowledge (*amor scientiae*) enabled them, despite the significant differences in their areas of specialization and vocational interests, to join together in a single corporate body that would serve to advance their mutual search for wisdom and truth.[104] Another view has emphasized the influence within the schools of a new concept of the unity of knowledge, based on the Aristotelian principle that all knowledge, in whatever field, must be capable of rational demonstration. Masters specializing in various subjects are thus said to have been bound together by common intellectual methods and aims to form the university where this unity of knowledge would be preserved within the diversity of faculties.[105] A more generally shared view claims that it was the desire for *laus et pecunia* as much as, if not more than, the *amor scientiae* or any similarity of method that defined the common interests embodied in the new institution. According to this third argument, it was the development of a vocational consciousness rooted in the tendency to view education as a means of social advancement and to conceive of knowledge as the *negotium scholaris*, as the common trade or business of scholars, that shaped the professional image and identity of the masters and motivated them to form the first universities.[106]

Each of these inspirations and motivations must certainly have had some influence within the schools, but none can satisfactorily explain the earliest expressions of the corporate will of the nascent university in Paris. In fact, the first statutes provide the best evidence of how those who formed the university defined their professional identity. Both the statutes promulgated in 1215 and, judging from the description of them in the papal decree *Ex litteris vestre*, those drawn up by the masters themselves before 1208 had been concerned primarily with teaching—with the issues of what should be taught, how, when, and by whom, and with the authority of masters over their students. Does this not suggest that the professional identity that the masters shared and that motivated them to form the university was based above all on their consciousness of their duties and responsibilities as teachers?

Teaching took precedence in the formation of the university. Whether members of the faculty of the arts, law, medicine, or theology, masters in Paris were conscious that they were involved in the common professional endeavor of teaching others what they themselves had been taught. It was the values, interests, and objectives these masters shared as teachers that motivated them to join together to form a single guild in order to reform the schools. As teachers and as reformers, they seem to have been inspired by a recognizable set of educational ideals: the essential value and integrity of all knowledge, the need to share one's learning willingly and freely (or, at least, without excessive concern for personal profit), and the importance of education to the improvement of society. Against the pressures of specialization and narrow professionalism, these were the higher ideals and purposes that the humanists and other critics of the schools had struggled to keep alive and, more importantly, that the moralists had helped to define in their lectures and had promoted in their sermons as a viable program for educational reform. The moralists may have had little success in exhorting scholars to improve their behavior, but they do seem to have been effective in inspiring the masters to join together, to assume their professional responsibilities as teachers, and to undertake the reform of the schools.[107] To them we owe no small debt of gratitude for the university.

Given their educational concerns and objectives, the moralists had especially good reason to be pleased by the formation of the university and by the statutes promulgated by Robert of Courson. What about the other critics of the schools? We know that Gerald of Wales was encouraged by developments in Paris and hoped that the newly established curriculum would prove beneficial to both theology and the liberal arts. Still, the criticisms that he and others had voiced about the decline of learning were never to be silenced. There would never be enough positions or rapid enough promotions to satisfy the ambitions of those who struggled to acquire learning in the university with the expectation of worldly rewards. The disgruntled successors of the humanists would continue to complain about specialization and professionalism. Nor would the foibles of academic life in the University of Paris cease to attract the attention of satirists. Rutebeuf and Rabelais were among those who carried on the satirical tradition begun by Walter of Châtillon and Nigel Wireker. And what of the monastic critics? It is to the monastic and religious orders that we must return to conclude this account of the origins of the university.

In August 1217, two years after Robert of Courson promulgated the statutes for the university, St. Dominic sent eight members of his newly founded order to Paris "in order that they might study, preach, and establish a convent."[108] By September these Dominicans had settled into a house near Notre Dame and the Hôtel-Dieu. Sometime during the following year they moved to a permanent home on the Left Bank that had been given to them by Master John of Barastre, a prominent theologian then holding the positions of royal chaplain and dean of St. Quentin, and by the university. Here, at the hospice and chapel of St. Jacques, the Dominicans established their own school, where, at the request of Pope Honorius III, their donor, Master John of Barastre, agreed to provide them with instruction in theology.[109] This arrangement made it possible for the Dominicans to hear the ordinary lectures given by the theology faculty in Paris without violating the decree prohibiting the members of religious orders from leaving their cloister to study. St. Jacques became the Dominican *studium generale*, the school where members of the Order of Preachers from throughout Europe came to study theology. By 1223 there were 120 members of the Dominican Order resident in Paris. Within a generation of their arrival, the Dominicans dominated the theology faculty in Paris.[110]

These events mark an important turning point in the history of the university. For more than a century the leaders of new religious orders had struggled against the growing influence of the schools and the new learning emanating from them. Cloister and school had been in opposition. Now, with the cooperation of the recently formed university and of the papacy, the new Order of Preachers had found a satisfactory means of reconciling the cloister and the school. Thanks to the link between St. Jacques and the university, the stability and routine of the cloistered life (*disciplina*) and the most advanced and sophisticated theological training of the schools (*doctrina*) could henceforth be combined. "To live a good life, to learn, and to teach," this was the ideal the Dominicans sought to fulfill in establishing their own house of study in Paris.[111] Philip of Harvengt and Stephen of Tournai would certainly have agreed with the ideal and applauded the institutional arrangement that brought learning back into the cloister.

Moreover, the Dominicans' program obviously had a general appeal. Other religious orders soon followed their lead and established similar houses of study in Paris. The Franciscans, who had arrived in Paris as early as 1219, took less than ten years—a short time considering their founder's emphasis on simplicity and resistance to learning—to organize their own school.[112] By 1254 other orders, including the Augustinians, Trinitarians, Premonstratensians, and even the Cistercians, had established houses of study in the city.[113] There had been some resistance. When, around 1245, the abbot of Clairvaux requested a subsidy from his daughter houses to establish a Cistercian school in Paris, at least one abbot, Arnulfus of Villers, steadfastly refused to contribute. Astonished by the novelty of the idea and concerned about its effect on the simplicity and humility of monks, he recalled the words of St. Bernard: "It is not the work of monks to teach, but to mourn."[114] But the fact that it was an abbot of Clairvaux seeking the subsidy shows how much things had changed. The appeal of the educational opportunities offered in Paris could no longer be resisted. A new and vital alliance was being forged between the cloister and the school. With the establishment of houses of study in Paris by nearly all the major religious and monastic orders, there was to be no further resistance to the continued growth and the expanding influence of the university and its learning, at least from them.

But there is another side to this history. The cooperation between the recently established university of secular masters and the new independent schools of the religious orders did not continue for long. No sooner did the Dominicans and Franciscans establish their houses in Paris than their interests and those of the other masters began to diverge. As separate communities with their own schools and teachers, the orders were not subject to the rules and regulations of the university. In a sense, each order had its own distinct and independent "university." Thus, when, as a result of a dispute over scholarly privileges, the university formally suspended lectures and dispersed from 1229 to 1230, the Mendicants felt no need to halt the instruction offered in their convents. Though these schools were intended primarily for members of the orders, those secular students who chose to remain in Paris were admitted to the lectures. Not surprisingly, when the secular masters returned to Paris in 1231, they soon began to feel the competition of the Mendicant schools. Since the masters who taught in the religious houses were financially supported by their orders, they could charge lower fees than the secular masters, most of whom were largely dependent upon student fees for their livelihood. Moreover, with the conversion of prominent masters such as John of St. Giles to the Dominicans and Alexander of Hales to the Franciscans, it was not long before the instruction available in the Mendicant houses of study could rival that in the university. Finally, in the 1250's the increasingly strained relations between the religious and secular masters broke out into an open and bitter conflict, irrevocably damaging the long-standing alliance between the papacy and the university that had been so important in helping the nascent corporation secure its autonomy and reform its own affairs.[115]

Admittedly, these events lie well outside the chronological scope of this book. They have been mentioned for what they suggest of the impact that monastic opposition had on the development of the schools prior to 1215. In an indirect and quite unintended way, the reformers' persistent struggle to keep the monks and regular clerics out of the schools and to keep secular students out of the cloister seems to have contributed to the formation of the university. Not only had monastic opposition to the schools provided an additional impetus to the masters' efforts to reform and to regulate their own affairs, but the exclusion of monks and regular clerics from the schools had also helped the masters to develop their own professional consciousness. Not bound by any strong ties to already existing orders, communities, or schools, the secular masters and scholars were motivated by their common professional identity and interests as teachers to form a single corporation. Given the later conflicts between the university and the *studia* of the Mendicant orders, it seems highly unlikely that a single guild could have formed had there been a sizeable number of monks or regular clerics among the masters teaching in Paris prior to 1215. There would probably have continued to be several separate schools, instead of a single autonomously functioning and legally recognized university. From this perspective, it may indeed have been fortunate that the Cistercians had been so critical and uncompromising toward the schools of Paris. Bernard of Clairvaux, as the most prominent critic of the schools – no less than his adversary Peter Abelard, as the first renowned Paris master – might then be counted among those who helped to shape the university.

NOTES

Notes

Printed sources are cited in full at the first reference in each chapter. Manuscript sources are cited by library call number; for a complete list of manuscripts cited, see p. 371. The following abbreviations are used in the Notes:

AESC	*Annales: Economies, sociétés, civilisations*
AHDLMA	*Archives d'histoire doctrinale et littéraire du moyen âge*
AHR	*American Historical Review*
BGPTM	*Beiträge zur Geschichte der Philosophie und Theologie des Mittelalters*
BIIRHT	*Bulletin d'information de l'Institut de Recherche et d'Histoire des Textes*
COCR	*Collectanea ordinis Cisterciensium reformatum*
CUP	*Chartularium Universitatis Parisiensis*, ed. H. Denifle and E. Chatelain (4 vols., Paris, 1889-97)
DNB	*Dictionary of National Biography*
DTC	*Dictionnaire de théologie catholique*
EHR	*English Historical Review*
Mansi	*Sacrorum conciliorum nova et amplissima collectio*, ed. J. D. Mansi (31 vols., Florence and Venice, 1759-98)
MGH SS	*Monumenta Germaniae historica: Scriptores* (in folio)
MRS	*Mediaeval and Renaissance Studies*
N&E	*Notices et extraits des manuscrits de la Bibliothèque Nationale*, ed. B. Hauréau (6 vols., Paris, 1890-93)
PL	*Patrologiae cursus completus: Series latina*, ed. J. P. Migne (221 vols., Paris, 1844-64)
RHE	*Revue d'histoire ecclésiastique*
Rolls Series	*Rerum Brittanicarum medii aevi scriptores or Chronicles and Memorials of Great Britain and Ireland during the Middle Ages*, published under the direction of the Master of the Rolls (244 vols., London, 1858-96)
RTAM	*Recherches de théologie ancienne et médiévale*

INTRODUCTION

1. Hastings Rashdall, *The Universities of Europe in the Middle Ages*, rev. ed. by F. M. Powicke and A. B. Emden (3 vols., Oxford, 1936), 3: 464.

2. *Ibid.*, pp. 459-64.

CHAPTER ONE

1. Alexander Neckham, *De laudibus divinae sapientiae*, ed. T. Wright, Rolls Series 34 (London, 1863), p. 453.

2. *Historia de vita et gestis Philippi Augusti*, ed. H. F. Delaborde, *Oeuvres de Rigord et de Guillaume le Breton* (2 vols., Paris, 1882-85), 1: 230.

3. *De nugis curialium* 5.5, trans. M. R. James (London, 1923), p. 248.

4. See J. W. Baldwin, "*Studium et regnum*: The Penetration of University Personnel into French and English Administration at the Turn of the Twelfth and Thirteenth Century," *Revue des études islamiques* 44 (1976): 199-215, and also Baldwin's more recent summary of his findings in "Masters at Paris, 1179-1215," in R. L. Benson and G. Constable, eds., *Renaissance and Renewal in the Twelfth Century* (Cambridge, Mass., 1982), pp. 154-58.

5. On the development of this role see S. d'Irsay, "L'Opinion publique dans les universités médiévales: Etudes sur l'activité politique de l'Université de Paris à ses débuts," *Revue des études historiques* 99 (1932): 237-56.

6. Otto of Freising, *Chronica* 6.18, ed. A. Hofmeister (Hannover and Leipzig, 1912), p. 278. See also *Chronica* 1.prol., p. 8, and *Gesta Friderici* 1.prol., ed. G. Waitz and B. von Simson (Hannover and Leipzig, 1912), p. 12.

7. *Cligès*, ll. 28-42, trans. W. W. Comfort, *Arthurian Romances* (London, 1914), p. 91.

8. On the idea of the *translatio studii* see A. G. Jongkens, "*Translatio studii*: Les Avatars d'un thème médiéval," in *Miscellanea mediaevalia in memoriam Jan Frederik Niermeyer* (Groningen, 1967). On its association with the political ideology of the period see W. Goez, *Translatio imperii: Ein Beitrage zur Geschichte des Geschichtsdenkens und der politischen Theorien im Mittelalter und in der frühen Neuzeit* (Tübingen, 1958), pp. 104-37.

9. For the development of Paris during this period, the latest and most comprehensive study is J. Boussard, *Nouvelle Histoire de Paris: De la Fin du siège de 885-886 à la mort de Philippe Auguste* (Paris, 1976). However, L. Halphen's older history, *Paris sous les premiers Capétiens (987-1223): Etude de topographie* (Paris, 1909), is still useful. On the development of the Right Bank, the commercial center of the city, see also A. Lombard-Jourdan, *Paris—Genèse de la Ville: La Rive droite de la Seine des origines à 1223* (Paris, 1976).

10. See W. M. Newman, *Le Domaine royal sous les premiers Capétiens* (Paris, 1937), pp. 98-99.

11. On these developments see R. Fawtier, *The Capetian Kings of France*, trans. L. Butler and R. J. Adam (London, 1960), pp. 185-87; F. Lot and R. Fawtier, *Histoire des institutions françaises au moyen âge*, vol. 2: *Institutions royales* (Paris, 1958), pp. 409-10; G. Tessier, *Diplomatique royale française* (Paris, 1962), pp. 133-252 *passim*; and, especially, E. Bournazel, *Le Gouvernement capétien au XIIe siècle, 1108-1180* (Limoges, 1975), pp. 18-27, 157-78.

12. Boussard, *Nouvelle Histoire de Paris*, pp. 299-327.

13. Peter Abelard, *Historia calamitatum*, ed. J. Monfrin (Paris, 1967), pp. 66, 70-71.

14. In 1107 Pope Paschal II confirmed the privileges of the abbey of Ste. Geneviève (*Cartulaire général de Paris, 528-1180*, ed. R. de Lasteyrie [Paris, 1887], p. 160, n. 142). Some scholars have assumed that these privileges included the right of the abbot to grant formal permission to teach (the *licentia docendi*). However, there is no clear evidence that the abbot ever actually exercised this right, if he had it, before 1227. In that year Pope Gregory IX issued a bull explicitly giving the abbot and canons of the abbey permission to license masters to teach theology, canon law, and the arts within their jurisdiction (*CUP* 1 no. 55, p. 111).

15. The independent school of Master Adam of Balsham – who was praised as a teacher by John of Salisbury, Godfrey of St. Victor, and Alexander Neckham – remained open longer than most such schools, probably from the early 1130's until Adam was elected bishop of St. Asaph, in 1175. On Adam and his school see L. Minio-Paluello, "The *Ars disserendi* of Adam of Balsham 'Parvipontanus,'" *MRS* 3 (1954): 116-69.

16. On the position of the scholasticus or *magister scolae* see E. Lesne, *Histoire de la propriété ecclésiastique en France*, vol. 5: *Les Ecoles de la fin du VIIIe siècle à la fin du XIIe siècle* (Lille, 1940), pp. 467-78.

17. On the Carolingian educational legislation and its impact see Lesne, *Les Ecoles*, pp. 15-32, and P. Riché, *Les Ecoles et l'enseignement dans l'Occident chrétien de la fin du Ve siècle au milieu du XIe siècle* (Paris, 1979), pp. 65-79.

18. The limited evidence about the teaching in these monastic schools and at the cathedral before 1100 is discussed in Lesne, *Les Ecoles*, pp. 197-202; Boussard, *Nouvelle Histoire de Paris*, pp. 108-12; and the dated but still useful study of L. Maître, *Les Ecoles épiscopales et monastiques de l'Occident depuis Charlemagne jusqu'à Philippe-Auguste (768-1180)* (Paris, 1865; rev. ed., 1924), pp. 96-100.

19. On Reims, in addition to Lesne, *Les Ecoles*, pp. 276-96, see the two articles of John R. Williams, "The Cathedral School of Rheims in the Eleventh Century," *Speculum* 19 (1954): 661-77, and "The Cathedral School of Reims at the Time of Master Alberic, 1118-1136," *Traditio* 20 (1964): 93-114.

At Laon, learning was supported by an excellent library established in the ninth century. See the recent study by J. J. Contreni, *The Cathedral School of Laon from 850-930: Its Manuscripts and Masters* (Munich, 1978). See also Lesne, *Les Ecoles*, pp. 299-310, and the chapter on the schools in S. Martinet, *Montloon: Reflet fidèle de la montagne et des environs de Laon de 1000 à 1300* (Laon, 1972), pp. 95-111, as well as the review of this book by R. Kaiser, "Laon au XIIe et XIIIe siècles," *Revue du Nord* 56 (1974): 421-26, which explains how religious and urban conflict affected education at the cathedral school. On the important intellectual achievements of the school under Anselm of Laon see F. Bliemetzrieder, "Autour de l'oeuvre théologique d'Anselme de Laon," *RTAM* 1 (1929): 435-83; B. Smalley, *The Study of the Bible in the Middle Ages* (Notre Dame, Ind., 1964), pp. 49-51; and O. Lottin, *Psychologie et morale aux XIIe et XIIIe siècles*, vol. 5: *Problèmes d'histoire littéraire: L'Ecole d'Anselme de Laon et de Guillaume de Champeaux* (Gembloux, 1959). A revised assessment of Laon as a center of biblical scholarship in the early twelfth century has recently been put forth by V. I. J. Flint, "The 'School of Laon': A Reconsideration," *RTAM* 48 (1976): 89-110.

The prominence of the school of Chartres begins with Master Fulbert, a student of Gerbert, who taught in the early decades of the eleventh century. On

Fulbert's teaching see H. C. MacKinney, *Bishop Fulbert and Education at the School of Chartres* (Notre Dame, 1957), and F. Behrends, *The Letters and Poems of Fulbert of Chartres* (Oxford, 1976). On the subsequent history of the school see Lesne, *Les Ecoles*, pp. 152–73, and A. Clerval, *Les Ecoles de Chartres au moyen âge du Ve au XVIe siècle* (Chartres, 1895). Since the publication of R. W. Southern's 1970 article on Chartres, there has been much debate about the importance of the school of Chartres in the twelfth century. See note 43 below for the relevant citations.

20. The relevant section of the *Historia calamitatum* can be found in J. Monfrin's edition (Paris, 1967), pp. 63–89. There are two excellent and handy translations: *The Story of Abelard's Adversities*, trans. J. T. Muckle (Toronto, 1964), which has very useful notes, and *The Letters of Abelard and Heloise*, trans. B. Radice (Harmondsworth, 1974), pp. 57–85.

There has been much debate about the authenticity of the *Historia calamitatum* and of other letters attributed to Abelard. For a summary of the debate up to 1972 see J. Monfrin, "Le Problème de l'authenticité de la correspondance d'Abélard et d'Heloise," in *Pierre Abélard–Pierre le Vénérable: Les Courants philosophiques, littéraires et artistiques en Occident au milieu du XIIe siècle*, Colloques internationaux du Centre National de la Recherche Scientifique 546 (Paris, 1975), pp. 409–24. In the same volume, John Benton mounted a new and serious assault on the authenticity of the letters: "Fraud, Fiction and Borrowing in the Correspondence of Abelard and Heloise," pp. 469–506. But in a more recent article, "A Reconsideration of the Authenticity of the Correspondence of Abelard and Heloise," in *Petrus Abelard: Person, Werk und Wirkung*, ed. R. Thomas, Trierer Theologische Studien 38 (Trier, 1980), Benton explains that he has changed his mind and why he now accepts the generally held opinion that Abelard did write the *Historia calamitatum* and the other letters attributed to him.

21. *Historia calamitatum*, ed. Monfrin, p. 63.

22. On the revival of dialectic, see D. Knowles, *The Evolution of Medieval Thought* (New York, 1962), pp. 93–106. On the reasons for the subject's appeal to ambitious young men, see R. W. Southern, *The Making of the Middle Ages* (New Haven, 1953), pp. 176–84.

23. On the wandering of the young scholars of this time in search of the great masters see M. D. Chenu, "Les *Magistri*: La 'Science' théologique," in *La Théologie au douzième siècle* (Paris, 1966), pp. 23–29.

24. The social background of these men and their impact on the schools is discussed in G. Duby, "Youth in Aristocratic Society," in *The Chivalrous Society*, trans. C. Postan (Berkeley, 1977), pp. 112–22; see especially the suggestive remark on Abelard, p. 114, n. 9.

L. Minio-Paluello, "Nuovi Impulsi allo studio della logica: La Seconda Fase della riscoperta di Aristotele e di Boezio," in *La Scuola nell'occidente latino dell'alto medioevo*, Settimane di Studio del Centro Italiano di Studi sull'alto medioevo 19 (Spoleto, 1972) 2: 742–66, gives a good survey of the phases in the recovery of Aristotle's logical writings and comments on their importance relative to other inspirations in the development of disputation. A helpful assessment of Abelard's importance and originality as a logician is the article of N. Kretzmann, "The Culmination of the Old Logic in Peter Abelard," in Benson and Constable, eds., *Renaissance and Renewal in the Twelfth Century*, pp. 488–511. Although Abelard knew some of the "new logic," the recovery of Aristotle's logical writings had only a limited influence on his thought. See the introduction by L. M. de Rijk to his critical edition of Abelard's *Dialectica* (2d ed., Assen, 1970), pp. xvi-xviii.

25. See D. Luscombe, *The School of Peter Abelard: The Influence of Abelard's Thought in the Early Scholastic Period* (Cambridge, 1969), and N. Häring, "Abelard Yesterday and Today," in *Pierre Abélard–Pierre le Vénérable*, pp. 341-403.

26. *Historia calamitatum*, ed. Monfrin, pp. 64-65. Corbeil, like Melun, was a royal fief, and it has been suggested that Abelard had the benefit of the patronage of someone at the Capetian court. See Muckle, *The Story of Abelard's Adversities*, p. 14, n. 7.

27. William's teaching during this period is also discussed in a letter written by a German student to his patron, which can be found printed in P. Jaffe, *Bibliotheca rerum Germanicarum* (6 vols., Berlin, 1864-73), 5: 285-87.

28. *Historia calamitatum*, ed. Monfrin, pp. 66-67.

29. Abelard (*Historia calamitatum*, ed. Monfrin, pp. 68-69) is especially bitter and harshly critical in his characterization of Anselm of Laon. For a fairer assessment of him as a scholar and teacher see the works cited in note 19 above.

30. *Historia calamitatum*, ed. Monfrin, p. 70.

31. *PL* 178, 371D-372B.

32. *Die Exempla des Jakob von Vitry*, ed. G. Frenken (Munich, 1941), p. 123.

33. *Gesta Friderici* 1.49, ed. Waitz, pp. 69-70.

34. *Metalogicon* 2.10, ed. C. C. J. Webb (Oxford, 1929), pp. 77-78.

35. *Cartulaire de l'église Notre-Dame de Paris*, ed. B. Guérard (4 vols., Paris, 1850), 1: 339.

36. On this school see L. M. de Rijk, "Some New Evidence in Twelfth-Century Logic: Alberic and the School of Mont Ste. Geneviève," *Vivarium* 4 (1966): 1-58.

37. *Metalogicon* 2.10, ed. Webb, pp. 77-83.

38. R. L. Poole, "The Masters of Paris and Chartres in John of Salisbury's Time," *EHR* 35 (1920), reprinted in A. L. Poole, ed., *Studies in Chronology and History* (Oxford, 1934), pp. 223-47, claims that John of Salisbury was studying with Gilbert of Poitiers and William of Conches at Chartres from 1138 to 1140. R. W. Southern has convincingly challenged this view in his "Humanism and the School of Chartres," pp. 71-73 (see n. 43 below). But some scholars, including Nicholas Häring and Peter Dronke (see n. 43 below), persist in dividing John's education between Chartres and Paris.

39. *Metamorphosis Goliae*, ed. R. B. C. Huygens, *Studi medievali* ser. 3, 3.2 (1962): 770-71. On the dating of the poem see J. F. Benton, "Philology's Search for Abelard in the *Metamorphosis Goliae*," *Speculum* 50 (1975): 199-217.

40. On the identification of Robert Pullen with Robert Amiclas, I agree with Poole, "The Masters of Paris and Chartres," pp. 244-46, and R. B. C. Huygens, ed., "Guillaume de Tyr étudiant: Un Chapitre (XIX.12) de son 'Histoire' retrouvé," *Latomus* 21 (1962): 827.

41. Huygens, "Guillaume de Tyr," pp. 811-29.

42. My interpretation of these sources concurs, on most details, with that advanced by R. W. Southern in his article "The Schools of Paris and the School of Chartres," in Benson and Constable, eds., *Renaissance and Renewal in the Twelfth*

Century, pp. 129–33, which appeared after this chapter was written. I remain unconvinced, however, by Southern's conclusion (p. 132) that the *Metamorphosis Goliae* hints that in 1142 the schools of Paris were in a state of decline.

43. On the limitations of cathedral schools generally and of Chartres specifically see R. W. Southern's controversial article, "Humanism and the School of Chartres," in *Medieval Humanism and Other Essays* (New York, 1970), pp. 61–85. Southern's general thesis that the main purpose of cathedral schools was "to provide fairly elementary instruction at the diocesan level" (p. 74) has withstood other scholars' challenges to some of his specific arguments about inflated reputation of Chartres as a center of learning; see P. Dronke, "New Approaches to the School of Chartres," *Anuario de estudios medievales* 6 (1969): 117–40, and N. Häring, "Chartres and Paris Revisited," in J. R. O'Donnell, ed., *Essays in Honour of A. C. Pegis* (Toronto, 1974), pp. 268–328. More balanced views of the significance of the school of Chartres are offered in the recent articles of J. Chatillon, "Les Ecoles de Chartres et de St. Victor," in *La Scuola nell'occidente latino dell'alto medioevo* (Spoleto, 1972), pp. 795–839, and R. Giacone, "Masters, Books and the Library at Chartres According to the Cartularies of Notre-Dame and Saint-Père," *Vivarium* 12 (1974): 30–51. Southern compares Paris and Chartres in detail in his more recent article, "The Schools of Paris and the School of Chartres."

Some scholars have made a strong case that the school of Chartres, even if not able to rival Paris institutionally, did embody an important intellectual tradition with its own coherent set of methods and ideas. See E. Jeauneau, *Lectio philosophorum: Recherches sur l'école de Chartres* (Amsterdam, 1973), especially the article, "Note sur l'école de Chartres," published originally in *Studi medievali* 3d ser. 5.2 (1964): 821–65; and T. Gregory, *Anima Mundi: La Filosofia de Guglielmo de Conches e la scuola di Chartres* (Rome, 1955). Southern challenged even this concept of the school of Chartres in the Stenton Lecture he gave at the University of Reading in 1978; see his *Platonism, Scholastic Method and the School of Chartres* (Reading, 1979).

44. N. Häring, ed., "A Latin Dialogue on the Doctrine of Gilbert of Poitiers," *Mediaeval Studies* 15 (1953): 252.

45. Letter 136, *The Letters of John of Salisbury*, ed. and trans. W. J. Millor, H. E. Butler, and C. N. L. Brooke (2 vols., London, 1955: Oxford, 1979), 2: 7; *CUP* 1.intro. no. 19, pp. 17–18.

46. *CUP* 1.intro. no. 22, p. 24.

CHAPTER TWO

1. The older view of C. E. Du Boulay (Bulaeus), *Historia Universitatis Parisiensis a Carolo Magno ad nostra tempora* (6 vols., Paris, 1665–73), who argued that the university was first established on Mont. Ste. Geneviève, and of C. Thurot, *De l'organisation de l'enseignement dans l'Université de Paris au moyen âge* (Paris, 1850), who attributed its origin to the union of the schools of logic on the Mont with the school of theology at Notre Dame, are discussed and refuted by H. Denifle, *Die Entstehung der Universitäten des Mittelalters bis 1400* (Berlin, 1885), pp. 671*ff.* Most later scholars have agreed with Denifle in emphasizing the role of the cathedral schools in the development of the university. See, for example, Hastings Rashdall, *The Universities of Europe in the Middle Ages*, rev. ed. by F. M. Powicke and A. B. Emden (3 vols., Oxford, 1936), 1: 276–78; C. H. Haskins, *The Rise of Universities* (New York, 1923; reprint ed., Ithaca, 1957), p. 14; A. Gabriel, "The

Cathedral Schools of Notre-Dame and the Beginning of the University of Paris," in *Garlandia: Studies in the History of the Medieval University* (Notre Dame, 1969), pp. 39-64; and A. C. Cobban, *The Medieval Universities: Their Development and Organization* (London, 1975), pp. 76-79.

2. J. Boussard, *Nouvelle Histoire de Paris: De la Fin du siège de 885-886 à la mort de Philippe Auguste* (Paris, 1976), pp. 204-18, 329-30. Cf. Rashdall, *The Universities of Europe in the Middle Ages* 1: 276-77.

3. It is certainly significant that the earliest colleges, or *hospicia*, endowed for poor scholars were located on either the Ile de la Cité or the Right Bank. On the foundation of these colleges see Rashdall, *The Universities of Europe in the Middle Ages* 1: 497-505. The arrival of the Dominicans in Paris is discussed below, pp. 312-14.

4. As Gaines Post has written ("Alexander III, the *Licentia docendi*, and the Rise of the Universities," in C. H. Taylor, ed., *Haskins Anniversary Essays* [Boston, 1929], p. 265), "no university arose from the mere expansion of a cathedral school proper into a *studium generale*, but rather from the concentration of a large number of masters and students whose conditions favored them." As late as 1229, when conditions in Paris were unfavorable, the masters suspended their teaching, left the city, and did not return for almost two years.

5. Peter Abelard, *Historia calamitatum*, ed. J. Monfrin (Paris, 1967), p. 65.

6. Throughout the twelfth century there was much debate about whether canons regular were to be ranked as monks or as clerics. On how the canons perceived themselves and their educational role see the important study of C. W. Bynum, *Docere verbo et exemplo: An Aspect of Twelfth-Century Spirituality* (Missoula, Mont., 1979). On how they were perceived by reformers and canonists, see the excellent chapter on the status of canons regular in J. C. Dickinson, *The Origins of the Austin Canons and Their Introduction into England* (London, 1950), pp. 197-223.

7. *PL* 171, 141-43.

8. Most of these were in northern France, but daughter houses were also founded in England, Scandinavia, and Italy. Significantly for the history of the schools, in 1148 the abbey of Ste. Geneviève, which had jurisdiction over the Left Bank, was reformed by the Victorines and became part of the order. See F. Bonnard, *Histoire de l'abbaye et de l'ordre des chanoines réguliers de S. Victor de Paris* (2 vols., Paris, 1904-8), 1: 141-90.

9. *Tractatus de immutatione ordinis monachorum*, *PL* 202, 1313B. A late-twelfth-century Victorine chronicle names eleven distinguished disciples of Abbot Gilduin, including Hugh, Achard, Thomas, Adam, and Richard. The text from MS. Paris BN lat. 15009 is cited by Dickinson, *Origins*, pp. 284-85.

10. See B. Smalley, *The Study of the Bible in the Middle Ages* (Notre Dame, 1964), pp. 83-195, and Henri de Lubac, *Exégèse médiévale* (4 vols., Paris, 1959-64), 3: 287-372, 387-403.

11. Peter Lombard arrived with a letter of introduction from Bernard of Clairvaux: Ep. 410, *PL* 182, 618.

12. *Oeuvres de Robert de Melun*, ed. R. M. Martin, Spicilegium Sacrum Lovaniense 13 (Louvain, 1932), 1: ix.

13. On the Comestor's association with St. Victor, see Smalley, *Study of the Bible*, pp. 178-80, and I. Brady, "Peter Manducator and the Oral Traditions of Peter Lombard," *Antonianum* 41 (1966): 483-90.

14. B. Smalley, *The Becket Conflict and the Schools* (Oxford, 1973), p. 30.

15. For example, the *Tractatus de immutatione* (see n. 9 above) describes William as "vir admodum litteratus et religiosus" and says of Hugh that "scientia litterarum et humili religione maxime effloruit."

16. *Didascalicon* 5.8, ed. C. Buttimer (Washington, 1939), pp. 108-9.

17. For the history of the school see Bonnard, *Histoire* 1: 85-140, and J. Chatillon, "De Guillaume de Champeaux à Thomas Gallus: Chronique d'histoire littéraire et doctrinale de l'école de Saint-Victor," *Revue du moyen âge latin* 8 (1952): 139-62, 247-72. Also see the more recent interpretive studies by Chatillon, "Les Ecoles de Chartres et de Saint-Victor," in *La Scuola nell'occidente latino dell'alto medioevo*, Settimane di Studio del Centro Italiano di Studi sull'alto medioevo 19 (Spoleto, 1972), 2: 802-39; and by M. D. Chenu, "Civilisation urbaine et théologie: L'Ecole de Saint-Victor au XIIe siècle," *AESC* 29 (1974): 1253-63.

18. R. Baron, "L'Influence de Hugues de Saint-Victor," *RTAM* 22 (1955): 55.

19. The account is found in the letter that accompanies Lawrence's *reportatio* of the lectures on which Hugh based his important *Summa de sacramentis*. The letter has been edited by B. Bischoff, "Aus der Schule Hugos von St. Viktor," in A. Lang et al., *Aus der Geisteswelt des Mittelalters (BGPTM* Supplementband 3.1, Munster, 1935), pp. 246-50.

20. *Didascalicon*, ed. Buttimer, pp. 2-3.

21. See *The Didascalicon of Hugh of St. Victor*, trans. J. Taylor (New York, 1961), pp. 3-7, 28-36; G. M. Paré, A. Brunet, and P. Tremblay, *La Renaissance du douzième siècle: Les Ecoles et l'enseignement* (Paris and Ottawa, 1933), pp. 94-108.

22. *Didascalicon* 1.2, ed. Buttimer, p. 6. Hugh quotes Boethius, *In Porphyrium dialogi* 1.3.

23. *Didascalicon* 1.4, ed. Buttimer, p. 11; trans. Taylor, p. 51.

24. *Didascalicon* 1.5-11, ed. Buttimer, pp. 12-22.

25. *Hugonis de Sancto Victore Opera Propaedeutica*, ed. R. Baron (Notre Dame, 1966), pp. 193-94. This account of the origins of the arts is also found in an additional chapter included in some manuscripts of the *Didascalicon* and in Buttimer's edition (pp. 130-32).

26. See G. R. Evans, *Old Arts and New Theology: The Beginnings of Theology as an Academic Discipline* (Oxford, 1980), pp. 27-37.

27. *Didascalicon* 2.16, ed. Buttimer, p. 34. For the significance of Hugh's departure from the more traditional "Platonic" division of philosophy see M. T. d'Alverny, "La Sagesse et ses sept filles: Recherches sur les allégories de la philosophie et des arts libéraux du IXe au XIIe siècle," *Mélanges Felix Grat* (2 vols., Paris, 1946-49), 1: 246-378, and Chenu, "Civilisation urbaine et théologie," pp. 1256-60.

28. See, for example, William of Conches, *Philosophia seu Summa philosophiae*, ed. C. Ottaviano (Naples, 1935), pp. 24-28.

29. *Epitome Dindimi in philosophiam*, ed. Baron, pp. 201-2.

30. *Didascalicon* 2.17, ed. Buttimer, pp. 35-36. Cf. William of Conches, *De philosophia mundi*, *PL* 173, 43.

31. *Didascalicon* 3.3, ed. Buttimer, p. 53.

32. *Ibid.*, 3.4, p. 55; trans. Taylor, p. 89.

33. *Didascalicon* 3.3, ed. Buttimer, p. 53.

34. *Ibid.*, 3.4, pp. 54-55.

35. *Ibid.*, 3.5, pp. 55-56.

36. *Ibid.*, On the significance of Hugh's distinction between "agere *de* arte"

and "agere *per* artem," see R. W. Hunt, "The Introduction to the 'Artes' in the Twelfth Century," in *Studia mediaevalia in honorem admodum Reverendi Raymundi Josephi Martin* (Bruges, 1948), pp. 99*ff.*

37. See, for example, Adelard of Bath, *De eodem et diverso* (c. 1116), ed. H. Wilner, *BGPTM* 4.1 (1903): 17.

38. *Didascalicon* 3.6, ed. Buttimer, p. 57. The sources of this idea are discussed by Taylor, *Didascalicon*, p. 213, n. 49.

39. *Didascalicon* 3.12, ed. Buttimer, p. 62. Hugh attributes the lines to a "sapiens quidam." Cf. John of Salisbury, *Policraticus* 7.13, ed. C. C. J. Webb (2 vols., Oxford, 1909), 2: 145. The lines are also quoted anonymously in one of Peter Comestor's sermons to scholars, *Qui non humiliaverit, PL* 198, 1730D.

40. *Didascalicon* 3.13, ed. Buttimer, p. 62. Hugh's bitterness suggests that he himself might have felt betrayed by former students who claimed his authority for their erroneous opinions. Perhaps this explains why Hugh, as Lawrence of Westminster recounts, took such care correcting his students' notes.

41. *Historia calamitatum*, ed. Monfrin, pp. 68-69.

42. *Didascalicon* 3.13, ed. Buttimer, pp. 63-64. On the relationship between Peter Abelard and the school of St. Victor see D. Luscombe, *The School of Peter Abelard: The Influence of Abelard's Thought in the Early Scholastic Period* (Cambridge, 1969), pp. 183-97.

43. *Didascalicon* 3.18, ed. Buttimer, p. 69.

44. *Ibid.*, 3.19, p. 69. Hugh's discussion of the value of exile includes a rare autobiographical reference. For an interpretation of this reference and of Hugh's origins see J. Taylor, *The Origins and Early Life of Hugh of St. Victor: An Evaluation of the Tradition* Texts and Studies in Medieval Education 5 (Notre Dame, 1957), especially pp. 51-54.

45. Smalley, *Study of the Bible*, pp. 105-6.

46. *Didascalicon* 6.3, ed. Buttimer, p. 115.

47. See the valuable discussion of the sixth book of the *Didascalicon* in Paré et al., *La Renaissance*, pp. 218-29.

48. *Didascalicon* 5.3, ed. Buttimer, pp. 96-97. Cf. *De arca noe moralis, PL* 176, 674A. In *Didascalicon* 4.1, p. 70, Hugh compares Scripture to a honeycomb and the writings of the philosophers to a whitewashed wall of clay. Scripture, he insists (*Didascalicon* 5.7, p. 106), is not to be read as literature and judged by the "colore dictaminis" but should be studied for the correction of morals.

49. *Didascalicon* 5.10, ed. Buttimer, pp. 111-12.

50. *Richard de Saint-Victor Liber Exceptionum*, ed. J. Chatillon (Paris, 1958). Chatillon discusses the plan and scope of Richard's scholarship in detail in his excellent introduction, pp. 7-96. See also Smalley, *Study of the Bible*, pp. 106-11. On Richard's sermons and the importance of preaching at St. Victor see Chatillon, "Sermons et prédicateurs victorins de la seconde moitié du XIIe siècle," *AHDLMA* 40 (1965): 7-60.

51. Godfrey of St. Victor, *Fons philosophiae*, ed. P. Michaud-Quantin, in *Analecta mediaevalia Namurcensia* 8 (1956): 35-64; trans. E. A. Synan, *The Fountain of Philosophy* (Toronto, 1972).

52. *Fons philosophiae*, ll. 21-44, ed. Michaud-Quantin, p. 36. Cf. *Microcosmos* 1.55, ed. P. Delhaye (2 vols., Lille, 1951), 1: 73.

53. *Fons philosophiae*, ll. 97-128, ed. Michaud-Quantin, pp. 38-39.

54. *Ibid.*, ll. 148-52, p. 40.

55. *Ibid.*, ll. 246-76, pp. 43-44. Cf. John of Salisbury, *Metalogicon* 2.10, ed. C. C. J. Webb (Oxford, 1929), pp. 76-83.

56. *Fons philosophiae*, ll. 277-96, ed. Michaud-Quantin, pp. 44-45. Cf. John of Salisbury, *Metalogicon* 2.10 and 3.3, ed. Webb, pp. 81 and 134. On this school see L. Minio-Paluello, "The 'Ars disserendi' of Adam of Balsham 'Parvipontanus,'" *MRS* 3 (1954): 116-69.

57. *Fons philosophiae*, ll. 769-836, ed. Michaud-Quantin, pp. 62-64.

58. P. Glorieux, ed., "Le 'Contra quatuor labyrinthos Franciae' de Gauthier de Saint-Victor," *AHDLMA* 27 (1952): 187-335. On this treatise see P. Glorieux, "Mauvais Action et mauvais travail: Le 'Contra quatuor labyrinthos Franciae,'" *RTAM* 21 (1954): 179-93. It is useful to compare Walter's treatise to the more moderate criticism of the teaching of the time made by his more learned contemporary John of Cornwall, *Eulogium ad Alexandrum III papam quod Christus sit aliquis homo*, ed. N. M. Häring in *Mediaeval Studies* 13 (1951): 253-300. Still, the common charge that Walter was totally ignorant of scholastic theology requires revision, in light of the evidence recently made available by Jean Chatillon's edition of twenty-one of his sermons: *Galteri a Sancto Victore et quorundam aliorum sermones ineditos* (Turnholt, 1975), pp. 11-185.

59. See especially *Contra quatuor labyrinthos Franciae* 4.1, ed. Glorieux, p. 270.

60. It was while he was away from St. Victor that Godfrey wrote his other major treatise, the *Microcosmos*. See *Le Microcosmos de Godfrey de Saint-Victor*, ed. P. Delhaye (2 vols., Lille, 1951).

61. Boussard, *Nouvelle Histoire de Paris*, pp. 229-30. On Absalon of St. Victor see P. Courcelle, "La Culture antique d'Absalon de Saint-Victor," *Journal des savants* (1972): 270-91. On Thomas Gallus see G. Théry, "Thomas Gallus, aperçu biographique," *AHDLMA* 12 (1939): 141-208, and J. Chatillon, "De Guillaume de Champeaux à Thomas Gallus," pp. 268-72.

CHAPTER THREE

1. Bernard of Clairvaux, *Ad clericos de conversione* 21.37, ed. J. Leclercq and H. Rochais, *S. Bernardi opera*, vol. 4 (Rome, 1966), p. 113.

2. Geoffrey of Auxerre, *De vita et miraculis S. Bernardi* 49, ed. R. Lechat, *Analecta Bollandiana* 50 (1932): 115-16. Cf. *S. Bernardi vita prima* 7.13, *PL* 185, 423-44.

3. On Bernard's activities during these years see E. Vacandard, *Vie de Saint Bernard* (2 vols., Paris, 1920), 1: 282-91 and 2: 1-69. On the politics of the schism, see H.-W. Klewitz, "Das ende des Reformpapsttums," *Deutsches Archiv* 3 (1939): 371-412; reprinted in *Reformpapsttums und Kardinalkolleg* (Darmstadt, 1957), pp. 207-53.

4. Ep. 372, *PL* 182, 533AB.

5. Abelard refers to Bernard's visit in a letter written to his disciples sometime before the Council of Sens. The letter has been edited by R. Klibansky, "Peter Abailard and Bernard of Clairvaux: A Letter by Abailard," *MRS* 5 (1961): 6-7.

6. "Exemplo sit sancti Bernardi, qui cum scolas logice Parisius ingressus fuisset, aliquos scolares deo lucraturus, post disputationem rogavit eum magister ut determinaret. Cum tamen in scolis nunquam audisset, respondit: 'Audite, qualiter deus contra vos argumentatur. Ipse quidem proponit vobis legem, assumit transgressionem, concludet penam eternam, argumentando in hunc modum: "Lex quam dedi tibi, dicit non peccabis. Tu autem huius precepti prevaricator es,

ergo tu dampnaberis"'" (Jacques of Vitry, *Cum egrediemini*, MS. Paris BN lat. 17509, f. 32rb).

7. This is suggested by C. E. Du Boulay (Bulaeus), *Historia Universitatis Parisiensis a Carolo Magno ad nostra tempora* (6 vols., Paris, 1665-73), 2: 10-11.

8. J. Leclercq, *The Love of Learning and the Desire for God*, 2d ed., trans. C. Misrahi (New York, 1974).

9. See U. Berlière, "Ecoles claustrales au moyen âge," *Bulletin de l'Académie Royale de Belgique, Classe des Lettres*, 5th ser. 7 (1921): 551.

10. M. Gibson, *Lanfranc of Bec* (Oxford, 1978), pp. 34-38; R. W. Southern, *Saint Anselm and His Biographer* (Cambridge, 1963), pp. 30-34, 194-204.

11. On this legislation see E. Lesne, *Histoire de la propriété ecclésiastique en France*, vol. 5: *Les Ecoles de la fin du VIIIe siècle à la fin du XIIe siècle* (Lille, 1940), pp. 1-27.

12. Peter Damian praises Abbot Desiderius for closing the "school for boys" (*PL* 145, 621). On the school of Monte Cassino at this time see H. Bloch, "Monte Cassino's Teachers and Library in the High Middle Ages," in *La Scuola nell'occidente latino dell'alto medioevo*, Settimane di Studio del Centro Italiano di Studi sull'alto medioevo 19 (Spoleto, 1972), 2: 582-605.

13. J.-M. Canivez, ed., *Statuta capitulorum generalium ordinis Cisterciensis 1116-1220*, vol. 1 (Louvain, 1936), 1134.78, p. 31.

14. *Gesta abbatum Lobbensium MGH SS* 21: 327; Lesne, *Les Ecoles*, pp. 362-64.

15. See Uldaric of Cluny, *Antiquiores consuetudines Cluniacensis monasterii* 3.8, *PL* 149, 742C, and N. Hunt, *Cluny Under Saint Hugh, 1049-1109* (Notre Dame, 1968), pp. 96-99.

16. *Gesta abbatum Lobbensium, MGH SS* 21: 327.

17. Several examples are cited by P. Riché in his article, "L'Enfant dans la société monastique au XIIe siècle," *Pierre Abélard—Pierre le Vénérable: Les Courants philosophiques, littéraires et artistiques en occident au milieu du XIIe siècle* (Paris, 1975), pp. 692-93. See also Berlière, "Ecoles claustrales," pp. 570-72, and Lesne, *Les Ecoles*, pp. 432-41, 450-52. A notable example is provided by the life of a certain Abundus (d. 1228), who had been sent as a boy to the Cistercian house in Villers-en-Brabant to study mathematics and who, contrary to the wishes of his merchant father, chose to enter the order (*Ex gestis sanctorum Villariensium, MGH SS* 25, 232; discussed by H. Pirenne, "L'Instruction des marchands au moyen âge," *AESC* 1 [1929]: 20-21).

18. For recent assessments of this activity see J. Leclercq, "The Renewal of Theology," in R. L. Benson and G. Constable, eds., *Renaissance and Renewal in the Twelfth Century* (Cambridge, Mass., 1982), pp. 68-87; and the studies in M. B. Pennington, ed., *One Yet Two: The Monastic Tradition, East and West* (Kalamazoo, 1976).

19. Geoffrey of Auxerre, *De vita et miraculis S. Bernardi* 10, ed. Lechat, pp. 93-94. Cf. *Vita prima* 3.9, *PL* 185, 231D.

20. Vacandard, *Vie de Saint Bernard* 1: 35-63.

21. *Dialogus* 2.prol., *PL* 66, 128A. On the importance in the monastic tradition of this account of Benedict's conversion see Leclercq, *The Love of Learning*, pp. 13-30. The enduring influence of Benedict's example is evident in the life of Arnulfus, abbot of the Cistercian house of Villers-en-Brabant from 1271 to 1276, who, we are told, chose to enter the cloister rather than to study at the University of Paris "in imitation of the example of St. Benedict, who, abandoning school,

consecrated himself entirely to the religious life" (*Chronica Villariensis*, *MGH SS* 25, 210).

22. *Regulam S. Benedicti*, preface.

23. Ep. 106, *PL* 182, 242A.

24. Ep. 412, *PL* 182, 621D.

25. Ep. 327, *PL* 182, 533AB.

26. See E. T. Little, "Relations Between St. Bernard and Abelard Before 1139," in M. B. Pennington, ed., *Saint Bernard of Clairvaux: Studies Commemorating the Eighth Centenary of His Canonization* (Kalamazoo, 1977), pp. 155-68; and A. Borst, "Abailard und Bernard," *Historische Zeitschrift* 186 (1958): 497-526.

27. These meetings are mentioned in a letter from the French episcopacy to Innocent II reporting on the events of the Council of Sens (Ep. 337, *PL* 182, 541B).

28. According to the *Vita prima* 3.5, *PL* 185, 311, Bernard had been benevolent and Abelard repentant. Abelard writes, in his letter to his disciples (Klibansky, "Peter Abailard," p. 6), that Bernard had pretended to be a "very good friend" (*amicissimus*).

29. *Contra quedam capitula errorum Abaelardi*, Ep. 90, *PL* 182, 1053-72.

30. Klibansky, "Peter Abailard," pp. 6-7.

31. Ep. 188, *PL* 182, 353AB.

32. Ep. 332, *PL* 182, 537C.

33. Ep. 193, *PL* 182, 359B.

34. Ep. 332, *PL* 182, 537D-538A.

35. Ep. 189, *PL* 182, 355D.

36. Ep. 187, *PL* 182, 349-50.

37. For an analysis of these nineteen propositions and of the issues of the conflict see E. T. Little, "Bernard and Abelard at the Council of Sens," in *Bernard of Clairvaux: Studies Presented to Dom Jean Leclercq* (Washington, D.C., 1973), pp. 55-71.

38. William of St. Thierry's letter is printed among those of Bernard of Clairvaux (Ep. 326, *PL* 182, 532A).

39. Ep. 190, *PL* 182, 1055-56, 1061-62. See A. Victor Murray, *Abelard and St. Bernard: A Study in Twelfth Century "Modernism"* (Manchester, 1967), pp. 72-88.

40. See G. R. Evans, *Old Arts and New Theology: The Beginnings of Theology as an Academic Discipline* (Oxford, 1980), pp. 79-90.

41. The letter begins, "Habemus in Francia novum de veteri magistro theologum" (1055A). Mockery pervades throughout, as in the outburst, "O alterum Aristotelem!" (1059B).

42. Ep. 337, *PL* 182, 540CD.

43. Ep. 338, *PL* 182, 543A.

44. Ep. 192, *PL* 182, 358D-359A; Ep. 330, 536A; Ep. 331, 537A; Ep. 332, 538A; Ep. 336, 540A; and Ep. 338, 543D.

45. Ep. 330, *PL* 182, 536B; Ep. 336, 540A; and Ep. 338, 543D.

46. Ep. 330, *PL* 182, 536B.

47. Ep. 189, *PL* 182, 354CD; Ep. 330, 535D.

48. The papal bulls can be found in *PL* 179, 515-17.

49. See D. Luscombe, *The School of Peter Abelard: The Influence of Abelard's Thought in the Early Scholastic Period* (Cambridge, 1969), pp. 14-59.

50. On Gilbert's association with Paris see above, pp. 22-24. On Gilbert's teaching and the Council of Reims see A. Hayen, "Le Concile de Reims et l'erreur théologique de Gilbert de la Porrée," *AHDLMA* 10-11 (1935-36): 29-102, and the articles cited in n. 62 below.

51. *Vita prima*, *PL* 185, 312.

52. *Historia pontificalis*, ed. and trans. M. Chibnall (London, 1956), pp. 15-28.
53. *Ibid.*, cap. 8, p. 16.
54. *Ibid.*
55. *Ibid.*, cap. 8, pp. 17-18.
56. *Ibid.*, cap. 9, pp. 19-20; translation mine.
57. *Gesta Friderici* 1.48-61, ed. G. Waitz (Hannover and Leipzig, 1912), pp. 74-88.
58. *Ibid.*, 1.60; trans. C. C. Mierow, *The Deeds of Frederick Barbarossa* (New York, 1963), p. 99.
59. *Historia pontificalis* cap. 12, ed. Chibnall, pp. 26-27; *Gesta Friderici* 1.61, ed. Waitz, p. 88.
60. *Gesta Friderici* 1.52; trans. Mierow, p. 88.
61. *Ibid.*
62. For other views of the significance of the conflict between Bernard and Gilbert see N. Häring, "The Case of Gilbert de la Porrée, Bishop of Poitiers," *Mediaeval Studies* 13 (1951): 1-40, and J. Leclercq, "Textes de Saint Bernard and Gilbert de la Porrée," *Mediaeval Studies* 14 (1952): 106-28.
63. See G. Constable, "Twelfth Century Spirituality and the Late Middle Ages," *MRS* 5 (1971): 27-60.
64. See J. Chatillon, "L'Influence de S. Bernard sur la pensée scolastique aux XIIe et XIIIe siècles," *Analecta sacri ordinis Cisterciensis* 9 (1953): 270-71; and J. R. Sommerfeldt, "Bernard of Clairvaux and Scholasticism," *Papers of the Michigan Academy of Sciences, Arts and Letters* 48 (1963): 265-77.
65. Ep. 205, *PL* 182, 372-73.
66. B. Smalley, *The Becket Conflict and the Schools* (Oxford, 1973), pp. 40-42.
67. Ep. 250, *PL* 182, 450.
68. Ep. 250, *PL* 182, 451A.
69. *Sermones in Cantica canticorum* 36.2, ed. J. Leclercq and H. Rochais, *S. Bernardi opera*, vol. 2 (Rome, 1958), p. 4. See Chatillon, "L'Influence de S. Bernard," pp. 272-74.
70. *Sermones in Cantica* 36.3, ed. Leclercq and Rochais, pp. 5-6.
71. *Ad clericos de conversione* 17.30, ed. Leclercq and Rochais, pp. 106-7.
72. Notably absent from this list and chapter is the great English Cistercian evangelist, St. Aelred of Rievaulx. He was little concerned with the schools, though in a treatise to his sister on the religious life he does state his opposition to public teaching within the cloister (*De institutione inclusarum*, ed. C. Dumont [Paris, 1976], p. 52).
73. See pp. 202-3.
74. J. Leclercq, "Virgile en enfer d'après un manuscrit d'Aulne," *Latomus* 17 (1953): 731-36. For several examples of similar visitations in the eleventh century see R. I. Moore, *The Origins of European Dissent* (New York, 1977), pp. 23-24.
75. Caesarius of Heisterbach, *Dialogus miraculorum* 1.32, ed. B. Strange (2 vols., Cologne, 1851), 1: 36-38.
76. J. Leclercq, "Lettres de vocation à la vie monastique," *Analecta monastica* 3d ser. 37 (1955): 169-97.
77. Ep. 2, *PL* 184, 293.
78. Ep. 2, *PL* 184, 294.
79. On Isaac of Stella see L. Bouyer, *The Cistercian Heritage*, trans. E. A. Livingstone (Westminster, Md., 1958), pp. 161-89, and the introduction to the

first volume of the (still incomplete) edition of Isaac's sermons by A. Hoste and G. Salet, *Isaac de l'Etoile, Sermons* (Paris, 1967), pp. 7-63. Cf. the interpretation of Isaac's career advanced by G. Raciti, "Isaac de l'Etoile et son siècle," *Cîteaux* 12 (1961): 281-306 and 13 (1962): 19-34, 133-45, 205-16.

80. Sermo 48, ed. Raciti, p. 288.

81. Isaac criticizes the monks for being "curiosi auditores" (*ibid.*).

82. Sermo 48, ed. Raciti, p. 289.

83. *Ibid.*, p. 290.

84. Isaac writes, "*Instabant*, igitur, *tempora periculosa* (2 Tim. 2.1), et intrabunt subversores veritatis scripturarum dicta suis sensibus accommodantes, quibus hec nostra licentiosa libertas fore poterit pernitiosa auctoritas" (Sermo 48, ed. Raciti, p. 290). Raciti ("Isaac de L'Etoile et son siècle," p. 297) argues that Isaac was almost certainly present at the Council of Reims.

My interpretation of this sermon differs from that of Raciti (*ibid.*, pp. 19-34), who dates the work to 1166 and argues that the leaders of the Cistercian order, led by Geoffrey of Auxerre, Bernard's biographer and successor as abbot of Clairvaux, forced Isaac to change his teaching amidst the Christological controversies that raged after the death of Peter Lombard.

85. See Leclercq, "The Renewal of Theology," pp. 74-87.

86. William of St. Thierry's education remains an issue of controversy. The argument that he studied at Laon was advanced by J.-M. Dechanet, *Guillaume de Saint-Thierry, l'homme et son oeuvre* (Bruges, 1942), pp. 10-15, and in his article, "L'Amitié d'Abélard et de Guillaume de Saint-Thierry," *RHE* 35 (1939): 762-67. Cf. the views first advanced by M.-M. Davy in the introduction to her translation of the *Epistola ad fratres Monte Dei: Un Traité de la vie solitaire* (Paris, 1946), pp. 17-18, and more recently in the unpublished doctoral dissertation of S. Ceglar, "William of St. Thierry: The Chronology of His Life" (The Catholic University of America, Washington, D.C., 1971). See also J. Leclercq, "Etudes récents sur Guillaume de Saint-Thierry," *Bulletin de la Société Internationale pour l'Histoire de la Philosophie Médiévale* 19 (1977): 49-55.

87. Ep. 326, *PL* 182, 532A.

88. *Disputatio adversus Petrum Abaelardum*, *PL* 180, 249B.

89. *Ibid.*

90. *Ibid.*, *PL* 180, 250A.

91. *Ibid.*, *PL* 180, 269C.

92. *Ibid.*, *PL* 180, 269D-270A.

93. *De erroribus Guillelmi de Conchis*, *PL* 180, 334A. Cf. William of Conches, *Philosophia seu Summa philosophiae*, ed. C. Ottaviano (Naples, 1935).

94. *De erroribus Guillelmi de Conchis*, *PL* 180, 334BC.

95. *Deux Traités sur la foi*, ed. M.-M. Davy (Paris, 1959), pp. 24-91.

96. On William of St. Thierry's theology see M.-M. Davy, *Théologie et mystique de Guillaume de Saint-Thierry*, vol. 1: *La Connaissance de Dieu* (Paris, 1954). On the *Aenigma fidei* see also M.-M. Davy, "La Connaissance de Dieu d'après Guillaume de Saint-Thierry," *Recherches de science religieuse* 28 (1938): 430-56; and E. R. Elder, "William of St. Thierry: Rational and Affective Theology," in E. Elder et al., eds., *The Spirituality of Western Christendom* (Kalamazoo, 1976), pp. 85-105.

97. *Aenigma fidei* 41, ed. M.-M. Davy, *Deux Traités sur la foi* (Paris, 1959), p. 128.

98. *Ibid.*, 40-52, pp. 126-38.
99. *Ibid.*, 47, p. 132.
100. *De sacramentis altaris* cap. 11, *PL* 180, 359A-360B.
101. See Dechanet, "L'Amitié d'Abélard et de Guillaume de Saint-Thierry," pp. 769-73. William explicitly names and condemns Abelard's *Sic et non* in his letter to Bernard of Clairvaux (Ep. 326, *PL* 182, 532D-533A).
102. *Expositio super Cantica canticorum*, *PL* 180, 504C. Cf. his *De natura et dignitate amoris* 25, in M.-M. Davy, ed., *Deux Traités de l'amour de Dieu* (Paris, 1953), p. 100.
103. See *De natura et dignitate amoris* 31, ed. Davy, p. 110. Cf. *Epistola ad fratres Monte Dei* 32-34, ed. M.-M. Davy (Paris, 1940), pp. 86-89.
104. Sermo 1 (in festo S. Benedicti), *PL* 185, 101BC.
105. See the survey of the use of the term *philosophia* in J. Leclercq's *Etudes sur la vocabulaire monastique du moyen âge* (Rome, 1961), pp. 39-67, 156-57, as well as the same author's article, "Maria christianorum philosophia," *Mélanges des sciences religieuses* 13 (1956): 102-5, and H. Rochais, "Ipsa philosophia Christus," *Mediaeval Studies* 13 (1951): 244-47.
106. Ep. 75, *PL* 202, 522C.
107. Letter 144 in *The Letters of Peter the Venerable*, ed. G. Constable (2 vols., Cambridge, Mass., 1967), 1: 354.
108. Letter 115, ed. Constable 1: 306.
109. On Guerric of Igny's life see P. R. Milcamps and P. A. Dubois, "Le Bienheureux Guerric: Sa Vie, son oeuvre," *COCR* 19 (1957): 207-71.
110. *PL* 185, 1-214.
111. Sermo 1 (in festo S. Benedicti), *PL* 185, 99-103. See J. Leclercq, "Guerric et l'école monastique," *COCR* 19 (1957): 238-48.
112. On Adam of Perseigne's life see J. Bouvet, "Biographie d'Adam de Perseigne," *COCR* 20 (1958): 16-26, 145-52.
113. Bouvet, "Biographie d'Adam de Perseigne," p. 17.
114. *Historia Occidentalis* cap. 9, ed. J. F. Hinnebusch (Fribourg, 1972), pp. 102-3.
115. Thirty of these letters are found in *PL* 211, 583-694. The remaining letters, as well as emendations of those printed by Migne in the *PL*, have been edited by J. Bouvet in ten fascicules of the *Archives historiques de Maine*, vol. 13 (1951-61). A complete critical edition of the letters in chronological order and with a French translation is being published by J. Bouvet in *Sources chrétiennes* (Paris, 1960-).
116. The others, according to Jacques of Vitry, were Masters Stephen Langton, Walter of London, Robert of Courson, Alberic of Laon, John of Liro, and John of Nivelles.
117. Ep. 1, *PL* 211, 666-68; ed. Bouvet, *Archives*, fasc. 1 (1951), pp. 12-17.
118. Ep. 1, *PL* 211, 666; ed. Bouvet, *Archives*, fasc. 1 (1951), p. 15.
119. Ep. 1, *PL* 211, 667A-668A; ed. Bouvet, *Archives*, fasc. 1 (1951), p. 16.
120. Ep. 36 (13), Adam de Perseigne, *Lettres*, vol. 1, ed. J. Bouvet (Paris, 1960), p. 200.
121. Ep. 35 (11), ed. Bouvet, *Lettres* 1: 180-93.
122. Ep. 36 (13), ed. Bouvet, *Lettres* 1: 200-202.
123. Ep. 67, ed. Bouvet, *Archives*, fasc. 10 (1961), p. 614.
124. *Ibid.*, p. 616.

125. *Ibid.*, p. 613.

126. "Nunc autem in schola Christi potes videri Christi auditores" (*Ibid.*, p. 615).

127. Ep. 30, ed. Bouvet, *Archives*, fasc. 5 (1955), pp. 215-31.

128. *Ibid.*, p. 224.

129. See B. Lohr, "The Philosophical Life According to Adam of Perseigne," *COCR* 24 (1962): 225-42.

130. "Un Sermon inédit d'Adam de Perseigne," ed. D. Matthieu, *COCR* 4 (1937): 106-11, 194-99.

131. *Ibid.*, p. 107. Cf. Guerric of Igny, Sermo 1 (in festo S. Benedicti), *PL* 185, 99-103.

132. "Un Sermon inédit," ed. Matthieu, p. 108.

133. *Ibid.*

134. *Ibid.*, p. 109.

135. *Ibid.*, p. 198.

136. *Ibid.*

137. *Ibid.*, p. 199.

138. Leclercq, *The Love of Learning*, p. 251.

139. See above, p. 25.

140. Ep. 73, *PL* 202, 520; *CUP* 1.intro. no. 22, p. 24.

141. Sermo 12, *PL* 202, 670A.

142. Sermo 86, *PL* 202, 898CD.

143. *Mosaici tabernaculi mystica et moralis expositio*, *PL* 202, 1059A.

144. *De disciplina claustrali*, ed. G. de Martel (Paris, 1977), pp. 152-54.

145. Ep. 7, *PL* 203, 58D-59A.

146. *Ibid.*, 59B.

147. For Philip of Harvengt's praise of Paris see Ep. 3, *PL* 203, 31D; *CUP* 1.intro. no. 51, p. 50, and Ep. 20, *PL* 203, 165D; and *CUP* 1.intro. no. 52, p. 51. For his view of the value of studying the liberal arts see Ep. 4, *PL* 203, 32-34; *CUP* 1.intro. no. 53, pp. 53-55. For another interpretation of the significance of Philip's favorable attitudes toward the schools see J. LeGoff, "How Did the Medieval University Conceive of Itself?" in *Time, Work and Culture in the Middle Ages*, trans. A. Goldhammer (Chicago, 1980), pp. 126-27.

148. In addition to Philip's letters see his treatise *De institutione clericorum* caps. 23-32, *PL* 203, 693-708.

149. *De institutione clericorum* cap. 30, *PL* 203, 703D.

150. See *Decretum* 2.7, q.1, *PL* 187, 765A. Although this decree does not explicitly mention canons regular, the closing of the school at St. Victor is probably a good indication of the prevailing attitude to public teaching in Augustinian houses.

151. A. L. Gabriel, "The Role of the Canons of Prémontré in the Intellectual Movements of the Twelfth and Thirteenth Centuries," in *Gedenkboek Ordre von Prémontré, 1121-1171* (Averbode, 1971), p. 204. On the attitudes of the Premonstratensians to the schools, see also J. F. Murphy, "The Premonstratensian Canons in the Renaissance Century," *Analecta Praemonstratensia* 23 (1957): 259-67.

152. The statutes promulgated by Robert of Courson at the Councils of Paris (1213) and Rouen (1214) are discussed below, pp. 303-4.

CHAPTER FOUR

1. Alexander Murray, *Reason and Society in the Middle Ages* (Oxford, 1978), p. 220.

2. Guibert of Nogent, *De vita sua* 1.4, ed. G. Bourgin (Paris, 1907), pp. 12-13.

3. John of Salisbury, *Metalogicon* 1.2, ed. C. C. J. Webb (Oxford, 1929), p. 9.

4. Murray, *Reason and Society*, pp. 292-312.

5. Walter of Châtillon, *Stulti cum prudentibus* 4, ed. Karl Strecker, *Moralisch-Satirische Gedichte Walters von Châtillon* (Heidelberg, 1929), no. 4, p. 64. Cf. Juvenal, *Satires* 1.30.

6. On the connections between the revival of satire and the Gregorian Reform see H. Schüppert, *Kirchencritik in der lateinische Lyrik des 12. und 13. Jahrhunderts*, Medium Aevum Philologische Studien 23 (Munich, 1972), and J. A. Yunck, *The Lineage of Lady Meed: The Development of Medieval Venality Satire* (Notre Dame, 1963), pp. 45-99. Also useful in showing the impact of the reform on thought and expression is K. J. Leyser, "The Polemics of Papal Revolution," in B. Smalley, ed., *Trends in Medieval Political Thought* (Oxford, 1965), pp. 42-64.

7. On Walter's career see F. J. E. Raby, *A History of Secular Latin Poetry in the Middle Ages*, 2d ed. (2 vols., Oxford, 1957), 2: 190-204; Schüppert, *Kirchencritik*, pp. 29-30; and J. Hillegouarc'h, "Un Poète latin du XIIe siècle: Gautier de Lille, dit Gautier de Châtillon," *Bulletin de l'Association Guillaume Budé* 4th ser. 1 (1967): 95-115.

8. *Dilatatur inpii* 8, ed. Strecker, no. 9, p. 106.

9. *A la feste* 13, ed. Strecker, no. 13, p. 125.

10. *Felix erat studium*, ed. Strecker, no. 11, pp. 113-15.

11. *Tanto viro locuturi* 14, ed. Strecker, no. 1, p. 8.

12. *Ibid.*, 17, p. 8.

13. *Ibid.*, 27, p. 13.

14. *Missus sum in vineam*, ed. Strecker, no. 6, pp. 82-88.

15. *Felix erat studium* 14, ed. Strecker, p. 115: "Superficietenus libri nunc leguntur, / et magistri nomine plures abutuntur."

16. *Stulti cum prudentibus* 26-28, ed. Strecker, no. 4, pp. 69-70. Walter's criticism of the schools of France for teaching young nobles the vice of homosexuality echoes Juvenal's second satire, especially his attack on the corrupting influence of Rome on the morality of youth (ll. 160-70).

17. *Inter curas hominum* 2, ed. Strecker, no. 7a, p. 97.

18. *In domino confido*, ed. Strecker, no. 3, pp. 38-52.

19. *Ibid.*, 4, p. 40.

20. *Ibid.*, 6-14, pp. 41-43.

21. *Ibid.*, 18, p. 44.

22. *Ibid.*, 20, p. 45.

23. *Ibid.*, 24-33, pp. 46-49.

24. On Peter the Painter see Raby, *Secular Latin Poetry* 2: 26-30. His poems were first identified by Hauréau, *N&E* 5 (1891): 211-38. Other poems of Peter's have been edited by C. Fierville, "Notices et extraits des manuscrits de la Bibliothèque de Saint-Omer, nos. 113 et 710," *Notices et extraits des manuscrits de la Bibliothèque Nationale et autres bibliothèques* 31 (1884): 129-32; J. Werner, *Beiträge zur Kunde der lateinischen Literatur des Mittelalters* (Aarau, 1905), pp. 139*ff*; and A. Boutemy, "Quelques Oeuvres inédites de Pierre le Peintre," *Latomus* 7 (1948): 51-69.

25. *Cur ultra studeam?*, ed. Werner, pp. 139-41.

26. *Temporibus nostris mutari*, ed. Fierville, pp. 130-32.

27. Raby, *Secular Latin Poetry* 2: 171-80; Wilhelm Meyer, *Die Oxforder Gedichte des Primas* (Göttingen, 1907; reprint ed., Darmstadt, 1970). Typical of Hugh of

Orléans's attacks on patrons are *Egregius dedit hanc*, ed. Meyer, no. 19, pp. 35-40, and *Vir pietatis inops*, ed. Meyer, no. 15, pp. 77-79.

28. *Ambianis, urbs predives*, ll. 31-56, ed. Meyer, no. 18, pp. 27-28; trans. H. Wieruszowski, *The Medieval University* (Princeton, 1966), pp. 134-35.

29. *Ambianus, urbs predives*, ll. 58-62, ed. Meyer, no. 18, p. 28.

30. *Ibid.*, ll. 94-117, p. 29. Cf. the interpretation of Raby, *Secular Latin Poetry* 2: 178-79.

31. *Metamorphosis Goliae* 56-57, ed. R. B. C. Huygens, *Studi medievali* ser. 3, 3.2 (1962): 771-72. On the interpretation of this poem see J. Benton, "Philology's Search for Abelard," *Speculum* 50 (1975): 199-217; and Winthrop Wetherbee, *Platonism and Poetry in the Twelfth Century: The Literary Influence of the School of Chartres* (Princeton, 1972), pp. 127-34. Both argue that the bride searching for Abelard is Philology. Cf. P. Dronke, *Abelard and Heloise in Medieval Testimonies* (Glasgow, 1976), pp. 16-18, who persists in the traditional view that the bride is Heloise.

32. K. Strecker, *Die Apocalypse des Golias* (Rome and Leipzig, 1925). On the interpretation of this obscure poem see Raby, *Secular Latin Poetry* 2: 214-19, and F. X. Newman, "The Structure of Vision in 'Apocalypsis Goliae,'" *Mediaeval Studies* 29 (1967): 113-23.

33. *Ut veram fatear*, ed. A. Wilmart, "Le Florilège mixte de Thomas Bekynton," *MRS* 4 (1958): 83-84.

34. A critical edition of the poem was published by K. Strecker, "Quid dant artes nisi luctum!" *Studi medievali* new ser. 1 (1928): 386-91. See also the valuable study of the poem's concluding line by S. Kuttner, "Dat Galienus opes et sanctio Justiniana," in A. B. Crisafalli, ed., *Linguistic and Literary Studies in Honor of Helmut S. Hatzfeld* (Washington, D.C., 1964), pp. 238-46.

35. *Meum est propositum* 8, ed. Strecker, p. 387.

36. *De palpone et assentatore*, ed. T. Wright, *Latin Poems Commonly Attributed to Walter Map* (London, 1841), pp. 106-30.

37. *Mundus a munditia* 8, ed. G. M. Dreves et al., *Analecta hymnica medii aevi* 21 (Leipzig, 1895), no. 206, p. 144. On Philip of Grève's poetry and career see Raby, *Secular Latin Poetry* 2: 227-35, and Schüppert, *Kirchencritik*, pp. 44-46.

38. *Si mundus viveret* 5, ed. Dreves et al., no. 214, p. 150.

39. *Veritas, aequitas* 5.2-3, ed. Dreves et al., no. 184, p. 128.

40. *De Artium conditione*, ed. Dreves et al., no. 230, p. 161.

41. *Sepe de miseria*, ed. A. Hilka and O. Schumann, *Carmina Burana* (Heidelberg, 1931) 1.3, no. 220, pp. 77-78. Cf. Abelard's account of the opening of his school at the Paraclete in the *Historia calamitatum*, ed. J. Monfrin (Paris, 1967), p. 94: "Tunc autem precipue ad scolarum regimen intolerabilis me compulit paupertas, cum 'fodere non valerem et mendicare erubescerem' [cf. Luke 16.3]. Ad artem itaque quam noveram recurrens, pro labore manuum ad officium lingue compulsus sum." On the Archpoet see Raby, *Secular Latin Poetry* 2: 180-89, and on the social background of him and other goliards P. Dronke, *The Medieval Lyric*, 2d ed. (Cambridge, 1977), pp. 21-22.

42. C. H. Haskins drew on these letters for his article "The Life of Medieval Students as Illustrated in Their Letters," *AHR* 3 (1897): 203-29.

43. *Exul ego clericus*, ed. Hilka and Schumann, 1.2, no. 129, p. 214. Other examples include *Artifex qui condidit* and *Sacerdotes et levite*, *ibid.*, nos. 224 and 225. Cf. *Ecce homo sine domo*, ed. Hauréau, *N&E* 6 (1893): 318.

44. P. Lehmann, ed., *Parodistische Texte* no. 19 (Munich, 1923), pp. 70-72. On

the origins and uses of medieval parody see P. Lehmann, *Die Parodie im Mittelalter* (Munich, 1922).

45. *Evvangelium*, ed. Lehmann, p. 71.

46. *Ibid.*

47. *Ibid.*

48. *Ibid.*, p. 72.

49. *Ibid.*

50. "Hinc nimirum studia sequi mente pura, . . . quod sola pauperies vita sit secura" (*Felix erat studium* 3, ed. Strecker, no. 11, p. 113).

51. *In sublimi solio*, ed. Hauréau, *N&E* 6 (1893): 306-8.

52. There are two nineteenth-century editions of *Hora nona sabbati*: Hauréau, *N&E* 6 (1893): 310-17, and Wright, *Latin Poems*, pp. 251-57.

53. *Hora nona sabbati* 8, ed. Hauréau, p. 311.

54. *Ibid.*, 14, p. 312.

55. *Ibid.*, 40, p. 315.

56. *Ibid.*, 53, p. 317.

57. The *Geta* has been critically edited by E. Guilhou and printed in G. Cohen, *La "Comédie" latine en France au douzième siècle* (2 vols., Paris, 1931), 1: 1-57 (with a French translation), and, more recently, by K. Bate, *Three Latin Comedies* (Toronto, 1976), pp. 15-34.

58. *Geta*, ll. 155-65, ed. Bate, pp. 20-21.

59. *Ibid.*, l. 231, p. 24.

60. *Ibid.*, ll. 385-95, pp. 29-30.

61. *Ibid.*, l. 429, p. 31.

62. *Ibid.*, ll. 443-50, pp. 31-32.

63. Cf. the view of Raby, *Secular Latin Poetry* 2: 58.

64. On John of Hauteville see Raby, *Secular Latin Poetry* 2: 100-102, and the introduction to the critical edition of the poem by P. G. Schmidt, *Johannes de Hauvilla Architrenius* (Munich, 1974), pp. 14-117.

65. *Architrenius*, ed. Schmidt, pp. 163-77.

66. *Ibid.*, 3.17, l. 341, p. 173.

67. *Ibid.*, 3.21, ll. 401-3, p. 175.

68. *Ibid.*, 5.3, ll. 72-84, pp. 198-99.

69. Cf. the *Anticlaudianus* of Alan of Lille, which probably inspired John of Hauteville's *Architrenius*. See the pertinent remarks of J. J. Sheridan in the introduction to his translation of the *Anticlaudianus* (Toronto, 1973), pp. 24-38. Other sources and influences are discussed by Schmidt, intro. to *Architrenius*, pp. 52*ff.*

70. The *Speculum stultorum* was first printed by T. Wright ed., *Anglo-Latin Satirical Poets and Epigrammatists of the Twelfth Century*, Roll Series 59 (2 vols., London, 1872), 1: 3-145. This has been superseded by the new critical edition of J. H. Mozley and R. R. Raymo, *Nigel de Longchamps, Speculum Stultorum* (Berkeley, 1970). There are also two good English translations of the poem: G. W. Regenos, *The Book of Daun Brunel the Ass* (Austin, 1959), and J. H. Mozley, *A Mirror for Fools* (Notre Dame, 1963).

71. *Speculum stultorum*, ll. 1178-96, ed. Mozley and Raymo, p. 57.

72. Jacques of Vitry, *Proverbium est* (*ad pueros et adolescentes*), MS. Paris BN lat. 17509, f. 150va.

73. *Speculum stultorum*, ll. 1199-1220, ed. Mozley and Raymo, pp. 57-58.

74. *Ibid.*, ll. 1521-30, p. 65. In the schools, the English had already acquired a reputation for drinking, as John of Salisbury notes in another of his letters to Peter of Celle: "Ceterum novit experientia vestra, 'quia non in solo pane vivit homo,' et quod potationis assiduitas apud extera nationes Anglos insignes" (Letter 33, *The Letters of John of Salisbury*, ed. and trans. W. J. Millor, H. E. Bulter, and C. N. L. Brooke [2 vols., London, 1955; Oxford, 1979], 1: 56-57).

75. *Speculum stultorum*, ll. 1573-74, ed. Mozley and Raymo, p. 66.
76. *Ibid.*, ll. 1925-36, pp. 73-74; trans. Regenos, pp. 97-98.
77. *Ibid.*, ll. 1997-2017, p. 75; trans. Regenos, pp. 100-101.
78. *Ibid.*, ll. 2023-38, pp. 75-76.
79. *Ibid.*, ll. 2413-60, pp. 85-86.
80. *Ibid.*, ll. 3893-94, p. 117. Explaining the title of his poem in a letter to William of Longchamp, Nigel writes less optimistically. Although he hoped that men might learn from observing "as in a mirror the foolishness of others and [might] correct their own folly," he knows that fools, "no matter how much they may have been taught by the foolishness of others," seldom learn (Wright, ed., *Anglo-Latin Satirical Poets*, 1: 3-4).
81. Wright, ed., *Anglo-Latin Satirical Poets*, 1: 4.
82. *Ibid.*, pp. 9-10; trans. (with emendations) by Regenos, p. 24.
83. On this work see the excellent introduction by A. Boutemy to his critical edition, *Nigellus de Longchamp dit Wireker Tractatus contra curiales et officiales clericos* (Paris, 1959), pp. 3-75.
84. *Tractatus*, ed. Boutemy, pp. 157-59.
85. *Ibid.*, p. 203.
86. *Ibid.*
87. *Ibid.*, p. 204.
88. *Ibid.*, p. 205.
89. On the life of Nigel Wireker see Boutemy's introduction to the *Tractatus*, especially pp. 13-25 and 35-45.
90. Charles Homer Haskins characterized the satirists as "spokesmen of the poorer class of clerks, often also the looser and wandering element, who missed the wealth and ease that came with promotion and willingly turned against their ecclesiastical superiors" (*The Renaissance of the Twelfth Century* [Cambridge, Mass., 1927], p. 187). The idea of a counterculture of amoral young men has gained currency largely from Helen Waddell's book *The Wandering Scholars* (London, 1932). On the myth of an "order" of wandering scholars or goliards see Raby, *Secular Latin Poetry* 2: 338-41. An excellent summary of what is known of the identities and careers of the satirists is Schüppert, *Kirchencritik*, pp. 28-32.
91. Wright, ed., *Anglo-Latin Satirical Poets*, 1: 10.
92. *Florebat olim studium*, ed. A. Hilka and O. Schumann, *Carmina Burana*, 1.1, no. 6, pp. 7-8; trans. G. F. Whicher, *The Goliard Poets* (New York, 1965), p. 142.
93. R. W. Southern, *The Making of the Middle Ages* (New Haven, 1953), p. 154.

CHAPTER FIVE

1. On the applicability of the term "humanism" to the twelfth century, see my article "The Twelfth-Century Renaissance," in W. T. Treadgold, ed., *Renaissances Before the Renaissance* (Stanford, 1984), pp. 114-43.
2. J. de Ghellinck, *L'Essor de la littérature latine au douzième siècle* (2 vols., Brussels, 1946), 1: 109-72.
3. B. Smalley, *The Becket Conflict and the Schools* (Oxford, 1973), pp. 10-15.
4. *Metalogicon* 2.10, ed. C. C. J. Webb (Oxford, 1929), pp. 77-83. See above, pp. 22-23.
5. *Metalogicon* 2.10, ed. Webb, p. 78.
6. *Ibid.*, pp. 79-80. On William of Conches's influence on John see H. Liebeschütz, *Medieval Humanism in the Life and Writings of John of Salisbury* (London, 1950), pp. 84-89.

7. *Metalogicon* 2.10, ed. Webb, p. 80. On Thierry of Chartres see A. Vernet, "Une Epitaphe inédite de Thierry de Chartres," in *Recueil de travaux offert à M. Clovis Brunel* (2 vols., Paris, 1955), 2: 660-70; and R. W. Southern, "Humanism and the School of Chartres," in *Medieval Humanism and Other Essays* (New York, 1970), pp. 68-70. Peter Helias was a renowned grammarian whose commentary on Priscian (the *Summa Prisciani*) became the standard textbook on the subject; see R. W. Hunt, "Studies on Priscian in the Eleventh and Twelfth Centuries," *MRS* 1 (1943): 194-231. Hardewin the German is otherwise unknown.

8. *Metalogicon* 2.10, ed. Webb, pp. 80-81.

9. The statutes stipulated that a scholar had to spend five years attending lectures in theology and a total of eight years in study before he could lecture publicly as a theologian. See below, p. 306.

10. Ep. 361, *PL* 182, 562.

11. On these years see *The Historia Pontificalis of John of Salisbury*, ed. and trans. M. Chibnall (London, 1956), and R. L. Poole, "John of Salisbury at the Papal Court," *EHR* 38 (1923), reprinted in A. L. Poole, ed., *Studies in Chronology and History* (Oxford, 1934), pp. 248-58.

12. On the dating of this exile see G. Constable, "The Alleged Disgrace of John of Salisbury," *EHR* 69 (1954): 67-76.

13. John complains about these trifles at several places in his writings; see especially *Policraticus* 1.intro., ed. C. C. J. Webb (2 vols., Oxford, 1909), 1: 15, and *Metalogicon* 4.42, ed. Webb, pp. 218-19.

14. *Policraticus* 1.intro., ed. Webb 1: 14.

15. See Liebeschütz, *Medieval Humanism*, pp. 41-44; Smalley, *The Becket Conflict*, p. 90; and Walter Ullmann, *Law and Politics in the Middle Ages* (London, 1975), pp. 255-59.

16. On John of Salisbury's use of the term "Epicurean" see Liebeschütz, *Medieval Humanism*, p. 78, and Smalley, *Becket Conflict*, p. 91; see also R. Jungkuntz, "Fathers, Heretics and Epicureans," *Journal of Ecclesiastical History* 17 (1966): 3-10.

17. *Policraticus* 7.8, ed. Webb 2: 122.

18. See B. Munck-Olsen, "L'Humanisme de Jean de Salisbury: Un Ciceronien au 12e siècle," in *Entretiens sur la renaissance du 12e siècle*, ed. M. P. de Gandillac and E. Jeauneau (Paris, 1968), pp. 53-69; and Liebeschütz, *Medieval Humanism*, pp. 63-68 and 79-84.

19. *Policraticus* 7.9, ed. Webb 2: 125.

20. *Ibid.*, 7.10, 2: 133.

21. *Ibid.*, 7.11, 2: 136.

22. *Ibid.*, 7.12, 2: 137-38. Cf. Juvenal, *Satires* 2-3.

23. *Policraticus* 7.12, ed. Webb 2: 144-45. Cf. *Metalogicon* 1.3, where John accuses the Cornificians of having attended the schools "quando in liberalibus disciplinis littera nichil erat et ubique spiritus querebatur, qui (ut aiunt) latet in littera" (ed. Webb, p. 10).

24. *Policraticus* 7.13, ed. Webb 2: 145.

25. *Ibid.*, 7.14, 2: 152. John attributes the idea to Quintilian (*Institutio oratoria* 2.9), but he may have got it from his teacher William of Conches. See E. Jeauneau, "Deux Rédactions des gloses de Guillaume de Conches sur Priscien," *RTAM* 27 (1960): 224.

26. *Policraticus* 7.15, ed. Webb 2: 156-57.

27. See *Metalogicon* 4.42, ed. Webb, pp. 216-19.

28. On the more theoretical aspects of the work see D. P. McGarry, "Edu-

cational Theory in the *Metalogicon* of John of Salisbury," *Speculum* 23 (1948): 659–75.

29. *Metalogicon* 1.1, ed. Webb, p. 6; trans. D. P. McGarry (Berkeley, 1955), p. 11.

30. *Metalogicon* 1.2, ed. Webb, p. 8; trans. McGarry, p. 12.

31. *Metalogicon* 1.2, ed. Webb, p. 9.

32. *Ibid.*, 1.3, p. 12.

33. *Ibid.*, 1.4, pp. 15–16.

34. *Ibid.*, 1.5, p. 20.

35. John's criticisms of the Cornificians echo those made by other masters, including his teachers William of Conches and Thierry of Chartres, about students who made it almost impossible for them to teach the liberal arts. See J. O. Ward, "The Date of the Commentary on Cicero's *De inventione* by Thierry of Chartres and the Cornifician Attack on the Liberal Arts," *Viator* 3 (1972): 219–21. According to John of Salisbury, such garrulous students ultimately did drive both William of Conches and another grammarian, Richard the Bishop, from the schools (*Metalogicon* 1.24, ed. Webb, p. 57). Another of John's teachers, the theologian Robert of Melun, who is criticized in the *Metalogicon* for a lack of classical learning (*Metalogicon* 2.10, ed. Webb, pp. 78–79), voices similar complaints about the difficulties of teaching ignorant students too lazy to learn but too quick to challenge a master (*Sententiae* 1, ed. R. Martin [Louvain, 1947], pp. 4–7, 15).

36. *Metalogicon* 1.6, ed. Webb, pp. 20–21.

37. William of Conches, *De philosophia mundi* 1.pref., *PL* 172, 43.

38. *Metalogicon* 1.1, ed. Webb, p. 7; trans. McGarry, p. 10.

39. *Metalogicon* 1.7, ed. Webb, p. 22.

40. *Ibid.*, 1.8–11, pp. 23–30.

41. *Ibid.*, 1.12, pp. 30–31; trans. McGarry, p. 36.

42. *Metalogicon* 1.23, ed. Webb, pp. 52–53.

43. *Ibid.*, 1.24, pp. 53–57. John seems to have known of Bernard's teaching only by reputation. The *Metalogicon* does not refer to any works of the master. Until recently, it was generally assumed that writings by Bernard did not or do not exist. This assumption has been strongly challenged by P. E. Dutton in his article "The Uncovering of the *Glosae super Platonem* of Bernard of Chartres," *Mediaeval Studies* 46 (1984): 192–221. If the attribution stands when the work has been edited, there will finally be direct evidence of Bernard's teaching.

44. *Metalogicon* 1.24, ed. Webb, p. 57.

45. *Ibid.*, 2.6, pp. 69–71.

46. *Ibid.*, 2.7, pp. 72–73.

47. *Ibid.*, 2.10, pp. 78–83.

48. *Ibid.*, 2.10, p. 83; trans. McGarry, p. 100.

49. *Metalogicon* 2.12, ed. Webb, pp. 83–84.

50. *Ibid.*, 2.17–18, pp. 91–97. See L. Denis, "La Question des universaux d'après Jean de Salisbury," *Revue des sciences philosophiques et théologiques* 16 (1927): 425–34.

51. *Metalogicon* 2.19, ed. Webb, p. 97.

52. *Ibid.*, 3.1, p. 120.

53. John writes that Abelard "ad puerilem de generibus et speciebus, ut pace suorum loquar, inclinavit opinionem" (*Metalogicon* 3.1, ed. Webb, p. 120). On the brilliance of Abelard's solution to the question of universals see N. Kretzmann, "The Culmination of the Old Logic in Peter Abelard," in R. L. Benson and G. Constable, eds., *Renaissance and Renewal in the Twelfth Century* (Cambridge,

Mass., 1982), pp. 491-94; and on the importance of his theory, also see M. T. Fumagalli, *La Logica di Abelardo* (Florence, 1964); and J. Jolivet, *Arts du langage et théologie chez Abélard* (Paris, 1969).

54. *Metalogicon* 3.5, ed. Webb, p. 139.

55. *Ibid.*, 3.3, p. 134.

56. *Ibid.*, 4.3, p. 167. On the *Ars disserendi* see L. Minio-Paluello, "The *Ars disserendi* of Adam of Balsham 'Parvipontanus,'" *MRS* 3 (1954): 116-69.

57. *Metalogicon* 4.24, ed. Webb, p. 191.

58. *Ibid.*, 4.27, pp. 193-94.

59. *Ibid.*, p. 4.

60. *Ibid.*, 3.pref., p. 119.

61. *Ibid.*, 3.4, pp. 135-39.

62. *Ibid.*, p. 136; trans. McGarry, p. 167. On the significance of this metaphor see E. Jeauneau, "'Nani gigantium humeris insidentes': Essai d'interprétation de Bernard de Chartres," *Vivarium* 5 (1967): 79-99, and "Nains et géants," in *Entretiens sur la renaissance du 12ᵉ siècle*, pp. 21-38.

63. *Metalogicon* 4.40, ed. Webb, pp. 212-13.

64. Letter 136, *The Letters of John of Salisbury*, ed. and trans. W. J. Millor, H. E. Butler and C. N. L. Brooke (2 vols., London, 1955; Oxford, 1979), 2: 7. See above, p. 25.

65. Letter 185, ed. Millor et al. 2: 223-25.

66. Letter 209, *ibid.*, pp. 314-39.

67. Letter 225, *ibid.*, p. 395.

68. Letter 271, *ibid.*, pp. 548-49.

69. Quoted in Smalley, *Becket Conflict*, pp. 107-8.

70. The text of the bequest can be found in the *Cartulaire de Notre Dame de Chartres*, vol. 3, ed. E. de Lepinois and L. Merlet (Chartres, 1865), p. 202. It has been reprinted by C. C. J. Webb, "Notes on Books Bequeathed by John of Salisbury to the Cathedral Library of Chartres," *MRS* 1 (1941): 128-29.

71. Peter's life must be pieced together from the evidence he provides in his letters. For other interpretations see J. A. Robinson, "Peter of Blois," *Somerset Historical Essays* (London, 1921), pp. 100-140 and the entry for Peter by C. L. Kingsford in the *DNB* 45 (1896): 46-52. On Peter's service at Canterbury see C. R. Cheney, *English Bishops' Chanceries* (Manchester, 1950), pp. 33-35, and *Hubert Walter* (London, 1967), pp. 158-71. My interpretation of the life and letters of Peter of Blois owes a great deal to R. W. Southern's article "Peter of Blois: A Twelfth Century Humanist?" in *Medieval Humanism and Other Essays* (New York, 1970), pp. 105-32, and also to Southern's comments on Peter's scholarship in *The Making of the Middle Ages* (New Haven, 1953), pp. 210-17.

72. In one of his letters Peter of Blois explains that his purpose in making the collection is threefold: "quod formam dictandi praescribo simplicibus, quod publicae utilitati munus devoti laboris et officium charitatis impendo" (*PL* 207, 289D). On the nature and purpose of the collection see Southern, "Peter of Blois," pp. 113-22, and the same author's earlier article "Some New Letters of Peter of Blois," *EHR* 53 (1938): 412-24. See also the more recent study of E. C. Higonnet, "Spiritual Ideas in the Letters of Peter of Blois," *Speculum* 50 (1975): 218-44.

73. Southern, "Peter of Blois," p. 114.

74. Ep. 101, *PL* 207, 311-14; excerpts were reprinted in *CUP* 1.intro. no. 25, pp. 27-29.

75. Ep. 101, *PL* 207, 312D-313B. Cf. *Metalogicon* 2.9, ed. Webb, pp. 76-77,

and *Policraticus* 7.2, ed. Webb 2: 98–99. This plagiarism was first remarked upon by P. Delhaye, "Un Témoignage frauduleux de Pierre de Blois sur la pédagogie du XIIe siècle," *RTAM* 14 (1947): 329–31. We know from a letter he wrote to John of Salisbury that Peter had read the *Policraticus* (Ep. 22, *PL* 207, 32A).

76. The list includes one modern author, Hildebert of Le Mans, and seven classical historians: Pompeius Trogus, Josephus, Suetonius, Egesippus, Quintus Curtius, Tacitus, and Livy. Cf. *Policraticus* 8.18, ed. Webb 2: 364, where the seven classical authors are given in the same order, followed by Serenus and Tranquillus, whom Peter does not list. On this plagiarism see Southern, "Peter of Blois," pp. 117–18.

77. Ep. 81, *PL* 207, 249–51.

78. Ep. 131, *PL* 207, 386C.

79. Ep. 51, *PL* 207, 154–57.

80. Ep. 6, *PL* 207, 18AB. Note the two possible allusions to the story of Brunellus, the hundred-year-old ass. See above, pp. 121–25.

81. Ep. 76, *PL* 207, 232B.

82. Ep. 8, *PL* 207, 21–24.

83. *Ibid.*, 23B.

84. *Ibid.*, 24A.

85. Ep. 26, *PL* 207, 91–92. On Peter's knowledge of and attitudes to civil law see Southern, "Peter of Blois," pp. 107–9.

86. Ep. 26, *PL* 207, 91B.

87. *Ibid.*

88. Ep. 140, *PL* 207, 416–22.

89. *Ibid.*, 416D.

90. *Ibid.*, 419C.

91. Ep. 14, *PL* 207, 42–51, and Ep. 150, 440B–441C.

92. Ep. 9, *PL* 207, 24–27.

93. As Southern has shown, Peter of Blois knew and used the *Verbum abbreviatum* of Master Peter the Chanter; see "Peter of Blois," p. 124. On his knowledge of theology also see Southern, "Some New Letters," pp. 416–24.

94. Ep. 23, *PL* 207, 83A.

95. Ep. 60, *PL* 207, 180D–181A.

96. Robinson, "Peter of Blois," p. 139.

97. Southern argues that from the mid-twelfth century the English increasingly regarded all the French, even those who were subjects of the English king, as foreigners. See his important article, "England's First Entry into Europe," in *Medieval Humanism*, pp. 141–47.

98. Ep. 92, *PL* 207, 289–91.

99. *Ibid.*, 290D.

100. *Ibid.* Cf. *Policraticus* 6.15, ed. Webb 2: 41.

101. The autobiography was edited by J. S. Brewer and printed in the first of the eight volumes of the collected works of Gerald of Wales, which were edited consecutively by Brewer, J. F. Dimock, and G. F. Warner and published collectively as number 21 of the Rolls Series, *Giraldus Cambrensis Opera* (London, 1861–91); H. E. Butler has translated the *De rebus* as *The Autobiography of Giraldus Cambrensis* (London, 1937). On Gerald of Wales see, especially, the important new biographical study by R. Bartlett, *Gerald of Wales, 1146–1223* (Oxford, 1982).

102. *De Rebus* 1.1, ed. Brewer, pp. 21–22.

103. *Ibid.*, 1.2, p. 23.

104. *Ibid.*, 1.6, p. 34. On this controversy see F. M. Powicke, "Gerald of Wales," *Bulletin of the John Rylands Library* 12 (1928): 394–95.

105. *De rebus* 1.9–10, ed. Brewer, pp. 42–43. On Angevin policies in Wales see W. L. Warren, *Henry II* (London, 1973), pp. 153–69.

106. *De rebus* 2.1, ed. Brewer, p. 45.

107. *Ibid.*, 2.1–4, pp. 46–49.

108. Powicke, "Gerald of Wales," p. 143.

109. John Baldwin rightly lists Gerald as a member of the circle of Peter the Chanter in *Masters, Princes and Merchants: The Social Views of Peter the Chanter and His Circle* (2 vols., Princeton, 1970), 1: 41–43. On Gerald's use of Peter's *Verbum abbreviatum* see also the references cited in note 130 below.

110. *De rebus* 2.6–7, ed. Brewer, pp. 54–56.

111. *Expugnatio Hibernica* 2.20, ed. A. B. Scott and F. X. Martin (Dublin, 1978), pp. 188–89.

112. *De rebus* 2.8, ed. Brewer, p. 57.

113. *Ibid.*, 2.24, p. 87.

114. *Ibid.*, 2.16, pp. 72–73.

115. *Ibid.*, 3.1, p. 89.

116. On the teaching of William de Montibus see H. MacKinnon, "William de Montibus: A Medieval Teacher," in T. A. Sandquist and M. R. Powicke, eds., *Essays in Medieval History Presented to Bertie Wilkinson* (Toronto, 1969), pp. 32–45. MacKinnon offers a synopsis of the conclusions reached in his unpublished doctoral dissertation, "The Life and Works of William de Montibus" (Oxford University, 1959).

117. On the dispute and its resolution see the articles of M. Richter, "Canterbury's Primacy in Wales and the First Stage of Bishop Bernard's Opposition," *Journal of Ecclesiastical History* 22 (1971), and "Professions of Obedience and the Metropolitan Claim of St. David's," *National Library of Wales Journal* 15 (1967–68). On Innocent III's involvement see C. R. Cheney, *Innocent III and England* (Stuttgart, 1976), pp. 134–40.

118. *De rebus* 3.3, ed. Brewer, p. 93.

119. *Ibid.*, 3.18, p. 119.

120. Powicke, "Gerald of Wales," p. 400. For a more sympathetic view of Gerald's Welsh identity see M. Richter, "Gerald of Wales: A Reassessment on the 750th Anniversary of His Death," *Traditio* 29 (1973): 379–90, the same author's book *Giraldus Cambrensis: The Growth of the Welsh Nation* (Aberystwyth, 1972), and Bartlett, *Gerald of Wales*, especially pp. 9–25 and 45–57.

121. *Itinerarium Kambriae*, ed. J. F. Dimock, *Opera* 6: 3–4; trans. L. Thorpe, *The Journey Through Wales and the Description of Wales* (London, 1978), pp. 63–64. The quotation is from Aulus Gellius, *Noctes Atticae* 16.8.

122. *Itinerarium*, ed. Dimock, p. 5; trans. Thorpe, p. 69.

123. *Descriptio Kambriae*, ed. J. F. Dimock, *Opera* 6: 157–8; trans. Thorpe, p. 213.

124. *Descriptio*, ed. Dimock, p. 164; trans. Thorpe, p. 217.

125. *De principis instructione*, ed. G. F. Warner, *Opera* 8: 1–329. On this work see K. Schnith, "Betrachtungen zum Spätwerk des Giraldus Cambrensis: *De principis instructione*," *Festiva Lanx. Festgabe Johannes Spörl* (Munich, 1966), pp. 53–66, and Bartlett, *Gerald of Wales*, pp. 69–100.

126. Ep. 24, ed. Brewer, *Opera* 1: 273–89. On Gerald's relationship with Walter Map see the reevaluation of A. K. Bate, "Walter Map and Giraldus Cambrensis," *Latomus* 31 (1972): 860–75. On the sources of the ideas Gerald uses to defend the arts in this letter see R. H. Rouse and M. A. Rouse, "The *Florilegium Angelicum*," in J. J. G. Alexander and M. T. Gibson, eds., *Medieval Learning and Literature: Essays Presented to R. W. Hunt* (Oxford, 1976), pp. 89–91. And on

his extensive use of florilegia for his classical references see A. A. Goddu and R. H. Rouse, "Gerald of Wales and the *Florilegium Angelicum*," *Speculum* 52 (1977): 488-521.

127. *Speculum duorum*, ed. Y. Lefevre and R. B. C. Huygens (Cardiff, 1974), pp. 168-75.

128. Gerald's remarks on Hubert Walter's ignorance are in his collection of invectives, the *Invectionum* 1.5, ed. J. S. Brewer, *Opera* 3: 29-31. He devotes a complete chapter of the *Speculum ecclesiae* to proving the superiority of secular to monastic bishops (*Speculum ecclesiae* 2.25, ed. J. S. Brewer, *Opera* 4: 75-81).

129. *Speculum duorum*, ed. Lefevre and Huygens, p. 248.

130. See E. M. Sanford, "Giraldus Cambrensis' Debt to Petrus Cantor," *Medievalia et Humanistica* 3 (1945): 16-32, and A. Boutemy, "Giraud de Barri et Pierre le Chantre: Une Source de la *Gemma ecclesiastica*," *Revue du moyen âge latin* 2 (1946): 45-62.

131. *Gemma ecclesiastica*, ed. J. S. Brewer, *Opera* 2: 5-7.

132. *Ibid.*, 2.35-36, pp. 341-48.

133. *Ibid.*, 2.37, pp. 348-49.

134. *Ibid.*, p. 349. This Master Mainerius probably can be identified with William of Tyre's master Mainerus and the Manerius named in the *Metamorphosis Goliae*, discussed above, pp. 22-23.

135. *Gemma ecclesiastica* 2.37, ed. Brewer, pp. 349-50.

136. *Ibid.*, pp. 350-51.

137. *Ibid.*, p. 351.

138. R. W. Hunt, ed., "The Preface to the 'Speculum Ecclesiae' of Giraldus Cambrensis," *Viator* 8 (1977): 204. The badly-damaged preface is now comprehensible, thanks to Hunt's masterly reconstruction and valuable commentary.

139. Ed. Hunt, pp. 205-6. On this Master Martin see Hunt's commentary in "Preface," p. 197.

140. Ed. Hunt, p. 206.

141. *Ibid.*, pp. 204-5, 209.

142. *Ibid.*, p. 209.

143. This part of the manuscript of the *Speculum ecclesiae* is severely damaged. As reconstructed by Hunt (p. 209), it reads: "[die]bus hiis nostris ultimis a summo pontifice Honorio [qu]i mandatum nuper [ema]navit, ut clerici red[ditus] . . . stitis bene—." Here, at the point where Gerald begins to transcribe the bull, the text breaks. The bull *Super speculam* can be found in *CUP* 1 no. 32, pp. 90-93.

144. Ed. Hunt, p. 209.

145. *Ibid.* Cf. *CUP* 1 no. 11, pp. 70-71, and *CUP* 1 no. 20, pp. 78-79.

146. Gerald refers to this work as "Super librum Aristotilis quendam de Anima" (p. 210). On this quotation see Hunt, "Preface," pp. 199-200.

CHAPTER SIX

1. J. Longère, *Les Oeuvres oratoires de maîtres parisiens au XIIe siècle* (2 vols., Paris, 1975). An indispensable resource for the sermons of the period is the recently completed catalogue of sermons compiled by J. B. Schneyer, *Repertorium der lateinischen Sermones des Mittelalters* (5 vols., *BGPTM*, Munster, 1969-75). Two older works on preaching that are still useful are L. Bourgain, *La Chaire fran-*

çaise au XIIe siècle (Paris, 1879), and A. Lecoy de la Marche, *La Chaire française au moyen âge, spécialement au XIIIe siècle*, 2d ed. (Paris, 1886). Sermons have provided useful evidence for the history of the University of Paris in the thirteenth century in M.-M. Davy's important study (though it was, unfortunately, based on a unique manuscript), *Les Sermons universitaires parisiens de 1230-1231* (Paris, 1931), and in the broader, less systematic article of C. H. Haskins, "The University of Paris in the Sermons of the Thirteenth Century," *AHR* 10 (1904): 1-27. More general histories of the university, like H. Rashdall's *The Universities of Europe in the Middle Ages*, rev. ed. by F. M. Powicke and A. B. Emden (3 vols., Oxford, 1936), and A. Luchaire's *L'Université de Paris sous Philippe Auguste* (Paris, 1899), used sermons primarily as sources for stories illustrative of university life, rather than for attitudes or ideas about learning and teaching.

2. The author of the *Metamorphosis Goliae* describes Peter Lombard as "Celebrem theologum . . . Lombardum," ed. R. B. C. Huygens, *Studi medievali* ser. 3, 3.2 (1962): 771.

3. See I. Brady, "Peter Lombard: Canon of Notre Dame," *RTAM* 32 (1965): 277-95, and the same author's *prologomena* to the new edition of the *Sententiae*, *Magistri Petri Lombardi Parisiensis episcopi Sententiae in IV libris distinctae*, Spicilegium Bonaventurianum 4 (Grottaferrata, 1971): 8-45. These correct the biographical information found in P. Delhaye, *Pierre Lombard: Sa Vie, ses oeuvres, sa morale* (Montreal-Paris, 1961).

4. For Peter Lombard's sermons see Brady, *Sententiae*, pp. 93-112. His list corrects and updates that found in the *DTC* 12 (1935), 1961-62, and used by D. van den Eynde in *Miscellanea lombardiana* (Novarra, 1957), pp. 58-60. In addition to the 26 sermons printed in *PL* 171 (and incorrectly attributed to Hildebert of Lavardin), four others have been edited: one by Hauréau, *N&E* 3 (1891): 223; two by van den Eynde, *Miscellanea lombardiana*, pp. 75-87; and one by H.-M. Rochais, "Une Collection de textes divers de S. Bernard dans le manuscrit Tours 343," *RTAM* 29 (1962): 106-11. Of the four that remain unedited, I have been able to consult the two in MS. Paris BN lat. 13374, ff. 46v-49v (which also contains the 26 printed in *PL* 171).

5. This account is found in a sermon exemplum of Jacques of Vitry. See G. Frenken, *Die Exempla des Jacob von Vitry* (Munich, 1914), pp. 100-101. Cf. the accounts of Caesarius of Heisterbach, *Dialogus miraculorum*, ed. B. Strange (2 vols., Cologne, 1851), 1: 371-72, and Stephen of Bourbon, *Anecdotes historiques*, ed. A. Lecoy de la Marche (Paris, 1877), p. 418.

6. See V. Mortet, *Maurice de Sully (1160-1196): Etude sur l'administration episcopale pendant la deuxième moitié du XIIe siècle* (Paris, 1890), and C. A. Robson, *Maurice of Sully and the Medieval Vernacular Homily* (Oxford, 1952).

7. The vernacular version of Maurice of Sully's sermons for Sundays and feasts has been edited, along with the Latin preface (*Evangelistis evangelizare*), by Robson, *Maurice of Sully*. I have also consulted the Latin version found in MS. Oxford Bodl. Laud lat. 105, as well as several other MSS. containing his sermons. For a further comparison of his preaching to other masters, see Longère, *Oeuvres oratoires*, 1: 14-18.

8. Discussed above, pp. 16-17.

9. The sixth known chancellor, Bernard Chabert (c. 1205-1206), was also a theology master, but there are no sermons or other of his works extant. See

P. Glorieux, *Répertoire des maîtres en théologie de Paris au XIIIe siècle* (2 vols., Paris, 1933-34), 1: 260.

10. Odo's letter to the pope is printed in J. B. Pitra, ed., *Analecta novissima spicilegii Solesmensis altera continuatio* 2 (Tusculum, 1888; reprinted 1967), pp. xxxix-xl. See Mortet, *Maurice de Sully*, pp. 155-57.

11. For the evidence of Odo's career see L. Hödl, *Die Geschichte der scholastischen Literatur und der Theologie der Schlüsselgewalt*, vol. 1: *Von ihren Anfangen an bis zur Summa Aurea des Wilhelm von Auxerre* (*BGPTM* 38.4, Munster, 1960), pp. 116-41; and J. Leclercq, "Lettres d'Odon d'Ourscamp, cardinal cistercien," *Analecta monastica* ser. 3, *Studia Anselmiana* 37 (Rome, 1955): 145-57.

12. Odo's *Quaestiones* have been edited by Pitra in *Analecta*, pp. 4-187. On the question of their authenticity, see I. Brady, "Peter Manducator and the Oral Teachings of Peter Lombard," *Antonianum* 41 (1966): 454-90.

On Odo's preaching see M. M. Lebreton, "Recherchers sur les mss, des sermons des différents personnages du XIIe siècle nommés Odon," *BIIRHT* 3 (1954): 33-54. Of the 19 sermons attributed to Odo of Soissons, 17 are an Ourscamp manuscript now in Cambrai (MS. Cambrai B. 561), 6 in MS. Paris BN lat. 14954 (including the two not in the Cambrai MS.), and 2 in MS. Paris BN lat. 13578. Only one has been edited, by Pitra, *Analecta novissima* 2: xlii-xlvi. Jean Chatillon has concluded that Odo probably preached the sermon *Adorna thalamum* at St. Victor while he was chancellor: see J. Chatillon, "Sermons et prédicateurs victorins," *AHDLMA* 32 (1965): 31, 54-55.

13. On Peter Comestor's life see Brady, "Peter Manducator," pp. 483-90, and Longère, *Oeuvres oratoires*, 1: 20-21.

14. B. Smalley, *The Study of the Bible in the Middle Ages* (Notre Dame, 1964), pp. 178-80, 196-263; R. M. Martin, "Notes sur l'oeuvre littéraire de Pierre le Mangeur," *RTAM* 3 (1931): 54-66; and A. Landgraf, "Recherches sur les écrits de Pierre le Mangeur," *RTAM* 3 (1931): 292-306. On his Gospel commentaries see Smalley, "Peter Comestor on the Gospel and His Sources," *RTAM* 46 (1979): 84-130.

15. For a list of Peter's sermons see M.-M. Lebreton, "Recherches sur les manuscrits contenant des sermons de Pierre le Mangeur," *BIIRHT* 2 (1943): 25-44, and the additions and corrections in *BIIRHT* 4 (1955): 35-37. Of Peter Comestor's 160 sermons, a total of 107 have been printed in *PL* 198, 1723-1844, and in *PL* 171 (among those attributed to Hildebert of Lavardin). Two of the largest unpublished manuscript collections are Clairvaux manuscripts now in Troyes (MSS. Troyes 425 and 1515). Other major collections are found in MS. Paris BN lat. 2950, ff. 1-163v, and MS. Oxford Bodl. Laud misc. 484, ff. 1-191v. In addition to these, I have consulted the following manuscripts containing sermons attributed to Peter Comestor: MS. Oxford Bodl. Laud lat. 105; MS. Paris Maz. 1005; MSS. Paris BN lat. 13586, 14470, 14589, 14590, 14925, 14954, and 16463.

16. MS. Cambridge UL Ii.1.24, ff. 117ra-123ra, has 40 sermons attributed to "Magister Hilduinus," and MS. Paris Maz. 774, ff. 168r-205va, has 42 sermons attributed to "Magister Hyduinus cancellarius parisiensi." I have also consulted MS. Paris BN lat. 3733, ff. 90v-125r, which contains 29 of these sermons without attribution. On Chancellor Hilduin and his preaching see Longère, *Oeuvres oratoires* 1: 21-22.

17. *CUP* 1.intro. no. 50, pp. 49-50.

18. On the life and writings of Peter of Poitiers see P. S. Moore, *The Works of Peter of Poitiers, Master in Theology and Chancellor of Paris (1193-1205)* (Washington, D.C., 1936); his sermons are discussed on pp. 122-44. The primary manuscript of Peter of Poitiers's sermons is MS. Paris BN lat. 14593. 56 of these 59 sermons are also found without attribution in MS. Oxford Bodl. Laud misc. 269 (a manuscript cited by neither Moore nor Longère). I have also consulted MS. Paris Maz. 1005, ff. 98rb-115rb, which contains anonymous versions of ten of these sermons, and MS. Oxford Bodl. e museo 82, which has three.

19. See n. 9 above.

20. On Prévostin's life and work see G. Lacombe, *La Vie et les oeuvres de Prévostin*, Bibliothèque thomiste 11 (Le Saulchoir, 1927); his preaching is discussed on pp. 182-200. See also Longère, *Oeuvres oratoires*, 1: 23-25. I have found many errors in Lacombe's list of Prévostin's sermons; some of these have been corrected by Schneyer, *Repertorium* 4: 870-76. I have consulted eight manuscripts containing a total of 61 sermons likely to belong to Prévostin: MS. London BM Add. 18335; MS. Oxford Bodl. 548; MS. Paris Ars. 543; and MSS. Paris BN lat. 3818, 13586, 14804, 14859, and 18172. Further work is needed on the attribution of several of these sermons. For an example of the satirical tone Prévostin uses in some of his preaching, see the excerpts from the sermon *Nolite me vocare Noemi* published by Hauréau, *N&E* 3 (1891): 165-66.

21. *Metalogicon* 2.10, ed. C. C. J. Webb (Oxford, 1929), p. 82.

22. On Bernard of Clairvaux's intervention on Robert Pullen's behalf, see below, pp. 64-65.

23. See F. Courtney, *Cardinal Robert Pullen: An English Theologian of the Twelfth Century* (Rome, 1945). Cf. B. Smalley, *The Becket Conflict and the Schools* (Oxford, 1973), pp. 39-50.

24. These important *Sentences* are printed in *PL* 186, 639-1010, and discussed by Courtney, *Robert Pullen*, pp. 55-276, and Smalley, *Becket Conflict*, pp. 40-45.

25. Pullen's sermons are discussed in Appendix 1 of Smalley, *Becket Conflict*, pp. 242-46. The 19 sermons ascribed to Robert Pullen are found in MSS. Lambeth Palace 458 and Hereford Cathedral o.2.viii; I have used the Lambeth manuscript. Smalley (pp. 245-46) convincingly refutes the attribution to Pullen of another collection of 26 sermons addressed to monks.

26. All 199 sermons of Raoul Ardent can be found in *PL* 155, 1301-1626 and 1667-2118. The long-lost preface to the collection has recently been discovered and edited by G. Wolf, "La Préface perdue des sermons de Raoul Ardent, chapelain de Richard I," *AHDLMA* 46 (1980): 35-39. On his preaching see Longère, *Oeuvres oratoires* 1: 30-31. On the *Speculum universale* see J. Grundel, "Das *Speculum universale* des Radulfus Ardens," *Mitteilungen des Grabmann-Instituts der Universität München* 5 (1961), the same author's article, "L'Oeuvre encyclopédique de Raoul Ardent, le *Speculum universale*," *Cahiers d'histoire mondiale* 9.3 (1966): 553-70, and also his recent book-length study, *Die Lehre des Radulfus Ardens von den Verstandestugenden auf dem Hintergrund seiner Seelenlehre* (Munich, 1976).

27. J. Baldwin, *Masters, Princes and Merchants: The Social Views of Peter the Chanter and His Circle* (2 vols., Princeton, 1970), 1: 39-40.

28. See Wolf, "Préface perdue," pp. 37-38. See also A. Vernet, "Le Lieu de sépultre de Raoul Ardent," *AHDLMA* 46 (1980): 40-44. Raoul Ardent's *obit* was edited and first discussed by M.-T. d'Alverny, "L'Obit de Raoul Ardent," *AHDLMA* 15-17 (1940-42): 403-5.

29. See n. 10 above.

30. Stephen of Tournai, Ep. 60, *PL* 211, 353.

31. For the life and legend of Simon of Tournai, see J. Warichez, "Simon de Tournai," *Biographie nationale de Belgique* 22 (1914): 543-53, and the same author's introduction to his edition of the *Disputationes*, Spicilegium sacrum Lovaniense 12 (Louvain, 1932). The sermon *O Sapientia* is edited by Warichez in this volume, pp. 301-7.

32. On Alan of Lille's life and works see M.-T. d'Alverny, *Alain de Lille, Textes inédits avec une introduction sur sa vie et ses oeuvres* (Paris, 1965), pp. 11-29, and the same author's article, "Maître Alain–'Nova et Vetera,'" *Entretiens sur la renaissance du douzième siècle*, ed. M. P. de Gandillac and E. Jeauneau (Paris, 1968), pp. 117-45. G. Raynaud de Lage, *Alain de Lille poète du XIIe siècle* (Montreal-Paris, 1951), is still useful, although much of the information is outdated. For the more recent evidence of Alan of Lille's long life span see P. Delhaye, "Pour la fiche Alain de Lille," *Mélanges de science religieuse* 20 (1963): 39-51. On his association with the Cistercians see J. M. Trout, "The Monastic Vocation of Alan of Lille," *Analecta Cisterciensia* 30 (1974): 46-53. Cf. P. Glorieux, "Alain de Lille, le moine à l'abbaye du Bec dans sa jeunesse," *RTAM* 39 (1972): 51-62.

33. For a list of Alan of Lille's sermons see d'Alverny, *Textes inédits*, pp. 129-50. One collection of 27 sermons, known as the *Liber sermonum*, is found in several MSS. alone or with the *Summa de arte praedicandi*. Of these, 9 have been edited: 3 in *PL* 210, 195-98, 221-23, and 226-28; 3 by d'Alverny, *Textes inédits*, pp. 241-51; and one each by Hauréau, "Mémoire sur la vie et quelques oeuvres d'Alain de Lille," *Mémoires de l'Académie des Inscriptions et Belles-Lettres* 32 (Paris, 1886): 18-19; by L. Hödl, "Eine unbekannte Predigtsammlung des Alanus von Lille," *Zeitschrift für katholische Theologie* 80 (1958): 516-27; and by P. Glorieux, "Alain de Lille, docteur de l'Assomption," *Mélanges de science religieuse* 8 (1951): 16-18. For the remaining 18, I have consulted MS. London BM Add. 19767, ff. 52r-99r. Of the more than 60 other sermons that have been attributed to Alan of Lille, only 17 have been edited: 9 in *PL* 210, 197-221 and 223-26; 6 by d'Alverny, *Textes inédits*, pp. 251-85; another by the same author, "Un Sermon d'Alain de Lille sur la misère de l'homme," in *Literary and Historical Studies in Honor of Harry Caplan*, ed. L. Wallach (Ithaca, 1966), pp. 515-35; and another also by d'Alverny, "Variations sur un thème de Virgile dans un sermon d'Alain de Lille," in R. Chevallier, ed., *Mélanges offerts à André Piganiol* (Paris, 1966), pp. 1517-28. For the unedited sermons, I have used MS. London BM Add. 19767 and MSS. Paris BN lat. 3818, 13586, 14859, 16463, and 18172. Alan's *Summa de arte praedicandi* is printed in *PL* 210, 110-98; I have also consulted the version in MS. London BM Add. 19767, ff. 1-52.

34. On Alexander Neckham's life and works see R. W. Hunt, "Alexander Neckham" (D.Phil. dissertation, Oxford University, 1936); J. C. Russell, "Alexander Neckham in England," *EHR* 47 (1932): 260-68; and W. Hunt, "Alexander Neckam," *DNB* 14 (1894): 154-55.

35. On Neckham's sermons and preaching see R. W. Hunt, "Alexander Neckham," pp. 90b-99, and Schneyer, *Repertorium* 1: 271-77. I have used the primary manuscript of his Oxford sermons, MS. Oxford Bodl. Wood empt. 13 (56 sermons, 13 of questionable attribution), and MS. London BM Harley 335 (11 sermons, 3 questionable). I have also consulted the florilegium of Neckham's works found in MS. Cambridge UL Gg.6.42, which contains excerpts from his sermons.

36. See F. M. Powicke, *Stephen Langton* (Oxford, 1928); the same author's

later article "Bibliographical Note on Recent Work upon Stephen Langton," *EHR* 48 (1933): 554–57; F. A. Cazel, Jr., "The Last Years of Stephen Langton," *EHR* 79 (1964): 673–97; and Baldwin, *Masters, Princes and Merchants* 1: 25–31.

37. See Smalley, *Study of the Bible*, pp. 196–263.

38. On Langton's *Quaestiones* see Baldwin, *Masters, Princes and Merchants* 1: 30 and 2: 19–20, n. 134. I have consulted the largest collection, those *Quaestiones* found in MS. Cambridge St. John's Coll. 57, ff. 147r–346v.

39. On Langton's preaching see, in addition to Longère, *Oeuvres oratoires* 1: 27–29, the major study of P. Barzillay Roberts, *Stephanus de Lingua-Tonante: Studies in the Sermons of Stephen Langton* (Toronto, 1968), which includes a complete listing of sermons attributed to Langton and a detailed analysis of the 122 sermons that are attributed to him in more than one copy. Barzillay Roberts has also edited several of Langton's sermons. Her edition of his inaugural sermon (*Legimus filios Israel*) as theology master first appeared in *Studies*, pp. 226–37. Three other Paris sermons are edited in her article "Master Stephen Langton Preaches to the People and Clergy: Sermon Texts from Twelfth-Century Paris," *Traditio* 36 (1980): 237–68. Her edition of *Legimus filios Israel* is also printed in *Selected Sermons of Stephen Langton* (Toronto, 1980), pp. 17–35, a volume that includes editions of three sermons Langton preached as archbishop. I have concentrated my studies on the sermons found in the following Paris manuscripts: MSS. BN lat. 16463 (50 sermons), 14859 (36), 14470 (35), 14593 (19), 3495 (17), 14525 (5), and 12420 (4).

40. For the life of Jacques of Vitry see P. Funk, *Jakob von Vitry: Leben und Werken* (Leipzig, 1909). See also *The Historia Occidentalis of Jacques de Vitry*, ed. J. Hinnebusch, *Spicilegium Friburgense* 17 (Fribourg, 1972), pp. 3–7, and E. W. McDonnell, *The Beguines and Beghards in Medieval Culture* (New Brunswick, N.J., 1954), pp. 20–39. On his origins and early career, also see J. Benton, "Qui étaient les parents de Jacques de Vitry?" *Le Moyen Age* 70 (1964): 39–47.

41. On Jacques of Vitry's preaching see Longère, *Oeuvres oratoires* 1: 31–33. Jacques explains the plan of his vast collection of sermons in the prologue to the *Sermones vulgares*, in Pitra, ed., *Analecta novissima* 2: 189–93. Excerpts from the *Sermones vulgares* can also be found in this volume, pp. 346–442. I have used the version of the *Sermones ad status* in MS. Paris BN lat. 17509. The *Sermones dominicales* were edited by Theodore Lyngam (Theodorus Lundanus), *Jacobi de Vitriaco Sermones in epistolas et evangelia dominicalia totius anni* (Antwerp, 1575).

The exempla from the *Sermones ad status* have been edited by T. F. Crane, *The Exempla or Illustrative Stories from the Sermones Vulgares of Jacques de Vitry*, Publications of the Folk-Lore Society 26 (London, 1890), and those from the *Sermones communes* by G. Frenken, *Die Exempla des Jacob von Vitry*, Quellen und Untersuchungen zur lateinischen Philologie des Mittelalters 15 (Munich, 1914), and also by J. Greven, *Die Exempla aus den Sermones feriales et communes des Jakob von Vitry*, Sammlung mittellateinischer Texte 9 (Heidelberg, 1914).

42. *Historia Occidentalis*, ed. Hinnebusch, especially pp. 89–106.

43. For the sermons of Geoffrey of Troyes see Schneyer, *Repertorium* 2: 159–64. The three primary manuscripts of his sermons are MSS. Paris BN lat. 3563 and 13586 and MS. Reims 581. Copies of some sermons are also found in MSS. Paris BN lat. 14593, 14954, and 16463 and in MS. Troyes 425, in each case among sermons of known Paris masters. Only one of these sermons has been edited, by Hauréau, *N&E* 2 (1891), 301–4.

44. *Historia Occidentalis* cap. 9, ed. Hinnebusch, pp. 102–3. The masters named include Stephen Langton and Robert of Courson. On the preaching com-

mitment of Paris masters, see Longère, *Oeuvres oratoires* 1: 35-44, and Baldwin, *Masters, Princes and Merchants* 1: 107-17.

45. *Verbum abbreviatum* cap. 1, *PL* 205, 25.

46. On the development of preaching technique, see Longère, *Oeuvres oratoires* 1: 44-62; Barzillay Roberts, *Stephanus de Lingua-Tonante*, pp. 77-132; and J. Leclercq, "La Magistère du prédicateur au XIIIe siècle," *AHDLMA* 15 (1946): 105-47.

47. *Summa de arte praedicandi* cap. 1, *PL* 210, 111D.

48. *Ibid.*, 112AB.

49. *Ibid.*, 113CD.

50. *Ibid.*, capp. 39-48, *PL* 210, 184-98.

51. "Qui enim bene vult docere populum sibi commissum, considerare debet IIIIor: locum, tempus, qualitatem personarum, quantitatem docendorum" (*Quis putas est*, MSS. Oxford Bodl. Laud misc. 269, f. 64va, and Bodl. e museo 82, f. 61rb-va).

52. On the use of exempla, see J.-T. Welter, *L'Exemplum dans la littérature religieuse et didactique du moyen âge* (Paris, 1927); for the frequent citations of Gregory the Great's dictum, pp. 68-78. See also J. A. Mosher, *The Exemplum in Early Religious and Didactic Literature in England* (New York, 1911), and Longère, *Oeuvres oratoires* 1: 58-63.

53. Quoted from Smalley, *Study of the Bible*, pp. 253-54. On Stephen Langton's use of exempla, see Barzillay Roberts, *Stephanus de Lingua-Tonante*, pp. 94-100, and her article, "Master Stephen Langton Preaches to the People and Clergy," *Traditio* 36 (1980): 241-42.

54. "Sic et predicator sermonem facturus et verba sacri eloquii propositurus laicis, variis exemplis reficere debet auditores" (*Ad te domine*, MS. Cambridge UL Gg.6.42, f. 161r). On his use of exempla, see R. W. Hunt, "Alexander Neckham," pp. 95-103.

55. *Cum egrediemini*, MS. Paris BN lat. 17509, f. 32rd; ed. Crane, *Exempla*, p. 12. On Jacques of Vitry's use of exempla see the works of Crane, Frenken, and Greven cited in n. 41 above.

56. On the legend see M. Schwob, *La Légende de Serlon de Wilton, abbé de l'Aumône* (Paris, 1899). On the early life of Master Serlo see A. C. Friend, "Serlo of Wilton: The Early Years," *Bulletin Du Cange* 24 (1954): 85-110. His poems have been edited by J. Oberg, *Serlon de Wilton Poèmes latins* (Stockholm, 1965).

57. Stephen of Bourbon, *Anecdotes historiques*, ed. A. Lecoy de la Marche (Paris, 1877), pp. 18-19.

58. For these handbooks and manuals, see H. Caplan, *Mediaeval Artes praedicandi: A Hand-list*, Cornell Studies in Classical Philology 25 (Ithaca, 1934), and *A Supplementary Hand-list* (1936). On their influence on the development of preaching technique see E. Gilson, "Michel Menot et la technique du sermon médiéval," *Les Idées et les lettres* (Paris, 1932), pp. 93-154, and T. M. Charland, *Artes praedicandi: Contribution à l'histoire de la rhétorique au moyen âge*, Publications de l'Institut d'Etudes Médiévales d'Ottawa 7 (Ottawa-Paris, 1963). See also the comments of Lecoy de la Marche, *La Chaire française*, pp. 332-35.

59. See, for example, Peter the Chanter, *Verbum abbreviatum*, *PL* 205, 56-82, and Alan of Lille, *Summa de arte praedicandi*, *PL* 210, 182-84. Cf. Guibert of Nogent, *Quo ordine sermo fieri debeat*, *PL* 156, 21-25.

60. *Quis vestrum habebit amicum*, ed. Lyngam, p. 514.

61. *Attendite vobis*, MS. Paris BN lat. 12420, f. 55vb.
62. *Super canticum canticorum* 5.9, MS. Oxford Magdalen Coll. 149, f. 144r.
63. *Qui timet Deum*, *PL* 155, 1320A.
64. *Cum sero esset*, *PL* 155, 1866D-1867A.
65. See, for example, the complaints against fame-seeking preachers made by Raoul Ardent, *Confido de vobis*, *PL* 155, 1371C, and by Jacques of Vitry, *Sublevatis Iesus oculis*, ed. Lyngam, pp. 519-20. See also Longère, *Oeuvres oratoires* 1: 41.
66. *Glosa super psalmos*, MS. Oxford Bodl. 284, f. 280ra-b.
67. Raoul Ardent, *Designavit Iesus*, *PL* 155, 1469C-1470A. The debate over payment for preaching is discussed by Baldwin, *Masters, Princes and Merchants* 1: 108-9.
68. *Deum time*, MSS. Paris BN lat. 13586, p. 2, and Reims 581, f. 31rb.
69. On the problem of academic discipline in Paris see Baldwin, *Masters, Princes, and Merchants* 1: 137-49.
70. *Obsecro vos fratres*, ed. Lyngam, p. 131. Cf. Jacques's sermon *Inclina Domine aurem tuam*, *ibid.* p. 795, where the ears are said to symbolize monks.
71. *Veni in ortum meum*, MSS. Paris Maz. 774, f. 173va; BN lat. 3733, f. 102v, and Cambridge UL Ii.1.24, f. 145vb.
72. For examples of this debate see the treatises of Rupert of Deutz, *Altercatio monachi et clerici, quod liceat monacho praedicare*, *PL* 170, 537-42, and Honorius Augustodunensis, *Quod monachis liceat praedicare*, ed. J. A. Endres, *Honorius Augustodunensis* (Munich-Kemptem, 1906), pp. 147*ff.* See also M. D. Chenu, *La Théologie au douzième siècle* (Paris, 1966), pp. 225-33, and G. Constable, "Renewal and Reform in Religious Life," in R. L. Benson and G. Constable, eds., *Renaissance and Renewal in the Twelfth Century* (Cambridge, Mass., 1982), pp. 51-56.
73. "Sunt autem duo genera contemplativorum. Alii enim sunt claustrales, alli vero scolares. Claustrales vacant orationi, scolares vero lectioni" (*Exsulta satis filiae Syon*, MSS. Paris Maz. 774, f. 178va; BN lat. 3733, f. 93v; and Cambridge UL Ii.1.24, f. 168vb).
74. Peter Comestor, *Oblatus est, quia voluit*, MS. Paris BN lat. 14589, f. 30va. Cf. *PL* 198, 1747A, and *Qui sedes super cherubim*, *PL* 171, 412D. Peter of Poitiers, *Cum obtuleris sacrificium*, MS. Oxford Bodl. Laud misc. 269, f. 35rb.
75. *Qui descendunt mare*, MSS. Paris BN lat. 3495, f. 202r, and BN lat. 14804, f. 160rb; both manuscripts contain sermons elsewhere attributed by name to Stephen Langton.
76. *Vinum non habent*, MS. Paris BN lat. 13586, p. 153.
77. See, for example, Hilduin (n. 73 above); Peter Comestor, *Egredimini filiae Sion*, *PL* 198, 1773AB; and Prévostin, *Egredimini filie Syon*, MS. London BM Add. 18335, f. 2v.
78. *Fili, si oblita*, Ms. Paris BN lat. 14925, f. 185rb-va. Cf. *Tolle filium tuum*, *PL* 198, 1797D. On this maternal imagery see C. W. Bynum, *Jesus as Mother* (Berkeley, 1982), pp. 113-25.
79. *Attendite ad petram*, MSS. Paris Maz. 774, f. 182va-b, and Cambridge UL Ii.1.24, f. 144ra-va. Cf. Hilduin, *Ortus conclusus soror mea*, MSS. Paris Maz. 774, f. 188ra-vb; BN lat. 3733, ff. 112r-113r; and Cambridge UL Ii.1.24, f. 149va-150ra. In this sermon Hilduin describes Augustine's spiritual children as scholars, canons, and prelates.
80. Cf. the interpretation of Longère, *Oeuvres oratoires* 1: 368-71.
81. *Fili, sedisti ad mensam*, *PL* 171, 650D.

82. See, for example, *Que est ista*, MS. Oxford Bodl. Wood empt. 13, f. 53r; *Omnia tempus habent* (to Cistercians), f. 60r; and *Ego sum pastor bonus*, f. 86r.

83. *Homo quidam nobilis*, MSS. Paris BN lat. 14593, ff. 124va and 295ra, and Oxford Bodl. Laud misc. 269, f. 14ra.

84. *Exsulta satis filia Syon*, MSS. Paris Maz. 774, f. 178vb; BN lat. 3733, f. 93v; and Cambridge UL Ii.1.24, f. 168vb.

85. Cap. 25, *PL* 186, 939D.

86. *Intravit Ihesus in quoddam castellum*, MS. London Lambeth 458, f. 137r, and *Aiel de Bethel*, f. 140v. See Smalley, *Becket Conflict*, pp. 43–48.

87. Raoul Ardent, *In illo tempore*, *PL* 155, 1426B. On Stephen Langton see Smalley, *Study of the Bible*, pp. 249–53.

88. *Regula pastoralis* 1.1, trans. H. Davis (Westminster, Md., 1950), p. 21.

89. An excellent example is found in Jacques of Vitry's sermon *ad prelatos et sacerdotes, Si sponderis pro amico*, MS. Paris BN lat. 17509, f. 8va.

90. Geoffrey of Troyes, *Domini patres*, MS. Reims 581, f. 111vb. Cf. Maurice of Sully, *Evangelistis evangelizare*, ed. Robson, in *Maurice of Sully*, p. 55.

91. See A. Murray, *Reason and Society in the Middle Ages* (Oxford, 1978), pp. 293–309.

92. *Qui descendunt mare*, MSS. Paris BN lat. 3495, f. 202v, and BN lat. 14804, f. 160va.

93. *Summa de arte praedicandi* cap. 44, *PL* 210, 192B: "sacerdotes nostri temporis sunt senes elementarii, centum annorum pueri." Cf. Peter Comestor, *Sederunt in terra*, *PL* 198, 1823B.

94. *Benedicite, Anania, Azaria*, MS. Paris BN lat. 17509, f. 28ra.

95. For these charges see below, pp. 267–68.

96. *Absterget Deus omnes*, MS. Paris Maz. 774, f. 201vb.

97. *Descendente Jesu de monte*, *PL* 155, 1749BC.

98. *Cum egrediemini*, MS. Paris BN lat. 17509, f. 31va–b; ed. Crane, *Exempla*, pp. 11–12. The story is from the *Vitae patrum*, *PL* 73, 158.

99. *Domini patres*, MS. Reims 581, f. 106vb. Cf. Peter Comestor, *Audi, filia, et vide*, *PL* 171, 905D, and Jacques of Vitry, *Fratres, non cessamus*, ed. Lyngam, p. 910.

100. *Adorna thalamum*, MS. Cambrai B. 561, f. 103va.

101. *Accesserunt ad Jesum*, *PL* 155, 1461D–1462A. Cf. *Designavit Jesus et alios*, 1465B.

102. *Beati servi illi*, MS. Oxford Bodl. Laud misc. 269, f. 13rb. This warning is missing from the two versions of the same sermon found in MS. Paris BN 14593, ff. 123va and 294va.

103. *In ecclesiis benedicite*, MS. Oxford Bodl. Laud misc. 269, f. 66va.

104. C. W. Bynum, *Docere verbo et exemplo: An Aspect of Twelfth Century Spirituality* (Missoula, Mont., 1979).

105. Ed. Robson, *Maurice of Sully*, pp. 55–56.

106. See, for example, Robert Pullen, *Et lectulum Salomonis*, MS. London Lambeth 458, f. 152r; Odo of Soissons, *Applica ad te Aaron*, MS. Cambrai B. 561, 106vb, and *Quecumque seminaverit homo*, f. 124rb–va; Prévostin, *Nolite me vocari Noemi*, MSS. Paris BN lat. 14804, f. 110va, and Paris Ars. 543, f. 225va; and Peter of Poitiers, *Ignis in altari*, MSS. Paris BN lat. 14593, f. 8rb–va, and Oxford Bodl. Laud misc. 269, f. 83va.

107. See above, pp. 208-9.

108. See, for example, *Gratias ago Deo meo*, ed. Lyngam, p. 835, and *Fratres, non cessamus*, p. 910.

109. *Meus est galaad*, MS. Oxford Bodl. Laud misc. 269, f. 10ra. Cf. *In sole posuit*, MSS. Paris BN lat. 14593, ff. 129va and 300ra; Paris Maz. 1005, f. 111vb; and Oxford Bodl. Laud misc. 269, f. 23vb.

110. *Sentite de Domino*, MS. Reims 581, f. 78ra.

111. *Factum est in die*, MS. Troyes 1515, f. 81ra-b.

112. *Erat quidam regulus*, ed. Lyngam, p. 887. Cf. Stephen Langton, *Super manus nostras*, MS. Paris BN lat. 16463, f. 95rb: "liber laicorum est pictura clericorum vero scriptura."

113. Raoul Ardent states the first principle succinctly: "Majoris enim efficiae sunt in subjectis exempla, quam verba." (*Exeuntes duo ex discipulis*, *PL* 155, 1861A). Two typical examples of the second are: "Qui enim aliud docet et aliud facit, non omnino veritatem docet, quia quod docet verbo, destruit exemplo" (Prévostin, *Christus passus est*, MS. Paris Ars. 543, f. 208ra); and "Restat autem et eius doctrina contemptibilis sit, cuius vita despicabilis invenitur" (Peter of Poitiers, *Ignis in altari*, MSS. Paris BN lat. 14593, ff. 7vb and 33rb, and Oxford Bodl. Laud misc. 269, f. 83ra.) Jacques of Vitry frequently combines the two arguments, as, for example, in one of his *Sermones dominicales*: "Melius siquidem docet vita quam litera, melius docent opera quam verba, melius fama bona quam lingua. Cuius enim vita despicitur, restat ut eius praedicatio contemnatur. Utrumque tamen necessarium est doctori bona, scilicet, vita et sana doctrina" (*Vado ad eum*, ed. Lyngam, p. 479).

114. *Homo quidam peregre*, MS. Paris BN lat. 2950, f. 77v.

115. *Sacerdotes nescientes Dominum*, MS. London Lambeth 458, f. 129r.

116. *Ibid.*

117. *Homo quidam peregre*, MS. Paris BN lat. 2950, f. 77v.

118. *Gratias ago Deo meo*, ed. Lyngam, p. 835: "Ex quo patet, quod sicut peccat qui scit et non vult docere proximum, sic qui non scit et vult magister esse."

119. *Ecce dies veniunt*, MS. Paris BN lat. 3818, f. 6v. Cf. Alan's *Summa de arte praedicandi* cap. 36, *PL* 210, 181A.

CHAPTER SEVEN

1. *Qui non humiliaverit*, *PL* 198, 1730D-1731A.

2. *Legimus filios Israel*, ed. P. Barzillay Roberts, *Stephanus de Lingua-Tonante: Studies in the Sermons of Stephen Langton* (Toronto, 1968), p. 233.

3. *Beati servi illi*, MSS. Oxford Bodl. Laud misc. 269, f. 12rb-va, and Paris BN lat. 14593, ff. 123ra and 293va. On the use of distinctions as a rhetorical device in twelfth-century sermons see J. Longère, *Les Oeuvres oratoires de maîtres parisiens au XII*[e] *siècle* (2 vols., Paris, 1975), 1: 55, and R. H. Rouse and M. A. Rouse, "*Statim Invenire*: Schools, Preachers, and New Attitudes to the Page," in R. L. Benson and G. Constable, eds., *Renaissance and Renewal in the Twelfth Century* (Cambridge, Mass., 1982), pp. 214-18.

4. *Beati servi illi*, MSS. Oxford Bodl. Laud misc. 269, f. 13ra, and Paris BN lat. 14593, ff. 123rb and 294vb.

5. *Cum esset Iesus annorum duodecim*, ed. T. Lyngam, *Jacobi de Vitriaco Sermones in epistolas et evangelia dominicalia totius anni* (Antwerp, 1575), pp. 131-36.

6. *Ibid.*, p. 134.

7. This sermon is discussed at length below, pp. 246–52.

8. *Qui sedes super cherubim*, *PL* 171, 413A.

9. *Egredimini filiae Sion*, *PL* 198, 1773D–1774A.

10. *Percutiet Deus omnes*, MS. Paris BN lat. 17509, f. 100ra.

11. Peter of Poitiers gives an especially bleak account of academic life: "Nobis quoque scolaribus hac vigilia competit vigilare, quatinus omnes labores et studia ad deum qui summe bonum est referamus. Quia certe si tot carnis macerationes, tot spiritus afflictus, tot frigora et lucubrationes in hieme, tot fervores in estate, tantam victus parcitatem, tantam longam in aliena terra peregrinationem, tantam diuturnam a parentibus et amicis et propinquis vel notis separationem, pro his que in hac vita speramus sustinemus, miserabiliores sumus omnibus hominibus" (*Beati servi illi*, MSS. Oxford Bodl. Laud misc. 269, f. 13va, and Paris BN lat. 14593, ff. 123va and 294va).

12. *Discipuli cum Domino*, MS. London Lambeth 458, f. 116r.

13. *Abeuntes Pharisaei consilium*, *PL* 155, 2116D–2117C.

14. *Legimus filios Israel*, ed. Barzillay Roberts, pp. 235–37.

15. *CUP* 1.intro. no. 4, p. 5. While serving as papal legate (c. 1185), Stephen of Tournai wrote a letter to Fulco, *magister scholarum* at the cathedral school in Orléans, ordering that a cleric be granted a *licentia docendi* unless "ad tale regimen scholarum minus idoneum ostendatis" (Ep. 115, *PL* 211, 404).

16. *Legimus filios Israel*, ed. Barzillay Roberts, pp. 235–36.

17. *Fiduciam talem habemus*, *PL* 155, 2035AB. Both this sermon and that of Jacques of Vitry on the same theme (see n. 18 below) suggest that the use of the adjective *idoneus* in this context was inspired by 2 Corinthians 3.5–6.

18. *Fratres, fiduciam talem habemus*, ed. Lyngam, p. 751.

19. *Cum factus esset*, *PL* 155, 1738D–1739A. Cf. *Exsurgens Petrus in medio fratrum*, *PL* 155, 1351A–1352A. Raoul also suggests thirty as the age for public preaching in his *Speculum universale* 9.37, MS. Paris BN lat. 3240, f. 11rb; cited from J. W. Baldwin, *Masters, Princes and Merchants: The Social Views of Peter the Chanter and His Circle* (2 vols., Princeton, 1970), 2: 90, n. 102.

20. *Ecce advenit Dominator*, ed. Lyngam, p. 136.

21. *Cum esset Iesus annorum duodecim*, ed. Lyngam, p. 136.

22. *Comede volumen istud* (*ad theologos et predicatores*), MS. Paris BN lat. 17509, f. 38rb.

23. *Maria unxit pedes Iesus*, MS. Paris BN lat. 14593, ff. 221ra–b and 342rb–va.

24. *Arbor si cecident*, MS. London Lambeth 458, ff. 149v–150r.

25. *Vinum non habent*, MS. Paris BN lat. 13586, p. 154. Cf. *Nolite me vocare Noemi*, MSS. Paris BN lat. 14804, f. 102va, and Paris Ars. 543, f. 226rb: "Quid dicam de theologis quorum plures discunt ut sciant quod est curiositas, vel ut sciantur quod est vanitas, vel ut vendant quod est simoniaca pravitas, et, quod deterius est, ut veniant magnos honores? Non discunt ut edificentur, quod esset prudens humilitas, vel ut edificent, quod esset fraterna caritas."

26. Cap. 7, ed. J. Hinnebusch, *The Historia Occidentalis of Jacques de Vitry* (Fribourg, 1972), p. 92. In one of his *Sermones dominicales*, Jacques of Vitry criticizes preachers and teachers for four bad motives: cupidity, vanity, curiosity, and heresy (*Abeuntes Pharisaei consilium*, ed. Lyngam, p. 903).

27. *Pone mensam, contemplare*, *PL* 171, 512CD. Prévostin uses the same story to warn against curiosity in *Egredimini filie Syon*, MS. London BM Add. 18335, f. 2v.

28. *Magnum quidem et difficile*, MS. London Lambeth 458, f. 110v. Cf. Peter

Lombard, *Assumpsi me spiritus*, ed. H.-M. Rochais, "Une Collection de textes divers de S. Bernard dans le manuscrit Tours 343," *RTAM* 29 (1962): 110.

29. *Egredimini filiae Ierusalem*, MS. London Lambeth 458, f. 143r.

30. *Miserunt Judaei ab Jerosolymis*, *PL* 155, 1692AB.

31. *Si videris sensatum*, MS. Paris BN lat. 17509, f. 30rb; J. B. Pitra, ed., *Analecta novissima spicilegii Solesmensis altera continuatio* 2 (Tusculum, 1888; reprinted 1967), p. 362.

32. *Obsecro vos fratres*, ed. Lyngam, pp. 130-31.

33. *Beati oculi qui vident*, *PL* 155, 2045BC.

34. *Misit Jesus discipulos suos*, *PL* 155, 1518B; *Omne datum optimum*, 1887CD; *Novissime recumbentibus undecim discipulis*, 1923D; *Cum venerit Paraclitus*, 1934D; and *Estote misericordes*, 1985BC.

35. *Convenerunt Pharisaei in unum*, *PL* 155, 2084B-D.

36. *Si videris sensatum*, MS. Paris BN lat. 17509, f. 29rb-va; ed. Pitra, p. 360. Cf. *Fratres, non cessamus*, ed. Lyngam, p. 910.

37. Teaching for monetary gain is mentioned or alluded to by Raoul Ardent, *Habentes donationes*, *PL* 155, 1740D, and *Abeuntes Pharisaei consilium*, 2117D; and by Jacques of Vitry, *Si sponderis pro amico*, MS. Paris BN, lat. 17509, f. 8rb, and *Fratres imitatores mei*, ed. Lyngam, p. 898.

38. *Utinam, fratres, argentum vestrum*, MS. Cambrai B. 561, f. 128va.

39. Peter of Poitiers, *Quasi modo geniti infantes*, MSS. Oxford Bodl. Laud misc. 269, f. 61ra-b; Bodl. e museo 82, f. 57va; and Paris BN lat. 14593, ff. 146rb and 320vb. Jacques of Vitry, *Cum esset Iesus annorum duodecim*, ed. Lyngam, pp. 133-34, and *Saecularia iudicia (ad judices et advocatos)*, MS. Paris BN lat. 17509, f. 35va.

40. *Qui habitat in adiutorio*, *PL* 198, 1765C.

41. *Apprehendunt septem mulieres*, *PL* 171, 478-79. This theme is the subject of a series of sermons by Peter Comestor found among those in MSS. Oxford Bodl. Laud misc. 484, ff. 1r-53v, and Troyes 425, ff. 34r-105rb. Other moralists to preach on this theme include: Prévostin, *Super excelsa mea*, MS. Paris BN lat. 14804, f. 95ra-b, *Sex annis seminabis*, MS. London BM Add. 18335, f. 9r-v, and *Venite, filii, audite*, MS. London BM Add. 18335, ff. 3r-4r; and Alexander Neckham, *Spiritus Domini replevit*, MSS. Oxford Bodl. Wood empt. 13, f. 104r, and London BM Harley 335, f. 3v.

42. *Omnia poma nova (ad theologos et predicatores)*, MS. Paris BN lat. 17509, f. 39ra. Cf. *Fratres, non cessamus*, ed. Lyngam, p. 911, and *Gratias ago Deo*, ed. Lyngam, pp. 835-36.

43. *Fili, mel invenisti*, *PL* 198, 1794B-D.

44. *Ibid.*, 1795A. On Peter Comestor's use of *distinctiones* see the remarks of Longère, *Oeuvres oratoires* 1: 55.

45. *Qui non humiliaverit*, *PL* 198, 1731-32.

46. *Recumbentibus undecim discipulis*, ed. Lyngam, p. 542.

47. *Omne quod natum est*, ed. Lyngam, pp. 409-10.

48. *Notum vobis facio Evangelium* (eleventh Sunday after Trinity), *PL* 155, 2027D. Cf. *Habent donationes*, *PL* 155, 1740CD.

49. *Notum vobis facio Evangelium* (nativity of St. Paul), *PL* 155, 1392D.

50. *Historia calamitatum*, ed. J. Monfrin (Paris, 1976), pp. 82-83.

51. *Audita feci tibi nova*, *PL* 171, 608D-609C. Cf. *Convertimini filii reverentes*, *PL* 171, 436B.

52. *Arbor si cecident*, MS. London Lambeth 458, f. 149v.

53. *Filius accrescens Ioseph*, MS. Paris BN lat. 14589, f. 40va.

54. *Non coques edum*, MSS. Oxford Bodl. Laud misc. 269, f. 43rb–va, and Paris BN lat. 14593, f. 310rb–va.

55. On this tradition see P. Courcelle, *Connais-toi toi-même: De Socrate à Saint Bernard* (3 vols., Paris, 1974–75).

56. The sermon, which probably dates from the same years as Innocent III's *De miseria* (c. 1195) has been edited and discussed by M.-T. d'Alverny, "Un Sermon d'Alain de Lille sur la misère de l'homme," in L. Wallach, ed., *Literary and Historical Studies in Honor of Harry Caplan* (Ithaca, 1966), pp. 515–35. Cf. *Summa de arte praedicandi* cap. 3, *PL* 210, 116–19.

57. M.-T. d'Alverny, *Alain de Lille, Textes inédits avec une introduction sur sa vie et ses oeuvres* (Paris, 1965), p. 272. See also d'Alverny's discussion of this sermon, pp. 145–47. Cf. *Summa de arte praedicandi* cap. 3, *PL* 210, 118B.

58. *Quasi modo geniti infantes*, MSS. Oxford Bodl. Laud misc. 269, f. 61rb–va, Bodl. e museo 82, f. 57va–b, and Paris BN lat. 14593, f. 320vb. Cf. Innocent III, *De miseria* 1.1, ed. M. Maccarrone, *Lotharii Cardinalis (Innocentii III) De miseria humane conditionis* (Lugano, 1955), p. 8.

59. *Quasi modo geniti infantes, ibid.*

60. *Cantate Domino canticum novum*, MS. Oxford Bodl. Wood empt. 13, f. 88r–v.

61. *De naturis rerum* cap. 173, ed. T. Wright, Rolls Series 34 (London, 1863), p. 283.

62. See especially books 2–4, ed. R. Bossuat, *Alain de Lille, Anticlaudianus: Texte critique avec introduction et des tables* (Paris, 1955): trans. J. J. Sheridan, *Alan of Lille, Anticlaudianus or The Good and Perfect Man* (Toronto, 1973).

63. *Ve vobis qui transitis*, ed. d'Alverny, *Textes inédits*, p. 274.

64. *Ibid.*, p. 275.

65. *Ibid.* Alan expresses similar views in his *Summa de arte praedicandi* cap. 36, *PL* 210, 180, and in the prologue to his theological summa, *Quoniam homines*, ed. P. Glorieux, "La Somme '*Quoniam homines*' d'Alain de Lille," *AHDLMA* 28 (1953): 119–20.

On the theme of despoiling the Egyptians, see H. I. Marrou, *Saint Augustin et la fin de la culture antique* (Rome, 1938), pp. 392–94, and B. Smalley, "Despoiling the Egyptians" (forthcoming). It is especially to be noted that Gregory IX uses the theme to begin his important decree to Paris theologians on the study of natural philosophy (1228), *CUP* 1 no. 59, pp. 114–16. Cf. *CUP* 1 no. 87, pp. 143–44.

66. "[N]on ut ibi figamus pedem, sed ut faciamus pontem" (*Ve vobis qui transitis*, ed. d'Alverny, p. 275).

67. *Quasi modo geniti infantes*, MSS. Oxford Bodl. Laud misc. 269, f. 61rb; Bodl. e museo 82, f. 57va; and Paris BN lat. 14593, f. 320vb.

68. *Arbor si cecident*, MS. London Lambeth 458, f. 148v.

69. *Nolite me vocare Noemi*, MSS. Paris BN lat. 14804, f. 102rb; and Paris Ars. 543, f. 226ra.

70. *Quasi modo geniti infantes* (n. 67 above).

71. *Nolite me vocare Noemi* (n. 69 above).

72. *Christus oris nostri*, MS. Cambridge UL Ii.1.24, f. 161va.

73. *Filius accrescens Ioseph*, MS. Paris BN lat. 14589, f. 40rb.

74. *PL* 198, 1727AB.

75. *PL* 171, 677B. On the *sophismata logicalia*, which were the school exercises

used by the masters of dialectic, see M. Grabmann, "Die Sophismataliteratur des 12. und 13. Jahrhunderts," *BGPTM* 37 (1940): 1-27.

76. On these translations and their impact in Paris see G. Leff, *Paris and Oxford Universities in the Thirteenth and Fourteenth Centuries* (New York, 1968), pp. 127-34 and 188-205. See also M.-T. d'Alverny, "Translations and Translators," in Benson and Constable, eds., *Renaissance and Renewal*, pp. 421-62, for a summary of the translations and their diffusion.

77. *Cum egrediemini*, MS. Paris BN lat. 17509, f. 31va; ed. Pitra, p. 366.

78. *Ibid.*, f. 31va-b; p. 366.

79. *Ibid.*, f. 31vb; pp. 366-67.

80. *Ibid.*, ff. 31vb-32ra; p. 367.

81. *Ibid.*, f. 32ra; pp. 367-68.

82. Leff, *Paris and Oxford Universities*, pp. 197-201.

83. *Cum egrediemini*, MS. Paris BN lat. 17509, f. 32ra; ed. Pitra, p. 368. Cf. Peter Lombard, *Audita feci tibi nova*, *PL* 171, 608D-609C.

84. *Cum egrediemini*, MS. Paris BN lat. 17509, f. 32ra; ed. Pitra, p. 368.

85. *Ibid.*

86. *Ibid.*

87. *Quaecumque scripta sunt*, ed. Lyngam, p. 19.

88. *Cum egrediemini*, MS. Paris BN lat. 17509, f. 32rb; ed. Pitra, pp. 368-69. Jacques of Vitry also uses the story of Jerome to illustrate the same point in *Quaecumque scripta sunt*, ed. Lyngam, p. 19.

89. *Cum egrediemini*, MS. Paris BN lat. 17509, f. 32rb-va; ed. Pitra, p. 369. On the theme of the captive woman see H. de Lubac, *Exégèse médiévale: Les Quatre Sens de l'Ecriture* (4 vols., Paris, 1959-64), 1: 290-304; and P. Courcelle, "Le Personnage de philosophie dans la littérature latine," *Journal des savants* (1970): 231-32.

90. Jacques of Vitry is quoting Isidore of Seville, *Sententiae* 3.13, *PL* 83, 685B-686A: "Ideo prohibetur Christianus figmenta legere poetarum, quia per oblectamenta inanium fabularum mentem excitant ad incentiva libidinum." This prohibition can also be found in Gratian, *Decretum* 1. D. 37, c. 15, *PL* 187, 207B. Stephen of Tournai argues that this decree prohibits bishops and priests from reading books of poetry but allows others to do so when applied "ad sacre doctrine usum" (*Die Summa des Stephanus Tornacensis über das Decretum Gratiani*, ed. J. H. von Schulte [Giessen, 1891], p. 55). Peter Comestor, *Converti me ad viam portae*, *PL* 198, 1727A, also warns against the study of the "figmenta poetarum."

91. *Cum egrediemini*, MS. Paris BN lat. 17509, f. 32vb; ed. Pitra, p. 370.

92. *Ibid.*, ff. 32vb-33ra; p. 371.

93. *Ibid.*, f. 33ra; p. 371. In the sermon *Quasi modo geniti infantes*, ed. Lyngam, p. 404, Jacques of Vitry stipulates the order in which these biblical books should be studied: first Proverbs, then Ecclesiastes, and last the Song of Songs.

94. See T. F. Crane, *The Exempla or Illustrative Stories from the Sermones Vulgares of Jacques de Vitry*, Publications of the Folk-Lore Society 26 (London, 1890), pp. 13-14. These exempla include an animal fable about a curious fox and a stubborn mule and the story of a simple rustic who, having dropped his axe from a bridge, is determined to wait until all the water has passed by to retrieve it. The former, Jacques explains, illustrates the foolishness of curiosity, the latter the stupidity of vainly seeking to know everything.

95. *Cum egrediemini*, MS. Paris BN lat. 17509, f. 31ra; ed. Pitra, pp. 365-66.

The prothemes of Jacques of Vitry's *sermones ad status* generally form an integral part of the subject of the sermon. Cf. what D. L. d'Avray and M. Tausche say about the prothemes to the sermons *ad coniugatos* in their recent article "Marriage Sermons in *ad status* Collections of the Central Middle Ages," *AHDLMA* 47 (1981): 86, n. 64.

96. *Cum egrediemini*, MS. Paris BN lat. 17509, f. 31ra; ed. Pitra, p. 365.

97. In MS. London BM Add. 18335, ff. 12r–14r, the sermon is the eighth of nineteen sermons entitled *Sermones prepositini accessus ad populum*. In MS. Paris BN lat. 13586, pp. 153–54, the sermon is anonymous but is found in a collection containing other sermons attributed to "Magister Prepositinus." On this manuscript see Hauréau, *N&E* 2 (1891): 300–323, and G. Lacombe, *La Vie et les oeuvres de Prévostin*, Bibliothèque Thomiste 2 (Le Saulchoir, 1927), pp. 191–92.

98. *Vinum non habent*, MS. Paris BN lat. 13586, p. 154. In the longer version of the sermon, in MS. London BM Add. 18335, ff. 13v–14r, Christ again speaks of his seven truly liberal arts, which are here symbolized by the spices that are mixed to prepare the wine of exultation referred to in the Song of Songs (8.2). The arts are also compared to the three gifts of the Magi: grammar, rhetoric, and dialectic are the gold; arithmetic and geometry, the myrrh; and music and astronomy, the frankincense. A significant distinction, not found in the other version, is also made between grammar and dialectic: "Grammatica igitur mores apponit, dialectica fidem" (f. 14r).

99. *Cum egrediemini*, MS. Paris BN lat. 17509, ff. 31vb–32ra; ed. Pitra, pp. 367–68.

100. *Si quis vult post me venire*, *PL* 171, 896D, and *Melior est canis*, *PL* 198, 1790A. Cf. *Laetare, Jerusalem*, *PL* 198, 1762CD.

101. *Cantate Domino canticum novum*, MS. Oxford Bodl. Wood empt. 13, f. 89r.

102. *Dixit Jesus discipulis*, *PL* 155, 1535C.

103. *Sentite de Domino*, MS. Reims 581, f. 78rb.

104. *Apud veteres in libro numeri*, MS. London Lambeth 458, f. 164r.

105. *Beatus et sanctus*, MSS. Oxford Bodl. Laud misc. 269, ff. 69vb–70ra, and Paris BN lat. 14593, f. 325vb.

106. *Gratia Dei sum*, MSS. Oxford Bodl. Laud misc. 269, f. 34vb, and Paris BN lat. 14593, f. 305va.

107. *Cum natus esset Iesus*, *PL* 155, 1731B.

108. Alan of Lille, *Cum natus esset Iesus*, MS. Paris BN lat. 3818, f. 19r: "Magi isti dicuntur non esse magi a magica arte, sed a maioritate scientie. . . . Isti instructi fuerunt et inspiratione divina et naturali philosophia." Cf. Jacques of Vitry, *Cum natus esset Iesus*, ed. Lyngam, p. 115.

109. Hilduin, *Surge illuminare Iherusalem*, MS. Paris Maz. 774, f. 194ra–b. Peter Lombard, *Congregabuntur filii Juda*, *PL* 171, 402D–403C. Cf. *Egredimini, filiae Sion*, *PL* 171, 352D, where Lombard calls philosophers, along with Jews and heretics, the enemies of the Church who "animarum salutem promittebant, de beatitudine ac justitia praecepta dabant, quam non conferebant sed auferebant."

110. *Congregabuntur filii Juda*, *PL* 171, 403C.

111. Peter Comestor, *Super tribus sceleribus*, *PL* 171, 677B. Cf. Stephen Langton, *Legimus filios Israel*, ed. Barzillay Roberts, p. 235.

112. *Comede volumen istum*, MS. Paris BN lat. 17509, f. 37ra–va. For his comments about the order in which to read the books of Solomon, see n. 93 above.

113. *Et lectulum Salomonis*, MS. London Lambeth 458, ff. 152v-153r.

114. *Accelera, tria sata*, *PL* 210, 209CD.

115. J. Leclercq, "L'Idéal du théologien au moyen âge," *Revue des sciences religieuses* 2 (1947): 121-48.

116. *Legimus filios Israel*, ed. Barzillay Roberts, pp. 230-33; see Baldwin, *Masters, Princes and Merchants* 1: 111-13.

117. *Legimus filios Israel*, ed. Barzillay Roberts, p. 233.

118. *Qui habitat in adiutorio*, *PL* 198, 1755CD.

119. *Quasi modo geniti infantes*, MSS. Oxford Bodl. Laud misc. 269, f. 61va-b; Bodl. e museo 82, f. 57vb; and Paris BN lat. 14593, f. 320vb.

120. *Ego Johannes vidi*, *PL* 155, 1514B.

121. On the theme of the richness of Scripture see, for example, Robert Pullen, *Sacerdotes nescientes Dominum*, MS. London Lambeth 458, ff. 129v-130r, and *Magnum quidem et difficile*, f. 112r; Peter Lombard, *Egredere de terra tua*, *PL* 171, 862C, and *Pone mensam*, 514D-515C; and Jacques of Vitry, *Quaecumque scripta sunt*, ed. Lyngam, p. 19. Peter of Poitiers uses the especially beautiful image of the flowers in the fuller's field (Isa. 7.3) in *Egredere in occursum*, MSS. Oxford Bodl. Laud misc. 269, f. 17ra; Paris BN lat. 14593, f. 296va; and Paris Maz. 1005, f. 102rb-va.

122. *Cum esset Iesus annorum duodecim*, ed. Lyngam, p. 135. Cf. *Proverbium est*, MS. Paris BN lat. 17509, f. 150va, and *Beatus qui vigilat*, f. 151va.

123. *Secundum multitudinem dolorum*, MSS. Oxford Bodl. Laud misc. 269, f. 30vb, and Paris BN lat. 14593, f. 303va.

124. *Accipe puerum istum*, MS. Troyes 1515, f. 9va.

125. *Non vos me eligistis*, MS. Paris BN lat. 16463, f. 139ra. Cf. *Preceptor tota nocte*, MS. Paris BN lat. 16463, f. 85ra, where Peter Lombard states that both the mechanical arts and Christian doctrine are better learned when taught from infancy, and *Homo quidam erat dives*, MS. Leipzig UB 443, f. 102v, cited by J. Longère, *Les Oeuvres oratoires des maîtres parisiens au XIIe siècle* (2 vols., Paris, 1975), 2: 301, n. 18.

126. *Beatus qui vigilat*, MS. Paris BN lat. 17509, f. 152rb.

127. *Si videris sensatum*, MS. Paris BN lat. 17509, f. 29ra-b; ed. Pitra, p. 359. Jacques cites as precedents several well-known patristic and classical examples, including Plato's choice of Socrates, Aristotle's of Plato, and the legend that both Plato and Pythagoras traveled to Egypt to learn their arts. See Hugh of St. Victor, *Didascalicon* 3.2, ed. C. Buttimer (Washington, 1939), pp. 48-52.

128. "Cum igitur omnia legere non possumus, utiliora legamus inter cuncta leges et percunctamur doctos" (*Si videris sensatum*, MS. Paris BN lat. 17509, f. 29va; ed. Pitra, p. 361). Cf. *Cum egrediemini*, MS. Paris BN lat. 17509, f. 33rb; ed. Pitra, p. 372.

129. *Venit Iesus a Galilea*, ed. Lyngam, p. 145.

130. *Circumdabo domum meam (ad fratres ordinis militaris)*, MS. Paris BN lat. 17509, f. 70ra-b.

131. *Saecularia justitia (ad judices et advocatos)*, MS. Paris BN lat. 17509, f. 35rb-va. Cf. *Comede volumen istud (ad theologos et predicatores)*, MS. Paris BN lat. 17509, f. 37rb. On the prohibition against clerics studying civil law, see Baldwin, *Masters, Princes and Merchants* 1: 86-87.

132. Preaching on the text of Mk. 11.17, Jacques says: "Videtur quod in Ecclesiis Dei, neque in aliis locis Deo consecratis liceat vendere candelas vel merces

etiam Deo offerendas, nec pueros docere, nec causas tractari, nec aliud officium, nisi pure Ecclesiasticum exerceri" (*Deus in loco sancto suo*, ed. Lyngam, p. 733). Still, Jacques may have found teaching in churches preferable to the situation he describes in Paris, where lectures were given in rooms upstairs from brothels (see *Historia Occidentalis* cap. 7, ed. Hinnebusch, p. 91).

133. "Locum ut non in locis publicis, non in sterquiliniis, non in compitis viarum, nec in plateis verba dei seminemus, sicut quidam nostrorum scolarium qui garrulitatem auctoritatem putant" (*Quis putas est*, MSS. Oxford Bodl. Laud misc. 269, f. 64va, and Bodl. e museo 82, f. 61va).

134. *Si videris sensatum*, MS. Paris BN lat. 17509, f. 30vb; ed. Pitra, p. 363.

135. *In paucis vexati*, MS. Paris BN lat. 17509, f. 82va; ed. Crane, *Exempla*, pp. 47-48.

136. *Provideat Dominus Deus* (*ad canonicos seculares*), MS. Paris BN lat. 17509, f. 24rb; ed. Crane, *Exempla*, p. 8.

137. Ed. G. Frenken, *Die Exempla des Jacob von Vitry*, Quellen und Untersuchungen zur lateinischen Philologie des Mittelalters 15 (Munich, 1914), pp. 146-47.

138. *Ibid.*, p. 139.

139. *Ibid.*, pp. 118-19.

140. *Ibid.*, pp. 137-38.

141. *Come eius sicut elate palmarum* (*ad monachos nigros*), MS. Paris BN lat. 17509, f. 48rb-va: "Multi vero viri prudentes et litterati in seculo religionem intrarent nisi timerent quod statim ad exteriora et secularia negocia mitterentur et quietem claustri amitterent."

142. *Veritas mea et misericordia*, MSS. Oxford Bodl. Laud misc. 269, f. 21rb-va; Paris BN lat. 14593, f. 298vb; and Paris Maz. 1005, f. 101rb.

143. *Utinam, fratres, argentum*, MS. Cambrai B.561, f. 128va: "Vidi multos, cognovi plurimos, immo video multos, cognosco plurimos in quorum labore non est veritas sed occasio in cordibus suis mendatium gestantes et vanitatem. . . . Adulterant enim studium non incedentes ex sinceritate."

144. See, for example, Raoul Ardent, *Cum factus esset Iesus annorum duodecim*, *PL* 155, 1738D-1739A; Prévostin, *Congregate illi*, MS. Paris BN lat. 18172, f. 51r; and Alexander Neckham, *Super ecclesiasten* 5 (*De vanitate curiositatis*), MS. Oxford Corpus Christi College 45, f. 184v.

145. *Homo quidam erat dives*, ed. Lyngam, pp. 717-18.

146. *Si videris sensatum*, MS. Paris BN lat. 17509, f. 30rb; ed. Pitra, p. 362.

147. *Scrutemur vias nostras*, MSS. Oxford Bodl. Laud misc. 269, ff. 41vb-42ra, and Paris BN lat. 14593, f. 309rb-va.

148. *Beati servi illi*, MSS. Oxford Bodl. Laud misc. 269, f. 13rb, and Paris BN lat. 14593, f. 294va.

149. *Scrutemur vias nostras*, MS. Oxford Bodl. Laud misc. 269, f. 42ra, and Paris BN lat. 14593, f. 309va. The example is introduced with the statement: "Sunt qui invidia cruciantur quod vitium in nobis scolaribus maxime dominatur."

150. Cap. 7, ed. Hinnebusch, pp. 90-93.

151. *Si videris sensatum*, MS. Paris BN lat. 17509, f. 30va; ed. Pitra, p. 362. Robert of Courson writes of masters actually buying audiences (*Summa*, MS. Paris BN lat. 14524, f. 49vb; cited by Baldwin, *Masters, Princes and Merchants* 2: 89, n. 92).

152. *Si videris sensatum*, MS. Paris BN lat. 17509, f. 31ra; ed. Crane, *Exempla*, p. 11.

153. *Beati servi illi*, MSS. Oxford Bodl. Laud misc. 269, f. 13rb, and BN Paris lat. 14593, ff. 123rb and 294rb.

154. *Scrutemur vias nostras*, MSS. Oxford Bodl. Laud misc. 269, ff. 41vb–42ra, and Paris BN lat. 14593, f. 309rb–va. Cf. *Veritas mea et misericordia*, MSS. Oxford Bodl. Laud misc. 269, f. 21rb–va; Paris BN lat. 14593, f. 298vb; and Paris Maz. 1005, f. 101rb.

155. *Nolite me vocare Noemi*, MSS. Paris BN lat. 14804, f. 102va, and Paris Ars. 543, f. 226rb.

156. *Historia Occidentalis* cap. 7, ed. Hinnebusch, p. 91.

157. *Qui sedes super cherubim*, *PL* 171, 413A.

158. *Beati servi illi*, MSS. Oxford Bodl. Laud misc. 269, f. 13va, and Paris BN lat. 14593, ff. 123va and 294va.

159. *Venit autem Amelech*, MS. London Lambeth 458, f. 177r.

160. *Paulus dicit: Omnes nos unum sumus*, MSS. Paris BN lat. 13586, pp. 85–86, and Paris BN lat. 3563, f. 37ra–rb.

161. *Si videris sensatum*, MS. Paris BN lat. 17509, f. 30vb; ed. Pitra, p. 363.

162. *Beatus qui vigilat*, MS. Paris BN lat. 17509, f. 152rb.

163. *Convertimini ad me*, *PL* 155, 1780D.

164. *Asperges me Domine*, MSS. Cambridge UL Ii.1.24, f. 156rb–va; Paris BN lat. 18172, ff. 62v–63r; and Paris Maz. 774, f. 117ra–b.

165. *Christus oris nostri*, MS. Cambridge UL Ii.1.24, f. 161rb.

166. *Excubate in custodiis* (*ad canonicos seculares et alios clericos*), MS. Paris BN lat. 17509, f. 20rb.

167. *Novate nobis novale*, MS. Paris BN lat. 14593, f. 67rb.

168. Alexander Neckham, *Ponite corda vestra*, MS. Oxford Bodl. Wood empt. 13, f. 112v; Peter of Poitiers, *Beati servi illi*, MS. Oxford Bodl. Laud misc. 269, f. 13rb; and Stephen Langton, *Viderunt eam hostes*, MS. Paris BN lat. 16463, f. 27rb–va.

169. "Sunt quidam qui ita gloriantur in vestibus . . . scilicet in lanis peccorum et in diversis tincturis pannorum, qui appariunt in cappa rubea modo in nigra. Et pauperes scolares . . . moriuntur frigore et fame, nec est qui compatiatur eis" (*Miser luxuriosus dicere potest*, MS. Paris BN lat. 14470, f. 212va–b.). This anonymous sermon is found among others known to belong to Peter Comestor and Stephen Langton, but it has not yet been attributed to a specific master.

170. *Erat homo ex Pharisaeis*, *PL* 155, 1951D–1952A.

171. *In ecclesiis benedicite*, MS. Oxford Bodl. Laud misc. 269, f. 66va. See passage quoted above, pp. 216–17.

172. See G. Lacombe, "Studies on the Commentaries of Cardinal Stephen Langton," *AHDLMA* 5 (1930): 61–62.

173. *Summa de arte praedicandi* cap. 36, *PL* 210, 181.

174. *Legimus in libro regem*, MS. London Lambeth 458, ff. 161v–162r.

175. Quoted from Smalley, *Study of the Bible*, p. 252. Cf. Jacques of Vitry, *Ascendens Iesus in naviculam*, ed. Lyngam, p. 853.

176. "Unde et quosdam audivimus cum de pluritate beneficiorum arguerentur, dicentes multis condempnare totum mundum. Nonne magistri theologie et alii innumeri sapientes plures habent prebendas et diversos tenent personatus et ecclesias?" (*Excubate in custodiis*, MS. Paris BN lat. 17509, f. 20rb).

177. On Stephen of Tournai's education see the biographical study of J. Warichez, *Etienne de Tournai et son temps* (Tournai, 1937), pp. 1–40. It was long

assumed that Stephen had also studied theology in Paris, a view asserted most confidently by J. H. von Schulte in the introduction to his edition of Stephen's *Summa, Die Summa des Stephanus Tornacensis über das Decretum Gratiani* (Giessen, 1891), p. xxiii. The detailed knowledge of the controversies among Paris theologians found in part 3 of the *Summa* seemed to support this view, but Stephen of Tournai's authorship of this part of the work is now seriously doubted. See S. Kuttner, "The Third Part of Stephen of Tournai's *Summa*," *Traditio* 14 (1958): 502-5. There is no other convincing evidence of an association with the schools of Paris before Stephen became abbot of Ste. Geneviève in 1176. Neither is there any certain evidence that Stephen had studied in the schools of Chartres, as argued by Warichez, pp. 29-40. Although two of his letters (Epp. 36 and 37 in the Migne edition, cited in note 178 below) suggest some formal ties with the chapter at Chartres, they do not specifically place him at the schools there.

178. The poem, *In commune theatrum*, has been edited by L. Auvray, "Une Poème rythmique et une lettre d'Etienne de Tournai," *Mélanges Paul Fabre* (Paris, 1902), pp. 284-90, and the *Summa* by von Schulte (see n. 177 above). Stephen's collection of more than 300 letters can be found in two separate editions: J. P. Migne, *PL* 211, and J. Desilve, *Letters d'Etienne de Tournai* (Valenciennes and Paris, 1893). On the value of these letters as a historical source see S. Scheler, *Sitten und Bildung der französischen Geistlichkeit nach den Briefen Stephanus von Tournai*, Historische Studien 130 (Berlin, 1915).

There are two major collections of sermons attributed to Stephen of Tournai. MS. Paris Ste. Gen. 1421 contains a unique collection of 45 sermons, only one of which appears elsewhere. The other collection, varying in size, is found in MSS. Paris Ars. 400 (29 sermons); Paris BN lat. 3733 (26 sermons); and Paris BN lat. 16463 (23 sermons); copies of several of these sermons also appear in other manuscript collections of the sermons of Paris masters, including MSS. Paris BN lat. 13586 and Paris BN lat. 18172. See J. B. Schneyer, *Repertorium der lateinischen Sermones des Mittelalters* (5 vols., *BGPTM*, Munster, 1969-75), 5: 509-13.

179. On Stephen of Tournai's stormy career as bishop see Warichez, *Etienne de Tournai*, pp. 246*ff.*, especially pp. 349-83, which recount his long struggle against communal emancipation.

180. Stephen's problems with Celestine III stemmed, apparently, from the circumstances of his election to the bishopric of Tournai. The chapter had originally elected Peter the Chanter, on behalf of whose election Stephen had written to the metropolitan, Archbishop William of Reims (Ep. 175, *PL* 211, 462; also in *CUP* 1.intro. no. 46, p. 46). On this disputed election and Stephen's subsequent troubles with Celestine III see, in addition to Warichez, *Etienne de Tournai*, pp. 320-21, the account in Baldwin, *Masters, Princes and Merchants* 1: 9-10.

181. Ep. 251, *PL* 211, 516, and *CUP* 1.intro. no. 48, pp. 47-48.

182. *Ibid.*

183. *Ibid.* This image of the torn garments of philosophy is taken from Boethius, *De consolatione philosophiae* 1.1. 22-24.

184. Ep. 251, *PL* 211, 516, and *CUP* 1.Intro. no. 48, p. 47.

185. *CUP* 1.intro. nos. 41-48, pp. 42-48.

186. For example, Stephen wrote several other letters of support for masters, e.g., an appeal to the archbishop of Reims to provide a benefice for a certain Master Hugo de Novaria (Ep. 105, *PL* 211, 394). Other significant examples of support of the schools include his intervention in 1176 to assist a scholar who had

been deprived of his inheritance because the judges—who were, according to Stephen, "illiterate and hated learned men"—refused to accept study as a legitimate excuse for absence from legal proceedings. In a letter to Archbishop William of Reims, Stephen warns that the action of the judges poses a potential threat to learning (Ep. 23, *PL* 211, 321-22). And, acting as papal judge delegate about 1185, Stephen orders the scholasticus of the cathedral of St. Croix, Orléans, to grant a *licentia docendi* to a certain Master G., who had previously been denied the right to teach in the diocese (Ep. 115, *PL* 211, 404).

187. *Diplomatum Belgicorum nova collectio*, ed. A. Miraeus and J. Foppens (Louvain, 1723), 2: 1197-98.

188. *Ibid.*, pp. 981-82.

189. *Iesus christus heri*, MSS. Paris BN lat. 3733, f. 85v, and Paris Ars. 400, f. 22vb.

190. *Postulavi patrem meum*, MSS. Paris BN lat. 3733, f. 77v, and Paris Ars. 400, f. 23vb.

191. *Accedite ad Dominum*, MS. Paris Ste. Gen. 1421, f. 26ra-b.

192. *Lingua canum tuorum*, MS. Paris Ste. Gen. 1421, f. 97rb.

193. *Dignus es, Domine*, MSS. Paris BN lat. 3733, f. 51r; Paris BN lat. 16463, f. 105va; and Paris Ars. 400, f. 13rb.

194. *Iesus christus heri*, MSS. Paris BN lat. 3733, f. 85v, and Paris Ars. 400, f. 22va-b.

195. *Ibid.*

196. *Facies tentorum in introitu*, MS. Paris Ste. Gen. 1421, f. 13rb.

197. *Mulierem fortem*, MSS. Paris BN lat. 3733, f. 88v, and Paris Ars. 400, f. 33ra-b.

198. For Stephen's remarks on the danger of public disputation see *Ponam te in superbiam*, MSS. Paris BN lat. 3733, f. 71r; Paris BN lat. 16463, f. 107ra; and Paris Ars. 400, f. 11ra; and *Iesus Christus heri*, MSS. Paris BN lat. 3733, f. 85v, and Paris Ars. 400, f. 22vb. In the second of these sermons, Stephen speaks approvingly of the action of a "christianissimus imperator" (Charlemagne?) who prohibited public disputation because of the danger it posed to faith.

199. See above, pp. 232-33.

200. *Cum esses iunior*, MSS. Paris BN lat. 3733, ff. 53v-54r; Paris BN lat. 16463, f. 132rb-va; and Paris Ars. 400, f. 26va. In other sermons, Stephen does not make as clear a distinction between physical and mental wandering: "Curiositas hominem extra se ducit ut alienam vitam inquirat. Per negligentiam fit deses circa se, per curiositatem vagatur extra se." (*Petrus quidem servatabur*, MS. Paris Ste. Gen. 1421, f. 83rb) and "Curiositas est in ludis, spectaculis, theatris, discurribus vagis, rebus novis videndis, rumoribus audiendis et recitandis" (*Maria Magdalena*, MS. Paris BN lat. 3733, f. 79r).

201. See note 203 below.

202. *Sapientia vincit malitiam*, MSS. Paris BN lat. 3733, ff. 63r-64r; Paris BN lat. 16463, 5ra-vb; and Paris Ars. 400, f. 28rb-vb.

203. "Sunt autem duo per maxima et ad nocendum pessima, quibus insidiis latens diabolus nititur ut interficiat innocentem. Alterum movet contra scolares, alterum contra claustrales. Cum enim due scole sunt, altera doctrine, altera discipline. In altera est auditorium veritatis, in altera exercitium virtutis. Singule si viam propositam habent, a qua deviare vel errare periculosum est et mortale. Scola doctrine et veritatis viam habet catholicam fidem, scola discipline et virtutis

sanctam operationem. Et quoniam neque doctrina sine disciplina, neque disciplina sine doctrina, neque virtus sine veritate, neque veritas sine virtute proficiunt ad salutem, una potest dici via propter eundem ad quem tendit finem, quamvis due dicantur propter geminam sollicitudinem. Via hec recta est, plana et munda. Recta sine errore, plana sine offensione, munda sine sorde. . . . Iuxta hanc viam tendit laqueos adversarius, et iuxta item scandalum ponit scolaribus in auditorio doctrine et claustralibus in exercitio discipline. Contra scolares movet heresim, contra claustrales ypocrism" (*Sapientia vincit malitiam*, MSS. Paris BN lat. 3733, f. 63r; Paris BN lat. 16463, f. 5ra; and Paris Ars. 400, f. 28rb).

204. For evidence of Stephen's diligent supervision of the studies of clerics at Ste. Geneviève, see the letters to Archbishop Absalon of Lund about the education of his two nephews, especially Epp. 80 and 111, *PL* 211, 376 and 400; *CUP* 1.intro. nos. 41 and 42, pp. 42-43. On the school of Ste. Geneviève under Abbot Stephen and on its importance to the history of the University of Paris, compare the recent assessment of J. Boussard, *Nouvelle Histoire de Paris: De la Fin du siège de 885-886 à la mort de Philippe Auguste* (Paris, 1976), pp. 332-34.

CONCLUSION

1. *The Historia Occidentalis of Jacques de Vitry* cap. 7, ed. J. Hinnebusch, Spicilegium Friburgense 17 (Fribourg, 1972), p. 92.

2. Cited from G. Lacombe and B. Smalley, "Studies in the Commentaries of Cardinal Stephen Langton," *AHDLMA* 5 (1930): 164. The comparison seems to have been a common one in the twelfth century. See, for example, the letters of Philip of Harvengt, *CUP* 1.intro. nos. 51-52, pp. 50-52. It was also used by Gregory IX in the thirteenth century (*CUP* 1 nos. 79 and 82, pp. 136-37 and 140).

3. J. W. Baldwin, "Masters at Paris, 1179-1215," in R. L. Benson and G. Constable, eds., *Renaissance and Renewal in the Twelfth Century* (Cambridge, Mass., 1982), pp. 148-51.

4. R. W. Southern, "The Schools of Paris and the School of Chartres," in Benson and Constable, eds., *Renaissance and Renewal*, p. 119.

5. Baldwin, "Masters at Paris," pp. 144-48.

6. Southern, "The Schools of Paris," p. 128, n. 44.

7. See above, pp. 261-63.

8. J. Boussard, *Nouvelle Histoire de Paris: De la Fin du siège de 885-886 à la mort de Philippe Auguste* (Paris, 1976), pp. 319-22. For comparisons between Paris and other French cathedral cities see Southern, "The Schools of Paris," p. 117, n. 7, and Baldwin, "Masters at Paris," p. 141, n. 12.

9. Boussard, *Nouvelle Histoire de Paris*, p. 380.

10. *Ibid.*, pp. 316-17.

11. To raise the twelve pounds for a full year's lease, John had to sell his horse. Letter 136, *The Letters of John of Salisbury*, ed. and trans. W. J. Millor, H. E. Butler, and C. N. L. Brooke (2 vols., London, 1955; Oxford, 1979), 2: 12-13.

12. J. W. Baldwin, *Masters, Princes and Merchants: The Social Views of Peter the Chanter and His Circle* (2 vols., Princeton, 1970), 1: 130.

13. F. M. Powicke, *Stephen Langton* (Oxford, 1928), p. 44.

14. *CUP* 1.intro. no. 55, p. 56.

15. Jacques of Vitry, *Historia Occidentalis* cap. 7, ed. Hinnebusch, p. 91.

16. In 1192 Stephen of Tournai, acting as papal judge delegate, absolved the abbot of St. Germain of any guilt in the affair (*CUP* 1.intro. no. 47, p. 47).

17. *Historia Occidentalis* cap. 7, ed. Hinnebusch, p. 90.

18. On the issue of jurisdiction over the issuing of the *licentia docendi* in this period, see the conclusions of Baldwin, "Masters at Paris," p. 143, n. 21.

19. On this distinction see S. d'Irsay, *Histoire des universités françaises et étrangères des origines à nos jours* (Paris, 1933), 1: 129-33, and the more recent article of L. Boehm, "Die *negotio scholaris*: Zur Entstehung von Berufsbewersstsein und Rechtsstand des Universitätsgelehrten im Mittelalter," in K. Schnith, ed., *Festiva Lanx: Johannes Spörl Festgabe* (Munich, 1966), pp. 29-52.

20. J. LeGoff, "The Universities and Public Authorities in the Middle Ages and Renaissance," in *Time, Work and Culture in the Middle Ages*, trans. A. Goldhammer (Chicago, 1980), p. 137.

21. The actual figures are 3 percent for the reign of Louis VII and 13 to 16 percent for that of Philip Augustus, compared to 29 percent for England during the same period. In the reign of Louis IX, 41 percent of the regalian bishops were from the ranks of masters. See Baldwin, "Masters at Paris," p. 154, and "*Studium et regnum*: The Penetration of University Personnel into French and English Administration at the Turn of the Twelfth and Thirteenth Centuries," *Revue des études islamiques* 44 (1976): 206-7.

22. Baldwin, "Masters at Paris," pp. 156-57, concludes that there were only two or three masters in the employ of Louis VII and about a dozen in that of Philip Augustus.

23. On the career of William the Breton see *Oeuvres de Rigord et Guillaume le Breton*, ed. H. F. Delaborde (2 vols., Paris, 1882-85), 1: lxxix-lxxx.

24. See B. Smalley, "Capetian France," in J. M. Wallace-Hadrill and J. McManners, eds., *France: Government and Society* (London, 1957), pp. 73-76.

25. On the building of the walls see Boussard, *Nouvelle Histoire de Paris*, pp. 319-27. On the impact the walls had on the schools see Baldwin, "Masters in Paris," pp. 140-41, and L. Halphen, "Les Origines de l'Université de Paris," in L. Halphen et al., eds., *Aspects de l'Université de Paris* (Paris, 1949), p. 20.

26. *CUP* 1 no. 10, pp. 69-70; H. Rashdall, *The Universities of Europe in the Middle Ages*, rev. ed. by F. M. Powicke and A. B. Emden (3 vols., Oxford, 1936), 1: 502-4.

27. *CUP* 1.intro. no. 50, pp. 49-50; Rashdall, *The Universities of Europe in the Middle Ages* 1: 501-2. It was Baldwin, "Masters at Paris," p. 141, who suggested that this foundation also originated under Capetian auspices.

28. Letter 255 (to Peter the Scribe), ed. Millor et al., 2: 394-95.

29. *CUP* 1.intro. no. 47, p. 47.

30. MS. Paris Maz. 178, f. 73va; cited in Baldwin, *Masters, Princes and Merchants* 2: 51, n. 55.

31. *Chronica*, ed. W. Stubbs, Rolls Series 51 (4 vols., London, 1868-71), 4: 120-21.

32. *CUP* 1 no. 1, pp. 59-61. On these privileges see P. Kibre, *Scholarly Privileges in the Middle Ages* (Cambridge, Mass., 1962), pp. 7-8 and 85-87, and Rashdall, *The Universities of Europe in the Middle Ages* 1: 294-98. On the general subject of clerical privileges see R. Génestal, *Le Privilegium fori en France du Décret de Gratien à la fin du XIV*[e] *siècle* (2 vols., Paris, 1921-24).

33. "Pro tenore siquidem privilegii, quod scolaribus Parisiensibus contulimus, nolumus ut canonici Parisienses et eorum servientes in hoc privilegio contineantur" (*CUP* 1 no. 1, p. 60).

34. On this point, I agree with Rashdall, *The Universities of Europe in the*

Middle Ages 1: 297-98, and disagree with LeGoff, who argues that Philip's privilege did recognize the legal autonomy of the university ("Universities and Public Authorities," p. 139).

35. *Oeuvres*, ed. Delaborde 1: 296-97.

36. *CUP* 1 no. 13, pp. 72-73.

37. See, for example, Halphen, "Les Origines," pp. 11-27, and E. Behler, "Die Entstehung der mittelalterlichen Universität von Paris," in H. Rahner and E. von Severus, eds., *Perennitas: Festschrift für Thomas Michels* (Münster, 1963), pp. 294-321.

38. According to Geoffrey of Auxerre, Pope Innocent II had himself built the fire in Rome for the burning of Peter Abelard's books. Geoffrey's letter can be found in V. Cousins, ed., *Abaelardi opera* (2 vols., Paris, 1849-59), 1: 70.

39. *Annales Reicherspergenses, MGH SS* 27, 471.

40. *CUP* 1.intro. no. 3, p. 4.

41. *CUP* 1.intro. no. 9, pp. 8-9.

42. *CUP* 1 no. 11, pp. 70-71.

43. This was the punishment that had been prescribed for such cases by the Lateran Council of 1139 (Mansi 21, 530).

44. *CUP* 1.intro. no. 5, pp. 5-6. On this decree, see Kibre, *Scholarly Privileges*, pp. 87-88.

45. *CUP* 1.intro. nos. 6 and 7, pp. 6-8.

46. *CUP* 1.intro. nos. 10 and 11, pp. 9-10.

47. *CUP* 1.intro. no. 13, pp. 10-11. The pope justifies his request on the grounds that providing such support for the study of theology is no less necessary than useful (*non minus necessaria quam utilis*) to the Church.

48. These policies first appear together in the decrees promulgated at the Lateran Council of 1179. See Mansi 22, 227, and *CUP* 1.intro. no. 12, p. 10.

49. On the influence of the *licentia docendi* in the development of the university compare the conclusions of Rashdall, *The Universities of Europe in the Middle Ages* 1: 282-83; P. Delhaye, "L'Organisation scolaire au XIIe siècle," *Traditio* 5 (1947): 253-61; and G. Post, "Alexander III, the *Licentia docendi*, and the Rise of the Universities," in C. H. Taylor, ed., *Anniversary Essays in Medieval History by the Students of Charles Homer Haskins* (Boston, 1929), pp. 255-77. Post writes (p. 264) that Alexander III's legislation "was the real beginning of active control of the teaching organization by the papacy, if only as a precedent." While this precedent was little used in the twelfth century, a recent article has shown just how important it became in the thirteenth. See A. Bernstein, "*Magisterium* and License: Corporate Autonomy Against Papal Authority in the Medieval University of Paris," *Viator* 9 (1978): 291-307.

50. *CUP* 1.intro. no. 4, pp. 4-5, and *CUP* 1.intro. no. 8, p. 8.

51. See G. Post, "Masters' Salaries and Student Fees in the Mediaeval Universities," *Speculum* 7 (1932): 181-98, and Baldwin, *Masters, Princes and Merchants* 1: 124-30.

52. On the enduring influence of this principle see G. Post, K. Giocarinis, and R. Kay, "The Medieval Heritage of a Humanistic Ideal: '*Scientia donum Dei est, unde vendi non potest*,'" *Traditio* 11 (1955): 195-234.

53. Mansi 22, 227, and *CUP* 1.intro. no. 12, p. 10.

54. *CUP* 1.intro. no. 15, p. 12. See Kibre, *Scholarly Privileges*, p. 86. Cf. Rashdall, *The Universities of Europe in the Middle Ages* 1: 291, n. 1.

55. *CUP* 1 no. 7., p. 66.

56. In 1212 Innocent III restricted the authority of the abbot of St. Victor, allowing him to absolve scholars only of sins committed in Paris (*CUP* 1 no. 15, p. 74).

57. For two examples of Innocent III's many efforts to secure benefices for Paris masters see *CUP* 1.intro. nos. 16 and 17, pp. 12-15.

58. *CUP* 1 no. 3, pp. 62-63.

59. B. Smalley, *The Becket Conflict and the Schools* (Oxford, 1973), p. 19.

60. *CUP* 1 no. 5, p. 65.

61. *CUP* 1 no. 8, pp. 67-68. On the significance of this decree, I am in agreement with G. Post, "Paris Masters as a Corporation, 1200-1246," *Speculum* 9 (1934): 421-45, and especially with P. Classen, "Die ältesten Universitätsreformen und Universitätsgründungen des Mittelalters," *Heidelberger Jahrbücher* 12 (1968): 72-92, who sees it as the *terminus technicus* of the university.

62. See Southern, "The Schools of Paris," pp. 114-21, and also the suggestive article by J. C. Russell, "The Early Schools of Oxford and Cambridge," *The Historian* 5 (1943): 61-73, reprinted in J. C. Russell, *Twelfth Century Studies* (New York, 1978), pp. 167-80.

63. To the list of masters of theology who served as chancellors of Paris between 1160 and 1210 should be added Master Bernard Chabert, who succeeded Peter of Poitiers and resigned in 1206 to become bishop of Geneva. See P. Glorieux, *Répertoire des maîtres en théologie de Paris au XIIIe siècle* (2 vols., Paris, 1933-34), 1: 260.

64. The decree begins: "Notum facimus universis quod nos residentiam cancellarii Parisiensis attendentes necessariam esse nostre Parisiensi ecclesie et cummunitati (*sic*) scolarium" (*CUP* 1 no. 6, p. 65). On this decree see G. Lacombe, *La Vie et les oeuvres de Prévostin*, Bibliothèque thomiste 11 (Le Saulchoir, 1927), pp. 39-42.

65. Although, it should be noted, John of Candeilles had been a master in the schools. See Glorieux, *Repertoire* 1: 270.

66. *CUP* 1 no. 14, pp. 73-74.

67. *CUP* 1 no. 16, p. 75.

68. *Ibid.*, pp. 75-76. The decree gives the chancellor the explicit right to license candidates independently in theology, law, and the arts, but not in medicine. However, it seems unlikely that the chancellor would have been intentionally denied this right in the case of a single Paris faculty.

69. *CUP* 1 no. 24, pp. 82-83. See Post, "Paris Masters as a Corporation," pp. 430-36.

70. *CUP* 1 no. 16, p. 76.

71. *CUP* 1 nos. 30-31, pp. 87-90. On the resulting conflict see Rashdall, *The Universities of Europe in the Middle Ages* 1: 309-11.

72. *CUP* 1 no. 79, pp. 136-39. See Rashdall, *The Universities of Europe in the Middle Ages* 1: 334-40, and Kibre, *Scholarly Privileges*, pp. 92-96.

73. Cf. Rashdall, *The Universities of Europe in the Middle Ages* 1: 309.

74. On the life and work of Robert of Courson see M. Dickson and C. Dickson, "Le Cardinal Robert de Courson: Sa Vie," *AHDLMA* 9 (1934): 61-142, and Baldwin, *Masters, Princes and Merchants* 1: 19-25.

75. *CUP* 1 no. 20, p. 78.

76. Baldwin, *Masters, Princes and Merchants* 1: 25.

77. *Ibid.*, pp. 63-157.

78. *Summa*, MS. Paris BN lat. 14524, f. 47ra-b; discussed by Dickson and Dickson, "Robert de Courson," p. 73, and Baldwin, *Master, Princes and Merchants* 1: 125-27.

79. Mansi 22, 831 (1213); Mansi 21, 459 (1131); Mansi 21, 528 (1139); Mansi 21, 1179 (1163). The decree was repeated at the Council of Rouen, which Robert of Courson convened in the following year (Mansi 22, 910). On the original prohibition see R. Somerville, "Pope Innocent II and the Study of Roman Law," *Revue des études islamiques* 44 (1976): 105-14.

80. Mansi 22, 838; also repeated at Rouen, Mansi 22, 911.

81. Mansi 22, 845. On the interpretation of this decree see Baldwin, *Masters, Princes and Merchants* 2: 55, n. 94, and G. G. Meersseman, "'In libris gentilium non studeant': L'Etude des classiques interdite aux clercs au moyen âge?" *Italia medioevale e umanistica* 1 (1958): 1-13.

82. Mansi 22, 854.

83. *Summa*, MS. Paris BN lat. 14524, f. 73rb-va.

84. Mansi 22, 824; also decreed at Rouen, Mansi 22, 903.

85. Mansi 22, 1015-18.

86. See Dickson and Dickson, "Robert de Courson," pp. 112-14, and Baldwin, *Masters, Princes and Merchants* 1: 22-23.

87. *Oeuvres*, ed. Delaborde, 1: 303-4.

88. Dickson and Dickson, "Robert de Courson," p. 99. For Courson's treatment of usury in the *Summa* see G. Lefevre, ed., *Le Traité de Usura de Robert de Courson* (Lille, 1902).

89. Dickson and Dickson, "Robert de Courson," pp. 97-99.

90. *Ibid.*, pp. 112-14.

91. *CUP* 1 no. 20, p. 78.

92. *Summa*, MS. Paris BN lat. 14524, ff. 49vb-50ra.

93. *CUP* 1 no. 20, p. 79.

94. *Ibid.*, p. 78. Cf. *CUP* 1 no. 16, pp. 75-76.

95. *CUP* 1 no. 20, p. 78. Cf. the interpretation of this decree advanced by G. Leff, *Paris and Oxford Universities in the Thirteenth and Fourteenth Centuries* (New York, 1968), p. 138.

96. *CUP* 1 no. 20, pp. 78-79; *CUP* 1 no. 11, pp. 70-71. On Robert of Courson's involvement in the Paris Council in 1210 and the prohibition against reading the *libri naturales* see Dickson and Dickson, "Robert de Courson," pp. 79-80 and 120-24.

97. *CUP* 1 no. 20, p. 79. On the customary hours of lectures see Rashdall, *The Universities of Europe in the Middle Ages* 1: 433-34.

98. *CUP* 1 no. 20, p. 79. On this meadow and the conflicts over it see Boussard, *Nouvelle Histoire de Paris*, p. 183, and Kibre, *Scholarly Privileges*, pp. 241-43.

99. *CUP* 1 no. 20, p. 79. Cf. *CUP* 1.intro. no. 5, pp. 5-6, and *CUP* 1 no. 7, p. 66.

100. "Nullus sit scolaris Parisius, qui certum magistrum non habet" (*CUP* 1 no. 20, p. 79).

101. *Ibid.*

102. *Ibid.*

103. As do, for example, Rashdall, *The Universities of Europe in the Middle Ages* 1: 286-88, and, more recently, A. Gabriel, "The Cathedral Schools of Notre

Dame and the Beginning of the University of Paris," in *Garlandia: Studies in the History of the Medieval University* (Notre Dame, 1969), p. 58, and P. Michaud-Quantin, "La Conscience d'être membre d'une *universitas*," *Miscellanea mediaevalia*, Veröffentlichungen des Thomas-Instituts an der Universität Köln 3 (Berlin, 1964): 1-14.

104. H. Grundmann, "Vom Ursprung der Universität im Mittelalter," *Berichte über die Verhandlungen der Sächsischen Akademie der Wissenschaften zu Leipzig, Philologisch-historische Klasse* 103, n. 2 (1957): 16-65.

105. L. Hödl, "Die dialektische Theologie des 12. Jahrhunderts," in *Arts libéraux et philosophie au moyen âge*, Actes du quatrième congrès international de philosophie médiévale, Montreal, 1967 (Paris, 1969), pp. 134-47.

106. Boehm, "Die *negotio scholaris*," pp. 34-48; LeGoff, "How Did the Medieval University Conceive of Itself?" in *Time, Work and Culture in the Middle Ages* (Chicago, 1980), pp. 122-34; and P. Classen, "Die Höhen Schulen und die Geselleschaft im 12. Jahrhundert," *Archiv für Kulturgeschichte* 48 (1965): 155-80.

107. For other views of the impact of preaching on professional consciousness see Michaud-Quantin, "La Conscience d'être membre d'une *universitas*," pp. 8-9, and Boehm, "Die *negotio scholaris*," pp. 39-40.

108. On the early years of the Dominicans in Paris see M.-H. Vicaire, *Saint Dominic and His Times*, trans. K. Pond (New York, 1964), pp. 260-66, and P. Mandonnet, *St. Dominic and His Work*, trans. M. B. Larkin (St. Louis, 1948), pp. 42-46.

109. Master John of Barastre may have been teaching already when Honorius III made his request in May 1221 (*CUP* 1 no. 44, pp. 101-2).

110. On the impact of the Dominicans on learning see Mandonnet, *St. Dominic*, pp. 175-92, and R. W. Southern, *Western Society and the Church in the Middle Ages* (Harmondsworth, 1970), pp. 296-99.

111. Vicaire, *Saint Dominic*, p. 261.

112. See J. R. Moorman, *A History of the Franciscan Order* (Oxford, 1968), pp. 123-33.

113. These orders, in addition to the Dominicans and Franciscans, are mentioned in a circular letter drafted by the University of Paris in 1254 concerning their grievances against the religious orders (*CUP* 1 no. 230, p. 253).

114. *Chronica Villariensis MGH SS* 25, 208. On some of the factors that motivated the Cistercians to establish a house of study in Paris see the suggestive article of D. Baker, "Heresy and Learning in Early Cistercianism," *Studies in Church History* 9 (1972): 93-107.

115. On this conflict see Rashdall, *The Universities of Europe in the Middle Ages* 1: 370-97. On its impact on the relationship between the university and the papacy see P. R. McKeon, "The Status of the University as *Parens scientiarum*: An Episode in the Development of Its Autonomy," *Speculum* 39 (1964): 651-75.

Manuscripts Cited

CAMBRAI B. 561

CAMBRIDGE

St. John's College 57
University Library (UL): UL Gg.6.42; UL Ii.1.24

LONDON

British Library (formerly: British Museum): BM Additional (Add.) 18335, 19767; BM Harley 335
Lambeth Palace 458

OXFORD

Bodleian Library (Bodl.): Bodl. 284, 548; Bodl. e museo 82; Bodl. Laud latin (lat.) 105; Bodl. Laud miscellaneous (misc.) 269, 484; Bodl. Wood emptorum (empt.) 13
Corpus Christi College 45
Magdalen College 149

PARIS

Bibliothèque Arsenale (Ars.): Ars. 400, 543
Bibliothèque nationale, Manuscrits latins (BN lat.): BN lat. 2950, 3495, 3563, 3733, 3818, 12420, 13374, 13578, 13586, 14470, 14524, 14525, 14589, 14590, 14593, 14804, 14859, 14925, 14954, 16463, 17509, 18172
Bibliothèque Mazarine (Maz.): Maz. 178, 774, 1005
Bibliothèque Ste. Geneviève (Ste. Gen.) 1421

REIMS 581

TROYES 425

TROYES 1515

Index

Index

Library of Congress Cataloging in Publication Data

Ferruolo, Stephen C., 1949-
The origins of the university.

Includes bibliographies and index.
1. Université de Paris—History. 2. Education, Medieval. I. Title.
LF2165.F47 1985 378.44'361 84-40445
ISBN 0-8047-1266-2